A History of the European Economy, 1000–2000

A History of the European Economy, 1000–2000

François Crouzet

University Press of Virginia
Charlottesville and London

The University Press of Virginia
© 2001 by the Rector and Visitors of the University of Virginia
All rights reserved
Printed in the United States of America
First published 2001

Design & Composition by Colophon Typesetting

ⓝ The paper used in this publication meets the minimum requirements of
the American National Standard for Information Sciences—Permanence of
Paper for Printed Library Materials, ANSI Z39.48–1984.

Library of Congress Cataloging-in-Publication Data

Crouzet, François, 1922–
  A history of the European economy, 1000–2000 / François Crouzet.
    p. cm.
Includes bibliographical references and index.
  ISBN 0-8139-2024-8 (cloth : alk. paper) — ISBN 0-8139-2025-6 (pbk. :
alk. paper)
  1. Europe—Economic conditions.   I. Title.
  HC240 .C763 2001
  330.94—dc21

                                                      00-051297

To my grandchildren

Contents

Maps

Tables

Acknowledgments

This book is derived from lectures I gave in October and November 1996 at the University of Virginia, Charlottesville. I therefore want to thank—for their invitation and welcome—the Corcoran Department of History; Professor Peter S. Onuf, who was then the chair; and Professor Ronald G. Dimberg, director, International Studies. I am also grateful to Professors John James, Mark Thomas, and Olivier Zunz, who very kindly attended my lectures and made many useful comments.

I am also indebted to friends who have been patient enough to read parts of the manuscript (or even the whole thing) and to criticize it—especially Elise S. Brezis, Pierre Mougenot, Patrick O'Brien—and also two anonymous commentators. As for the parts of the book that venture into medieval history, my daughter-in-law, Professor Elisabeth Crouzet-Pavan, has been an invaluable help.

Warm thanks are deserved by Marie-José Serizier for the preparation of the manuscript, which was continuously lengthened and recast. Professor Jean-Robert Pitte and Florence Bonnaud of the Laboratory of Cartography at the University of Paris–Sorbonne must also be thanked for the maps. The support of Professor Jean-Pierre Bardet, director of the Roland Mousnier Center at the University of Paris–Sorbonne, has been vital and most generous.

Richard Holway, editor for history and social sciences at the University Press of Virginia, Ellen Satrom, David Sewell, and all members of the press who have been involved in work on the book have shown much patience and understanding, for which I am most grateful.

Finally, like every time I have written a book, my wife has been most supportive and calmly endured the outbursts of bad temper that my work generated!

Introduction

In this short book, I try to outline the history of the European economy—which is somewhat different from an economic history of Europe. By "European economy," I mean a world economy in the sense of Fernand Braudel and Immanuel Wallerstein, one that is of course located in Europe and has some common aspects and some common institutions; one that is somewhat integrated, as its different parts are linked by trade and other relations more intensively than they are linked with other systems; and one that achieves some kind of organic unity (despite diversity, which is typical of Europe).

This economic Europe has rarely coincided with the geographical entity that has been and is called "Europe," and both have had uncertain and changing boundaries, especially to the east, toward Asia. Indeed, Europe, which makes up only 7 percent of the Earth's land surface, has been called a small peninsula of Asia, and no clear geographical boundary demarcates it from the rest of the Eurasian land mass. The Ural Mountains never were a barrier; for centuries, hordes of nomads from the steppes of central Asia invaded Europe, which suffered greatly from their incursions. This was one reason why, up to about 1700, Russia was not considered part of Europe; it entered thanks to Peter the Great and his successors but left after the Bolshevik Revolution of 1917, and whether it has reentered is not yet perfectly clear. Likewise, the Eastern European satellites of the Soviet Union were outside Europe from 1945 to 1989. During that period, Europe stopped at the Iron Curtain. Europe, thus, is the work of humans, not nature, and as such has always had a variable geometry.

According to one British writer, "whether Europe actually has a history in any conventional sense of the word is open to doubt. Certainly most historians do not seem to believe so."[1] This is a gross example of Euroskepticism. In my view, Europe has been a living entity from both the cultural and the economic points of view, and from both angles it covers about the same area. Europe is where one finds Romanesque abbeys, Gothic cathedrals, and baroque palaces in countries that have shared the experience of the Renaissance, the Enlightenment, and the romantic movement. This means, of course, western, central, and northern Europe, and it happens that for almost ten centuries the most active and dynamic centers—the leaders of the European economy—have been situated there.

A major problem is, therefore, ascertaining at what period a European economy—with the meaning I suggested—did emerge. The consensus is that this emergence, the birth of Europe, took place in the Middle Ages, and more precisely between the tenth and the thirteenth centuries. Indeed, there was no European economy or polity in antiquity. The Roman Empire, which identified for several centuries with the civilized world in the west, was a Mediterranean empire. Some of its most populated and richest provinces were in Africa and Asia. Its rule did not extend durably beyond the Rhine and the Danube, and in the British Isles, only England became part of it. Vast areas of central, northern, and eastern Europe never were under Roman rule and had almost no economic relations with the Roman world, even though some Roman artifacts have been found in Poland and along the shores of the Baltic, from which amber was sent southward. The border between Greco-Roman civilization and the so-called barbarian people passed through the heart of Europe, from the northwest to the southeast, through present-day Britain, Germany, Hungary, and so forth.

Europe was thus born amid the ruins of the Roman Empire, by a swing of that border, which henceforth ran from north to south, and by its eastward advance, as Germanic, Scandinavian, Hungarian, and Slavonic peoples were converted to Christianity, which extended far beyond the former limits of the Roman Empire. Still, the importance of the Roman heritage must not be overlooked; within Europe, there were for a long time significant differences between regions that had been strongly romanized (e.g., Italy, southern France) and those where Roman influence had been short-lived or nonexistent (e.g., Germany east of the Rhine).

On the other hand, another border, running from east to west, appeared to the south of Europe because of the Arab-Muslim conquests (seventh and eighth centuries) and, in the late Middle Ages, those by the Ottoman Turks. The unity of the Mediterranean world was destroyed, and Christendom suffered enormous losses of territory. Though the northward advance of the Muslims was decisively stopped by the Franks at the battle of Poitiers (732), and though Spain was reconquered rather early (largely by the thirteenth century), the Balkans remained under the Turks up to the nineteenth century, while North Africa and the Middle East were lost forever. The Mediterranean had lost its centrality and become a fluctuating border, even a battlefield. Moreover, an increasing division developed between the Roman Catholic Church in the west and the Greek Orthodox churches in the east, which led to a final schism in the eleventh century and contributed to the creation of a strong contrast between western-central Europe and eastern Europe. Nonetheless, up to the sixteenth century, trade relations with the eastern Mediterranean remained vital for western Europe. Indeed, during most of the long period considered, "Europe" means its western and central parts plus Italy, Iberia, and Scandinavia—roughly Latin Christendom. Still, an effort has been made not to forget eastern Europe.

In my first chapter, I sketch the emergence of a European economy, which certainly had become a reality by the thirteenth century. In the second, I analyze the main characteristics of the economic system that had thus been built up, and that basically lasted, despite many changes, up to the eighteenth century. From an economic point of view, the conventional division between the late Middle Ages and the early modern period is artificial. I borrow this view from Marc Bloch and other historians; Rondo Cameron (1989) has rightly written: "From the viewpoint of the history of technology, there is no hiatus between medieval and modern times." And the institutions that had been established during the Middle Ages served as the framework of economic activity until the advent of the industrial and French revolutions.

The third chapter is devoted to the industrial revolution, the new economic system it created, and the latter's diffusion from the late eighteenth century to 1914. Finally, I survey the disasters that struck the European economy from 1914 onward, its renaissance after World War II, and its present crisis and decline.

I shall end this introduction with some cautionary remarks. In this work I try to consider Europe as a whole and to pay special attention to relations among its various parts: to intra-European trade—which developed early, particularly upon the base of differences in resources between northern and southern Europe; to the diffusion of institutions and technology; to migrations of labor and capital. I look for the forces that have bound together the regions of Europe and worked toward creating some kind of integrated (even loosely) European economy. But neither centrifugal forces nor connections with the outer world are overlooked. The great non-European civilizations have had a strong influence upon Europe at several stages of its development, even though Europe eventually established a technological, economic, and military ascendancy over them (a problem that is considered herein). Moreover, since the sixteenth century, some parts of Europe have had close links with the Americas; and, at times, an Atlantic economy may have had more reality than a European one. This history of the European economy tries to be non-Eurocentric.

Third, I have to briefly mention the geographical factor, which is important but often neglected by economists and social scientists. It has been rightly rehabilitated by David Landes in *The Wealth and Poverty of Nations* (1998). On the other hand, geographical determinism must be carefully avoided. Despite its small size, Europe has an amazing diversity in landscapes, climates, natural resources, and languages. This diversity has stimulated trade relations, specialization, geographical division of labor, and therefore productivity gains. Some writers also see it as a factor behind the political fragmentation that has prevailed in Europe and that can be considered either a source of progress or a cause of disasters.

Actually, Europe is made up of several long west-east zones. The far north, from Scotland to Scandinavia and northern Russia, has inhospitable highlands and, in some regions, subarctic conditions. Then, the great northern European plain extends fanlike from London and Paris to central and southern Russia. Large areas of those plains have fertile soils, excellent for cereal cultivation, but some others are less favored. The climate gradually changes from maritime (mild winters, cool summers) in the west to continental (cold winters, hot summers) in the east. These plains are crossed by several large—and navigable—rivers, which flow from the south or southeast toward the north or northwest. The plains are bounded to the south by a succession of low mountains, hills, and plateaus, from central France through Germany to Bohemia, separated by a number of gaps and basins. Farther south stands a barrier of high mountains—the Pyrenees, the Alps, and the Carpathians. However, the Alps, though the highest, can be passed or skirted without too much difficulty; moreover, they are neither a desert nor an isolated area, and they have played an important role in the history of Europe, of which they are an integral part. Still, the Alpine system is a great divide, from both the climatic and cultural points of view. It demarcates Mediterranean Europe, the most distinctive region of the Continent. The land is much more broken than in the north, with mountain ranges (actually prolongations of the Alpine system), hills, and coastal plains, which are generally small (the main exception is the Po valley in northern Italy). The climate appears idyllic to northerners: *"Kennst du das Land, wo die Zitronen blühn? / Im*

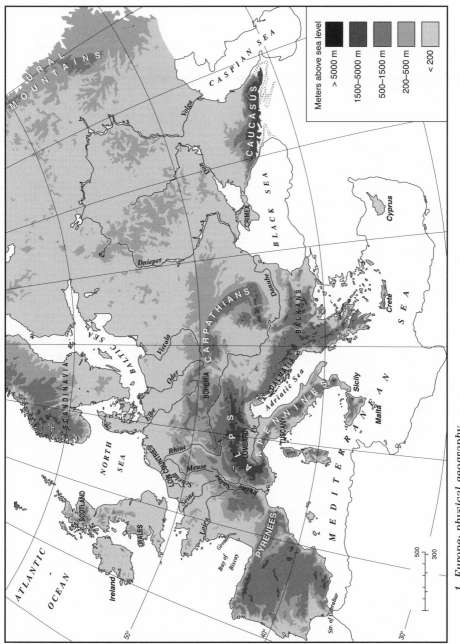

1. Europe: physical geography

Meters above sea level
> 5000 m
1500–5000 m
500–1500 m
200–500 m
< 200

URAL MOUNTAINS
CASPIAN SEA
Volga
Don
CAUCASUS
CRIMEA
BLACK SEA
Cyprus
Dnieper
Danube
CARPATHIANS
BOHEMIA
BALKANS
Vistula
Oder
BALTIC SEA
Elbe
SCANDINAVIA
DALMATIA
Adriatic Sea
APENNINES
ALPS
LOMBARDY
TUSCANY
Sicily
Malta
Crete
MEDITERRANEAN SEA
Seine
Rhine
Meuse
Scheldt
Saône
Rhône
NORTH SEA
LOW COUNTRIES
SCOTLAND
WALES
Ireland
Loire
Gironde
Bay of Biscay
PYRENEES
ATLANTIC OCEAN
Str. of Gibraltar

500
300

50°
40°
30°

dunkeln Laub, die Goldorangen glühn" (Goethe, "Mignons Lied"[2]). In fact, summers are hot and dry, soils often thin and liable to suffer from erosion or exhaustion, so that conditions for agriculture (except for vines and olive trees) are not too favorable in most places. Moreover, minerals, coal especially, are much more abundant in northwestern and central Europe than in the Mediterranean regions.

Altogether, Europe enjoys a moderate, temperate climate (except in the far north), and most of it is suited to cultivation. It has neither deserts nor disease-ridden tropical areas (nor the multiple cropping that continuous warmth makes possible in the latter). It has rich mineral resources. On the other hand, vast areas are not very fertile; the climate is somewhat too wet in the west, too cold in winter in the east, too dry in summer in the south; and the vagaries of the weather cause sharp fluctuations in harvests. On the whole, the natural endowment is not particularly generous. The wealth of Europe was much more the hard work of people than the bounty of nature.

A special advantage must, however, be mentioned: Europe is a peninsula, surrounded on three sides by seas. Moreover, its coasts are jagged, with many large and small peninsulas, many large and small offshore islands. The Mediterranean, Baltic, and Black Seas are three "great lakes," thanks to which maritime influences—not only climatic, but also economic—penetrate the Continent, where, except in Russia, no place is really far from the sea. Though for centuries the large majority of Europeans never had a glimpse of salt water, the sea has been a major determinant of Europe's history, working for both union and division. However, it would be too deterministic to see Europe as naturally outward looking, as more prepared for overseas trade and expansion than other continents.

A last cautionary remark is about the difficulties and dangers in using place- and country names when considering a very long time period. Up to the nineteenth century, "Germany," "Italy," and "Romania" were only geographical expressions, not the names of states. In other cases, names have changed: "Bohemia" is the present-day Czech Republic; the "United Provinces" (in short, "Holland"), the Kingdom of the Netherlands. Boundaries have undergone countless changes. France expanded significantly eastward between the fifteenth and the eighteenth centuries. The southern Netherlands of the sixteenth and seventeenth centuries included today's Belgium and also a stretch of northern France. Some states have disappeared—definitively, like the Venetian Republic and the Hapsburg or Austro-Hungarian empire, or temporarily, like Poland, which did not exist as a state from 1795 to 1919 or from 1939 to 1945. Many others emerged in the twentieth century.

Moreover, from the economic historian's point of view, some large natural and cultural areas that transcend the boundaries of states are actually more important, in many instances, than political units—at least up to the consolidation of nation-states in the nineteenth century. The Baltic, Rhenish, Alpine, western Mediterranean, and Balkan areas are prominent examples.

A final note is that this book is an essay and not an attempt to deal systematically with all aspects of the Continent's economic history over ten centuries.[3] Scholars have engaged in complex controversies about most problems that are considered, but lack of space does not permit me to do justice to—or even to mention—most of their views.

Abbreviations

CAP	Common Agricultural Policy	IMF	International Monetary Fund
CEEC	Central and Eastern Europe Countries	ITR	information-technology revolution
ECB	European Central Bank	MNC	multinational company
ECE	east-central Europe	NATO	North Atlantic Treaty Organization
ECSC	European Coal and Steel Community	NEP	New Economic Policy
ECU	European currency unit	OECD	Organization for Economic Cooperation and Development
EEC	European Economic Community		
EFTA	European Free Trade Area	OEEC	Organization for European Economic Cooperation
EMS	European Monetary System		
EMU	Economic and Monetary Union	OPEC	Organization of Petroleum Exporting Countries
EPU	European Payments Union	PPP	purchasing power parity[4]
EU	European Union	TFP	total factor productivity[5]
FDI	foreign direct investment	U.K.	United Kingdom of Great Britain and Northern Ireland (adjective form)
GATT	General Agreement on Tariffs and Trade		
GDP	gross domestic product	U.S.	United States of America (adjective form)
GNP	gross national product	USSR	Union of Soviet Socialist Republics

*A History of the European
Economy, 1000–2000*

One

The Emergence of a European Economy, Tenth through Thirteenth Centuries

The Heritage from the "Dark Ages"

The abolition of the western Roman Empire in AD 476 and its replacement by the so-called barbarian kingdoms had no serious economic significance. The economy of late antiquity survived, but it was an exhausted, degenerate economy; its decline, which had started during the great crisis of the third century, continued—and may have worsened. Population had been falling since the third century due to invasions, insecurity, and heavy taxation, and because the Roman view of marriage worked in favor of low birthrates. The immigration of the so-called barbarians—about one million of them—who settled within the empire had no significant positive impact. The fall in population was dramatically aggravated by successive outbreaks of plague, which came from the east and raged from the 540s to 614, especially in southern Europe. Italy, the heart of the former Roman civilization, was struck while it was also suffering badly from the last Germanic invasion—by the Lombards, who destroyed the old elites. The plague hit hard in the Byzantine Empire as well. These two regions, which had resisted economic regression, were together the worst struck by the plague. The population of Europe (west of the Urals) in c. AD 200 has been estimated at 36 million; by 600, it had fallen to 26 million; another estimate (excluding "Russia") gives a more drastic fall, from 44 to 22 million.[1] Moreover, evidence from contemporary skeletons reveals a poor state of health, chronic malnutrition, and high children's mortality.

As a consequence, cultivated areas contracted, and wilderness, especially forests, expanded. Scattered human communities lived in isolated clearings, practicing subsistence agriculture. In the parts of Europe that had not belonged to the Roman Empire, population density was very low and agriculture was primitive, mainly based on slash-and-burn techniques. This low level of population and of material culture prevailed in Scandinavia; in the areas east of the Elbe, which were mainly inhabited by Slavic people; and in the Balkans, which Slavs occupied almost entirely in the seventh century (in the steppes of southern Russia there were Ural-Altaic nomads, who lived from stock raising). In those vast areas—many of which had been devastated by successive invasions—the mode of life was simple, based on the tribe and the kinship group. The basic units were hamlets, where a small number of families lived and, often, farmed the land collectively; not fully sedentary, they moved their habitat from time to time.

Even in the west, there was a regression in technology (with some exceptions, as Germanic peoples were better than the Romans at working iron): a number of skills were lost, the production and trade of artifacts (mostly made in rural estates' workshops) fell, and the whole way of life was reduced to a lower plane. The most advanced sectors of the economy disappeared, including banking, which had been fairly developed in the Greco-Roman world. The ruling aristocracy was uncultured, unruly, violent. The use of writing became increasingly rare. Ignorance, barbarity, and brutality prevailed, particularly in the Frankish kingdom (France plus parts of Germany), which was the largest in western Europe.

The Christian west was backward and poor relative to the Byzantine Empire and the Muslim world (not to mention the distant civilizations of India and China)—and it was to remain so for centuries. Indeed, Paul Bairoch (1997) has written that, up to the fifteenth century, what was essential in world history was happening in Asia. Europe, certainly, was on the periphery of the civilized world and of a world trade system centered in Asia. The Byzantine Empire, although attacked by many enemies and restricted in the seventh century to Asia Minor, the southern Balkans, Greece, and southern Italy (which had been reconquered in the sixth century), retained an active and relatively sophisticated economy, with luxury industries, much trade, and large towns.[2] Constantinople and Córdoba (the latter in Muslim Spain) were by far the largest cities in Europe. In the former western empire, on the other hand, urban life had greatly deteriorated. Though most Roman cities had survived, particularly those with bishops' sees, they had greatly dwindled in size and population and, behind their walls, did not have much economic function; rich landowners had deserted them to live on their estates.[3] By 600, the population of Rome, once at least half a million, had fallen to 50,000.

On the northern fringe of the empire and in the Balkans, urban life had been destroyed, and non-Roman Europe did not have any proper cities before it was Christianized.

The status of trade—especially long-distance trade—has been a matter of scholarly controversy. According to Henri Pirenne, relations between western Europe, on one hand, and Byzantium and the eastern Mediterranean, on the other, had been fairly well maintained up to the Arab conquests and invasions of the sixth and seventh centuries, which interrupted Christian seaborne trade and therefore brought about a definite discontinuity between ancient and medieval Europe. Actually, long-distance trade between East and West had been declining before the Muslim invasions, and the latter did not destroy it altogether, as ascendancy at sea belonged to the Byzantines and not to the Arabs. Nonetheless, trade became more insecure; moreover, Byzantium tried for fiscal reasons to restrict it to ports it controlled in southern Italy, while, as mentioned above, southern Europe suffered much from plagues and other disasters, and western Europe was very poor. What trade there was consisted of small quantities of luxury goods—mostly spices and silk fabrics from the East and even the Far East (they had come through central Asia or the Persian Gulf and Iraq)—carried mainly by Jewish and Syrian merchants. But references to those merchants disappear after the sixth century. By 670–680, there were signs of trade contraction: parchment replaced papyrus (from Egypt) at the chancellery of Frankish kings; and in northern countries, wax candles replaced oil lamps for lighting churches. On the other hand, from the late sixth century, Byzantine artifacts penetrated in eastern Europe as far as the Baltic coast in return for slaves, furs, and honey.

After this long depression, which signaled a break between antiquity and the Middle Ages, and a nadir, possibly c. 600, there was from the seventh century onward a recovery, as a new economy began to emerge. Change became more pronounced in the eighth century, when the Carolingian kings established a new political order. They conquered and Christianized Germany between the Rhine and the Elbe as well as Austria. The contemporaries of Charlemagne (768–814) used the word "Europa" for his empire, which was the first European political construction (indeed, the six countries that established the Common Market in 1957 coincided roughly with its territory!). It also was an economic space and a cultural community.

Thanks to better security, fewer famines, the absence of plagues, and the Christianization of marriage, which gradually created a new demographic system with high fertility rates, population started to increase in

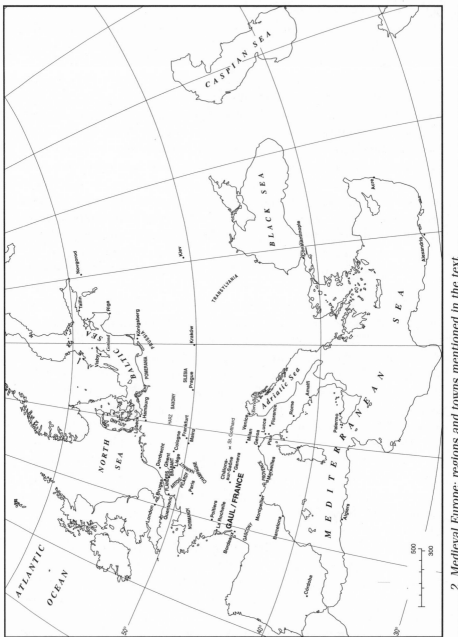

2. *Medieval Europe: regions and towns mentioned in the text*

northern Gaul and Germany. According to one estimate mentioned earlier, the population of Europe ("Russia" excluded) rose from 22 million c. 700 to 25 million c. 800, and 28 million c. 900 (see table 1.1, below). Charlemagne's empire may have had 15 to 18 million inhabitants, which was more than the late Roman Empire. Nomadism decreased, people were more firmly settled, and more land was brought into cultivation again (or even for the first time). Though extensive tracts of the Carolingian empire remained empty wilderness, there also were some well-populated areas. Patterns of landownership and tenancy changed according to a mix of Roman traditions and Germanic customs; the manorial system developed and expanded (but it did not prevail everywhere). There was some progress in farming techniques, and water mills, which had been used in the late Roman Empire but in small numbers, became quite numerous; European creativity was raising its head.[4] There also was some new life in towns (mainly in the area between the Rhine and the Seine), and peasants came to urban markets to sell their surplus output, receiving specie in return.

Trade with the eastern Mediterranean was carried on by some seaports of southern Italy under Byzantine control, and by Torcello, one of the islands in the Venetian lagoon, where people from the mainland had taken refuge after the Lombard invasion of 568–569 and established several small towns. Torcello has long been a lost city (with only two churches now standing), but recent research shows that in the seventh and eighth centuries it was a *magnum emporium* for trade with Byzantium (Crouzet-Pavan). Some other European ports also traded with the East, North Africa, and Muslim Spain, and new overland routes were opened from Byzantium through Slav countries to Cologne or Mainz on the Rhine, and through Russia to the Baltic. Slaves, who had been captured from pagan peoples, were a major item in this traffic, and many were sold to Muslim Spain. Still, the aggregate volume of east-west trade remained minute.

A new development was the opening of trade routes in northern Europe by the Frisians, people who lived on the marshy coast between the Scheldt River and the Jutland peninsula and for whom the sea—for both fishing and trading—was a major resource. Using boats with one large square sail, they traded with England, France, Germany, and Scandinavia, and traveled far into the Baltic Sea, thus creating a new east-west axis along which there was a circulation of western goods (coarse woolens from Flanders, weapons, tin from England, wine, salt), Nordic produce (furs, wax, honey, amber), slaves, and Oriental luxuries. The island of Gotland, in the Baltic Sea, was a major emporium, and a number of new ports *(wiks)* were established on the coasts of the Channel and the North

Sea (e.g., Duurstede-Dordrecht, in the Rhine delta, and Quentovic); they were the forerunners of the trading towns of northern Europe. In fact, northwestern Europe, especially the area between the Rhine and the Seine that was the center of Carolingian power and civilization, had become the most dynamic area of the Continent; there was a shift away from the Mediterranean, the focus of classical civilization. Around 800, the population of northwestern Europe surpassed that of the Mediterranean region. There also was some internal trade in bulk goods, particularly among the dispersed estates of great monasteries.

A proof of the break with the ancient world is the monetary revolution. The Roman monetary system had somehow survived, but in a degenerate form: gold coins were not minted anymore, while silver coins were of light weight and contained a good deal of lead. Charlemagne replaced this system with a new, monometallist one (793–794), using silver, with the *denarius* (penny in England) as the basic unit; it was to last for most of the Middle Ages, as the silver standard was more suitable to the realities of the time and to the resources of Europe, which had a number of silver mines (though the major center for silver mining was then in central Asia) but little gold. Still, a shortage of precious metals prevailed, and they had an enormous purchasing power. Moreover, large quantities of those metals were hoarded in the treasures of churches, monasteries, and princes. Specie circulation was restricted to the elite and to estate traders, who were selling high-value products. Transactions of lesser folk were too small for the use of even the tiniest coin: payments to their lords were in kind or labor, and barter deals were frequent.[5]

To the east of the Carolingian empire, there was also some economic progress from the seventh century onward, thanks to the end of invasions. Population increased and became more settled. Around villages, land was more regularly cultivated, and itinerant farming was relegated to peripheral areas; iron plowshares and sickles came into use among most Slavic peoples.

Though Charlemagne's empire remained poor and backward if compared with contemporary China or the Muslim world, some foundations of the European economy were nevertheless laid down from the seventh century to the beginning of the ninth, and the changes that started then were to continue for long afterward. However, from the mid-ninth century to the mid-tenth, there was a serious setback, for two main reasons.

First, the West suffered new invasions from all directions: by the Norsemen or Vikings from the north (and also from the west, as they attacked the Atlantic coast), by Saracens from the south, and from the east by the Hungarians (or Magyars), who settled in the Middle Danube plain, from which they made raids in Germany and as far as central France. The Vikings (mainly from Denmark) started raids against England and then Ireland in 793 and attacked the Continent from 810 onward; they plundered and destroyed all concentrations of wealth, especially seaports, cities, and monasteries; they greatly harmed the trade that was developing in the northern seas. As for the Muslims, an invasion of Gaul had been beaten off at Poitiers in 732, but in the ninth century they occupied Sicily and other islands in the Mediterranean. Many Muslim immigrants settled in Sicily, where they introduced new plants—lemons, oranges, cotton, sugarcane, and mulberries—as well as silkworms. In the tenth century, Palermo may have had more inhabitants than any Christian town but Byzantium. This relative prosperity is clear proof of the Muslim world's economic advance. As the Muslims had gained the ascendancy at sea, they made raids—mainly to capture slaves—on the coasts of Christian countries, which were deserted by their inhabitants; Rome was sacked in 846. In the tenth century, the Saracens established bases in Italy and southern France (especially at La Garde Freinet, overlooking the present resort of St. Tropez, which they occupied from 890 to 972), from which they launched raids into the hinterland as far as Switzerland.

The second reason for the setback was the breakdown of the Carolingian empire; by 843 (when the grandsons of Charlemagne partitioned his empire), the dream of a "kingdom of Europe" was over, and the very notion of the "state," which had been crucial to the Greco-Roman world, and which the Carolingians had attempted to restore, faded away. Moreover, in the successor kingdoms, as central power crumbled away, power was "privatized" to the benefit of thousands of local potentates; anarchy, violence, and insecurity prevailed.

Henceforth, Europe would never be subject to one single ruler. The Holy Romano-Germanic Empire, which revived the Carolingian dream in the tenth century, had under its control (a weak one, most of the time) only Germany and northern Italy. The plurality of centers of power and the decentralization of decisions characteristic of Europe have, like the European legal systems, their roots in the late and post-Carolingian age. They then survived the emergence of strong nation-states, of which Europe was to have many, whether large or small. This decentralized system, which resembles the competitive model in economics, is often seen as giving Europe an advantage over large, unitary, centralized, autocratic empires like China. There was no central power that could universally thwart innovation and dissent or impose complete obedience and conformity, while competition between states, once they had emerged, was liable to stimulate innovation. Thus, pluralism and political fragmentation were one source of European (particularly western European) economic progress—and also of political liberties. On the other hand, fragmentation and competition had a destructive potential, particularly in the numberless wars—or the thousand-year-long European civil war—that have devastated Europe for centuries. The rise of nation-states involved additional dangers; their absence during the period that will be now considered may have been one factor contributing to the remarkable achievements that started around 1000.

Earlier on, however, the new invasions caused extensive destruction; part of the West's precious metals stock was lost—as booty, ransom, or tribute. Many people were slaughtered, and many others panicked and fled their homes; population fell in some areas, and though others hardly suffered, the population leveled off for a century.

However, these disasters should not be overestimated; many of the aforementioned changes went on continuously or started again when there was a lull. When the Vikings settled in some western countries—such as Normandy, England, and Sicily—they established well-ruled states. They also turned from pirates to traders, associating plunder and commerce. In order to sell their booty in the Baltic Sea area, they created trading ports along its coasts and developed a network of relations with the hinterland. Vikings from Sweden navigated the rivers of Russia, founding Novgorod, Kiev, and other towns on their banks. In the eighth and ninth centuries, they had relations with Persia through the Caspian Sea and the Volga. Then they reached the Black Sea and sold furs and slaves to the Byzantines and the Muslims, in exchange for spices and silks. Large quantities of ninth- and tenth-century *dirhems* (Muslim silver coins) have been discovered in Scandinavia and northern Russia along with jewelry of Oriental make. Also in the ninth century, the *Rus*, as they were called, made Kiev the center of a loosely organized state, the first "Russian" state, and they were soon assimilated into its Slavic population. In the tenth century, trade revived in the North and Baltic Seas.

In the Adriatic, the island of Rialto (part of Venice) rose by trading in salt, slaves, and timber. Located at the center of the lagoons, it attracted population at the expense of the other towns, eventually superseding Torcello and in 828 becoming the seat of the dukedom. Venetian ships at first carried goods locally, and then in the Adriatic, but some of them sailed to the eastern Mediterranean as early as the ninth century. However, the volume of Venice's trade remained limited up to the eleventh century, though its traffic, through the Adriatic, benefited from the Muslim mastery of the western Mediterranean.

An Age of Demographic Expansion

Indeed, around 950, the worst was over, and conditions were present for a "great leap forward," a long period of change and expansion that created the traditional European economy. Common features were found in almost all parts of Europe, as they were grounded in similar material cultures and institutions.[6] Of course, the process was neither regular (there may have been accelerations in the late eleventh and the late twelfth centuries, as well as some setbacks caused by famines) nor uniform all over Europe: because of geographical and historical circumstances, some areas progressed early, while others were laggards; some of the most vigorous growth spurts took place in late-starting regions, for example, in the countries east of the Elbe in the twelfth century.[7] Overall, though, the trend was unmistakable.

Key to this trend was the simple fact that advancements could occur, due to the end of invasions and external threats. The Scandanivians and Hungarians settled down and converted to Christianity. The Saracens were expelled from their bases in Provence (972). Sicily was reconquered by the Christians (1072). Muslim piracy was reduced, and activity revived along the Christian coasts of the western Mediterranean. The Slavic people of eastern Europe and the Balkans were also Christianized from the ninth to the eleventh century. Perhaps using new resources obtained from the rise of the slave trade with the rich Muslim world, they organized into principalities and kingdoms, where some towns were established, and they became sedentary. Princes granted land to their faithful warriors, whose estates were cultivated by slaves or bonded peasants in a situation reminiscent of western feudal society. Indeed, within two centuries (and mainly in the tenth), Christian Europe's area doubled, and it expanded from the Elbe to the Volga, from the Danube to the polar circle, even though the material culture in this "new Europe" was lower than in the west.

Moreover, western and central Europe were not to suffer any more invasions, particularly by nomads from central Asia, who were truly dangerous enemies. Eastern Europe was less fortunate and was indeed a vast glacis that served to protect the west. In the twelfth century, the Petchenegs and other tribes devastated the Balkans but were eventually repelled. In the thirteenth century, however, the Russian state of Kiev was destroyed by the Mongols under Batou Khan, Genghis Khan's grandson; most of Russia fell under Mongol rule; and the country was only to enter Europe four centuries later. From 1236 to 1242, raids by Mongols brought devastation to Poland, Hungary, Silesia, Bohemia, and parts of the Balkans down to the Adriatic. It seems that Batou Khan had projects to attack

Europe, but after 1242 the Mongols turned eastward and conquered China. Still, in the fifteenth and sixteenth centuries, the Balkans were to be conquered by the Ottoman Turks, who—like the Tartars of southern Russia—continued to threaten Poland and central Europe until the late seventeenth century. On the other hand, as early as the end of the eleventh century, during the First Crusade, western Europe had shown its ability to project its military power to distant lands (from which it was also obtaining the goods it needed).

Another factor is the "feudal peace" that might be said to accompany "feudal anarchy." The many local skirmishes between feudal lords may have been less destructive than the large-scale warfare that developed after large states had revived. The building of numerous fortified castles—which started everywhere c. 950–970—provided some security in the countryside, even though they were at first rudimentary (with a wooden keep) and symbolic of the usurpation of royal power by feudal lords. The "peace movements" that the church sponsored also contributed to this time of possibility.

As for positive factors, we shall follow Douglass North and Robert Thomas: "A growing population was the exogenous variable that basically accounts for the growth and development of Western Europe" from the tenth to the thirteenth centuries. Admittedly, some writers have given priority to improvements in technology and higher agricultural productivity, without which demographic growth would soon have stopped. Still, population seems the *primus movens,* the determinant variable, the engine of progress in agriculture and of what have been called the commercial and urban revolutions. Moreover, according to North, population growth brought about changes in relative prices, which contributed to the development of institutional innovations.

How to explain this demographic growth that generated more producers and consumers? First, over history, fertility has always tended to outstrip mortality, resulting in net population growth—except when catastrophes struck. Secondly, at this time, the last invasions had come to an end, a degree of security prevailed, and some areas of order were created. There were no terrible, pan-European epidemics between the eighth and the fourteenth centuries, while there was a warming up of the climate from the tenth century onward, especially north of the Alps. Nutrition may have improved thanks to new plants, like peas and lentils, and the creation of new settlements gave more opportunities to make a living.

Moreover, since Carolingian times, western Christendom had been developing its own system of values and its own demographic model. Polyg-

_____ Table 1.1 _____

The population of Europe, AD 1–1995 (figures are in millions of
inhabitants)

Year AD	Europe, territory of the former USSR excluded	Europe, to the Ural Mountains	Year AD	Europe, territory of the former USSR excluded	Europe, to the Ural Mountains
1	31	31	1340	74	—
200	44	36	1400	52	60
400	36	31	1500	67	81
600	22	26	1600	89	100
700	22	—	1650	—	105
800	25	29	1700	95	120
900	28	—	1750	111	140
1000	30	36	1800	146	180
1100	35	44	1900	295	390
1200	49	58	1950	395	—
1250	57	—	1995	581	—
1300	70	79			

_____

Source: Bardet and Dupâquier, vol. 1 (1997), p. 33, table 1, and p. 29. Figures for Europe exclusive of
the former USSR come from J. N. Biraben, "Essai sur l'évolution du nombre des hommes," *Population*
34, no. 1 (1979): 13–25. Those for Europe to the Urals are from C. McEvedy and R. Jones, *Atlas of
World Population History,* 1978.

Maddison (1998) gives somewhat different figures for Europe, the former USSR excluded:

Year AD	Population in millions	Year AD	Population in millions
50	34	1280	68
960	40	1500	72
1000	45	1650	91

amy, contraception, abortion, infanticide, and desertion of children were
banned; the church's doctrine on marriage—that it be monogamous, ex-
ogamous, and indissoluble—was enforced. The nuclear family grew
stronger and became dominant (except among Slavic people). This system encouraged procreation and the acceptance of children (at the same
time a means of birth regulation, based on late marriages, was emerging).
There was an increase in birth and fertility rates, while death rates are

likely to have fallen, though infantile and juvenile mortality remained terribly high. Evidence from cemeteries shows a clear improvement of physical conditions from the eleventh to the thirteenth century; the average age at death may have risen.[8]

It is of course difficult to estimate the increase in numbers. In England, where some reliable data are available, population (which may have already risen from 250,000 c. 600 to 750,000 c. 950) increased by a factor of three or even four between the Norman conquest (1066) and the early fourteenth century; it likely rose from one million (it was 1.1–1.2 million in 1086) to 3.4–4.5 million (some writers go as far as 5 or 6 million in 1340). Progress was likely slower on the Continent, but the kingdom of France may have had 5 million inhabitants c. 1000 and 15 million or more c. 1300. Europe (including Russia) may have had 35 million people c. 950 and 79 million c. 1300; its population more than doubled.[9]

Thus, population grew markedly, but it did not explode like that of the Third World in the late twentieth century; Europe's rate of growth was well below 1 percent per year (possibly as low as 0.2 to 0.3 percent). This growth was more remarkable for its long duration than its rapidity, which also changed over time. Growth started in areas close to the Mediterranean and was slow at first; then it spread northward and accelerated, with a peak from 1100 to 1150; it slowed down in the second half of the thirteenth century. Historians speak of *monde plein*, a full world, in reference to western and central Europe around 1300; from the tower or spire of a village church, several others could be seen (this is a trait of the European identity). Rural population in several areas actually reached levels close to those of the eighteenth century, but the Celtic fringes of the British Isles, Scandinavia, and most of east-central and eastern Europe retained low densities. This increased population was mobile; it is a serious mistake to believe in the immobility of the medieval (and early modern) peasantry. Many people migrated to the towns and to the "frontier" (in the American sense) in eastern Europe and elsewhere. This stimulated intra-European trade, and all in all the rise of a market economy was a direct response to population growth. Moreover, a bigger population provides more opportunities for innovation, with more people generating more ideas.

Some historians also stress social changes as a factor behind economic expansion. With the collapse of central governments, landowners became feudal lords and masters of castles. They strengthened their hold over peasants and imposed upon them additional exactions. This enabled them to create new equipment—such as mills, ovens, wine presses, and bridges—and establish and protect markets. Peasants were thus prompted to produce more and to sell their crops, to be able to pay their new charges. There was also the proliferation of small princely courts, which indulged in conspicuous consumption of luxuries, thereby increasing demand, plus the massive building of castles, churches, and monasteries. Thus, heavy expenditure by the aristocracy contributed to the economic dynamism that prevailed from the tenth century onward.

Change and Progress on the Land

While the number of Europeans increased, institutional structures that were to last a long time were being established. The variety of local experiences and the time lags between regions were immense, but simplification is not too misleading, as most changes ran along parallel lines. Owing to the primacy of agriculture, the most important of these structures was in the countryside: the manorial system, which developed gradually over several centuries.

Large estates with from several hundred to tens of thousands of acres, the owners of which dominated the local peasantry, had existed in most of Europe for a long time; they had expanded during the early Middle Ages, and the power of their lords had increased accordingly. However, up to about the year 1000, small and medium freeholders had survived in large numbers, particularly in Germany and along the coasts of the northern seas. In the classical (or bipartite) estate of the eighth to the ninth centuries, which existed mainly in northern France and in western Germany (to some historians, it was the exception rather than the rule), arable land was divided in two separate but linked components, plus the *saltus* or *incultum*, of woods and rough pasture, where peasants had won rights. The demesne (a third or less of the estate's arable land), on one hand, was cultivated for the sole benefit of the lord; the tenants' holdings, on the other, had been granted to peasants (freemen or slaves) in return for dues and labor services; and the link between the two was that the tenants (and not gangs of slaves, like in the Roman Empire) cultivated the demesne under their labor services. During the chaos and violence of the ninth, tenth, and eleventh centuries, the numerous lords of manors, who built castles, took over most of the state's powers (including the right to command, to judge, and to punish) and revenues; thanks to their retinues of professional warriors, they dominated the countryside around their seats. With wide powers over both land and people, they were able to impose new constraints and new burdens (particularly monopolies of equipment like mills, ovens, etc.) upon the inhabitants of their manors and the areas around their castles, and to reduce some of them (but rarely the majority) to the status of serfs, who belonged from birth to their lord, were bound to the land, and bore the heaviest burden of dues and services. Many freeholders and freemen put themselves under the protection of lords, who took over their land in return.

At the same time, chattel slavery died out—rather quickly in most of France (between the 930s and the 1030s), but more slowly in some parts of southern Europe. The church forbade the enslavement of Christians, with the result that any slaves had to be imported from pagan countries; these were expensive to buy and to maintain and less productive than serfs. The distinction between freedom and slavery, which had long been a basic trait of society, gave way to one between warriors and peasants. Together, the chaos of the period, the scarcity of labor, and the abundance of land made the manor an efficient mode of production, and serfdom an efficient institution: serfs gave labor services in return for land, protection, and justice, and the risk of holdings being deprived of labor was much reduced.

However, from the eleventh century onward, the rise of a market economy, towns, and trade, and the improved productivity of agriculture resulted in a disaggregation of manorialism. A crucial element—the sharing of inputs in the form of labor services—disappeared, as such forced labor was far less productive on demesne farms than hired (i.e., free) labor.[10] Those services were bought back by many tenants. On the other hand, demesnes contracted, and increasingly lords leased them out for rent to farmers (who paid a fixed rent) or to sharecroppers (the latter were numerous in southern France and Italy, especially for vine growing and stock raising). In the twelfth century, many lords obtained less income from their demesnes than from feudal exactions.

Tenant lands, meanwhile, became more and more divided as population increased. In thirteenth-century northern France, most holdings had from ten to fifty acres. Despite the fact that on smaller properties it was impossible to make a living, tenants were able to improve their position. In fact, they became quasi-owners, as their land could be inherited by their children or sold; tenure was de facto in perpetuity. In late thirteenth-century France, 80 percent of land was cultivated by peasants under one of several secure forms of tenure. Admittedly, tenants still had to pay various dues, which could be heavy, but they were codified by customs and were increasingly paid in money, rather than in kind or in labor. Moreover, the real value of monetary dues (which were fixed) fell greatly in the thirteenth century, owing to fast-rising prices. In the twelfth and thirteenth centuries, there was also a withering away of serfdom in western Europe: the increase in population and abundance of labor had made it unnecessary; besides, serfs resented their status and were ready to buy their liberty, either on an individual or a collective base. In 1315, the king of France freed all the crown's serfs, and in 1318 he asked feudal lords to follow his example. A kind of spontaneous agrarian reform had made the manor a less oppressive institution.

This emergent late manorial system endured in France up to the French Revolution, and later in some other countries, but it was in a state of constant, though gradual, evolution. The sharp fall in population that occurred after the mid-fourteenth century only accentuated the trends of change that had prevailed beforehand, as it again created a shortage of labor in relation to land. Lords had to moderate their demands in order to attract and retain tenants; the extraction of direct labor from the latter almost died out, as did the direct cultivation of demesnes, which were increasingly farmed out; and serfdom approached extinction in western Europe. Developments in eastern Europe were inverse, and serfdom (which had emerged later, in Poland, e.g., in the twelfth century) greatly progressed in the late Middle Ages and the early modern period. In the Balkans from the thirteenth century onward, landownership, which had previously been vested in the village community, became the province of princes and noblemen, and the formerly free peasantry fell into a status close to serfdom (see below).[11]

As it survived, the manorial system was a mixed system that combined large estates and tiny peasant-owned plots, but almost everywhere large landowners leased out their land. The result was that small family farms were dominant, with millions of small entrepreneurs who were free men and able to respond to incentives. This system was rational, adapted to the conditions of the time, and able to produce surpluses and to become market oriented; it was not inimical to change. Needless to say, there were many local variants, and some countries around the periphery—the Celtic fringe, Scandinavia, Friesland, the Balkans—never manorialized properly.

A major consequence of population growth—and also of the increased flexibility of the manorial system—was a powerful impetus to clear the wilds and wastelands (especially forests) that had been so extensive in the Dark Ages. Around 1000, half of France was forested (complete with marshes, wetlands, and heaths), and the ratio was markedly higher east of the Rhine. This movement toward clearing had started in the eighth century, revived markedly after 950, peaked in the twelfth century, and continued in the thirteenth, though it slowed down in the densely populated parts of western Europe, where some shortages of timber and of pastureland were felt (still, land improvement continued in northern Italy). It was helped by improved and more powerful equipment, thanks to which stumps could be rooted out and heavy soils turned over (more on this below).

Clearings took several forms. In many villages, a good deal of land was cleared on the outskirts of fields already under cultivation. On a grander scale were frontierlike movements, which involved the creation of new villages, the inhabitants of which often had migrated from far away. The most important case was the settling by Germans of the countries to the east of the Elbe and later of the Oder.

At the start of this migration, a crucial episode of European history, those areas were sparsely populated by seminomadic Slavic tribes at a low level of material culture. Peasants lived in small villages and used primitive agricultural techniques; they cultivated poor varieties of cereals, such as millet, on the light soils that their crude tools could turn over, or they lived from pig breeding and the exploitation of forest resources. Cultivation was itinerant, and most of the land was waste. From 1150 onward, knights and peasants from Germany, where population had increased, penetrated east of the Elbe; a century later, they crossed the Oder into Pomerania. Thanks to better armaments, they drove off, exterminated, subjugated, or assimilated the Slavic population. This *Drang Nach Osten* (eastward push) went on farther east; Prussia (where Königsberg was founded in 1240) and the Baltic countries, which had been pagan, were conquered and Christianized by military religious orders and by crusaders. In the late Middle Ages, however, the border between Germans and Slavs was stabilized.

These conquests brought about significant economic changes. German princes and abbeys (many of the latter were founded beyond the Elbe) "imported" colonists from western Germany and from the Low Countries; some groups of Germans even settled in Hungary and Transylvania. Population increased markedly: twelve hundred villages were founded in Silesia between 1200 and 1350. Farming techniques and rural landscapes were completely changed as well. The new settlers introduced western equipment and methods (wheeled plows, water mills, three-year rotations), cleared up much woodland and cultivated heavy soils, grew wheat instead of millet, and lived in large villages surrounded by open fields. Soon they had surpluses of grain to send down the rivers to ports on the Baltic coast, for export. A large area of Europe that had been rather wild was thus integrated into its expanding economy.

There also was a frontier in Spain, with the *Reconquista* (or reconquest) by Christians of the Arabs (most of it was completed by the mid-thirteenth century) and its repeopling by immigrants (many of them from France).[12] The draining of marshes and reclamation of land from the sea—by systematic diking—on the coasts of the Low Countries was an important development, and many wetlands were also conquered in the Po valley of northern Italy. Those achievements were the work either of initiatives by peasant communities or of organized settlement by lords, who attracted settlers by offering them various advantages, and who used middlemen *(locatores)* to recruit and settle them. Some monastic orders also played a role, especially the Cistercians, who built their abbeys in the wilderness and created large farms around them. Europe thus expanded both internally and externally, and the cultivated area increased between 10 and 30 percent, depending upon the country. Georges Duby wrote that the clearance movement was the most decisive and spectacular development in the European economy between 900 and 1500. However, by 1300, large tracts of land were still covered by forests, and the latter retained a key role in the economy, as suppliers of food for humans (game, fruits, mushrooms), of pasture for pigs and horses, and of wood—which was the only source of heat and a basic material.

Moreover, from the mid-tenth century to the late eleventh—and even earlier in some areas—there had been a reorganization of human settlements and a large increase in their number—which were most durable. One major factor was the proliferation of fortified castles; people congregated around them, in "boroughs" (some of them became towns), partly under pressure by lords who wanted to control more closely their subjects, and partly because the latter wanted security—and also services, which priests, craftsmen, and others provided. The establishment of a network of rural parishes, completed in the eleventh and twelfth centuries, was another factor. The building (in stone) of countless Romanesque churches contributed to the fixing around them of human habitats. Some settlements also developed close to monasteries, and many, of course, in connection with the clearing up of land. The European village can be said to have been born in the tenth century, and in the twelfth, village communities became organized and recognized. They had rights over common lands and, in open-field regions, coordinated operations on arable land.

This development displayed several regional patterns. In Mediterranean Europe, there was *incastellamento,* that is, the concentration of population in large fortified villages, sited on tops of hills; below them, cereals, vines, and olive trees were mixed in enclosed and irregular fields. In the twelfth to the thirteenth centuries, terraced fields were built in all Mediterranean countries, of which they became typical. In the wide plains of northern and northwestern Europe, many people who had previously lived in dispersed farmsteads also concentrated in villages, which were smaller than in the south (two to three hundred inhabitants) but generally compact—nucleated or clustered. They were surrounded by open, unenclosed large fields, divided into long and narrow strips, which were farmed in unison but not communally in the strict sense. Street villages, with one long strip of land behind each farmhouse, were typical of German colonization in the east, but were also found elsewhere. As for western parts, along the Atlantic, their population was scattered in hamlets or isolated farmsteads, and the fields were enclosed by hedges or stone walls. This gradually developing *bocage* landscape was also found in some areas of recent settlement. In the poorer areas like the Scottish Highlands, the system of infield-outfield was practiced, and in the forests of Scandinavia, Finland, and Russia, where land was plentiful, a primitive system of slash-and-burn agriculture continued to prevail. It is, however, simplistic to reduce the almost infinite variety of European rural landscapes to a few, well-demarcated major systems (open fields in the north, enclosed fields in the south, *bocage* in the west); there were enclaves (e.g., enclosed fields in hilly areas of the open-field zone) and transitional types, plus the special cases of mountains, where people lived mainly from stock raising. Moreover, even though in some areas the rural landscape had hardly changed since Roman times, in many others it was being developed (one might say "constructed"—though not to its final stage) during this period. Those diversified and humanized landscapes, which were the patient work of generations, have largely survived up to very recent times, when the demands of modern machinery brought about serious changes. As for villages, almost all current settlements were in existence by the early fourteenth century.

Another major development was the diffusion from the tenth century onward, and from the region between the Loire and Rhine Rivers, of several technological advances that had emerged during the earlier period. Often interdependent, they as a whole made it possible to feed many more people. One was the heavy-wheeled plow, with its asymmetrical iron share, moldboard, and coulter, which had been invented in southern Germany. It made deep furrows and turned the sod over and was capable of breaking and turning heavy but fertile soils, which had previously been left uncultivated. It spread in the plains of northern and central Europe, from the eighth century onward, but the traditional unwheeled "scratch" plow —with wooden share—continued to prevail in southern Europe, where soils were thin (and even in the north on light soils, in hilly regions, and among poor peasants, as the new plow needed a strong team of animals to pull it).[13] The efficiency of the plow was much increased by the substitution, again mainly in the north, of horses for oxen as draft animals.

This was made possible by the introduction (in the ninth century, possibly from China) of the collar resting on the horse's shoulders, instead of the throat-and-girth harness, which increased by a factor of four or five the power of horses. Transport benefited from this innovation, of course, particularly as it was combined with those of the stirrup and the nailed horseshoe. For cultivators, horses were more expensive and more fragile than oxen, but they were much faster; time spent on plowing could be reduced and the number of tillings could be increased, making the soil more productive. By 1200, plowing with horses was widespread in northern France, in the Low Countries, and in southern England. Meanwhile, the harnessing of oxen also improved, as their yoke was put on their horns and then on their forehead instead of their withers; because several pairs of them could be harnessed in file, they were often preferred to work heavy soils.

Another innovation of Carolingian times (it was used in the ninth century on large estates in fertile areas of northern France) was the three-field rotation: a field was cultivated for two consecutive years (with one sowing in the fall, the next one in the spring) and then left fallow during the third, whereas formerly it had been left fallow every other year. Under its classical form—in northeastern France and southern England, for example—the territory of a village was divided into some large fields made up of parallel long strips (each peasant held one or more in each field); each of them was entirely—and compulsorily—devoted to one stage of the ternary rotation. The advantage of this new system was that the ratio of land under cultivation rose from 50 percent to 66 percent of the arable area, and with it rose the yield per unit of labor and capital. The most advanced areas—like Flanders—experimented with more complex crop rotations and fertilizing techniques; in the thirteenth century, forage plants were cultivated on the fallows around Flemish towns. By that time the three-field rotation was practiced in regions from England to Poland, but not everywhere. The hilly regions of Atlantic and central Europe, which were unsuited to open fields, had small and enclosed fields cultivated with light plows, pulled by a single animal, on a two-field rotation. In southern Europe, because of its dry climate, spring-sown cereals could not grow and ripen before the summer's drought; with some exceptions, it had to keep to the old and less-productive two-field rotation. There was indeed a close—but not perfect—relationship among the use of horses for plowing, the wheeled plow, the three-course rotation, and the open fields (long strips of land reduced the number of times the plow had to turn, which saved both time and land). This system gradually emerged from the ninth to the thirteenth century, but once put together the interdependence of its elements made it last long; in many parts of Europe it survived up to the nineteenth century.

Consideration must also be given to the improvement of tools (hoes and pitchforks were made of iron, instead of wood), the invention of new ones (e.g., the harrow), and practices such as marling and the irrigation of meadows. As demand increased with population, and as labor was becoming abundant, cultivation was more carefully done: for example, a fourth tilling was added before the autumn sowing. Altogether, from the ninth to the thirteenth century, there was a transition from an extensive agriculture to a relatively intensive one, as the gardens belts around many villages show. Productivity improved, particularly as concerns yields (i.e., crop-seed ratios). According to some historians, they rose from about 2 to 1 in Carolingian times to an average 4 or 5 to 1 in the late twelfth century, but it has been argued that Carolingian yields were underestimated, and that yields increased only between 25 and 50 percent. Such a rise remains substantial and was one factor behind the reduction in labor services and in direct farming of demesnes. Still, there was much diversity in yields at local levels.

A last development was the expansion of rich crops like wheat, which gives white bread, and oats, and the corresponding retreat of poorer ones, such as rye and barley; in general cereals progressed northward and eastward. Vine growing, in an early stage, also extended in the same directions. Wine was necessary for Christian services and wanted by the aristocracy; many towns had their belts of vineyards, even in Flanders and England. Later, however, when transportation had improved and competition from more suitable climes was felt, vineyards retreated to the Paris, Reims, and Moselle areas, while there was a great expansion in southwestern France, which exported wine by sea to northern countries. Viniculture is labor intensive and market oriented and was a great help to many small peasants. Cultivation of textile plants, like flax and hemp, and dyestuffs, like woad, also expanded, and in the thirteenth century sheep raising, for producing wool, became very important in England, in tandem with the growth of the woolens industry in Flanders, where English wool was exported—a clear connection between the progress of agriculture and of manufacturing. There also was some intensification in stock raising: clearings much reduced the herds of swine and cattle that had roamed forests and wastelands; animals then grazed on fallow lands or on meadows, and some were fattened to be sold to butchers. In mountainous countries from Norway to southern Italy, there was much transhumance in order to provide food to animals year-round. It was to develop greatly in the fourteenth and fifteenth centuries, in the entire Alpine belt.

Most of it was short distance, from one village to its upland meadows, where cattle were sent to pasture in the summer, but there was also some long-distance traveling—mainly of sheep—on the Spanish *meseta,* between Provence and the Alps, and in other areas.

It is therefore a mistake to consider medieval (and early modern) agriculture as a subsistence, self-sufficient kind of farming, and peasants as backward and resistant to all innovations. A large share of output was of course consumed by the cultivators, but a growing percentage was sold on the markets (which multiplied around fortified sites beginning in the ninth and tenth centuries), because of both demand by the towns and peasants' needs for cash. And some produce—wine, wool, grain, cattle—was carried to its markets over long distances. The market and monetary economy gradually penetrated the medieval countryside. A recent study has shown that in England, in the matter of draft animals, the peasantry was more technologically progressive and willing to change than other sections of society.

Indeed, technological progress was not foreign to medieval people—and this point must be stressed. As Joel Mokyr (1990) wrote, "Dark ages Europe managed to break through a number of technological barriers that had held the Romans back"—for complex reasons, which are connected with manorialism, Christianity (values such as respect for manual labor, subordination of nature to man, and the concept of linear time), and some freedom of enterprise. Mokyr has stressed the amazing technological achievements of medieval Europe, which came about despite an uncongenial context of insecurity at times, and a primitive economic and cultural environment at the start. And David Landes (1998) has described medieval Europe as "one of the most inventive societies which history had known," as it made "the invention of invention." Europeans were equally good at borrowing from others (classical antiquity, Asian and Islamic societies) and at creating their own technology. Moreover, their achievements were practical and aimed at modest goals but were able eventually to transform daily existence; medieval engineering easily surpassed the work of the Greco-Roman world.

Before considering some of those achievements in the nonagricultural sectors, the importance of the water mill—with vertical overshot wheel and complicated gearing for power transmission—must first be stressed.[14] The number of mills increased fast from the tenth to the thirteenth century; England had almost six thousand of them in 1086, and twelve thousand by 1300, though the latter figure included a number of windmills that had been introduced in the late twelfth century from Iran; tide mills were also used on the coasts.[15] Poland had some water mills in the twelfth century, but they only became widespread in the thirteenth and four-teenth centuries.

The main use of mills was, of course, to grind grain, but they were soon used for industrial purposes—to crush ores; to forge iron (first mention in 1104); to full woolen cloth; to make paper, oil, tan, and so forth. They were also driving pumps—for drainage purposes, such as in the Low Countries. Most mills were in the countryside, but many were set up in towns or in their suburbs. Mills were labor saving, so that much labor was freed for other purposes. Medieval Europe was the first society to build an economy on nonhuman power, as opposed to one built on the backs of slaves and coolies (Mokyr 1990). Still, some time lags behind other civilizations persisted; after the reconquest of Sicily and Spain from the Muslims, some skills—especially irrigation techniques—were lost; gunpowder, which was described in China in approximately AD 44, was not used in Europe before the 1320s. But even so, by the late Middle Ages, Europe had the ships and weapons to dominate the world.

Towns and Industries

Though agriculture remained by far the largest sector, the others, which formerly had been tiny, grew faster. In the early Middle Ages, the urban tradition of antiquity had been partly destroyed; even though continuity in towns' history is nowadays stressed, they had very small populations and military, political, and religious rather than economic functions. However, from the tenth century, first in Italy and then elsewhere, a sharp change occurred. Old cities revived and grew, particularly by the extension of suburbs (boroughs) outside their old walls, close to a monastery, a market, a bridge, or a port site. Later on, suburbs often were included within new fortifications, as medieval towns were invariably surrounded by walls. Moreover, many new towns emerged, some of them boroughs that grew next to a castle or a monastery, especially on sites suitable for trading. Cities like Ghent and Bruges were born from the conjunction of a castle and a *portus*. There were also "planted towns," created ex nihilo by the decision of some prince or lord particularly in areas of new settlement or for military reasons (the *bastides* of Gascony, which was disputed between the kings of France and England). They often had gridiron patterns, like later American towns.

A second generation of cities was thus born in the regions that had belonged to the Roman Empire, and cities emerged in vast areas of central, eastern, and northern Europe, where they had previously been absent. As mentioned earlier, in the eastern regions of German settlement, peasants produced for sale, and trading towns (with a mainly German population) were established; moreover, a string of port towns appeared on the coasts of the Baltic Sea—from Lübeck (founded 1143) to Riga (1201) and Reval (Tallin, 1270). In Poland, protourban fortified sites *(castra)* that acted as administrative centers and local markets became proper towns, inhabited by craftsmen and traders, during the eleventh and twelfth centuries; foreign merchants—mostly Germans—were attracted by the offer of privileges, and eventually by the granting of self-government (like in western cities). By the twelfth century, Poland had some large towns, like Kraków. The urban network that was thus set up —with a peak of new foundations in the twelfth century—was to last up to nineteenth-century industrialization; 93 percent of the European towns with more than 20,000 inhabitants in 1800 had been in existence by 1300.

This proliferation of towns resulted from the revival of long-distance trade. It is not the case that the merchants who carried it on had been at first itinerants—peddlers on a larger scale—who went to procure goods where they were produced and carried them to where they would be sold, and who eventually settled where they had some permanent shelter and warehouse. Actually, most such traders has been *ministeriales,* servants of the clerical and lay aristocracy, who bought and sold goods for their masters' account at the local level. Some of them extended the range of their business to interregional and even transcontinental trade. But the origins of merchants were diverse, and they included Jews, whose communities in southern Europe, the Rhineland, and Champagne played some role.[16] Merchants often settled in ancient cities, which, with their clergy and nobility, were centers of consumption, the more so when they also had the court of some king or great lord.

Urban demand also stimulated handicrafts. Actually, one major novelty of the eleventh and twelfth centuries was that the making of manufactured goods, which hitherto had been carried on within the framework of the manorial system, often in the manor's workshop by members of the lord's *familia,* passed into the hands of independent craftsmen. Many of them (such as smiths, wheelwrights, potters, etc.) stayed in villages, and coarse textiles were made everywhere in peasants' households, but much handicraft moved to towns, which also had many services—commercial, political, juridical, and educational, for example. The identity of towns was thus enhanced, even though they often retained agricultural activities, with gardens and vineyards around their walls or even inside them. There was a complex interplay between the rise of towns and the expansion of agriculture: their markets were outlets for the countryside's surpluses, without which their population could not have been fed (and the penetration of the monetary economy in villages was reinforced). They also absorbed some of the rural surplus population. On the other hand, urban elites, in collaboration with some princes and lords, created a new infrastructure: markets were established, roads and waterways improved, new laws and a new judiciary introduced. Consequently, transaction costs were reduced, and trade, both interregional and transcontinental, was stimulated. Towns were the birthplace of capitalism, both effect and engine of economic expansion.

Of course, the urban network varied in density; the latter was correlated with the rural population's density and the level of development in the region. So Highlands Britain, Scandinavia, the Balkans, some parts of the Mediterranean zone, and Russia had few towns (and backward economies), while the most urbanized countries were also the most densely populated. Europe had two areas where urbanization started and reached its highest level: Flanders (with its clothing towns) and northern Italy, both fertile and "industrial" regions where major trade routes also converged.[17] Moreover, in Italy, the Roman urban network had not been too much obliterated, relations with the more advanced economies of Byzantium and Islam had been maintained, and the landed aristocracy resided in towns. It was also in Italy that the "communal revolution" started in the late eleventh century and freed cities from bishops' or princes' authority. Many Italian—and also German—towns became city-states, independent republics. Even under powerful monarchies, as in England and France, towns had a degree of self-government. This liberty that cities enjoyed was a specific and vital character of Europe's history. It created a major contrast with China, where urban life was controlled by bureaucrats and landowners; where any entrepreneurial activity was precarious, liable to extortions by the bureaucracy; and where no independent middle class of traders and manufacturers could develop. Moreover, city-states (and all urban centers)—which were relatively small units—may have had an advantage as loci of technological creativity.

Some towns became rather large: by 1300, Venice, Milan, and Genoa had about 100,000 inhabitants each; and Paris, capital of a large state, was the biggest city in the West, and even bigger than Constantinople, with possibly 200,000 people.

However, such "giants" were very rare: by 1300, Europe had about 6,000 towns, but only 100 of them had more than 10,000 inhabitants (and only a score over 25,000), even though the number of these relatively large cities had more than doubled since 1100; another 100 to 150 had between 5,000 and 10,000 people. Most towns were quite small, basically big villages with a market and some craftsmen. Therefore, the degree of urbanization must not be overestimated: c. 1300, only 10 percent of Europe's population lived in towns (but 25 percent in Flanders, Brabant, and northern Italy—and more in some areas of those regions, e.g., in the *contado* of Florence). Population grew somewhat faster in towns than in the countryside, but only because of constant immigration from the latter, as towns had a surplus of deaths over births.

At first, trade was the reason towns grew, but soon they concentrated the production of craftsmen-manufactured goods for local consumption and also in many cases for export to distant markets, as textile fabrics—and their raw materials—were not bulky and could be easily transported, even overland. The making of woolen cloths was the largest medieval industry; they were made everywhere, but from the eleventh century onward, woolens were produced for export in large quantities in the towns of Flanders and the neighboring areas, where the first "industrial" cities emerged.[18] The main centers were originally in Artois, at Arras and St. Omer, and then the focus moved northward to Ypres, Ghent, and Bruges; eventually, cloth making spread to nearby provinces such as Picardy, Champagne, Hainaut, and Brabant. Cloths were standardized but of good quality (largely made from English wool), and exports were mainly of gray cloths, which were sold at the fairs of Champagne (see The Growth of Trade, below) to Italian merchants, who had them dyed and finished, and exported them to the Levant. Northern Italy (including Tuscany) also developed, somewhat later, a large textile industry of its own—and was the only European country to make silks.

Actually, production of silk and weaving of silk fabrics had long been a Chinese monopoly, and silks were exported from China to the Middle East and the Roman Empire, through central Asia, along the famous "silk road" (indeed, there were several routes, including one by sea). Raw and spun silk was also imported from China, and silk weaving developed during the Roman Empire period in Egypt and Syria, then in Constantinople. But supplies were expensive and irregular, and in the mid-sixth century, the Byzantine emperor Justinian sent to China some monks (Buddhist or Christian) who managed to smuggle back some silkworm eggs plus the know-how to breed worms (an early case of government-sponsored industrial espionage!). The production of raw silk and the silk industry spread to Greece, Sicily, and Muslim Spain (in the eleventh century). Silk weaving—with raw silk imported from Sicily, southern Italy, the Levant, and China—emerged in Lucca in the twelfth century.[19]

The rise of the woolen industry was helped by inventions from the eleventh and twelfth centuries: the spinning wheel (which at least doubled productivity relative to the distaff-and-spindle method), the horizontal pedal loom for weaving, the water-powered fulling mill (mentioned in England in 1185). The widening of markets through the growth of trade stimulated the diffusion of those—and other—inventions. Moreover, there was a growing and extensive division of labor in textile production, resulting in higher productivity and lower costs; this division was largely by gender: spinning was done by women; weaving, dyeing, and finishing by men. This was a major change from the early Middle Ages, when women, often gathered in the workshops (typically called *gynecea*) of rural estates, dominated textile work. The shift in the gender organization of textile production came when the latter moved to towns.

Nontextile industries were less important, but the working of leather was widespread, and there was a strong increase in the production of iron and other metals. Metals were much more widely used than in antiquity, particularly in the countryside, though there was not much technical progress in the making of iron, which was by a direct process with a low hearth and a wind furnace (blast furnaces developed in the fourteenth century). Still, German miners' search for and working of metallic ores in the mountains of central Europe (Harz, Carpathians) contributed to the opening of those regions. There was some concentration of metalworking in districts that made quality products, thanks to the quality of their ores and the skills of their workers, such as Liège and the Meuse valley (christening fonts cast in Dinant are found in churches far away), or Milan and Brescia, which made renowned armors and weapons.

Building was also very active, especially for military and religious purposes: enormous fortresses and large and splendid churches sprang up everywhere in Europe starting in the early eleventh century.[20] A contemporary chronicler, the monk of Cluny, Raoul Glaber, wrote (before 1031): "One could have said that the world shook itself to throw off its decrepitude and to don a white mantle of churches." Thousands and thousands of the latter are still standing from Sweden to Portugal, from Scotland to Poland, as proof of this birth of a new Europe. Progress was also qualitative: in the ninth century, buildings were wooden (except churches); from the eleventh century, stone and masonry prevailed, and monuments became bigger and better decorated. In the twelfth century, the Roman craft of brick making was revived in northern Europe, and the "Gothic revolution" started: thanks to ogival vaults and flying buttresses, tall, solid, and well-lighted churches could be built. By that time, building technology, which involved much division of labor, had clearly overtaken that of antiquity. And by the thirteenth century, western Europe had many highly skilled craftsmen, including sculptors, enamelers, gold- and silversmiths, stained glass–makers, and painters of illuminated manuscripts.

Another development that started in the twelfth century and progressed in the thirteenth was the emergence in industry and trade of a new pattern of organization, the guild system, which, like the manor, was to last for centuries.[21] Though this system did not spread to all trades or to all places, and though it took various forms, it was widespread, with three main characteristics (plus a religious aspect). First, in each town, only members of the relevant guild might practice a trade; guilds had a hierarchical organization and their leaders had police powers with the support of the town's authorities; and work was regulated in order to restrain competition and fraud, and to guarantee the quality of products. This was, of course, in accordance with the ideal of stability that prevailed, but inimical to innovation—and to production on a larger scale than the family workshop (the number of apprentices and workmen whom one master could employ was restricted). The trend toward corporatism and regulation was to be strengthened during the hard times of the late Middle Ages. However, regulations were far from being strictly respected, and in the textile industries they did not prevent the emergence of practices that became important: merchants came to control the whole process of production, and the artisans who worked for them were no more than wage earners. They also, of course, commercialized manufactured goods, which, together with the raw materials for their production, played an increasing role in "international" trade.

The Growth of Trade

The expansion of commerce was an engine of growth for the whole economy, but the former was also helped by some of the institutional and technological innovations mentioned above as well as the increase in population and production, including the creation of agricultural surpluses.

Trade growth, initiated in the tenth through eleventh centuries, blossomed in the thirteenth; it started at the periphery of Europe, from seaports—mostly in southern Italy, which had maintained relations with Byzantium and Muslim countries. Amalfi was the most important: it had made agreements with its Muslim neighbors so that its ships could navigate the Strait of Messina, and it traded with North Africa and even Egypt. However, those southern ports were too far from northwestern Europe, and they were soon superseded by more northerly ones: Pisa, Genoa (which dominated trade in the western Mediterranean), and Venice. A trade treaty with Byzantium of 992 (followed by another one in 1082) gave privileges and tax exemptions to the Venetians—actually a quasimonopoly of the empire's trade; in the twelfth century they received privileges in Acre and other ports in the crusaders' states. Indeed, from the late eleventh century, commercial expansion by Europeans went hand in hand with their military counteroffensive against Islam, especially the Crusades (and the reconquest of Sicily and Crete), which changed the political and economic balance of power to the advantage of Christians, so that Italian cities and merchants took over the long-distance Mediterranean trade. According to Arab writers, in the early eleventh century the Mediterranean was a Muslim lake where a Christian "cannot float a plank" (actually, most goods were carried to the west on ships from the eastern Mediterranean); at the end of the century, "the sea belongs to the Rûm" (Romans, i.e., Christians). Moreover, the Crusades stimulated shipbuilding—to transport crusaders and pilgrims—and the making of weapons, to the benefit mainly of Italian cities. As for the crusaders who returned home, they had acquired a taste for a more sumptuous and refined way of living, which increased the demand for luxuries.

Eventually, however, the Crusades ended in failure: Acre, the last western Christian stronghold in the Holy Land, fell to the Muslims in 1291. Still, Christians retained their ascendancy at sea, and they were allowed to trade in the Muslim-controlled ports of Egypt and the Levant.[22] Muslim countries kept to their passive role of intermediaries between the Indian Ocean and the Mediterranean, and their trade did not generate a powerful merchant elite, like in Italy. On the other hand, the Crusades of reconquest in the Iberian Peninsula were a success—and also a commercial reconquest. Muslim Spain had been closely linked with the Muslim East, while Christian Spain (and Portugal) was integrated into the European economic sphere and developed its trade with northern Europe. This contributed to the opening of the Atlantic, of which the most striking example—a sea route from Italy to Flanders and England—will be discussed again later.

Long-distance trade in the Mediterranean was mainly a transit trade in goods that came from far away—from India, Southeast Asia, and China—and that Italian ships loaded at Alexandria and other ports in the Levant; Italian merchants then redistributed them all over Europe.[23] However, ships and merchants from Barcelona, Montpellier, and Marseilles had a share in this traffic. And the overland routes, from Constantinople and Black Sea ports to Kiev, Novgorod, Kraków, Prague, and ports on the Baltic coast, remained active until the Mongol invasion; a more southerly route passed through Transylvania and reached Hungary. But land traffic was much smaller than seaborne trade: Austria and southern Germany were wholly supplied through Venice with goods from the East.

The main goods traded were the same as in the early Middle Ages, but in much larger quantities: silks and other luxury fabrics, raw silk, spices (especially pepper, of which medieval people were very fond[24]), perfumes, ivory, and precious stones. There were also wines from Crete and Greece, currants, oranges, raw cotton, and, from Asia Minor, bulk cargoes of alum, which was necessary for dyeing textiles. Europeans exported woolens and linens, metals, weapons, salt, and slaves. In the eleventh century, Venice sent slaves from Dalmatia to Muslim countries. In the thirteenth century, after the Fourth Crusade (1204), Venetians and Genoese bought slaves in their Black Sea trading posts; they sold the men in Egypt and the women in Italy, Marseilles, and Barcelona, as domestic servants. Europeans also exported silver, as the balance of trade was against them. This represented a significant change relative to the early Middle Ages, when Europe only exported primary goods (and slaves) to the more developed Byzantine and Muslim countries; in the thirteenth century, Muslim industry had declined and the West had become an exporter of manufactures; this reversal was to become more pronounced later on.

With widened horizons in the thirteenth century as a consequence of the Fourth Crusade, Venice and later Genoa established a colonial empire of trading posts in the former Byzantine Empire; their merchants and ships entered the Black Sea and in its eastern ports made contacts with Asian merchants, who had been able to travel so far thanks to the peace that prevailed in the Mongol empire. The Muslim Middle East was thus left out of the loop. A few Westerners traveled as far as China—the best known being the Venetian Marco Polo, who wrote his *Book of Marvels* after returning from a long stay in China (1275–1291). In volume this Black Sea trade was marginal (and would stop in the fifteenth century), but it was a bold initiative and a forerunner of the fifteenth-century "discoveries" that resulted from efforts to establish direct relations with India and China. As an aside, it is worth mentioning that, in 1291, the Genoese Vivaldi brothers disappeared off the coast of Morocco while attempting to circumnavigate Africa.

This glamorous long-distance trade with the East and its role as engine of growth for the European economy as a whole must not be overestimated. Its volume remained quite small (and much smaller than traffic in the Indian Ocean); it has been estimated that, c. 1300, imports into Italy from the East did not exceed five thousand tons per year (and were basically of luxuries). And as the West needed to have goods to export in return, the case has been made that the urban renaissance in the Low Countries and the fast growth of woolen cloth production there were the forces that generated the expansion of trade.

At any rate, one must certainly not neglect the intra-European, inter-regional trades, which also grew quickly starting in the late eleventh century.[25] Their rise resulted from the variety of resources and climatic conditions, and from the fact that areas of high population density could more efficiently produce labor-intensive goods, which they exchanged for land-intensive produce from regions that were less densely settled. Moreover, there were improvements in land transport, thanks to the shoulder collar and the iron horseshoe as well as to the building of many bridges.[26] Still, bulk goods could circulate over long distances only by river or by sea, but their passage was eased by a "nautical revolution" in the thirteenth and fourteenth centuries, which included the invention of the hinged sternpost rudder (which replaced the steering oar), the use of the compass, maps (*portulans*), and rutters (published sailing directions), and the building of larger sailing ships—the nave or round ship and the cog, which was invented in the north but spread to the Mediterranean (it was derived from Viking boats, but was broader and higher).[27] New commercial techniques invented by Italian merchants are mentioned in chapter 2. Though many merchants traveled with their goods, by the thirteenth century most trading houses operated from one city and had agents and factors in other places.

One of the intra-European trades was the export of salt and wine from the French Atlantic coast to England and Flanders (later to Germany and the Baltic as well); c. 1250, more than a thousand ships from the north entered the port of La Rochelle each year, and in the early fourteenth century, Bordeaux exported on average more than 80,000 200-gallon tuns of wine per year (105,000 in 1305–1309).[28] A different trade developed in the North Sea and the Baltic following the integration into Christian Europe and development of large territories east of the Elbe. They exported—down rivers and then by sea—grain, herring, wool, furs, hides, and forest products to the "advanced" and urbanized countries, such as Flanders and the rest of the Low Countries, which sent in return woolens and other manufactures. At the crossroads of traffic with the Baltic, Germany, France, England, and the Mediterranean stood the Flemish city of Bruges (and its outer harbors of Damme and Sluys), which was a center both of redistribution for many goods and of the textile industry; it also became, in the late fourteenth century, the largest money market in Europe. However, Bruges had neither ships nor seamen; its trade was dominated by foreigners—Germans at first, and later Italians.

Northern European trade extended up to Novgorod, in Russia, and was largely handled by merchants from German cities, of which Lübeck was the most important. A major hub of their Baltic trade was the port of Visby, on the island of Gotland. In the late twelfth century, the German

cities on the Baltic coast united in a league; then, in the thirteenth century, the merchants of Lübeck concluded a treaty with those of Hamburg
and of other towns (including some along the Rhine). This union, which
came to be called the Hansa, joined between seventy and eighty trading
towns, but it only was a very loose confederation, and its commercial
techniques were less sophisticated than those of Italian merchants. The
Hansards were granted privileges in various ports, especially London and
Bruges, and their ships sailed as far as French and Iberian ports. From
Flanders to the eastern Baltic, they created a northern maritime culture,
complete with towns that had many similar features: brick houses with
high gables, belfries, and Gothic churches with wide naves and large win-
dows still display the stamp of the Hansa.

The most populous and active part of medieval Europe stretched
from southeastern England through the Low Countries, a large slice of
France, and the Rhineland (this was for long the heart of Europe) to Tuscany, but there were two regions that in all respects had become the most
active, advanced, and rich: northern and central Italy, Flanders, and con-
tiguous areas in present-day Belgium and northern France. This bipolarity
was to last up to the sixteenth century and was an important aspect of Europe's history. A major breakthrough was thus achieved when a connection between those two poles was established. A number of fairs were held
along the roads from the North Sea to the Mediterranean, but around
1180, the fairs of Champagne (at the southern fringe of the most developed areas of northwestern Europe) became by far the most important
and the great mart of European trade; there were six of them each year,
in four different towns east of Paris.[29] Merchants from the north brought
woolens and linens, which they sold to Italians, who had come with silks,
spices, and other products from the Orient; Jews, Germans, and men from
southern France also attended. Hides, furs, dyes, and metals were also
traded. The fairs benefited from protection by the counts of Champagne,
who gave safe-conducts to merchants and appointed some wardens of the
fairs, who became a tribunal, "a kind of supreme court of Europe's trading world" (Carpentier and Le Mené).

Travel between Italy and the fairs was at first by sea to the ports of
Provence, and then on land along the Rhône and Saône valleys or through
passes in the western Alps, but it was made easier by the opening of a direct route through the central Alps. Some cattle breeders from what is now
central Switzerland wanted to sell their animals in populous Lombardy, so
between 1218 and 1230 they created a road over the St. Gotthard pass,
including a stone bridge over a dangerous torrent, the Reuss. This route
was soon used as a shortcut by merchants and proved a major development

in European economic history. It also started the integration of Switzerland (as it later became known) into the European economy.

Still, the importance of the fairs of Champagne did not last very long; in the late thirteenth century, their banking activities, involving new techniques of credit, prevailed over the purely commercial role, and they ceased to take place around 1320, eventually replaced to some degree by new fairs: at Châlon-sur-Saône, farther south, and at Geneva. In the fifteenth century, Geneva, at the crossroads of several major trading routes, was to be the place where Italian merchants met those from France, southern Germany, and Flanders. However, the deathblow for the fairs of Champagne had come earlier, from the opening of the direct sea route through the Straits of Gibraltar, from the Mediterranean to the Atlantic and the North Sea, especially the port of Bruges.[30] The passageway was inaugurated in 1277 by Genoese and was in regular use by the early fourteenth century (Venetian ships followed from 1317 onward). There was, of course, a connection with the progress in shipping and navigation that has been mentioned, and also with the Reconquista in Spain, thanks to which Christian ships could sail through the Straits of Gibraltar.[31] Needless to say, the opening of direct relations between two maritime spaces —the Mediterranean on one hand, the Atlantic and the northern seas on the other—which had hitherto been separated had a profound impact on European history.

Farther east, meanwhile, there was a lot of overland traffic through passes in the Alps, from Venice to southern Germany (which had rich silver and copper mines) and the Rhineland. The city of Frankfurt had fairs, through which relations developed with the Hansa on one hand, Hungary and Poland on the other, while Cologne was the intermediary between Flanders and Germany. Part of the traffic that had gone to the Champagne fairs was thus diverted toward a new axis from Italy to the Low Countries through the Alps and the Rhineland.

Most historians agree that by the thirteenth century (and possibly as early as the twelfth), thanks particularly to the fairs of Champagne, an integrated European market—a *respublica mercantaria,* or a European "world economy" (in the Braudelian sense)—had emerged, despite the divisions and fights between nations and states. From the eastern Mediterranean to the eastern Baltic and the Black Sea, there were increasing flows of goods and circuits of trade. No quantitative measurement is possible, but the case of England is illustrative: during the thirteenth century, its overseas trade increased threefold (after adjustment for inflation).

Contributing to this integration was the diaspora across Europe of Italian (often called "Lombards") businessmen, as well as some Iberians. Most

of them were small businessmen who were ubiquitous in dispensing consumer credit, as pawnbrokers and usurers. Others were proper merchants,
and some were agents of a few "supercompanies."[32] The latter were involved in commodity trading (e.g., exports of grain from Sicily), but they
were also bankers, and they became involved in dealings with princes (the
kings of England, particularly) as tax farmers and lenders of money.
Around 1340, the Bardi company, from Florence, had three hundred
agents scattered across Europe. However, these large companies failed in
the 1340s, a symptom of the economic malaise that antedated the Black
Death. Still, a kind of international trading community had emerged,
making easier the diffusion of new commercial and financial techniques.

Of course, integration remained loose and most trade took place over
short distances, in low-value, locally or regionally produced goods, though
this meant that countless small markets and small merchants existed.
Moreover, though money had not been widely used in the eleventh century, except as a standard of value, in the thirteenth the monetarization
of the economy was achieved. As the number of transactions multiplied,
the circulation of specie became much more intense (in Poland, large-
scale minting of silver coins had started in the late eleventh century). The
eleventh-century shortage of silver was alleviated by the opening of new
mines on the Anglo-Scottish border (where mining boomed from 1135
to 1225), in Italy, and in central Europe (in Freiberg, Saxony, in 1160, and
later in Bohemia). Large silver coins *(gros)* could thus be minted, a process
that began in Italy in the early thirteenth century and later in other countries (1266 in France). Moreover, thanks to increased trade with North
Africa, gold from the Sudan arrived in Europe, allowing gold coins to be
minted in the West (particularly Italian cities) for the first time since the
seventh century. The florin was first coined in Florence in 1252, Genoa
minted gold at the same time, and Venice followed in 1284. Though gold
did not circulate much outside Italy before the fourteenth century, Marc
Bloch, taking into account some other innovations (including non-
metallic money), wrote of a thirteenth-century "monetary revolution"; it
established a bimetallic monetary system that was to last long. The quantity of money in circulation and—likely—the latter's velocity markedly increased during the thirteenth century. On the other hand, the number
of minting authorities fell: there had been an enormous number earlier
on, when feudal lords took over the state's powers (and many coins of
poor quality were then issued), but when strong states emerged again,
their princes (especially the kings of England and France) imposed the
exclusive use of their money in the lands they ruled and claimed a monopoly over minting.

A New Europe

Around 1300, after three creative centuries—at the grassroots level, without constraints by nonexisting states—Europe was densely populated, mobile, active, and dynamic. Literacy, schooling, and the use of writing and reckoning had revived remarkably. Beginning in the late twelfth century, the need for accurate accounting in business developed; the introduction, c. 1202, of Arabic numerals made counting, calculating, and measuring much easier. New mentalities—ones that were not at all "medieval" in the common meaning—were emerging. Later, time measurement became an interest. The first mechanical, weight-driven clocks were made in the late thirteenth century, and their use spread during the fourteenth (watches and spring mechanisms would appear in the fifteenth century). Landes (1983) has demonstrated their importance, as both a symptom and a proof of technological progressiveness; they were the "greatest achievement of medieval mechanical ingenuity." Their making demanded a high level of precision and thus served as an example for all other machinery. Clockmakers were to be the pioneers of mechanical engineering, and clocks a monopoly of Europe for centuries. The invention of spectacles in late thirteenth-century Pisa was also important: it at least doubled the working life of craftsmen and literate people. Altogether, there was a trend toward rationality, to the idea that nature could be mastered and its forces harnessed for human uses.[33]

Europe had traveled a long way from the "barbarism" of the seventh century, and from the tenth to the early fourteenth century its economy changed in depth and greatly expanded. The question now is whether there was economic growth, that is, sustained increase in per capita product. Some writers doubt it: expansion of production was extensive, involving large increases in the numbers of people at work, so productivity gains were small, especially in the dominant agricultural sector, despite innovations, as their diffusion was generally slow; also, the economy was dualist, with the dynamic sector in a minority position. Moreover, by the late thirteenth and early fourteenth centuries, overpopulation and diminishing returns were threatening.[34] Nonetheless, there is little doubt that per capita income increased. G. D. Snooks (in Maddison and Van der Wee) has calculated that in England it almost trebled between 1086 and 1330, despite a population growth of the same order. He believes that similar progress took place in Flanders, northern France, Lombardy, and Tuscany. Many scholars have been skeptical (to say the least), but Ian Blanchard, while writing that "inevitably such a calculation is fraught with difficulties," suggests that Snooks's conclusions are supported by other ev-

idence. Angus Maddison (1998) has estimated that per capita GDP increased by one-fourth in Europe (Russia excluded) from 960 to 1280, but
that China, under the Song dynasty, did better, enjoying an intensive
growth and reaching a higher level of product per head. Undoubtedly,
Europeans of all ranks were living better by 1250 than by 950—thanks to
technological progress (especially the three-field system and the new
sources of power) and the diffusion of the market economy, which had
reduced transaction costs and promoted specialization.

However, at the mid-fourteenth century, Europe was to be struck by a
terrible disaster—the Black Death—which killed one-third of its population and caused, of course, a serious fall in output and a protracted stagnation. Still, the technological and institutional progress and the increase
in knowledge that had been achieved before this disaster were not destroyed, and when population and production recovered, it was largely
within the framework that had been created before the plague. The European economy of the late Middle Ages and the early modern period,
which will be considered in the next chapter, was not fundamentally different from the one that had emerged in the thirteenth century.

This economic—and social—order, which thus prevailed in Europe
for at least eight centuries, is often called "feudalism." In a stage theory
of history, feudalism is the intermediate regime between slavery, which
was typical of the ancient world, and capitalism, which prevailed in the
modern era but will eventually be superseded by socialism. Feudalism is
the system appropriate to a "natural economy": land is almost the only
source and embodiment of wealth, agriculture is by far the dominant sector, goods are not commodities, and labor is provided not by wage contract but by compulsory service; there is a concentration of both wealth
and power in the hands of large landowners, to whom the bulk of the
working population is subjugated, particularly by serfdom; and large estates are the typical form of economic organization, though small units
of production are dominant.

On the other hand, many historians who are concerned with precision consider the essence of feudalism to be the fief—the knightly estate
charged with obligations of military service. Therefore, the words "feudal" and "feudalism" must be reserved for societies where fiefs play a major
role, where the usual functions of government have become vested in feudal lordships, where the social order rests upon links between man and
man—obedience and fidelity on one side, protection on the other—and
where the dominant economic organization is the manor.

This restrictive use of "feudalism" is the most sensible, inasmuch as the
so-called feudal economies "were seldom wholly or even mostly natural"

(Postan 1983), without surpluses and markets. However, it greatly restricts the extension of feudalism, both in time (from the tenth to the twelfth century in most of western Europe) and in space, as manorial estates were never universal in Europe. On the other hand, the manor, under changing forms, long survived fiefs and knightly service, that is, feudalism in the strict sense. Conversely, according to Karl Marx himself, capitalism was born in Italian cities of the twelfth and thirteenth centuries.

Altogether, there was in Europe (but not everywhere) after 1000, for some time, an economic, social, and political system that can be called "feudal," but some of its features died out early, and others survived long. The transition from feudalism to capitalism, which has so much aroused Marxists, was so protracted that the concept is not very useful. The European economy of the late medieval and early modern times was a complex mixture. It makes more sense to call it just the "traditional European economy."

Two

Change and Continuity in the European Economy, Fourteenth through Eighteenth Centuries

---

The last chapter stressed that there was a block in European history from the thirteenth or fourteenth centuries to the eighteenth that transcends the old division between Middle Ages and early modern times. During this long period, the European economy went through many significant changes—an endless dynamism that is its striking and unique feature; but it also retained some common and permanent basic characteristics, even though there were serious differences in the economic history of Europe's different parts. Alfred Chandler has written: "The American businessman of 1840 would find the environment of fifteenth-century Italy more familiar than that of his own nation seventy years later." And in England, strong similarities can be observed between the late medieval and seventeenth-century economies. Admittedly, one can object that there was a sharp break in the sixteenth century because of the "discoveries" of faraway lands, the rise of oceanic trades, the inflow into Europe of precious metals and the inflation that they fueled, and also the Reformation, which divided Europe in two hostile camps. The importance of those developments cannot be denied, but they were parts of the unceasing flow of major and minor changes that Europe underwent without any radical alteration in the structures and workings of its economy. "In the *material* things of life the great break came in the eighteenth century" (Pounds).

This chapter will first present the dynamic and positive aspects of European economic history. The second part will analyze the handicaps that contributed to inertia and immobility in the long run, but that did not prevent all economic growth.

Progress in Technology

The first point is that the technological creativity that medieval Europe had displayed was unabated. Moreover, while in earlier centuries Europe had borrowed greatly from Asian technologies, henceforth it pulled ahead on its own steam; by 1500, it had achieved at least parity with the most advanced parts of the Asiatic world, and then it widened the gap by moving ahead of them. It has been argued that Europe's advantage, when its colonial expansion started, was mainly in armaments and military organization, while in GNP per capita the difference with India or China was small, and that the West needed Asian goods, a need which was not reciprocated. Actually, by 1200, the Islamic world had lost its momentum in technology. China's economic zenith had been reached in the twelfth century; in the fourteenth century and later, under the Ming and Qing, an increasingly bureaucratic, centralized, and introverted system inhibited change. Unlike China, which fell into a "high level equilibrium trap" (Elvin), in other words, a situation where technology is fairly advanced but where further progress does not give any return in the short run, Europe did not stop: it had taken "its stand under the signs of uninterrupted change" (Braudel). Moreover, by 1500, the European world had become integrated enough that new technologies spread quite fast, thanks to migration of skilled labor. Some migration was spontaneous: miners and glassworkers from Bohemia and Germany, ironworkers from the Liège area, and Italian silk weavers went to other countries. But there were also many refugees fleeing religious (rather than political) persecution; in the late sixteenth century, Protestant textile workers left the southern Netherlands in large numbers, settling in Holland and England; a century later, around 1685, they were followed by French Huguenots, who also went to Switzerland and Prussia. Skilled workers (as well as entrepreneurs) could also be suborned by agents of a foreign government that wanted to establish or improve some branch of manufacture. This was how the making of plate glass was started in France, thanks to Venetian experts (1665). In the eighteenth century, the French government, among others, sponsored a great deal of industrial espionage in England, which had then become the leader in technology.

On the other hand, surprisingly, there were fewer macroinventions, fewer major breakthroughs than in the early Middle Ages. Progress consisted largely of microinventions, of improvements to existing techniques. This confirms the idea of continuity, as major discontinuities with the past result from macroinventions. During the Renaissance, the profession of engineer emerged (this was a weakening of the classical dichotomy between thinkers and makers), but the machines engineers invented and built were mainly for public works and for erecting monuments; some of their bold ideas could not be turned into reality because of constraints in workmanship and materials (the flying machines and submarines that Leonardo da Vinci designed are typical). The "scientific revolution" of the seventeenth century, the creation of modern science by Galileo, Descartes, Newton, and others, had very little impact upon technology at the time, except some applications of mathematics (and astronomy) to civil and military engineering, navigation, and mapmaking. Some scientists took much interest in practical problems, but with few concrete results.

Let us now consider briefly the main innovations. In agriculture, the "new husbandry" emerged, but only in Flanders, Holland, and England; it was almost ignored in the rest of Europe (see below). In power generation, there were improvements of water and windmills (like the replacement of wind post-mills by tower-mills), but none of them was revolutionary. The mining of coal and its use, for both domestic and industrial purposes, greatly increased in Britain—but only in Britain, though important progress was achieved in mining techniques first in central Europe in the fifteenth century, later in England.[1] In the iron industry, a major advance took place in the fourteenth and fifteenth centuries, with the introduction (first in the Rhineland and the Liège district) of the blast furnace, where high temperatures could be obtained, thanks to water-driven bellows; it produced pig iron, which had to be refined to get bar iron, but the latter was of better quality and cheaper than it had been when made in traditional Catalan forges (by the eighteenth century, few of the latter were in operation). Consideration must also be given to the invention of rolling, slitting, wire-drawing mills—to process metals—and of reverberatory furnaces, to produce nonferrous metals and also glass, ceramics, and the like.

Connected with metalworking was the invention of printing with movable type (1453), the first great European invention for which the name of the inventor—Johannes Gutenberg—is known. It is one of the greatest inventions of all times, with far-reaching cultural consequences, but a tiny direct economic impact despite a fast expansion: in 1480, 110 European towns had printers, and by 1500, their number had risen to 236. The invention of gunpowder (which may have come from China), the development of artillery (first used in 1326–1327) and of portable firearms (fifteenth century), and their continuous improvement caused a complete change in warfare and had more direct—and indirect—economic influence. Also influential were spring-driven clocks and watches (mid-fifteenth century) and the making of scientific instruments, which was largely derived from clock making; it was perfected in south German cities (Augsburg,

Nürnberg) in the fifteenth and sixteenth centuries; it taught the wonders that precision can achieve and had spillover effects in manufacturing, like the improvement of lathes for making precision parts.

In contrast, textiles, the largest industry of the time, had only microinventions: the stocking frame or knitting machine (1589); the ribbon loom (1604), which could weave up to twenty-four ribbons simultaneously; some improvements in the spinning wheel (it was made foot operated in the sixteenth century, thanks to the treadle and crank); and the development in Bologna, Italy, from the fourteenth century on, of water-powered silk-reeling and -throwing mills, with complex machinery that could throw simultaneously thousands of threads, and that were forerunners of factories. Also, Europeans started to make cotton fabrics, in imitation of India.

Altogether, there were significant productivity gains in some areas, but there was also a spottiness, a lack of cumulative and interactive effects of technical change, of "chain reactions," so that "the productivity of the economic system as a whole made only very limited progress" (Cipolla).

Still, an exception to this generalization might be made in the case of shipbuilding and navigation technology, which achieved continuous and striking progress—in continuity with the nautical revolution of the thirteenth and fourteenth centuries, and also in correlation with geographical discovery and the growth of seaborne trade. "Maritime Europe" was created by exchanges of technology between its two major areas—the Mediterranean and the Atlantic and northern seas—after the opening of the sea route from Italy to Flanders. The lateen sail, which was Indian and Arabic in origin and had become typical of the Mediterranean, was taken up in the north. The carvel building technique, which superseded clinker planking, and thanks to which bigger and lighter ships could be built, spread from the north. Southern and northern influences met on the northern coast of Spain and in Portugal, where several important innovations were made, and eventually large ships were much alike, both in the Mediterranean and in the Atlantic. The best-known example is the caravel, which was developed by the Portuguese c. 1430 and became the instrument of the "great discoveries"; rather small and light, it was nonetheless fast, with two or three masts carrying lateen sails. However, the major invention, c. 1400, was the development of the three-masted ship with full rigging of both lateen and square sails, which was easy to handle (it could, unlike earlier ships, sail against the wind) and relatively fast. Among the early ones was the carrack, built in Basque ports but much used by both the Genoese and the Portuguese. The galleon came in the sixteenth century, and in the north the *holk (hourque)* replaced the single-masted cog. Meanwhile, the oared galley fell into disuse, except for warfare in the Mediterranean and the Baltic.

The three-masted ship made global sailing possible and the Europeans masters of the high seas—and therefore of the world—for several centuries. At first, ships were bifunctional, usable both for trade and in war; but with the introduction of heavy guns and also the decline of piracy, ships became specialized (by the mid-seventeenth century) as cargo ships or naval vessels. The average size of merchant ships was on the increase, as was the ratio between tonnage and number of sailors (i.e., labor productivity). One particularly notable design c. 1595 was the Dutch *fluyt* (flyboat in English), a long and flat-bottomed ship that was cheap to build and operate and carried a large cargo with a small crew; it was widely used in the seventeenth and eighteenth centuries, especially in the northern seas. Constant improvements in hull design, rigging, and armaments eventually produced in the eighteenth century what was perhaps the most sophisticated and complex masterpiece of pre–industrial revolution technology: the three-deck, three-mast ship of the line, carrying up to 120 guns and a 1,500-man crew. Ships also had better navigational tools and methods; by the early sixteenth century, the system of winds and undercurrents in the Atlantic was well understood; and compasses and navigational charts were improved. Starting in the fifteenth century, sea captains could easily estimate their current latitude using the cross-staff and later the astrolabe and the quadrant, but the calculation of longitude remained uncertain until the Englishman John Harrison built an accurate chronometer in 1763.

In contrast, there were few improvements in inland transport. River navigation was most active—and much cheaper than land transport (six to ten times less for the same weight)—but many rivers were difficult to navigate because of natural and/or manmade obstacles (such as dams for water mills). Though locks had been invented in the twelfth century, few canals were dug before the mid-1700s. The Languedoc canal, which opened in 1681 with 119 locks and linked the Mediterranean to the Atlantic, was a pioneering but isolated case of large-scale transport works.[2] Despite some improvements in the building of carts, wagons, and carriages, land transport lagged behind the remarkable growth of seaborne trade, which was an outstanding aspect of the period we are considering, one that has connections with progress in shipbuilding and navigation as well as commercial and financial techniques.

Important commerce-related innovations had started in the twelfth and thirteenth centuries and went on later, greatly facilitating the expansion of trade. In these matters, everything was invented and developed

by Italian merchants, including, first, several types of companies or partnerships for carrying trade. In the early ones, the agreement between
silent and active partners was temporary, valid for one venture only; but
in the twelfth century, some partnerships were regularly renewed and thus
durable. As early as the thirteenth century, then, some Italian trading and
financial companies had become very large and were operating in other
countries—as far away as England (so that some writers have called them,
rather anachronistically, the first "multinationals").[3] Secondly, Italians
developed insurance against risks at sea (which became common in the
Mediterranean after 1350, but only in the sixteenth century in northern
Europe), double-entry bookkeeping (it emerged in the early fourteenth
century; the first known example in England is from 1525), and the bill
of exchange, thanks to which payments could be made and funds transferred over long distances more easily than with the costs and risks involved in transporting specie.

The last development, the bill of exchange, appeared in the late thirteenth century and was the product of a long and rather complex
process connected with the trade fairs, especially those of Champagne,
where merchants needed to have ready money available. The first step,
in the twelfth century, was a contract of exchange concluded before a
public notary: a merchant would recognize that he received a sum in
specie and undertake to repay it at another place and in different coins,
at a rate of exchange laid down in the contract (and that actually embodied an interest). Thus, merchants who went to buy at the fairs could
get cash there. In a second step, after 1250, a letter—or order of
payment—was written by the seller of foreign currency to a correspon-
dent abroad to deliver the specie to the buyer (three different parties
were involved). Eventually, the large companies replaced these two doc-
uments with a single one: the bill of exchange, which is both a contract
(but with no intervention by a notary) and the order to a third party to
carry it out, and which is handed over directly to the creditor. Three
operations—exchange, credit, transfer—were thereby merged. Eventually, the church, which condemned lending at interest as usury, accepted the bill of exchange as legitimate because of the risk that was involved. Because all the business at the fairs of Champagne was on credit,
the fairs helped the bill of exchange's diffusion, and trading in those
bills developed. There was a setback in the use of bills after the decline
of the Champagne fairs and the failure of some large Italian companies
in the 1340s, but a revival came with the rise of the fairs in Geneva in
the fifteenth century and in Lyon in the sixteenth, with a great expansion all over Europe at that time. The bill of exchange ultimately became

the instrument for almost all important payments, at both the national and international levels.[4]

Italy also invented banking: it grew out of money changing, an important occupation beginning in the eleventh century due to the great diversity of coins (the word "bank" derives from the northern Italian term for the counter—*bancum*—of a money changer).[5] Some money changers who had safes accepted deposits by their customers and then made transfers from one account to another; they invested some of the deposited funds in trade operations, and they granted advances and overdraft facilities, thus creating new means of payment. The earliest deposit and giro banks emerged in Genoa c. 1150; Venice followed a century later, and then Florence, where techniques were improved, especially the use of written (instead of oral) giro orders, which are behind the origin of checks (the oldest one known was issued in 1374). In the fourteenth century, banking spread to southern Germany and the Low Countries (especially to Bruges), but on a lesser scale than in Italy.

In the fifteenth century, however, because of economic and political circumstances, banking suffered a serious confidence crisis. In Italy, the discredit of private banks led to the creation, generally by city councils, of many relatively large public deposit and giro banks; they acted as cashiers for city authorities and, of course, had private customers. The best known of them is the Casa di San Giorgio, in Genoa (1408).[6] In the second half of the sixteenth century, many new public banks were established in Italy, notably the Venetian Banco della Piazza di Rialto (1587). In addition, in the late 1400s and the 1500s, many Italian city councils created *monti di pietà,* or public pawnbroking institutions to grant inexpensive credit to modest-living and poor people.[7] The *monti* were imitated in other countries, especially in the southern Netherlands; they contributed to a decline of usury and a fall in interest rates.

Italians also invented "international banking," meaning houses involved in transfers of funds over long distances, in bills-of-exchange trading, and in arbitrage.[8] They were established by merchant-bankers who traded on a large scale and gradually developed their financial operations; indeed, up to the 1700s—and even later—many bankers remained merchants too. Such activities flourished mainly in Tuscany (in Siena, Pisa, Lucca, and Pistoia), but after 1300, the merchant-bankers of Florence established their primacy in connection with large imports of English wool for cloth making in their city, and large exports of Florentine cloth to many places around the Mediterranean. Some powerful family partnerships created networks of factors and agents in many towns, both north and south of the Alps. Quite early, merchant-bankers became involved in deals with kings and princes, to whom they made loans or advances on taxes, and also with the Holy See, to which they transferred taxes and dues collected all over Latin Christendom. Though the three most powerful merchant-banks of Florence failed in the 1340s, Italian bankers—especially those from Florence—remained dominant in Europe in the fifteenth and sixteenth centuries; c. 1450, the house of Medici (established in 1397) was the most powerful house in the world.[9]

International banking was closely linked with large commercial fairs, at first those of Champagne and later the fairs of Geneva, which grew in importance starting in the late fourteenth century; they were a major outlet for Italian exports and a hub of financial deals, which large Italian houses controlled. They had close connections with the fairs of Antwerp and Bergen op Zoom, in the Low Countries, which were very important in the fifteenth and sixteenth centuries, and they also integrated the economies of Swiss towns into international circuits. Then, during the first half of the sixteenth century, the fairs of Lyon became the dominant center of international settlements thanks to Italian merchant-bankers—from Florence at first, but increasingly from Genoa, plus some bankers from southern Germany. They played a key role in the financing of French military campaigns in Italy. A parallel role was played, on the side of the Hapsburg enemies of France, by the fairs of Castile (the main one was at Medina del Campo), which became integrated into the European financial network in the early 1500s; Genoese bankers had there a dominant role. However, the fairs of both Lyon and Medina declined after midcentury, because, inter alia, both the French and Spanish crowns had defaulted on their debts. Meanwhile, Genoese bankers—whom France had tried to blackmail by banning them from Lyon—had created in 1535 their own fairs at Besançon, not far from Lyon, but outside the French kingdom. Eventually, in 1579, they transferred those fairs to Piacenza, in Lombardy. They were purely financial fairs, for multilateral settlements. From 1579 to 1627, Piacenza was the center for all international financial business, but its fairs declined fast afterward.

Meanwhile, Italian banking and trading practices had spread in Europe, generally introduced by Italian businessmen who had settled north of the Alps (and also attended fairs there). Indeed, up to the eighteenth century, the European economy worked with the stock of commercial and financial instruments and institutions that Italians had created and perfected before 1350. The main development was the diffusion in other countries of techniques such as the bill of exchange. However, from the sixteenth century onward, some significant innovations were made in northern Europe, where, formerly, trading techniques—especially those

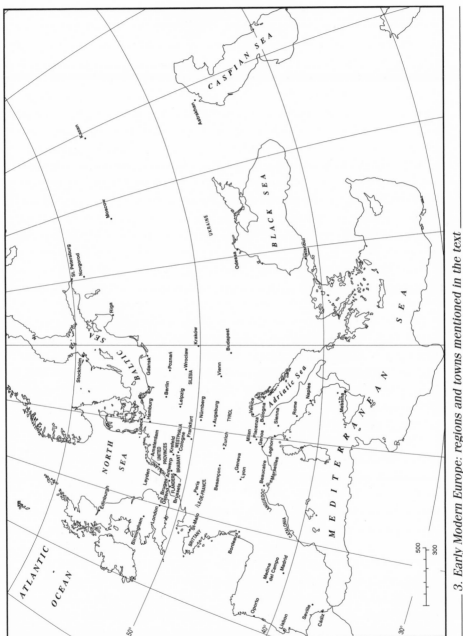

3. *Early Modern Europe: regions and towns mentioned in the text*

of the Hansards—had been rather primitive (admittedly, trade there was less complex than in Italy). Those changes were crucial to the development of an autonomous financial system in northwestern Europe.

In Antwerp, which was the economic capital of northern Europe for most of the sixteenth century, and in which merchants from many countries did business, transferability of trade bills was most useful, and the practice of endorsing bills of exchange emerged in the late sixteenth century. By 1600, it had become common; it made bills of exchange negotiable, with legal and financial security for their owners. By the same time, the discounting of commercial securities, of which the first known example dates from 1536, had also become common, and some businessmen specialized in buying and selling bills of exchange. From Antwerp, these new methods spread around northern Europe; for instance, they penetrated in England through the intermediation of English merchants who had close relations with Antwerp. The city thus played a key role in the deepening and widening of the "financial revolution" that had started in Italy.

Another innovation that took place in Antwerp was the opening in 1531 of the first modern *burse* (in Dutch, or bourse—exchange), which was a permanent market, open daily at fixed hours, where merchants met and did business—trading in bills of exchange and in various public financial instruments or securities issued by governments, institutions, or companies. This was an institutionalization of earlier informal arrangements that had existed in many towns; but, unlike many other "exchanges" where goods were traded (on samples), the Antwerp *burse* was purely financial. Thanks to this concentration of mercantile and financial transactions, prices of coins, prices of financial instruments, and rates of exchange were settled. In 1571, the Royal Exchange opened in London on the model of the Antwerp *burse*.

In the late sixteenth century, Amsterdam replaced Antwerp as the great mart of Europe. In 1609, the former's city council founded the Wisselbank—or exchange bank. In order to regularize the monetary situation, which was confused and unstable, the new bank was granted a monopoly over transactions involving gold and silver coins of high face value, and over paying large bills of exchange on Amsterdam; it also received deposits of specie and transferred funds from one account to another. It dealt, of course, in precious metals; in 1638, it was allowed to receive bullion or specie as security and to give negotiable receipts in return. It did not, however, make loans, except to the city of Amsterdam and to the East India Company. There was nothing very new in this system, which imitated that of the Banco della Piazza di Rialto. Nonetheless, all great merchants of Amsterdam opened accounts with the bank, and soon many foreign merchants followed, so that an increasing number of international transactions was settled through bills of exchange payable in Amsterdam or through giro operations at the bank, which became the leading international clearing institution. The Wisselbank was imitated in several German cities, such as Hamburg (1619). It was very useful to businessmen, though it did not create money.

The last stage, therefore, was the emergence of banknotes, which derived from the growing use in northwestern Europe of instruments with the bearer's clause. In London in the mid-1600s, many goldsmiths issued convertible cash notes or promissory notes payable to the bearer as receipts for deposits of valuables. These were the ancestors of banknotes, and those goldsmiths were the precursors of the banks of issue. However, the first such type of bank emerged in Sweden, where the government was engaged in an ambitious military expansion and needed money badly; in 1661, the Stockholm Banco, which had been established by a Dutch merchant, received a thirty-year monopoly over issuing "letters of credit" (printed notes to the bearer, which were convertible into copper); they were issued for loans to the king, but a panic broke out in 1663 and the bank closed in 1664.[10] The first great bank of issue was therefore the Bank of England, which was founded in 1694 as a wartime expedient but recently celebrated its third centenary.[11] It issued promissory notes to pay sums of specie to the bearer on demand, that is, true banknotes. Beginning in 1709, it had a monopoly over issuing notes in London, but its notes did not circulate much in the rest of the country. Gradually throughout the eighteenth century, it assumed some of the functions of a central bank, as both the bank of the English government (e.g., it managed its public debt) and the bank for London businesses; it became a lender of last resort. In France, meanwhile, the émigré Scottish financier John Law founded in Paris in 1718 a royal bank under the government's blessing; but he was overambitious, issuing far too many notes, and the venture ended in disaster as early as 1720, leaving a lasting distrust among French people of public banks and paper money. Only in 1776 was a new embryonic central bank established—the Caisse d'escompte—but it was suppressed during the French Revolution. A French central bank of issue, the Banque de France, was only established in 1800. In Spain, a royal bank had been founded in 1782.

In addition to such large public banks, there was an increasing number of private banks, which gradually separated from merchant houses; inter alia, they dealt in bills of exchange and discounted them. In the seventeenth century, Amsterdam private bankers "invented" acceptance credit to finance international trade; it would become common in the next century. There were also other agents of financial intermediation (like attorneys and *notaires*), such that eighteenth-century Britain, Holland, and France had active and flexible credit markets that served an increasingly large segment of the population.

The Bank of England was a joint-stock undertaking. Indeed, joint-stock companies, or corporations, were an invention of the early modern period, but their diffusion was limited, both because most firms were far too small—with at best a few partners—and because such companies were distrusted and could not be established without government's permission. Joint-stock companies were founded only when a large amount of capital was needed, especially for long-distance trades; the most famous are the English and the Dutch East India Companies (1600 and 1602), but some existed in mining, insurance, land reclamation, and other sectors.

Lastly, despite all these novelties, traditional structures persisted in trade and business. Two examples: Fairs long remained important, at the regional and international levels. The role of some great fairs, for trading in commodities and also as the hubs of international banking up to the early seventeenth century, has been mentioned earlier. Later on, however, international fairs declined in western Europe (with exceptions, like Beaucaire for trade in the western Mediterranean) to the benefit of towns. The main ones, such as Leipzig and Poznań, that emerged in the fifteenth century were orientated toward little-urbanized eastern Europe. The omnipresence of peddlers is also notable; they often came from mountainous, poor areas and diffused new products, including tobacco, handkerchiefs, and books.

Another development was the role of colonies of foreign merchants, who mainly settled in port cities, where they were often organized in "nations" that benefited from special status and privileges (on the other hand, they could also suffer from segregation). Italians, who could be found almost everywhere in northwestern Europe, and Hansards, who spread across northern Europe, are the most typical but not the only ones. In 1468, during festivities in Bruges, there was a parade that included 10 merchants from Venice, 22 from Florence, 108 from Genoa, 24 from Spain, 108 *osterlins* (men from the east, i.e., Germany and the Baltic), plus several Frenchmen and some Englishmen. In the eighteenth century, Bordeaux had colonies of English, Irish, Dutch, and German merchants, Cádiz a large French colony and a smaller English one, and Lisbon and Oporto many Britons.

Such diasporas were especially influential when they were strengthened by religion and kinship. In the Middle Ages, Jews had been generally persecuted—with many massacres, and total expulsion from some countries, especially England and France. Finally, they were expelled from Spain (1492) and Portugal. Some of the refugees from Iberia went to North Africa and the Ottoman Empire, but a number settled in northwestern Europe, mostly in Holland and in England, when Oliver Cromwell had authorized their reentry in 1655–1656.[12] In the early modern period, Jews—both Sephardim and Ashkenazim—made up a transnational network of businessmen spread across Europe. Most of them were petty traders, but their ranks included big international bankers and merchants, often specialized in trading precious metals, jewelry, diamonds, pearls, and coral. Some others were involved in war contracting, supplying armies with food, fodder, and horses. In the seventeenth century, "Court Jews" (factors) emerged in central Europe and were a great help to many princes.[13] Like some other minorities, Jews benefited from the porousness between family and commercial matters; from extensive networks that were at the same time family, information, and credit; and from secrecy in their correspondence, which often was in Hebrew or Yiddish. Still, the view of Werner Sombart, who maintained, against Max Weber, that Jews rather than Calvinists were the creators of capitalism, seems very far-fetched and biased.

The Armenian diaspora must also be mentioned. Armenians were intermediaries between Asia and Europe, and they were present along most routes that linked the two continents, first in many Italian and Mediterranean ports, then in the Balkans, Russia, and Amsterdam.

However, the most important diaspora, from an economic point of view, was that of the Walloons and Huguenots—Calvinists who fled persecution in the southern Netherlands and in France and immigrated to Protestant countries, especially Switzerland, Holland, and England. Émigrés and their descendants remained in close touch with relatives and friends who had stayed home (after ostensible conversion to Catholicism, in many cases); after persecution had abated, some members of émigré families went back to France to set up as bankers, particularly in Paris. Those strong, family-based networks, which had an excellent system of information, have been called the "Huguenot International" by Herbert Lüthy, but Martin Körner prefers the expression "International Protestant banking," the network of which is older and more widespread than the constellations of French Huguenot families. Actually, Protestant banking emerged during the French wars of religion, in the late sixteenth century, when some Swiss Protestant cities were the main financial supporters of the French Protestant party. Moreover, in the eighteenth century, Swiss Protestant merchants and bankers were to be found all over Europe, including Catholic countries other than France (e.g., Austria), and Switzerland had a surplus of capital that it exported. On the other hand, the role of French Huguenot financiers must not be underestimated; they were a great help to the French treasury in times of need, such as the difficult wars from 1689 to 1713, when they drained enormous funds from all over Europe for their persecutor, Louis XIV. In the eighteenth century, they financed foreign trade, notably the French East India trade, and knitted together European markets. Conversely, descendants of Walloon refugees and some Huguenot émigrés played a part, as directors or shareholders, in the foundation of the Bank of England.

New and Old Trade Routes

The major change in European trade resulted from the "great discoveries," which have been seen as creating a break between the late Middle Ages and subsequent centuries. In the sixteenth century, Europeans achieved the unity of the oceanic world and took over intercontinental trade: they established a direct, regular, and growing trade across the Atlantic and Indian Oceans with the Americas and Asia. This trade was stimulated by an increased differentiation in resources endowments, inasmuch as Europeans have always wanted things that only other continents could produce. Admittedly, in some respects, changes represented only a diversion of the traditional trade with Asia through the Middle East, or an invasion of the global system of trade that had developed for centuries in the Indian Ocean and the Chinese seas (and traffic among the countries that bordered them remained quite large). But henceforth Europeans bypassed intermediaries and instead collected Eastern produce at the source and in their own ships (this had been the aim of the explorers, Columbus included). On the other hand, trade with the Americas was completely new, and it developed in connection with colonialism, with the settlement in America of many Europeans, while also creating the Atlantic slave trade from Africa.[14] True enough, in the sixteenth and even the seventeenth centuries, the ocean trades were small in comparison with intra-European trade and generated only a very limited effect in Europe, but the advance of European settlements, especially in North America (which had been at first neglected), later caused a large increase in volume of this trade, and also its diversification.

The consequences of the discoveries were far-reaching for the European economy. The pioneers in the ocean trades were the Portuguese in the East Indies (a remarkable feat for a small and poor country of one million people) and the Spaniards in America, and they claimed monopolies over the lands they had first reached and over their trade. But beginning in the late sixteenth century, those monopolies were attacked by other seafaring people. The Dutch, the English, and the French penetrated the Asian and American spaces, captured some Portuguese and Spanish possessions, engaged in smuggling with the others, founded new settlements, and developed a large trade. The Spanish and Portuguese empires survived up to the Napoleonic wars, however, and were important for Europe's economy. Spain did not have large industries to supply its colonies—especially their population of European origin—with manufactured goods, and Portugal had even less; they had to import large quantities of goods from other European countries and reexport them to America (some others were smuggled into the colonies). This created important markets for Britain, France, the Netherlands, and (to a lesser extent) Germany.

On the other hand, Mexico and Peru had rich silver mines (especially the silver mountain of Potosí, which was discovered in 1545), and during the first half of the eighteenth century Brazil produced large quantities of gold. Most of those precious metals were shipped to Spain and Portugal, to the tune of about 73,000 tons of silver and 1,700 tons of gold over three centuries. There were fluctuations in the quantities shipped, but except during some decades in the early and mid-seventeenth century, there was no sharp and lasting drop; actually, arrivals in Europe were larger in the seventeenth century than in the sixteenth, and they increased again in the eighteenth.

Because of Iberia's negative balance of trade and Spanish military expenditures abroad, most of the precious metals that were imported into Spain and Portugal eventually found their way to other European countries. Recent analyses have shown, for example, that French gold coins of the mid-eighteenth century contained gold from Brazil (Morrisson, Barrandon, and Morrisson).

The sixteenth century was a period of inflation in Europe, with an increase in prices by a factor of three or four (the so-called price revolution).[15] The inflow of precious metals from America has long been held responsible for this inflation, according to the quantitative theory of money and buttressed by the price-specie-flow model; the dramatic, worldwide fall in silver's cost of production and in its purchasing power has also been seen as the underlying cause of the sixteenth-century global inflation.

However, it has also been pointed out that Europe's stock of precious metals, which was already large by 1500, only increased moderately during the sixteenth century—especially during its first half—while there was a stronger influx of treasure during the seventeenth century, when prices were falling or stagnating most of the time and when "morosity" had succeeded "prosperity." The inflow of metals does not match periods of price inflation (or deflation) in Europe as a whole, and monetarist interpretations of sixteenth- and seventeenth-century price history are not valid. The explanation is to be found in population growth, which was strong in the sixteenth century and weak or even negative in the seventeenth, and in the increased velocity of money circulation, which population growth induced and which fell when the latter halted. It is significant that prices of basic foodstuffs increased much more than those of other goods.

On the other hand, up to the late eighteenth century, silver from America was used by western Europeans to balance their trade with the Baltic, and still more with India and China, where demand for European goods was nil and where people were accustomed to hoarding.[16] China, across the Pacific, also received significant quantities of Mexican silver on the yearly galleon from Acapulco to Manila. So most American silver flowed to Asia, and Europe was mainly, in this respect, a transshipment region. Still, American treasure lubricated "the wheels of commerce" and helped to develop some trade flows.

Another important development was that European consumption patterns were markedly altered by growing imports, at falling prices, of produce that had previously been very expensive (sugar, cotton) or even unknown (tobacco, coffee, tea, cocoa), while there was a relative decline of spices—especially pepper—even within imports from Asia. Several types of "colonial produce" were addictive, semidrugs, and their consumption was also stimulated by fashion and by new forms or places of sociability that were associated with them (e.g., coffeehouses). Starting out as luxuries for the elite few, they spread downward in society, becoming necessities for ordinary people in the late eighteenth century—especially sugar and tea in Britain. In addition, Europeans tried making their own Oriental manufactures—chinaware or porcelain, and cotton fabrics—an important factor behind the start of the industrial revolution. Finally, in the eighteenth century, "colonial trade" of Britain and France particularly had become very large. From 1716–1720 to 1784–1788, France's trade outside Europe increased in volume more than fivefold; during the same period (up to 1786–1790), the volume of England's trade with America, Africa, and the East Indies increased four and a half times.[17] The Dutch, meanwhile, retained a large trade in colonial produce, and Denmark, Sweden, and Oostende entered the East India trade, especially the tea trade from China.[18] Colonial trade had many backward and forward linkages; it stimulated industries that exported to the colonies (hence a possible linkage in Britain with the industrial revolution) or processed colonial produce (sugar refining, for example); it also stimulated the production and trade of timber and other naval stores—to build merchantmen and warships (the latter intended to defend each power's colonies and trade and to conquer those of its rivals!).

Indeed, it has been maintained that Europe enriched itself and accumulated capital, thanks to its superiority in military and business technology, at the expense of the rest of the world, through the looting and mining of precious metals in America; the cultivation of plantations in the West Indies and the southern continental colonies by slaves (slavery is a theft of labor), on land stolen from Native Americans; and the gains of the slave trade. Though slavery is by no means specific to European expansion (it had existed for millennia in many regions, including Africa), the slave trade from Africa is a critical problem. It was established to provide manpower for plantations (mainly sugar plantations) in America. As plantations' slaves generally suffered a heavy demographic deficit, with a large excess of deaths over births, an increasing and massive transatlantic forced migration of labor took place: it is accepted that 11 to 12 million Africans were forcibly deported across the Atlantic from the 1400s to the 1800s. (About the same number was carried across the Indian Ocean by Muslim traders, but over a longer period.) The average death rate during those voyages was 14 percent.

Relations between the slave trade and the progress of western European economies have been much discussed. According to Eric Williams's thesis, as Britain was the foremost slave-trading country (ahead of Portugal and France), the large profits from that trade financed the British industrial revolution. Actually, little capital accumulated from the slave trade was invested into industry, inasmuch as profits from the trade were irregular and never abnormally high (though English slavers were the most efficient).

On the other hand, slavery and the slave trade cannot be isolated from the broader "Atlantic system," that is, the complex trading pattern that emerged after the "discovery" of America and that united it with Europe and Africa. Slavery and thus the slave trade played a central role in the development of that system, which has been described as slave based. They were essential to the extension of plantations, to the rise in the production and trade of colonial produce, and therefore to the growth of seaborne trade, which employed many Europeans and enriched European merchants.

Still, as we shall see, oceanic trade made up only a small percentage of Europe's total economic activity, even in the late eighteenth century.

It was one factor behind western Europe's development, among many others. From the point of view of industry, it was significant, but neither decisive nor vital, and profits from foreign trade—which, again, were not especially high—only financed a small share of total investment.

More generally, the significance of empire for economic growth was not large, except in the case of Britain. One reason is that Europeans quarreled about distant possessions, and the cost of their wars was high, especially for the defeated countries. Spain and Portugal actually became poorer because of their empires, and the balance sheet of the first French colonial empire is deeply in the red; its economic falloffs were limited, and the whole French Atlantic system collapsed in the 1790s during the French Revolution. Colonies did contribute to the enrichment and development of Britain—the most aggressive and successful imperial power—and also of Holland, but they were neither a necessary nor a sufficient condition for the industrial revolution; it is likely that the latter would have started even without colonial exploitation, and the peak of Britain's Caribbean and slave trades came when the industrial revolution was well under way. On the whole, the role of the "periphery" was "peripheral."

The rise of the direct ocean trade with Asia had as its counterpart the decline and eventual demise of the time-honored transit-trade through the Mediterranean in goods from the East, which had boomed in the fifteenth century. However, this did not happen instantaneously. True enough, the Portuguese tried to monopolize the East India trade by armed force, and in the early years of the sixteenth century (the first cargo of spices from Lisbon arrived in Antwerp in 1501) there was a sharp fall in the arrival of spices in the ports of the Levant and thus at Venice, with the last Venetian Flanders fleet sailing in 1532. But the Portuguese were unable to control the whole Indian Ocean, and the Mediterranean trade in spices revived at midcentury and remained very large (though, possibly, not as profitable as earlier on) up to the 1590s. It was the Dutch, who first entered the Indian Ocean in 1595, who destroyed the traditional spice trade at its source, by occupying the Spice Islands—or Moluccas— in 1605. After this, the sea route to and from the East around Africa definitively prevailed.

The Mediterranean and its ports—especially Venice—were thus deprived of their glamour trade. Still, a high-end trade was preserved with the Levant, from which Europe imported raw materials, such as raw silk and cotton, plus dried fruits, and to which woolens and other manufactures were exported. There was also much regional traffic in foodstuffs, for example, in grain from Sicily and elsewhere to supply Italian towns, and in salt. Alum, for the textile industry, which had long been obtained from Asia

Minor, was now exported from rich mines near Rome. However, trade suffered from recurrent warfare with the Ottoman Empire, from piracy by the Barbaresques (of Algiers), and from privateering by the knights of Malta. Moreover, the Mediterranean was increasingly penetrated in the late sixteenth century by Dutch and English ships; they brought supplies of goods of which southern countries were short, mostly grain and dried fish, but also woolens, which drove out Italian cloths. The first large-scale invasion was around 1590, when, after several harvest failures, Italian towns placed in Baltic ports orders for large quantities of grain, which Dutch ships alone were able to carry. After a lull, a more regular trade developed, and the Dutch and eventually the English took over much of the rich Levant trade.[19] This was a striking contrast with the late Middle Ages, when Genoese and Venetian ships went to England and Flanders, and a sign that the center of gravity of Europe's economy had shifted from south to north: starting in the seventeenth century, the most active port in the Mediterranean was Marseilles, which belonged to a non-Mediterranean power, while the Tuscan town of Livorno, which had become a free port in 1593, was the lynchpin of English trade with the Mediterranean; the latter was the largest seventeenth-century market for English woolens and for colonial produce reexported from England, on English ships.

On the other hand, both long- and short-distance trade along the northern and Atlantic coasts of Europe greatly increased.[20] It was mainly a trade in bulk goods for daily use that were exported from the countries around the Baltic, which had large surpluses of many primary products, to western Europe (mostly England and the Low Countries) and to the Mediterranean. This trade increased markedly from the fifteenth century onward and integrated the Baltic area into the European economy. It was an asymmetric trade, as Baltic countries exported much more in volume and value than they imported; and inter-Baltic trade was small, though Lübeck remained—at least in the sixteenth century—an important crossroads of traffic in all directions.

The engines of this trade were the western demand for bulk necessities and the wide gap between price levels of those commodities in, say, Gdansk and Amsterdam (this gap narrowed over time as transport costs fell and integration improved). At first, grain was the major item among those exports, but its trade was both large and irregular, both permanent and casual. There was a strong positive correlation between grain prices in the west (they fluctuated more wildly than those of any other commodity) and the volume of traffic, which thus moved in inverse ratio to western harvests. However, starting in the late seventeenth century, the grain trade declined, and exports from the Baltic became dominated by raw materials: iron, flax, hemp, potash, and, above all, such strategic materials as timber and other "naval stores" (pitch, tar) for shipbuilding. Indeed, the major maritime powers—which were in the west—did not have enough ship timber (Holland had none at all). As both the merchant fleets and the navies of those countries greatly expanded in the seventeenth and eighteenth centuries, the trade in timber and naval stores grew fast, helping to integrate into the European economy Sweden, Norway (masts were its specialty), and Russia. It also shifted some traffic from ports like Gdansk, which were the outlets of grain-growing areas, to places like Stockholm, Riga, and St. Petersburg, which had forests and mines in their hinterland. From south to north, or west to east, came traditional staples (salt and wine from the French Atlantic coast, Spain, and Portugal), which the northern countries could not produce for climatic reasons; also Spanish wool for the textile industries of England and the Low Countries. The fast rise of the fisheries—for herring in the North Sea and cod in the Atlantic—greatly stimulated the trade in salt, which in bulk was the main commodity going northward, but its relative importance in international trade declined. Once areas in Asia and the New World had been opened for trade, Asian and American products were reexported from Lisbon and Seville (which was replaced by Cádiz in 1685) to Antwerp and other northern ports. Later, in the eighteenth century, large quantities of sugar and coffee from the French West Indies were reexported from French ports, especially Bordeaux, to Holland, Germany, and the Baltic. Manufactured goods such as woolens and linens circulated both ways: from England, the Low Countries, and France to the Baltic, as well as to Spain and Portugal, to be reexported to their colonies.

Because almost all the large trade to and from the Baltic passed through the narrow channel of the Sund, between Denmark and Sweden, where ships had to pay tolls to the king of Denmark, their numbers are well known.[21] They rose from about 3,500 per year in the 1560s to more than 6,000 in the mid-1590s. After that point the number of passages declined, but the average tonnage of ships increased, so that the trade's total volume increased by a third in the first half of the seventeenth century. There was a depression in the late seventeenth century, particularly from 1690 to 1717 (3,700 ships in 1700), followed by a sharp recovery. The number of passages doubled then in the next fifty years, reaching 5,500 ships in the 1730s and a peak over 8,000 in 1780.

Most of the ships were Dutch. In the fourteenth and fifteenth centuries, however, the Hanseatic League had dominated trade in the Baltic and North Seas. Dutch competition emerged in the fifteenth century (indeed, the Dutch opened the route through the Sund), developed greatly

in the sixteenth century, and by the 1600s the Dutch practically monopolized the northern trades (as well as a good deal of the trade to and from
Atlantic ports): they had better ships (which did the return trip to and
from the Baltic within one season), their freights were lower, and they
were more aggressive in business. Moreover, German cities suffered
greatly from the Thirty Years' War (1618–1648). However, in the eighteenth century, the Dutch monopoly was eroded by the British and the
Scandinavians, except in the grain trade. Like the Mediterranean trade
in the Middle Ages, then, northern trades did see intense rivalries, but
no regional thalassocracy emerged in the Baltic.

The large increase in seaborne trade must not obscure the fact that
there was a good deal of intracontinental traffic. In fact, the two inter-
mingled; rivers and roads fed the seaports with goods to be exported, and
they redistributed within the Continent those that had been imported by
sea. Europe was crisscrossed by north-south and west-east trade routes, at
the crossroads of which a number of commercial towns, such as Cologne,
Frankfurt, Leipzig, Wrocław, and Kraków, prospered. The north-south relations were very active in the fifteenth and sixteenth centuries, when a
large share of trade between the two poles of the European economy—
the Low Countries and northern Italy—was overland, through the Bren-
ner and St. Gotthard passes and the Rhine, and when southern Germany,
rich from its mining and textile industries, was an economic satellite of
Venice. This trade was in woolen cloth, spices, metals from central European mines (especially copper), and metal goods. Trade and mining
brought great wealth to some merchants of southern Germany, the Fugger family of Augsburg being the most famous example, who became
merchant-bankers and played a vital role in financing "international"
trade (and also the wars against France of Emperor Charles V, to whom
they lent enormous sums). In the seventeenth century, however, this trade
fell sharply because of the economic decline of Italy and the devastation
of Germany by the Thirty Years' War.[22]

Farther east, there was some trade between southern Germany and
southern Poland, on the one hand, and Hungary, the Balkans, and the
Ottoman Empire on the other; it was largely carried on by Armenian,
Jewish, and Turkish merchants. Manufactures were sent southward, while
cattle and other primary produce (plus some Eastern luxuries) went
northward. In addition, furs from Siberia and silk from Iran reached Europe through Russia. This traffic was never large and declined after the
mid-seventeenth century, if not earlier. A special, quaint branch of overland trade was that in cattle, which could be carried over long distances,
as animals are self-propelled. The main areas for rearing cattle were

Denmark, which supplied Holland and also northern German towns; Hungary; and Switzerland, which supplied northern Italian and southern German cities.[23] In Britain, drovers took herds of cattle from Wales and Scotland to London. The continental cattle trade had its peak in the early seventeenth century with about 400,000 animals; then it declined somewhat but persisted.

It is almost impossible to measure the growth of Europe's trade, which was undoubtedly very large, several times higher than population growth. Still, Fernand Braudel has suggested a rough measurement, which is the fivefold increase in Europe's merchant shipping from 1600 to the 1780s. Foreign trade was the most dynamic sector of the economy, with repercussions that were both quantitative and qualitative, and in the seventeenth and eighteenth centuries it was seen as the driving force of a nation's power and prosperity. Despite this, many modern historians have stressed that Europe, even in the eighteenth century, remained basically agrarian. It had a dual economy where the modern sector—commercial and industrial—was much smaller than the traditional one. Moreover, Europe was divided into many quasi-self-sufficient and isolated small areas, and interregional and international trade was marginal; it only concerned the richer classes, and mainly those in towns, plus the armies and navies, while the masses lived in poverty. The largest part of trade was, by far, regional and local, organized around small towns. It has been observed that in their peak year, exports of grain from the Baltic—around which only a dozen towns had a significant foreign trade—were equivalent to the annual consumption of 750,000 persons, a small percentage indeed of western and southern Europe's population. (Still, the United Provinces would have starved but for imports of grain.)

However, several other necessities entered long-distance trade: salt, timber, metals, hemp, and others. And many people in the eighteenth century occasionally consumed luxuries such as spices and wine, plus sugar, tea, and coffee, while many peasants cultivated crops for sale to distant markets and many craftsmen used raw materials from far away. It is thus a mistake to think of a dual economy with two isolated sectors, and the modern, market sector was growing during the centuries we are considering, thanks to the expansion of foreign trade. Admittedly, one must be cautious in speaking of a world economy and of global business cycles. Rather, the focus should be on how the range of goods traded became wider and interaction between European regions became more frequent; they became more dependent upon each other's produce, and division of labor increased. The internationalization coefficient increased in the sixteenth century, and again (much more) in the eighteenth century. Particularly among southern, western, and northern Europe, links that had been rather tenuous by 1300 or 1400 became much stronger. The development of oceanic trades by western countries—and the progress that the latter achieved—would not have been possible but for this integration and the mobilization of northern Europe's resources. There was also an increase in the number of textile-manufacturing districts that competed on international markets.

The study of prices shows a growing degree of integration, not only within Europe, but also with some other parts of the world. It could be said that a world market for spices existed in the Middle Ages; discoveries and colonization created intercontinental markets for many tropical products, and by 1700 there was a round-the-world network of integrated markets, from Lima to Guangzhou via Europe, and from Acapulco to Guangzhou via Manila. Silver thus had the first truly global market! Still, owing to the high cost of road transport, many inland areas of Europe remained outside that network, almost isolated and self-sufficient, while maritime areas—especially large seaports—greatly benefited.

Moreover, in the eighteenth century, a sophisticated, smoothly functioning, efficient system of financial markets emerged in northwestern Europe, with Amsterdam and London as its centers.[24] Though information moved more slowly than it would later, market prices responded with rationality, and arbitrage was effective on the foreign-exchange markets. In addition, an integrated capital market funneled funds, mainly from Amsterdam, but also from Geneva and Frankfurt, to borrowers—impecunious governments (including Britain's), and also long-distance trades (capital from Geneva and Switzerland financed the French East India trade). Moreover, a multilateral system of settlements, through bills of exchange, had developed in the seventeenth century, so that trade imbalances (as between the Baltic and the west) did not require the shipping of specie. Altogether, in the early modern period, foreign trade was an engine of change, and even of growth, especially for industry.

Manufactures in Town and Country

There was a wide range of manufactured goods, but textiles remained by far the largest industry, employing 60–70 percent of the "industrial" labor force, and also the most complex. Despite some level of local production almost everywhere, it was not sufficient, and fabrics were bought from a number of large exporting areas, which sold quality goods for the well-to-do as well as cheap articles (e.g., linens were sent to America to clothe slaves).

The largest European textile industry remained that of wool, which had been an exporter since the Middle Ages, but it underwent constant changes. In the sixteenth century, traditional heavy woolen cloth lost ground in favor of the "new draperies," which were lighter (often worsteds), with brighter colors and many varieties; then came the "light draperies," made mainly from Spanish wool. In the eighteenth century, however, heavy cloth came back into demand. Moreover, delocalization was a constant feature of the wool industry due to acute competition, frequently changing fashion, a mostly low-skilled labor pool, and limited fixed capital; manufacturing frequently moved from places where labor costs had become too high toward locations where wages were lower. As some of the older centers declined, especially Flanders (at least its large cities, as manufacturing spread to small towns and the countryside), Brabant, and northern Italy, some new ones arose, like Leiden in Holland, Verviers in Belgium, Languedoc and other places in France, and Bohemia and Silesia in the east.[25] England, on the other hand, prohibited the export of its fine raw wool and instead developed the making of cloth, which at first was sent abroad to be dyed and finished but after the sixteenth century was exported in a fully finished condition. Despite ups and downs, England established and retained a leading position in the international trade of woolens and worsteds, but competition was intense between its many manufacturing districts.

The silk industry was for long an Italian monopoly, and Italians developed advanced technologies for silk-reeling and -throwing in mills, which were at first concentrated in Bologna (with 112 of them in 1583) and then spread to other towns, eventually to the hilly area below the Alps. In the second half of the sixteenth century, silk production at all levels (weaving included) boomed in Italy, especially in the north. But competition from other countries arose, often encouraged and protected by governments that were worried by heavy imports of Italian silks. The most successful competitor was Lyon, where Italian merchants and skilled workers introduced the industry; close to Italy, it could easily import raw and thrown silk to complete the silk that was produced in southeastern France. Lyon became the largest center in Europe for silk weaving, the largest maker and exporter of silk fabrics, and, in the eighteenth century, the fashion leader. Silk weaving also developed in Nîmes, London, Zurich, Krefeld, and Berlin. As a result, silk weaving collapsed in Italy in the seventeenth century, except for some niches (velvet in Genoa, e.g.), and Italy became mainly a producer and exporter of silk thread, a striking example of its deindustrialization.

Linens, from flax or hemp, were made almost everywhere, but mainly in a long, discontinuous belt that extended from Scotland, Ireland, and

Brittany to Holland, Westphalia, Bohemia, Silesia, and even to Russia. Large quantities of linens were sent to the Spanish colonies and the West Indies. The cotton industry was a latecomer, a case of import substitution following a "craze" (dating to the 1660s) for printed cottons that East India companies imported from India.[26] Eventually those Asian fabrics were prohibited in several countries where the spinning, weaving, and printing of cotton developed during the eighteenth century, mainly in England, but also in France, Catalonia, and Switzerland (where by 1770 it had become the main industry).[27] This was to have enormous consequences.[28]

The nontextile industries were by no means unimportant. They included the making, mainly in towns, of all kinds of consumption goods, both common and luxury (luxury trades greatly flourished in large cities like London and Paris), and also the production and processing of metals. Nonferrous metals were mainly produced in mountainous areas of central Europe (Harz, Erzgebirge, Slovakia) and in England.[29] Iron ore was found in many places but required wood and waterpower to be turned into iron, and the iron industry developed in widely scattered areas. Sweden and then Russia, which had huge forests, became large exporters of bar iron (indeed, Russia, c. 1800, was the largest maker of iron in the world). However, because of the large quantities of wood used by ironworks, the threat of a fuel shortage became serious in some areas during the eighteenth century. As for the secondary metal trades, they also were scattered, but some concentrations of them existed, such as around Liège, in the Rhineland (Siegerland), and around Birmingham. Europe's output of iron may have increased from 100,000 tons (or less) c. 1500 to 250,000 tons c. 1750 and 600,000 c. 1790. A new industry that emerged in the sixteenth century and then developed quickly was distilling, to make brandy, gin, whisky, vodka, and other spirits from wine, grain, fruits, or sugar. The Dutch played a key role in the diffusion of those new beverages.

As mentioned earlier, from the thirteenth century to the early 1700s, there was no large increase in industrial labor productivity, even in textiles, despite a number of innovations. On the other hand, there were significant changes in the organization of industry. First, a great deal of manufacturing—especially low-skilled work—moved from the towns to the countryside, where wages were lower and where the craft guilds could not enforce their restrictive practices.[30] Secondly, rural industry became organized under the *Verlag* or putting-out system, also called "commercial capitalism," which had emerged in the late thirteenth century in Flanders, Normandy, and England, where it had its fastest development.[31] Merchants—who were called "merchant-manufacturers"—could employ hundreds of people (including many women) who were no more than piecework wage earners, even though they generally owned the tools and simple machines (such as hand looms) on which they worked. Merchants controlled the whole process of production and sale, supplying workers with raw materials and marketing the goods that had been made according to their orders. This system spread to nontextile industries, like the making of shoes, tools, weapons, watches, and other metal artifacts. Nonetheless, the typical productive unit remained the small family workshop (as traditional technology did not generally allow for economies of scale), hence the expression "domestic system." Only in some branches did technical necessities impose a more centralized mode of production (in "protofactories" or "embryo-factories"): the furnace industries, with their ironworks, glassworks, and sugar refineries, were the most typical; breweries, paper mills, and silk-throwing mills can also be mentioned. Some other large undertakings were established by governments: dockyards for their navies (the earliest was in Venice), and the royal manufactures, which were founded in France and other countries in the seventeenth and eighteenth centuries, mainly for making luxury goods. The latter had large buildings and many workers but little machinery.

The rise of rural industries, which were both domestic and capitalist, which often worked for distant markets, and which peaked in the 1700s, is an important aspect of European economic history in the early modern period; it has been deemed distinctive enough, as a separate stage of economic evolution, to deserve a special name: "protoindustrialization." The late American scholar Franklin Mendels, who also observed a connection with the condition of population and agriculture, coined the term. Protoindustrialization developed mainly in districts where a dense rural population needed to supplement the meager incomes it derived from farming, either because the soil was poor and divided or because the country was fertile but overpopulated, with many landless and underemployed laborers. It also developed in symbiosis with the progress of commercial farming, so that its workers could be fed either in the same area or not far away; in the latter case, there was interregional reciprocity between agriculture and manufacturing. Moreover, Mendels maintained that protoindustrialization "prepared modern industrialization proper," that is, mechanized, factory industry. This view has been disputed, and protoindustrialization has been called "a concept too many." Several regions of protoindustrialization atrophied during the nineteenth century, while some regions of modern industrialization had not known protoindustrialization, so the latter cannot be seen as a precondition of proper industrialization.[32] Nonetheless, I find the concept useful, inasmuch as it has been qualified and refined by recent scholars, to show that protoindustrialization was a complex phenomenon with several variants. Most mining—of coal and metallic ores—carried on by tiny firms in rural surroundings was actually "protoindustrial" (it also employed female labor). Besides, it was a flexible system, well suited to reduce the chronic underemployment and seasonal unemployment of the rural labor force —laborers, small farmers, and their womenfolk. Protoindustrialization increased the quantity of work that was available to those people and resulted in an increase of product per capita. It also promoted the penetration of capitalism and of market relations in European economies. It is therefore important that in the eighteenth century, Europe, particularly the area west of the Oder, had a large number not only of industrial towns, but also of protoindustrialized rural districts.

Shifts in Economic Primacy

The last major changes in the European economy to consider are the shifts that occurred in the centers of economic power and wealth. They were much stressed by Braudel, who described a sequence of ascendancies, each one revolving around one dominant, large port city. Indeed, he overestimated such concentrations of power and overlooked the polynuclearity that persisted. Venice did not "dominate" Europe, even though it made handsome profits as the intermediary in the spice trade. Actually, words like "ascendancy" and "primacy" are ambiguous; in the economic field, they involve less hegemony than leadership, meaning a concentration of skills that guarantees higher levels of per capita wealth. On the other hand, from the late sixteenth century onward, there was a shift in the scope and degree of concentration of economic power, which became more pronounced in the seventeenth and eighteenth centuries; though other countries tried to imitate the leaders, various forces inhibited the convergence process. Moreover, Braudel did rightly stress the role played by force in the building of economic empires: opulence often was the product of successful aggression. As for Charles Kindleberger (1996), he considers that "it is the vitality and flexibility giving way to rigidity that determine the pattern" of rise and decline.

Medieval Europe, as we have seen, had two poles that were more advanced and richer than the rest: northern Italy and the Low Countries, especially Flanders. This bipolarity persisted in the late Middle Ages and the 1500s, particularly favoring Italy, which suffered less than other regions from the depression and wars of the 1350–1450 period, and which experienced, from 1454 to 1494, a period of peace, freedom, and prosperity. This was especially true for Venice, which greatly benefited from trade with the Orient (which it dominated) and had surpassed Genoa; all the evidence we have stresses its opulence in the fifteenth century, when many of its splendid buildings were erected. Moreover, Milan and Florence had become major centers of the textile industry, and Italians remained far ahead in banking and finance. Colonies of Italian merchants and money lenders had settled in all important centers of trade in western Europe, and large financial companies had risen again, especially in Florence (e.g., the house of Medici, which, however, failed in 1494). The court society that had grown in all large towns generated a growing demand for luxury goods—from silks to mirrors, glass, books, and paintings, of which many were exported, owing to the taste abroad for Italian fashions.

However, this ascendancy was undermined in the sixteenth century by a number of factors. There was of course the opening of the sea route to India and Southeast Asia by the Portuguese. Still, Italians—especially Genoese—contributed, thanks to their capital and expertise, to the financing first of the "discoveries," then of Spain's and Portugal's trade with their colonies, and the exploitation of America. Moreover, we have seen that the impact of the new route was delayed: Venice retained a large spice trade up to the end of the sixteenth century. Moreover, Venetians greatly developed their industries, especially wool, silk, glass, and printing. For a time, Venice, which had superseded the war-damaged cities of Lombardy, was the largest industrial city in Europe. In the early seventeenth century, however, the industries of Italy, including those of Venice, which suffered from constraints by craft guilds and from high wages, greatly declined under the competition of cheaper goods from northern Europe (and much know-how had been stolen by foreigners or defecting workers). The wool industry collapsed and the silk industry declined, with the production of raw silk and its throwing in mills being the only dynamic branch.

Moreover, Venice wore itself out with a succession of wars against the Turks, who seized its possessions in the eastern Mediterranean (Cyprus, 1571; Crete, 1669), while the Dutch, the English, and later the French captured much of the trade with the Levant. Overall, Italian shipping declined: there was a shortage of timber, and ship design was inferior to that of northern ships, which were better built, were faster, and had lower freights.

In addition, during the first half of the sixteenth century, Italy, which was rich but politically divided and militarily weak, had been a battleground between France and Spain; the latter won and imposed a stifling rule over most of the country. In some respects, however, the long *pax hispanica* was also a blessing, and the negative effects of the Counter-Reformation and the Inquisition have been overestimated; the condemnation of Galileo (1633) certainly did not kill Italian science, for example.

Actually, the worst calamity was the plagues that devastated the large cities between 1628 and 1657; as a consequence, it has been estimated that the population of northern and central Italy fell by 16 percent from 1600 to 1650. According to P. Malanima (in Maddison and Van der Wee), the period 1580–1650 saw a sharp fall in real income and the loss by Italy of its leadership. There was a recovery after the mid-seventeenth century, and population increased, but by 1750–1770 the level of real income was about the same as two centuries earlier. Since northern countries had progressed in the meantime, Italy had relatively declined.

Its recovery after 1650 was largely based upon the progress of agriculture, in which rich urban patricians heavily invested, leading to much land reclamation and improvement. Some writers have therefore used the word "refeudalization," but this is only valid for the kingdom of Naples, which was backward relative to central and northern Italy, and which Spanish rulers had heavily exploited. It was a land of large estates that employed wage earners in extensive wheat and olive-oil production. Their absentee landlords lived in the enormous capital (Naples was for a time the largest city in Christian Europe), which drained the resources of a depopulated countryside. The middle class did not engage in productive enterprises, the silk industry died out, foreign trade was in the hands of foreigners, and brigandage was rampant.

Besides the withdrawal toward the land, there was one into finance and rentier status, thanks to which Genoa, the old rival of Venice, retained an international role. Its bankers superseded those of southern Germany and Tuscany, whom the Spanish and French "bankruptcies" of the 1550s had badly hit; they became the bankers of the Spanish government and, from 1560 to 1627, helped to transfer American silver from Spain to its armies in the Low Countries. The silver was carried by land and sea from Seville to Barcelona and Genoa, but the transfer to Flanders was by bills of exchange, thanks to the surplus that Florence and Venice had in their trade relations with northern Europe. The exchange fairs of Piacenza were central in those operations. Their heyday—from 1579 to 1627—was the last episode in the history of traditional international banking under Italian control. Still, after transfers for Spanish accounts had stopped (after a new bankruptcy in 1627, the Spanish government shipped silver by sea to the Low Countries), Genoa remained an international financial market, lending money to many governments and cities until the French Revolution. Nonetheless, by the mid-seventeenth century, the economic glory of Italy was over, and the Mediterranean had become a backwater, outside the mainstream of history.[33]

One might have expected Portugal and Spain, which, thanks to their explorations, had conquered large overseas empires, to succeed Italy as economic leaders. They did not. Their economies were not advanced, not prepared for such a role, and they lacked capital and skilled manpower. The organization of their colonial trade followed unwise policies: a system of monopoly for one port—Lisbon and Seville (replaced by Cádiz in 1685)—and of convoys, or "fleets," for ships sailing to and from the colonies. Only in the eighteenth century did Spain somewhat liberalize its colonial trade. Though Portuguese and Spaniards carried home in their own ships the spoils of their colonies, they left their redistribution in Europe to other countries, which also supplied most of the manufactures that were reexported from the two countries to their colonies.

Moreover, Portugal was small and weak but displayed a lot of staying power; its resistance to the Protestant onslaught on Iberian empires, which started in the late sixteenth century, was protracted in the East Indies and successful in Brazil. Still, eventually it was made a satellite by England, as it needed the support from a major naval power, and then had to share with the British the gains from empire.[34] As for the Spanish empire, it was soon overstretched, with constant wars against the Turks, the French, and the rebels in the Low Countries; most of the treasure from America was exported to finance those campaigns. Spain did not invest enough in sea power and eventually lost control of the Atlantic in the mid-seventeenth century; it was also unable to prevent smuggling into its colonies.

Despite American treasure, the country was heavily taxed, and the Spanish government borrowed massively, suffered bankruptcies, and debased its currency. Inflation and the inflow of precious metals made Spanish industries uncompetitive and attracted imports of foreign goods. As for agriculture, irrigated areas suffered from the expulsion of the Moriscos. So, from the late sixteenth century onward, the Spanish economy regressed, famines and plagues caused depopulation, and the country became for a long time very poor. B. Yun (in Maddison and Van der Wee) estimates that from 1590 to 1630 Castile lost 20 percent of its population, and that its GDP fell by 15 percent; from 1630 to 1750, population recovered, but real GDP per capita fell by 17 percent. Spain was therefore stricken much harder than Italy.

By 1600, the southern pole of Europe's economy had thus almost died out. A mononuclear system replaced the bipolar one, and henceforth there was only one center of gravity, located in the north.[35] But it took some time to settle lastingly.

In the Middle Ages, Flanders was the major industrial region of Europe, and Bruges its commercial and financial metropolis. After the decline of the Champagne fairs, it was the major market for textiles in the Low Countries; it also had fully assimilated Italian innovations in business techniques. However, in the mid-fifteenth century, Antwerp took over Bruges's role: it had a better port and was closer to the clothing districts of Brabant, which were expanding, while Flanders was declining. From 1501 onward, it received a flow of spices from Portugal (though imports of spices overland from Venice went on) and, starting in the 1530s, a good deal of the silver and colonial produce that Spain imported from America and then reexported. It also was the staple port for English woolen cloths, which it finished and distributed (particularly in central Europe). By the mid-sixteenth century, Antwerp was at its peak and had become the commercial and financial capital of northern and western Europe, importing and reexporting all kinds of goods from the East Indies, America, England, Germany (copper, e.g.), and southern Europe. Still, it was a "passive" entrepôt that was dominated by foreign merchants and had neither merchant shipping of its own nor direct links with the non-European world. In the late sixteenth century, however, a native merchant elite emerged, and various industries grew fast. In Antwerp's hinterland, there was a mass production of woolens, linens, and many kinds of luxury goods (tapestries, jewelry, lace, etc.). Moreover, a money market developed to serve the large transit trade; it was dominated at first by Tuscan merchant-bankers, who came over from Bruges c. 1500, and later by Genoese; agents of south German bankers were also present in force. The innovations in financial techniques achieved in Antwerp during the sixteenth century (which have been mentioned earlier) played an important role in shaping modern banking—and bourses.

However, the primacy of Antwerp was destroyed by war. The Low Countries—present-day Netherlands, Belgium, and parts of northern France—were Spanish dominions. In 1572, large-scale rebellion broke out against Spanish rule primarily for religious reasons, as many people had converted to Protestantism. This started a bitter war that lasted almost eighty years (1572–1648) with only a twelve-year truce, 1609–1621. The Spaniards succeeded in reconquering the southern Netherlands, including Antwerp, which they took and sacked in 1585, but the northern Netherlands—or United Provinces—won their independence; they blockaded the Flemish coast and the estuary of the Scheldt, Antwerp's river; its seaborne trade was destroyed and its international role lost. The city's fortune had been short-lived, and the southern Netherlands suffered greatly from the Eighty Years' War.[36]

Antwerp's inheritance was taken over by the United Provinces, particularly Holland and the city of Amsterdam. Earlier on, the northern Netherlands had been less developed and less rich than the southern provinces, though the Dutch had gradually built a large merchant fleet that dominated the transport of produce from the Baltic, especially grain, and carried much of Antwerp's trade.[37] They also became dominant in fishing, curing, and selling North Sea herring. In the Middle Ages, herring had been caught mainly on the coasts of Skåne (southern Sweden), but starting in the fourteenth century fisheries were richer in the North Sea. The Dutch borrowed expertise from Flemish fishermen and developed new techniques of gutting and salting fresh herring, which they also did on board fishing boats; in the sixteenth century, they used special ships, the *busses,* from which other boats brought the catches on shore.

However, the fortune of the Dutch was born in revolution and war, from external, noneconomic circumstances. Their world trading position was forged during the Eighty Years' War (Israel); during the 1590s they rapidly extended their trade to the Mediterranean, the East Indies, and America. Moreover, as they successfully resisted Spain, while the latter subdued the southern provinces and Antwerp, there was a massive migration of Protestants from south to north, especially of merchants and craftsmen (particularly Flemish weavers), who brought with them capital, skills, and networks of trading relations. There were also Jews from Spain and Portugal (and from other countries, notably Germany, after 1630) and French Huguenots. This inflow of human capital was the single most important factor in the rise of Holland, and especially Amsterdam. Still, the role of the "native" element must not be overlooked. Immigrants gave a basic impetus, but they were a minority—though a significant one, possibly 125,000 persons, or 10 percent of the total population, from 1585 to the 1620s. By sheer numbers the local community became the driving force.

Other favorable factors were the abundance and cheapness of capital, weakness of guild regulations, religious tolerance, and high level of literacy that prevailed in the Dutch Republic; in the seventeenth century, Amsterdam surpassed Venice as the major center of book production in Europe. There was also a vast network of waterways and therefore cheap transport; a unique system of passenger transport on towboats, at low cost, was organized from town to town. And energy was available, thanks to windmills (about three thousand of them were used for industrial purposes in the seventeenth century in this windy country; they supplied as much power as fifty thousand horses) and to peat (for heat-using industries). In addition, many windmills were used for draining polders. In the seventeenth century, several countries called upon Dutch (and Flemish) engineers to drain marshes through windmills.

Moreover, the Dutch were both innovators and receptive to innovation.[38] They greatly improved their agriculture, which—as much grain was imported—specialized in commercial crops and dairy farming (some writers see this progress in farming as a major engine of growth). They mechanized some industrial processes, such as those used in shipbuilding, and won the primacy in shipping technology. As they did much bulk transport, for which low freights were crucial, they succeeded in lowering both shipbuilding costs and the size of crews, through the major invention of the *fluyt,* which has been mentioned earlier. They were also ahead in navigation techniques: starting in 1630, they applied mathematics to navigational measurements. In the field of business techniques, they created a powerful East India Company (VOK, 1602), and in finances, a consolidated public debt under the form of negotiable securities, the Amsterdam Wisselbank, and "price currents" or regular listings of the price of goods traded on the market and of exchange rates; such public lists were printed in Amsterdam beginning in the 1580s.[39] Other financial techniques, such as markets in futures, options, and various forms of derivatives, were also developed. The tulip-bulb mania from 1634 to 1636 was an early case of "bubble," or speculative boom and crash on futures markets. Altogether, the efficiency of markets was greatly improved.

However, one must also take into account the aggressive policies the Dutch followed to increase their commerce, thanks to close links between the republic's ruling oligarchy and the world of business. There was, of course, the closing of the Scheldt estuary, which ruined Antwerp and was made permanent by treaty in 1648. Then, because the Portuguese royal family had become extinct, Portugal was annexed to Spain, allowing the Dutch to enter the Indian Ocean in 1595, conquer the Spice Islands, and capture most of the East India trade (they even traded with Japan); they also tried, unsuccessfully, to conquer Brazil. Historians have discussed whether the wealth of Holland came mainly from the traditional and bulk "mother trades"—especially in grain from the Baltic and in herring from the North Sea—or from the "rich trades" in high-value products from the Indies and the Levant, which were largely established by force; the latter seems the more accurate view. But the export of home-produced goods must also be taken into account: butter, cheese, beer, gin, textiles, cut diamonds, Delft earthenware, and ships. Indeed, the interactivity of agriculture, industry, trade, and finance made the whole economy dynamic and integrated.

Amsterdam thus became, by the mid-1600s, the commercial and financial center of Europe and the world, the first true world entrepôt, more advanced and bigger than earlier great emporia and trading cities such as Venice. It was the world market for all possible commodities and an active transshipment center, with an enormous merchant fleet (the

Dutch had sixteen thousand ships in 1664, at least half of Europe's total seagoing tonnage, and unbeatably low freight charges) and powerful merchant elites. It also was the most suitable place to conduct international financial business, thanks to asset security and transferability, and it became the clearinghouse for most bills of exchange resulting from international transactions (many of them were actually settled in bills on Amsterdam) and the leading market for precious metals.[40]

Jan de Vries and Ad van der Woude have therefore maintained that the Dutch created a new type of economy, "the first modern economy," and that they—and not the British—achieved the break with the past that founded the modern economic system. This view has been rightly criticized by Herman van der Wee (1999): it is based upon criteria of modernity that could perfectly fit the advanced economies of Italy and the southern Netherlands during previous centuries; there was no discontinuity between those economies and that of Holland during its golden age, while the British industrial revolution was to be a definite break. Nonetheless, the Dutch economy stands out as it was no longer mainly agrarian, like in other countries, but was highly urbanized, highly dependent upon international trade and services, and based upon intermediation (the Dutch were, primarily, collectors and distributors). While the United Provinces was a small country, with only 2 million people c. 1700 (twice the size of the population c. 1600), it was a great power and the world economic leader, controlling the seaborne trade of many other countries, such as France, and infiltrating English, French, and Spanish colonies. Though in the sixteenth century Germany had been looking southward, to Italy, in the seventeenth most of Germany and central Europe gravitated toward the United Provinces. The latter had shaped a new European market, from the Baltic to the Mediterranean; it had eliminated regional ascendancies—Italian in the Mediterranean, Hanseatic in the Baltic. No power save nineteenth-century Britain has reached such a preponderance over world commerce. In the early seventeenth century, the United Provinces may have had 7–8 percent of European trade and a higher percentage of Europe's trade with the rest of the world. They also enjoyed a fast rise in per capita income.

Some historians have therefore wondered why Holland, which had achieved high levels in science and technology, and which had in Leiden the biggest concentration of textile industry in Europe, plus various other manufactures, did not start a full-scale industrialization, like England did in the eighteenth century. There were many reasons: the home market was narrow and many foreign markets were to be closed by protectionism; costs were higher than abroad, because industry was mainly in towns and wages high owing to heavy indirect taxation (so that labor-intensive industries could not compete with those of Britain); and there was a shortage of energy, with peat inadequate for the metal industries.

Therefore, a Dutch industrial revolution was not to be, and worse, the Dutch primacy did not last long: economic decline started in the late seventeenth century (c. the 1670s) and aggravated in the eighteenth. There was a leveling of trade expansion, because of both faltering demand, during the "seventeenth-century depression," and protectionism abroad. The five main "staple trades"—grain, herring, salt, timber, and textiles—declined. On the other hand, trade in colonial produce continued increasing (but part of it was in produce reexported from French or English ports). In the 1620s, Dutch trade had been more than twice that of England (by value); in the 1660s and 1690s, it was roughly 50 percent bigger; but in the 1750s it had fallen to three-quarters of English trade, and by 1790 to 40 percent (when actually, at constant prices, it was lower than a century earlier). Since the mid-eighteenth century, it also was inferior to the trade of France. Its profitability had deteriorated as well.

The main factor behind the decline was the burden of wars upon a small and overstretched country. Both England and France had become jealous of Dutch power and wealth. Under the influence of mercantilist views, they tried to reduce them through policies like the English Navigation Acts of 1651 and 1660, which aimed to oust the Dutch from their middleman function by reserving for English ships most of England's trade and the whole of its colonial traffic, and then through war. From the 1650s to the 1670s, there were three Anglo-Dutch wars, of which two were caused by blatant British aggression (the second resulted in the Dutch losing a small piece of real estate—Nieuw Amsterdam, i.e., New York). The third (1672), with the British in alliance with France, just aimed at dismembering and destroying the Dutch Republic. Then the United Provinces became allies, or rather satellites, of England against Louis XIV in two terribly expensive wars (1689–1713) that greatly increased the national debt, and therefore taxation, thus harming Dutch competitiveness. Industries declined one after the other, except a few, such as sugar refining, tobacco processing, and distilling. The tonnage of the merchant fleet fell after 1670, as we have seen. By the 1740s, which were a low point, after which a recovery took place, per capita income may have fallen by 15–20 percent.

Thus the Dutch golden age came to its end, though in the eighteenth century Holland remained a rich country. Because it had too much capital for internal investment and low interest rates, it became the banker of Europe and exported much capital, as mentioned earlier. England was the main outlet: it received half of Dutch foreign investment—in government, Bank of England, and East India Company stocks; by 1780, the Dutch held 80 percent of Britain's overseas debt. In the 1780s, the Dutch also bought French government stock. This is an interesting case of accumulation without growth and of rent-seeking behavior.[41]

Nonetheless, the center of Europe's economy, after having moved from Antwerp to Amsterdam, had shifted to London; Britain had emerged as the top nation. Though its economy had been commercialized early due to exports of wool, then woolens, and to the spread of the wool industry in the countryside, Britain had long been on the periphery of Europe. In the fifteenth and sixteenth centuries most woolen exports were sent to Antwerp, and London climbed to prosperity as a satellite of Antwerp. But after that town's fall, the English diversified their industry and trade, challenging the Iberian powers and expanding in America and in India, thanks to which they had, by the late seventeenth century, a large import and re-export trade in colonial produce. England had changed from an exporter of raw materials and importer of manufactures into an exporter of manufactured goods and importer of raw materials and colonial produce. Its total foreign trade, at constant prices, increased almost threefold during the seventeenth century (growth was especially fast from 1650 to 1700) and trebled again from 1700 to 1790. Its merchant shipping fleet grew from c. 50,000 tons in the 1570s to 200,000 in 1660, 450,000 in 1750, and more than one million in the 1780s. Moreover, from the mid-seventeenth century onward, agriculture became more market-oriented and diversified; cereal yields improved, and agricultural production was growing faster than population, so that the fear of famine vanished.

Around the same time, after 1688, during the wars against Louis XIV, there was in England a "financial revolution"; it created a new system of public finance based on the Dutch model. Its central piece was the national debt, which was serviced thanks to high (mostly indirect) taxation, so that, despite its fast accumulation, it inspired confidence and attracted capital (both British and Dutch). The English state was small but strong, the most effective fiscal state in Europe, and its sound finances were a major factor behind Britain's rise to world power. The new system mobilized efficiently the country's resources in wartime, particularly to build up the Royal Navy, which, as the biggest in numbers and the best in fighting capacity, won for Britain ascendancy at sea. Thanks to the latter Britain destroyed the first French colonial empire, in North America and India, and was the victor in the "Second Hundred Years' War" with France (1689–1815), which had largely economic motives. Although its rich Caribbean colonies gave France as large a foreign trade value as Britain's in the 1780s, this would be decimated during the French Revolution and Napoleonic wars, allowing Britain to capture a predominant share of international trade and services. Indeed, as early as 1713, it had become a great power, the leading trading and colonial country. The industrial revolution greatly strengthened this ascendancy, of course, which lasted up to 1914. However, Britain's primacy was different from that of previous leaders. It had a big port city in London, but behind it lay a relatively large territorial state, so that the country was able, up to the twentieth century, to withstand the military and political storms that had earlier stricken small, open, trading economies, such as Venice, the Hanseatic cities, and even Holland. Moreover, English wealth was based not only on trade, which is vulnerable, but upon technological superiority.

A sharp contrast can be drawn between England and France. The latter was much bigger and more populated: with around 20 million people in the seventeenth century and 28 million in 1789 (within its present frontiers), France had the biggest population in Europe. As a consequence, despite possibly suffering from overpopulation, it was the most powerful state in Europe and enjoyed long periods of political ascendancy during the seventeenth and eighteenth centuries. On the other hand, France never attained economic primacy or leadership, though it certainly had the biggest economy in Europe, including many large industries and —at least in the eighteenth century—a prosperous foreign trade. As for income per capita, it was, according to Paul Bairoch (1989), just above the European average in the late eighteenth century. Douglass North and Robert Paul Thomas have placed France among "the also-rans," and Braudel has stressed that the center of the European economy, which moved from Venice to London, never settled on French territory. Moreover, France was a constant borrower of foreign technology—Italian, then Dutch, and eventually English. Charles Kindleberger (1996) has also observed that France did not have—like Holland and England—one long rise followed by a long decline, but rather experienced a connected series of rises and declines (which went on during the nineteenth and twentieth centuries). Explanations have been found in structural (institutional, cultural, social) aspects of French history, such as its absolute monarchy, where economic and political freedom was restricted, or in its anticapitalist mentality, which was widespread among both elites and masses. But a major factor may have been the long succession of wars that aggressive neighbors—England, the Spanish and Austrian Hapsburgs, and later Germany—imposed upon the country.

We must, however, return to the seventeenth century, and stress that the vitality of Europe had then concentrated in a tiny fringe of its northwest—in Holland and England—and that those two countries' obvious growth may not have balanced the decline in southern countries and elsewhere (Germany, the southern Netherlands). Holland, however, was an entrepôt, like Venice had been, gaining its wealth from services as middleman. Those two facts illustrate first the continuity between late medieval and early modern economies: seventeenth-century capitalism was not markedly more advanced in the Protestant north than it had been in sixteenth-century Catholic Italy; there was more imitation and transfer than mutation. And secondly, they reveal the fragility of those economies, the uncertain and variable character of their growth. These are points that will be developed later.

Eastern Europe

We must, however, first consider a vast region, eastern and southeastern Europe, which has not been much mentioned earlier because it was not deeply affected by most of the changes discussed; it was and remained backward relative to the west.

The first—and possibly the main—factor behind this backwardness was that eastern Europe was invaded and subjugated by non-European conquerors, from which it was liberated only after several centuries. As a matter of fact, the transoceanic expansion of western Europe balanced out the heavy losses that Christendom had suffered on its eastern flanks beginning in the mid-thirteenth century, which had resulted in the subjugation and isolation of its Greek Orthodox sector. In this respect, it is worth mentioning that Orthodoxy—which prevailed in Russia and in the Balkans—imbued its faithful with a conservative mentality that was hostile to anything novel or foreign. Moreover, it did not postulate separation between spiritual and temporal powers, and this led to autocratic rule.

First, the Mongol invasion had destroyed the Russian state of Kiev (1241), with its prosperous towns, and for several centuries the wide plains of southern Russia were in the hands of the "Golden Horde"—nomadic Mongols and Tartars—who, up to the seventeenth century, also made devastating raids into Poland. However, surviving Russians had fled northward to the forested and marshy regions of central Russia, where soils were poor. The Mongols imposed tribute to those principalities but left them largely alone. They were quite backward economically; estates were practically self-sufficient, while towns and trade were far less developed than they had been in the Russia of Kiev. The only important trading town was Novgorod, in an out-of-the-way position to the northwest, which had relations with the Baltic area and with the Hanseatic League.

Eventually, Muscovy emerged as the leader and from the fifteenth century started to expand, mainly to the northwest, toward the Baltic, and to the south, toward the Black and Caspian Seas, against the weakened Golden Horde. The Russians took Kazan in 1551, Astrakhan in 1556, and peasants from Muscovy colonized the rich lands along the Volga, the Don, and the Dnieper. Siberia—out to the Pacific—was also conquered rather quickly. However, Russia did not reach the Black Sea coasts before the late eighteenth century: Azov was occupied in 1774, Crimea in 1783. The Ukraine did not become an exporter of wheat, through the Black Sea port of Odessa, until the nineteenth century.

The geographical factor contributing to Russia's retardation must be stressed: its handicaps were its immensity, a scattered population, transport difficulties (rivers freeze in winter), and remoteness from the major centers of economic activity. Late medieval Muscovy had few relations with other regions.[42] However, in 1553, a contact was made with the west, when ships of the English Muscovy Company visited the White Sea, but it was a tenuous link. Russia only became a European power when it conquered the Baltic countries in the early eighteenth century (however, the Baltic Sea freezes in winter, so that trade is interrupted); the 1703 founding of St. Petersburg, on the Gulf of Finland, was a landmark. Moreover, as was to happen again and again in Russia's history, Peter the Great was trying to "westernize" Russian society from above and by force—thus creating a sharp cultural division between Europeanized elites and the masses. Nonetheless, and despite later policies by "enlightened despots" (especially Catherine II, or Catherine the Great), eighteenth-century Russia had neither a free peasantry, nor a significant middle class, nor legal norms hospitable to private enterprise. Still, there was a start of industry, mainly textiles around Moscow and ironworks in the Ural Mountains, with a labor force mainly of serfs, bound to the works.

Europe suffered other serious losses as well, in its southeastern flank, owing to the unrelenting advance of the Ottoman Turks in the late Middle Ages and the sixteenth century. After building up a strong state in Asia Minor, they had crossed the Dardanelles in the mid-fourteenth century and methodically conquered the Balkans. They destroyed the kingdom of Serbia at the battle of Kosovo (1389) and crushed an army of western crusaders at Nicopolis (1396). Then they turned against the remnants of the Byzantine Empire and took Constantinople (renamed Istanbul) in 1453. The Geneose and Venetian "colonies" in the eastern Mediterranean were seized. In the sixteenth century, the Turks conquered most of Hungary (Buda was taken in 1541) as well as Romania, Crimea, and parts of southern Russia; their Tatar vassals harassed the frontiers of Poland.[43]

They were also strong at sea, but plans for raiding—and possibly invading —Italy were defeated by the Hispano-Venetian sea victory at Lepanto (1571). Still, the Turks remained a serious threat to their neighbors for a long time: as late as 1683, they besieged Vienna—unsuccessfully. But after 1600, the Ottoman Empire started to decay, while European military technology was increasingly superior. The rolling back of Turkish power started in the late seventeenth century, with the reconquest of Hungary (Buda was recaptured in 1686) and Croatia, but the liberation of the Balkans was not to take place before the nineteenth century (it was actually completed in 1912).[44]

There is a black legend about rule by the Turks, parts of which are untrue. They did not force the people they had conquered to convert to Islam, and they left a good deal of autonomy to the various ethnoreligious communities in their empire; a large majority of the Balkans' population remained Christian. Still, their rule was brutal, arbitrary, and fiscally demanding. Only subsistence agriculture could survive under the devouring state, which siphoned off any surplus to finance its army and bureaucracy; some crafts also survived, but they were left to minorities, as society in the Ottoman Empire was based on ethnic division of labor; this was not favorable to extension of enterprise, inasmuch as any accumulation invited seizure. Still, the Ottomans accepted Western merchants in their ports and there was some trading activity, especially to supply Istanbul, which recovered fast and with half a million inhabitants c. 1550 had become again, for a time, the largest city in Europe. Altogether, Turkish rule over southeastern Europe perpetuated there a high degree of economic backwardness.

Despite sporadic raids by Mongols and Tatars, conquest and oppression by alien rulers did not affect countries like Poland (which was then much larger than today), Bohemia, and Germany east of the Elbe—or, to use a recent expression, east-central Europe (ECE).[45] Those regions were somewhat "westernized"; since the Middle Ages, they belonged to the European trading system. Poland, which the Black Death largely spared, did relatively well in the fourteenth and fifteenth centuries and had its golden age in the sixteenth century. Population increased; agriculture made some progress: the three-year rotation spread, as did water mills (proof of the lag behind the west); and mining, handicrafts, interregional, and international trade expanded. The lifestyle at court, in the nobility, and in the growing towns drew closer to western norms. In the seventeenth century, however, first Germany and Bohemia and then Poland (which had annexed Lithuania[46]) were devastated by a succession of wars in which Sweden, Russia, and Turkey were also involved. War, plagues, and famines reduced population; both the area under cultivation and farm output fell back; and towns decayed.

Conversely, after 1721, there was a long period of peace, and economies revived. Exports from the Baltic ports to the west greatly increased; some landowners introduced new crops (clover, potato) and some new methods. There was a strong protoindustrialization in Bohemia and a rise of manufactures (mostly textiles) in Poland, within the framework of large estates. Population grew relatively fast in eighteenth-century eastern Europe, at 0.6 percent per year, versus 0.3 percent in northwestern Europe, because the East had retained the custom of marriage at puberty for women, while the West had adopted marriage at an older age. Eastern Europe's share of Europe's total population, which had been 28 percent c. 1400, reached 34 percent in 1800. The rise of a powerful Russian state, the reconquest of the Ukraine, and the definitive victory of sedentary societies over nomads also played a part in this expansion. Nonetheless, and despite the reforming efforts of some "enlightened despots," eastern Europe remained backward: its agriculture was extensive and primitive, and urbanization and population density were much lower than in the west.[47]

A major factor behind this backwardness was the area's so-called second serfdom, which also impacted Russia negatively. While peasants west of the Elbe—with few exceptions, mainly in Germany—were freemen (since the twelfth to the thirteenth centuries) and many were hereditary tenants (i.e., de facto owners of their small plots), ECE was under the system called *Gutsherrschaft*. This meant large manorial estates, of which a major part was in demesne and made up of large farms cultivated by the forced labor of serfs. This system was relatively new: it had emerged in the fifteenth and sixteenth centuries, as opportunities for landowners in the Baltic hinterland to sell grain in western markets had developed. Grain could be transported cheaply on large rivers, such as the Oder and Vistula, and their tributaries, to ports on the Baltic coast, and then loaded on Dutch ships, which had low freights. Those opportunities encouraged landowners to enlarge their demesnes and to increase the labor dues of their peasantry (many peasants, moreover, were only life tenants). In the late fifteenth and the early sixteenth centuries, Polish assemblies ("diets") restricted peasants' personal liberties, especially their right to leave their villages, and fixed to one day per week the minimum statute labor. This "second serfdom" or "manorial serf system" was counterproductive in the long run as it led to economic regression or at least stagnation (e.g., in most parts of Poland); it made the labor force immobile, the peasantry poor and passive. It also hampered the growth of towns and of a middle class while concentrating the ownership of land into a rather small number of magnates.

This "refeudalization" was often fostered and favored by princes, who used estate owners as agents of their power, particularly in Russia. In that immense country, where vast tracts of fertile land were available, thanks to the reconquest of the southern regions, peasants were tempted to run away and landowners tried to forbid them to move.[48] In this, the latter group was decisively supported by the state. The new Romanov dynasty had suppressed the ancient aristocracy and needed followers capable of acting as its local agents, especially to collect taxes, which were heavy because of large military expenditures. A new "feudal" nobility was created by land grants and the subjugation of the peasantry, which in the seventeenth century became bound to the land. This subjection was completed in the 1700s, especially by Catherine II; although celebrated by Western intellectuals as an enlightened and benevolent ruler, she finished making Russia an autocratic, despotic monarchy. Still, some signs of autonomous growth (in rural domestic industry, for example) appeared.

It must be mentioned that supporters of the "dependency theory" explain the economic backwardness of eastern Europe by its relations with the West. The weaker economies of the East were made into a semiperipheral, semicolonial area, reduced to primary production and to low— or nonexistent—rates of growth. Moreover, exports of grain to the West were instrumental in the rise of the "second serfdom." On the other hand, a large share of the population of the countries around the Baltic earned a living through large exports (of grain and also of other goods). Many historians also stress the underlying social and political conditions in eastern Europe that had prevailed in the Middle Ages, before the "second serfdom," as factors contributing to backwardness: by 1200 or 1300, Europe east of the Elbe had clearly been behind western regions.

However, a last point to stress is that, before the industrial revolution, differences in per capita incomes between countries were not large. According to Bairoch (1979), the ratio between the richest and the poorest European countries c. 1700 was 1 to 1.5–1.6 (it may have been higher between provinces within one country). Qualitative evidence suggests that the gap might have been wider, but not very much. This lack of divergence is a sign of weak growth—even in the so-called advanced countries.

Low Productivity and Its Consequences

A first—and obvious—character of preindustrial economies was the primacy of agriculture. A large majority of the population was work-

ing on and living off the land (indeed, this was a necessity owing to the
low productivity, a subject to which we shall return). According to Bairoch
(1997), 76–80 percent of Europe's population (Russia excluded) was engaged in agriculture c. 1700—hardly less than c. 1300. By the 1780s, the
ratio was two-thirds in France and larger in other countries, with the exception of Holland and Britain, where only half the population was employed in farming. Admittedly, many people in the countryside were involved part-time in industrial and services work, but this did not alter the
dominance of agriculture, which generated the largest share of national
income. It also was the leading sector, as the fluctuations of harvests had
a strong impact upon the rest of the economy.[49] Of course, European
economies, especially in the west, had much diversified since the early Middle Ages, but the importance of trade and manufactures must be neither
underestimated (inasmuch as they were powerful forces of change) nor
overestimated. Industry remained closely linked to agriculture, which, for
example, supplied most of its raw materials (wood, textile fibers, oilseeds,
dyestuffs); as humans and animals also supplied a good deal of power,
E. A. Wrigley (1987, 1988) has rightly called the preindustrial economies
"organic." Also, industry was often scattered over the countryside.

A corollary of agriculture's primacy was the low rate of urbanization.
Bairoch (1997) has estimated that in the eighteenth century, 12 percent of
Europe's population (Russia, with 3 percent, excluded) lived in towns of
5,000 inhabitants or more, which was hardly more than c. 1300 or 1500.
The share of towns with more than 2,000 people increased more markedly
—from 15 percent of total population c. 1500 to 24 percent c. 1800—but
many of those "towns" were just large villages (and almost all cities retained
some agricultural activity). As Europe's total population increased, the
urban population doubled in absolute numbers. The rate of urbanization
varied greatly from region to region; it increased markedly in England, but
it remained higher in Italy and Spain. A significant development was the
increase in the number of large towns, those with more than 100,000 inhabitants: six in 1500, seventeen in 1750, and twenty-two in 1800; this resulted from the fast growth of some capital cities and of several ports on
the Atlantic and North Sea coasts. Historians have debated the economic
impact of those large towns, particularly of capitals. Braudel has described
them as parasites that lived at the expense of their hinterlands and impoverished them. This seems true for cities like Madrid or Naples, but not
for Amsterdam, London, or Paris, which were dynamic centers of change
and growth; London, for example, created a national market in England.

Because towns had more deaths than births, increase in their population was only possible thanks to constant replenishment by immigrants

from the countryside. A city like eighteenth-century Bordeaux, which doubled in size, attracted people from all over the southwestern quarter of France. Indeed, population was on the move, and the old view that peasants were immobile is completely wrong.

A second and basic character of preindustrial economies was their low productivity, especially for labor, which was generally unskilled, uneducated, and often unable to work properly due to undernourishment. As a direct consequence, massive and omnipresent poverty was a general trait of traditional economies and societies, and it was made worse by underemployment and seasonal unemployment (traditional agriculture did not give work for more than half the year at best). Poverty among the masses was of course aggravated by the highly unequal income and wealth distribution; in societies that were fundamentally poor, a small number enjoyed affluence, even magnificence, but no redistribution could have cured the ills resulting from low productivity: average real incomes were bound to be very low, and a precarious living, close to the subsistence line, was inevitable for the majority of the people. In late seventeenth-century England, which was better off than the rest of Europe, half of the population could not live off its own resources and had to be helped by public or private charity. In eighteenth-century France, the top decile of the population received one half of total incomes, and the 70 percent at the bottom, one quarter (Morrisson and Snyder).

As for technology and equipment, they were crude, while land—the most important available natural resource—was badly utilized. Moreover, despite the inventions mentioned earlier, there was no decisive, overall improvement in labor productivity from the thirteenth to the eighteenth centuries.

This situation was particularly serious in the all-important sector of agriculture. Farming techniques and equipment were rudimentary—the wheeled, horse-drawn plow mentioned earlier was not used in most of Europe; very often plowing merely scratched the topsoil. Scythes were only used to mow meadows, and ears of grain were cut with sickles; sowing by hand-spreading seeds resulted in waste. Therefore, crop yields were poor: the ratio of seed to crop was 1 to 3 at worst, 1 to 7 (or rarely 10) at best, and 1 to 5–6 in many areas; this meant low yields per acre: 3 to 4 hundredweights for wheat. There has been much debate about those yields and whether they did or did not increase during the period we are considering; the conclusion appears to be—according particularly to B. H. Slicher van Bath—that yields doubled in western Europe from the twelfth to the late eighteenth century, but that there was not much progress from the sixteenth to the eighteenth centuries in most regions of France and

Germany. Still, there were marked regional and temporal variations, and high yields were obtained in the Île-de-France, where the proximity to Paris stimulated the emergence of large farms (often more than 500 acres) that were like grain factories with high yields and also produced fodder, straw, and meat for the capital. Likewise, in the Low Countries, particularly in Flanders, Brabant, and then north Holland, the increase in urban population intensified demand and stimulated gradual improvements in farming techniques. Already in the fourteenth century, some farmers took a catch crop of beans or peas on what had previously been fallow land, so that they fed more animals and obtained more manure. In Flanders, yields of 1 to 9–11 were found in the fifteenth century, and of 1 to 11–12 in the eighteenth. Altogether, between the twelfth and the eighteenth centuries, grain yields may have increased in those areas by a factor of 3 to 4.[50]

However, labor productivity improved far less (likewise in northern Italy) because the quantity of land available per person employed in agriculture was small. On the other hand, England had the advantage of a lower population density, and its labor productivity may have increased over 60 percent from 1650 to 1800, while grain production was moving steadily upward after 1500. As for France, Philip T. Hoffmann has suggested that the long-run rate of total factor productivity growth over three centuries up to 1789 was close to zero; some regions (Normandy, Île-de-France) had periods of fast growth, then suffered setbacks because of devastation in time of war, fiscal exactions, and high transport costs, which prevented progress in specialization and gains from trade.[51] Moreover, yields were very irregular from year to year, according to weather conditions.

Altogether, traditional agriculture—with some exceptions—was caught in a kind of vicious circle. Because of low yields, arable land had to be almost entirely devoted to bread grains. They gave their nourishment to the masses and, in many areas, were difficult and expensive to import; only the Baltic area had regular surpluses to export. Moreover, cereals supply the highest number of calories per unit of cultivated area. Because people wanted to eat white bread (which, actually, is the most cost-effective food—and the easiest to digest), wheat progressed, but it was grown mainly in southern countries and on fertile soils, such as in the Paris basin and on the loess belt of central Europe. On poor soils, under cool and wet climates, and in eastern Europe, rye, maslin (a mixture of wheat and rye), oats, barley, and buckwheat prevailed. As a result of cereals' dominance, animal fodder was limited to meadows, which were rarely extensive; to grazing the stubble after harvests; and to pasturing on fallow land. There were exceptions, of course; in some areas, grass pre-vailed over grain, and stock raising was the main activity: the mountain regions, where cereals did not grow except in a few spots, and the marsh-lands, especially along seacoasts. But such areas had a low population den-sity and, nonetheless, many of their inhabitants had to migrate, either for one season each year or for longer periods, as laborers, peddlers, or—in Switzerland—mercenaries in foreign armies. Though the association of grain growing and stock raising was a specific trait of European agricul-ture, the numbers of livestock were relatively low, and animals were small and skinny; consequently, there was a shortage of manure, which resulted in low yields and in the need to leave fields in fallow, to restore their fer-tility, one year out of two or three, so that output was restricted.

Still, agriculture was not unable to change; for example, Europe adopted new crops and new animals, which came from Asia in the Mid-dle Ages and later from America: rice, oranges, beans, tomatoes, tobacco, maize (corn), and potatoes.[52] But there were hindrances, so that neither corn nor potatoes were widely grown before the eighteenth century (when they helped to feed a growing population). Another achievement was the extensive land reclamation, from the late Middle Ages onward, especially in the Low Countries and in northern Italy, and also in many marshlands on the coast of western Europe. In addition, traditional farming often in-volved a skillful adaptation to the environment, based upon centuries-long experience, and a successful effort to preserve it. Still, there were cases of soil exhaustion, like in eighteenth-century Denmark, which suffered an ecological crisis because of deforestation and sand drifts.

Nonetheless, despite sharp regional variations in performance (e.g., in Italy, between Lombardy and the kingdom of Naples), and despite the variety of agricultural systems (as each small *pays*—of which there was a multitude—had its own), the tragedy of European economies was their dependence on low-productivity agriculture, even though it was by no means static.

Manufacturing, on the other hand, had craftsmen with highly so-phisticated skills, skills that have remained unequaled, but they worked mainly in the small sector of luxury trades; for most consumption goods, production techniques were often crude and followed an unchanging routine, and equipment was rudimentary: hand tools and simple ma-chines, like spinning wheels, hand looms, and foot-pedal lathes. Despite the use of water and windmills, human physical strength remained es-sential in most industrial processes, which were highly labor-intensive and therefore slow and expensive. Work was often seasonal and had to stop when watercourses of mills froze or dried up, or when laborers went back to the fields. As mentioned earlier, it was also the case that small family workshops were dominant in industry, despite its penetration by merchant capitalism and the emergence of some centralized, medium- or large-sized units of production, as generally existing technology did not allow for economies of scale. Circulating capital was much more important than fixed capital, of which industry had little—especially in its domestic branch—and more generally, fixed reproducible capital was mostly peripheral to production, being made mainly of buildings and ships. Still, it is likely that reproducible capital per capita increased. If "monuments" (churches, castles, etc.) are excluded, the level of net capital formation was very low (under 3 or even 2 percent of GDP), but gross capital formation may have been rather high, as most equipment was of poor quality, had a short physical life, and needed a good deal of maintenance. Moreover, metals remained "poor relatives" (Braudel); c. 1700, output of iron per capita and per year, though higher than c. 1300, was only four pounds. Traditional economies were still based upon wood—which Europe was lucky to be well provided with, except in its southern regions— both as a fuel and as a material. Large rafts, which floated downstream to bring firewood and timber to cities like Paris, could be seen on many rivers.

Productivity was also low in transports, especially land transport.[53] Infrastructure was poor and badly maintained: roads were just dirt tracks, rivers were strewn with obstacles, canals were rare outside the Po valley and the Low Countries, and ports lacked facilities. "Vehicles" had a modest carrying capacity; the remarkable advances that were achieved in shipbuilding and the art of navigation have been stressed earlier, but in the eighteenth century there were few merchant ships that could carry more than two or three hundred tons; only "East Indiamen" that circumnavigated Africa exceeded a thousand tons. Circulation of goods and people was slow, irregular, subject to the whims of the weather, and thus largely seasonal. Transport costs were high, especially on land (so that many rivers that now appear unnavigable were regularly used). Stagecoach services, which started in the west in the seventeenth century, were intended for mail and for well-to-do passengers.

The consequence was a fragmentation of the market, a juxtaposition of small regional units, which lived mainly upon their own resources. Europe had a market economy, of course, even in the huge, backward, and poor periphery of its southern and eastern regions (Poland was a large exporter of grain), and only some isolated inland areas, such as in mountainous regions, had a "subsistence economy" (still, large quantities of cheese from Switzerland traveled over long distances!). Though market participation certainly increased from the fifteenth century onward, the market economy was not fully developed; many producers, mainly in agriculture, were only marginally involved in it. Moreover, because information was rare and irregularly supplied, markets were unstable and unpredictable, and uncertainty and risk were stronger than in later periods—making possible both high profits and grievous losses. In short, economies lacked coherence.

Early modern Europe thus had a low-productivity economic system because most of its technology, though neither primitive nor static, remained rudimentary. Europe was inventive and innovative, and, since the early Middle Ages, its stock of techniques had been enriched and perfected; the many new inventions from the thirteenth to the seventeenth century have been mentioned earlier, but their spottiness and their slow introduction into practical use have also been stressed; they created a few new branches of industry (like hosiery), transformed some existing ones, and increased their productivity levels, but their effects upon the global economy were limited. There were few spin-offs or fallouts, few backward or forward linkages, even considering the inventions, of great import for the future, that were made in England c. 1700: the steam engines of Savery and Newcomen, and the coke-smelting of iron. Many inventions may have been too specialized to change the basic equipment and processes used by the majority of farmers and craftsmen.[54]

It would take much space to try to explain adequately the deficiencies in technological progress, rooted in the social, political, and cultural structures and institutions that Europe had inherited from the Middle Ages, which changed only slowly. The manorial system, or what remained of it, was, in some respects, an impediment to progress in agriculture, even though manorial dues had become very low in many parts of western Europe. Peasants also had to pay tithes to the church and taxes to the state, so that the total "fiscal" burden may have been, in seventeenth-century France, equivalent to 40 percent of their gross product. A serious flaw was certainly that, except in England, large landowners rarely took an interest in or invested in improving their estates; they only tried to obtain from them as much income as they could. As for peasants, it is a myth that they were irrational, custom bound, and stubbornly hostile to any change, and that they had no contact with the outside world. Still, they were mostly ignorant and poor, neither able nor willing to improve their tiny farms, except for a small number of large "capitalist" farmers who were market oriented, had some capital and equipment, and were agents of progress. Peasants were also prisoners of constraints often imposed by strong village communities; but it has been recently suggested that those communities, even though they opposed innovations like enclosures of communal property, were not a serious obstacle to improvements and growth. The open-fields system was not as rigid and innovation-crippling as often assumed: major changes in crop rotation were to be made within its framework. Altogether traditional rural society was neither rigid, nor stagnant, nor immobile, but it also was not very congenial to progress. Moreover, in eastern Europe, serfdom, which had died out in the west, developed east of the Elbe from the fifteenth century onward, and later in Russia, as has been mentioned. In towns, the monopolies and regulations that the craft guilds imposed hampered invention and innovation; as a consequence, much industry moved to the countryside, which reduced costs but due to the isolated rural environment hampered progress, except in some districts of dense protoindustrialization in England.

Politically, the period we are considering was marked by the rise of absolutist states (absolutist, but not despotic). They frequently engaged in warfare and therefore imposed heavy taxation upon their subjects. The "military revolution" of the seventeenth century made things worse in this respect, as permanent armies in peacetime and larger ones in wartime greatly increased military spending.[55] However, the inefficiency of their fiscal machinery and the web of privileges within society prevented princes from collecting as large a share of national product as modern states do, making budget deficits frequent and defaults on debt not rare. The French ancien régime collapsed because it did not tax its people enough, not because it taxed then too much. Governments, churches, and the upper classes also indulged in conspicuous consumption and in monument building, but not in productive investment. Still, according to Werner Sombart (1915), the luxury of princely courts helped to generate capitalism. Braudel, on the other hand, considered that it was parasitic and antieconomic. Some recent writers have revived the Sombart thesis.

On the other hand, from the sixteenth century onward, many governments tried to enforce "economic policies," with the idea of "developing" their countries and especially "encouraging" seaborne trade, in order to get more resources from taxation. Those policies were inspired by mercantilism, the dominant economic ideology of the period, which had a pessimistic and fixed view of economic affairs, one connected with the hard times that prevailed for most of the seventeenth century. World trade was seen as finite, as a zero-sum game, such that one country could only become richer at the expense of others. Also, state intervention was deemed necessary to prevent the national economy from deteriorating, and especially the balance of trade—the central concept of mercantilism—from becoming unfavorable. This meant restricting imports, stimulating exports, and encouraging import-substitution industries with the help of a panoply of prohibitions, tariffs, bounties, subsidies, regulations, privileges, monopolies, and eventually "war for trade" against commercial rivals.

Such policies were far from new. Since the late thirteenth century, governments had imposed customs duties on imports (and sometimes on exports). But in the seventeenth century, protectionism became more systematic and widespread, so that international integration of markets was restricted and Europe became a mosaic of protected markets. On the other hand, the incidence of mercantilism must not be overestimated. Jean-Baptiste Colbert (French minister of finance, 1661–1683) is often seen as the mercantilist par excellence, and "colbertism" is synonymous with an exacerbated mercantilism. Still, Colbert was no "colbertist"; he was far less interventionist than it is often assumed. Moreover, he had neither the means nor the money to fully implement most of his plans, and many of the trading and manufacturing companies he encouraged were not successful. This is typical of mercantilist policies, which, most times, were either ineffective (as governments did not have the means to enforce them) or clearly counterproductive. For example, Frederick II of Prussia and the Portuguese chief minister Pombal started a number of industries that hardly survived them.[56] In some cases, however, new industries were created, public works (e.g., canals) were achieved, and foreign trade increased (by the English Navigation Acts, for example). In the eighteenth century, government policies became more liberal, but altogether state interventions had a rather negative impact, inasmuch as they involved cooperation between government and rent-seeking interest groups of businessmen.

European societies also shared the values of a military and landed aristocracy, and a worldview that was deeply religious, conservative, and adverse to change. Trade and hand labor were despised. Men who had made money in business retired to buy land and live like gentlemen, so that economies suffered a loss of capital and talents (on the other hand, some noblemen were involved in business, such as mining, ironworks, shipping, and colonial trade). The idea of progress, of manipulating and transforming nature through rational investigation and experiment, only emerged slowly. However, mentalities were gradually changed—and not only among elites—by the Renaissance, the Reformation, the Enlightenment, and the seventeenth-century scientific revolution, which applied mathematics to the study of nature and developed the experimental method. Among those great cultural movements, Max Weber gave a special significance to the Calvinist Reformation, and his thesis has been recently rehabilitated by David Landes (1998). Calvinism stimulated literacy (for Bible reading) and generalized among its adherents the previously rare virtues of rationality, order, diligence, productiveness, and punctuality. The "new man," who was endowed with these qualities, created in Holland and Britain a new economy, while southern Europe saw much less change because of its Catholicism and reactionary anti-Protestant backlash. That Protestants played a significant role in sixteenth- and seventeenth-century western economies is not to be denied, but it can be argued that the new religion appealed to the kind of people —tradesmen, craftsmen—whose personal values were already conducive to hard work and business acumen. Moreover, all Calvinist countries were not economically successful. England was mainly Anglican, and its economic "divergence" did not develop until more than a century after its monarchs had imposed Protestantism.

On the whole, North and Thomas have been right to stress the role of institutional arrangements and property rights. European countries did not have the efficient economic organization that is the key to growth, and that only occurs when property rights make it worthwhile to undertake socially productive activity.[57] Intricate networks of privileges prevented the emergence of free and flexible markets and encouraged monopolies. Jean-Laurent Rosenthal's study of two French provinces shows that, before the French Revolution, drainage and irrigation projects—and more generally investment in agriculture—were crippled by the high transaction costs that were involved in improving land, particularly because of endless litigation over ill-defined property rights and because authority was too decentralized, which favored special interests.[58] In some countries, the protection of persons, property, and contract was not fully guaranteed, and rulers could unilaterally alter in their favor property rights. Holland and England were exceptions: they established institutions congenial to economic progress and so were the first countries to eventually break the vicious circle that had hampered economic growth.

Malthusian Traps

There is no proper theory of growth for preindustrial economies, but the model that has been widely accepted for some time is a Malthusian one: it hinges on the relationship between population and resources (i.e., land). In a mainly agricultural society, with low levels of productivity, the supply of cultivable land per capita of population is seen as the chief determinant of real incomes. This is sound, with some qualifications, and taking into account the North and Thomas interpretation.

Basically, preindustrial economies were fragile, unstable, and subject to recurrent crises, so that their growth could only be slow and irregular.

Of course, production and trade greatly increased between the eleventh and the eighteenth centuries, but mainly because of the upsurge in Europe's population, which rose from about 40 million to 200 million. So this was extensive, Smithian growth, rather than intensive growth, and increase in output or income per capita was in the long run much slower because of the Malthusian trap: population tended to grow faster than food production, while peasant holdings became smaller and smaller. Moreover, progress in technology and/or income caused higher birthrates. Therefore, economies were accident prone and expansion could only be temporary; it was periodically interrupted by crises and depressions resulting from the three scourges of famine, plague, and war.

When there was no famine, epidemic, or devastating war, European population had an excess of births over deaths (despite high infantile mortality) and therefore increased—though not very fast. One reason for this slowness was that western societies—and this was one major specificity —were able to limit fertility by delaying marriages (especially for women); smaller family sizes favored investment in human (and even physical) capital. Still, after the large-scale clearings of wasteland achieved in the twelfth and thirteenth centuries, not much new land was left to be put into cultivation in western Europe, and a high density of population had been reached. Indeed, the most fertile regions were overpopulated and suffered from a "land famine," which pushed up land prices and rents, increasing also the fragmentation of holdings. Moreover, we know that crop yields did increase slowly, except in some privileged areas, because of the vicious circle in which agriculture was caught. So by 1300 or even earlier, despite the technological progress that had been achieved, there were diminishing returns, as poor land was put into cultivation (especially under the three-year rotation) and pastures shrank.[59] In late thirteenth-century England, much arable land was undermanured, underrested, and overworked—in a word, exhausted—and yields fell off. After a long period of demographic growth, the pressure of population over resources, which had driven up prices even during the golden age of the thirteenth century (they had increased fourfold in England), was becoming acute, as was indicated by a serious famine in 1315–1317 in northwestern Europe. Available food supplies and real incomes per capita (especially wages) fell. In some areas, population may have decreased (but in some others, it continued to grow until the plague), and life expectancy as well. Moreover, wars broke out, especially between England and France, leading to heavier taxation, and climatic conditions deteriorated, becoming cooler and wetter. It has therefore been maintained that immiserization, which multiplied the numbers of the destitute weakened by nutritional deficiencies, created conditions for disaster. Actually, the plague, when it came, was an indiscriminate killer of rich and poor alike. Still, under-nourishment may have helped the diffusion of other diseases, while high population densities—especially the overcrowding of towns, the lack of hygiene, and the proliferation of rats and fleas—made contagion easier.[60]

Historians have no basis to assert that a Malthusian crisis as cata-strophic as the one that actually took place was inevitable, but they can at least suggest that, as the mid-fourteenth century drew nearer, Europe was locked into a Malthusian stasis, where further expansion was not pos-sible, and that a "correction" (as stock exchange analysts say nowadays) was bound to come—like three hundred years later, in the seventeenth century.[61] But one exogenous and fortuitous factor made it much more deadly than a mere Malthusian trap.

Disaster came by accident: in 1347 a ship sailed from a Black Sea port, where bacilli had been brought by some caravan from central Asia (a ran-som of commercial expansion), to Messina and Genoa. It carried the plague, both bubonic and pulmonary, the Black Death, which spread quickly all over Europe, especially along trade routes, though a few re-gions, notably Poland, were spared. There had been no plague in the West for six hundred years, and the people had no immunity. In four years, the Black Death (its peak was in 1348, and it stopped in 1350) killed a third of Europe's population: 25 million people, of a total of 80 million; in some places, including some large towns, the proportion reached one-half. But this was not the end: four renewed attacks of the plague took place dur-ing the second half of the fourteenth century, and there were three more in the early fifteenth century (the last general outbreak was in 1421–1423). The plague had become endemic, and there were further outbursts in the centuries that followed, particularly in the late sixteenth century and the early seventeenth, but they were localized—mainly in large towns—and less deadly. Eventually, however, quarantine measures in seaports and a sanitary cordon on the border between the Hapsburg and Ottoman Empires prevented the fatal disease from developing again in the West: London had its last outburst of plague in 1665, Paris in 1668; those at Marseilles in 1720 and Messina in 1742–1744 were the last in the West.[62] In the nineteenth century, only the Balkans and Russia suffered from the plague.

The population of Europe did not really recover before the 1420s, when it may have been 60 million (compared to 80 before the Black Death, i.e., a fall of a quarter). In France, which besides the plague was devastated by English armies, population did not start to recover before 1450, when it was a third lower than in 1340; in some provinces, it had fallen by half or even more. Paris, for example, had more than 200,000 inhabitants in 1328 and under 100,000 in the early fifteenth century. Altogether, northwestern Europe suffered most, though, in Italy, the population of Florence in 1427 was under half its 1338 level.

The dramatic fall in population disrupted all aspects of life and generated an economic depression that lasted well into the fifteenth century. Much marginal land was given up and thousands of villages were deserted and "lost," especially in England, Germany, and Scandinavia. Prices and rent fell roughly 50 percent on average; grain prices, however, fell more, so farmers converted land to pasture and the first enclosures of open fields took place, in order to facilitate stock raising. Meanwhile, there was an acute labor shortage, so real wages sharply increased: in late fifteenth-century England they were twice as high as before the plague, a level not to be reached again before the nineteenth century. The fall in output may have been less serious in industry than in agriculture: the cloth industry declined in Flanders but grew in England and in other places. Still, the depression was severe and protracted. It may have been aggravated by a shortage of precious metals from the mid-1300s to the mid-1400s, because several mines were exhausted and there was a drain of specie to the east. Governments were led to monetary mutations and debasement of the coinage, changes that hampered business. However, new silver mines were discovered in Tyrol and Saxony in the 1460s.

After 1450, however, came a long period of renewed expansion that supported the brilliant culture of the Renaissance. By the early sixteenth century, European population was roughly at its preplague level, and it continued to increase afterward, reaching 100 million for Europe (Russia included) c. 1600. The population of France doubled between 1420 and 1560. Trade, both intra-European and transoceanic, greatly increased, as did manufacturing output. Land that had been deserted was put back into circulation. Due to the increase in specie stocks and in the velocity of circulation, money penetrated more widely into economic circuits.

Eventually, however, food production lagged again behind a growing population; this explains the rise of grain exports from the Baltic to western and southern Europe, and, in combination with the inflow of precious metals from America, the sharp inflation of the sixteenth century. In the late sixteenth and early seventeenth centuries, overpopulation and immiserization prevailed again. There was no general disaster on the scale of the Black Death, but expansion came to a stop at dates that varied from country to country and ranged from the 1590s to the mid-1600s. Germany was a battlefield during the Thirty Years' War, which was, of course, accompanied by famines and epidemics; it lost at least 20 percent of its population, and the war left a long-term structural legacy. Poland, also involved in long wars, lost population as well. Spain and, to a lesser degree, Italy suffered from devastating plagues. In some French provinces, demographic expansion stopped around 1630, but in Langue-doc it went on until 1670, and the French kingdom's population, despite several severe short-term crises, was somewhat higher c. 1700 than c. 1600. In England, on the other hand, the fast population growth of the sixteenth century generated a sharp fall in living standards, as, up to 1650, food production failed to keep pace with this increase and cycli-cal food crises were fairly frequent. The population of England reached a peak in 1656 and then slightly declined for a quarter of a century, to recover afterward. Still, its growth rate was close to zero during the sec-ond half of the seventeenth century, despite the economic progress that was achieved after 1660.

Many historians consider most of the seventeenth century a somber period for Europe's economy, and its global income may have fallen.[63] However, pessimism must not be pushed too far, and the once fashion-able concept of a "general crisis" in the "tragic" seventeenth century has been given up. Exports of raw materials and naval stores from Baltic countries to the west went on increasing after 1650 (even though total traffic through the Sund declined), which is a sign of expansion in in-dustry and shipping. Despite the wars between France and the "maritime powers," trade with America increased; to take just one example, the merchant fleet of the port of St. Malo in Brittany (which was active in trade with Spain and its colonies) doubled between 1664 and 1683.

Recovery and expansion returned starting in the early eighteenth century—roughly from 1720, but with variations in dates from country to country. These forces were especially visible in regions that had suf-fered badly in the seventeenth century. In Spain, despite an increase in population, GDP per capita may have increased by 20 percent from 1750 to 1800, when, according to David R. Ringrose, the country's modernization started. The southern Netherlands (which had become Austrian) had a renaissance that prepared the success of Belgium in the nineteenth century; they had remarkable gains in agricultural pro-ductivity and technological progress in industry, while banks in Brus-sels and Antwerp developed links with the Amsterdam money markets. In Germany and Bohemia, protoindustrialization progressed greatly.[64] Eastern Europe had a fast growth in population (which almost dou-bled), especially in Russia, where fertile lands in the south were settled, and in Hungary. As for Britain and France, countless fine country and town houses, cities like Bordeaux and Bath, and the New Town of Edinburgh are clear evidence of their growing wealth—and of a "consumer revolution." According to Bairoch (1997), aggregate industrial production in Europe (Russia included) may have increased by a factor of five between 1700 and 1800. European population (west of the Urals) rose from 120 million c. 1700 to 140 million c. 1750 and 180 million c. 1800; its rate of growth accelerated from 0.3 percent per year during the century's first half to 0.5 percent during the second, mainly became of a decline in mortality (mostly among infants and children).[65]

The age of the Enlightenment was also one of prosperity, but there are signs that toward the century's end Europe was heading toward new troubles because population was growing too fast, as the Reverend Thomas Malthus stated in 1798; indeed, prices along with rents had been rising since the 1730s, real wages were under pressure, and the average height of humans was declining. There was an "industrious revolution," as people had to work harder and longer to preserve their standard of living. On the other hand, it has been maintained that the constraints that food supplies imposed upon the economy had loosened. There had been no pan-European famine since 1709–1710, thanks to improvements in market integration and transportation plus interventions by governments, which were by no means irrational and not always ineffective. New crops, especially potatoes, contributed to increased food supplies. Traffic through the Sund reveals that western Europe was becoming less dependent on grain imports, which is proof of an increase in its agricultural output. In France, according to recent estimates, eighteenth-century grain production increased at the same pace as population (which rose from 22 million c. 1700 to 28 million in 1789); total factor productivity in agriculture progressed at 0.3 percent per year during the decades before 1789, thanks to many small improvements; and if the bad harvest of 1788 contributed to the demise of the ancien régime, there was no starvation or mortality crisis in 1789. George Grantham sees no symptom of a high-pressure demographic system in prerevolutionary France and concludes that the view that eighteenth-century France suffered from overpopulation is "unproved." Nevertheless, in Britain, where agricultural improvements were achieved on a larger scale, grain production progressed more slowly than population, and the country, which had been an exporter of grain in the mid-eighteenth century, became a net importer. Wrigley and Schofield believe that the danger of Britain falling into a Malthusian trap was real.

However, Europe was this time to escape thanks to the agricultural and industrial revolutions, which indeed made possible both a large increase in population and, after a time, progress in real incomes for most Europeans.

The economic history of Europe from the Middle Ages to the eighteenth century is thus dominated by two very long cycles, which Rondo Cameron (1989) has called Europe's logistics, and the beginning of a third, and therefore by two protracted depressions, with the second cycle —and its phase of depression—shorter than the first.[66] Depressions may have had connections with changes in climate, which became cooler and wetter in the fourteenth century and again from the late sixteenth onward, during the "Little Ice Age," when many winters were harsh and glaciers moved forward in the Alps.

Moreover, preindustrial economies also suffered frequent but short crises roughly at least once in every decade, when bad weather (generally too much rain) caused a sharp fall in grain yields and output. The worst was when harvests failed two years in succession, so that real famine became possible. Food prices would rise sharply and be stirred up by speculation and by panic among ignorant people, who feared starvation. Price hikes, which could reach 80 percent within a short cycle in eighteenth-century France (and more in earlier periods), were out of proportion with falls in output, which were generally about 20 or 30 percent; markets, which often performed poorly and operated under ill-conceived regulations, were not able to generate the necessary intertemporal and spatial redistribution of food. Most of the population fell into misery, and many people did not have enough to eat.

Such "subsistence crises" were often accompanied by outbursts of hypermortality, when death rates rose to 70 or 100 per thousand, two or three times the normal level, while marriages, conceptions, and births decreased, so that a significant share of population in a region or even a country could be wiped out. In France between the beginning of 1693 and the end of 1695, the excess of deaths over births was 1.5 million, almost 7 percent of the total population of 22 million. Admittedly, this type of nationwide crisis was relatively rare, as most subsistence crises were regional. Moreover, population generally recovered quite fast from these short crises (except in some occasions when disasters accumulated) thanks to self-regulating mechanisms, especially lower marriage age after mortality peaks.

Many historians accepted that victims of mortality peaks had died from starvation per se, but some sharp rises in food prices were not followed by high death rates, and recent research has shown that there is no direct correlation between harvest failures and hypermortality crises. Shortages of food did not cause high death rates, except when epidemics broke out. Admittedly, underfed people were especially liable to contract epidemic diseases and to die in large numbers, and high bread prices drove many destitute people to take to the road, where they could diffuse diseases. On the other hand, after the early eighteenth century, both subsistence and demographic crises became milder, and the very existence of "subsistence crises" during that period has been disputed; even in the seventeenth century, large-scale famine was exceptional, so epidemics and war now appear as the great killers.

Indeed, war played a major but often neglected role in demographic and economic fluctuations, at least up to the end of the War of Spanish Succession (1713). Though the number of men killed in action was relatively small, many soldiers died from diseases. Civilian populations were the worst sufferers, however, even though massacres of civilians ceased after the mid-seventeenth century. The passing and quartering of troops had disastrous effects in the countryside: they ate peasants' reserves (including seeds for the next season), killed farm animals, and burned houses. Many peasants fled to the safety of towns, where overcrowding generated food shortages and epidemics.

Another traditional view that has been recently criticized is that during those "old type crises," as they have been called by E. Labrousse, the nonagricultural sector, especially industry, was bound to suffer as people devoted their entire income to buying food. Actually, the correlation between "harvest cycles" and "industrial cycles" is not close; the latter could be influenced by what happened in the agricultural sector, but also by other factors, particularly outbursts of speculation by merchants followed by crises in the credit system. At any rate, hypermortality crises were a cause of economic instability and recurrent recessions.

Finally, expansion was rarely general: the rise of new centers of trade and industry was often offset by the decline of areas that had earlier prospered; the successive delocalizations of the wool industry are good examples. At a more general level, in the seventeenth century the rise of northwestern Europe was offset by the waning of Italy, Spain, and Germany.

Growth Prevails

Under such circumstances—the extreme instability in the short run, the chaotic succession of crises and depressions—some writers have described preindustrial Europe as a blocked or jammed society and wondered whether it had any economic growth at all in the long run. Indeed, real wages moved counter to population: their increase often resulted from high mortality, not from better productivity; they may have been at their peak in the early fifteenth century, when population was at its lowest![67]

However, this view is too pessimistic—as is the concept of centuries-long "immobile history."[68] The Malthusian model has to be qualified; some Boserupian episodes, when population growth had positive effects, when it drove technological change and productivity gains, must be superimposed upon it (Komlos 1989). One must also take into account the expansion of international trade and of rural domestic industry, which created more employment and new sources of income in sectors where marginal productivity of labor was higher than in agriculture. The rise of rural industry reduced seasonal (winter) unemployment in the countryside and improved workers'—if not labor—productivity, thus increasing output, both aggregate and per capita. Moreover, even the Black Death did not destroy the knowledge, technology, infrastructure, and institutions that had been built up during the preceding period. In the long run, Europe accumulated human and physical capital, technological and scientific knowledge. Though fluctuations were many and sharp, at each secular peak and at each secular trough population and production (and the capital-labor ratio) were higher than last time. The institutional basis of modern capitalism was built up during this lengthy and agitated apprenticeship.

So there was no stagnation in the long run; instead of an unbroken vicious circle, preindustrial Europe went through a slowly ascending sine curve, and some growth took place. Landes (1969) has suggested that eighteenth-century incomes per capita were threefold higher than around the year 1000, and they were certainly higher than those of many Third World countries presently. As for Maddison, he has estimated that western Europe (in a broad sense: the area of the present European Union) had, from 1500 to 1820, a modest average rate of growth under 0.2 percent per year in its income per capita, so that the latter almost doubled over those three centuries. He puts at 0.1 percent per year the growth rates for 1000–1500 in western Europe, and for 1000–1820 in the rest of Europe.[69] From calculations that have been already mentioned and are, of course, problematic, the Australian economist G. D. Snooks has estimated that in England from 1086 to 1688 real per capita income rose at a rate of 0.3 percent per year and so increased almost sixfold in six centuries (certainly an overestimation), and he advances the notion that major continental countries may have had a similar growth. In France, agriculture may (at worst) have stagnated in the long run, but there was much progress of industry, trade, and services, from which even peasant incomes benefited. For Flanders and Brabant, Herman Van der Wee and J. Blomme (in Maddison and Van der Wee) have found that growth was very slow, though these areas had an advanced economy: from 1510 to 1812, physical product per capita increased 52 percent, a mean rate of growth of 0.14 percent per year. However, those provinces suffered many devastating wars, especially from 1568 to 1648 (Huy, a small town, was besieged seven times within forty years); their rate of growth from 1560 to 1610 was negative, and therefore their overall achievement over three centuries was remarkable.

Progress is moreover obvious from a qualitative point of view. There was a gradual improvement in housing, in the arrangement and furnishing of dwellings. Wood, adobe, and thatch were superseded by stone, brick, tile, or slate—except in the Alps, Scandinavia, and eastern Europe, where wood was superabundant. Glass windowpanes, chimneys, and stoves became widespread. Then, starting in the late seventeenth century in England and in Holland, and some time later in France and other countries, the "consumer revolution" began: an increase in the range, number, and value of household items owned by members of the middle—and even the working—class, and especially new products entering into everyday use, such as chests of drawers, mirrors, earthenware and china pieces and services, clocks, prints, and books. To this can be added the growing consumption of coffee, tea, and sugar.

Eighteenth-century Europe had an economy that was richer, more sophisticated, more specialized, more industrialized, and more urbanized (over 20 percent of urban population, against 15 percent c. 1500) than ever before. Moreover, Europe had become more advanced and richer than the rest of the world, even the great Asian civilizations of India (which was technologically backward) and China. Though population and GDP increased faster during the eighteenth century in China than in Europe, Chinese income per capita did not rise between 1400 and 1800, while the 0.2 percent per year that Europe achieved was unequaled in the rest of the world (except the future United States in the seventeenth and eighteenth centuries). Still, according to Bairoch (1979), the gap in GNP per capita between Europe and the rest of the world was not large (20 to 30 percent); Maddison (1998) sees the difference as bigger and western Europe well ahead of China by 1500. Still, possibly, c. 1750 more than 70 percent of world manufacturing output came from non-European (mainly Asian) countries.

Europe's economic structures, despite the generalization of market relationships, the monetization of production factors, and the commodification of labor, were not drastically different from those of earlier centuries, and the eighteenth century was rather the zenith of old-regime economies than the dawn of a new era—except in Britain, the most advanced of the national economies, where a revolutionary process had started in agriculture in the seventeenth century and was starting in industry at the mid-eighteenth century. The rest of western Europe, which was used to continuous change, was ready to follow after a short lag.

Three

The Age of Industrialization, 1760s–1914

Just as the Reverend Malthus was making his gloomy forecasts (1798), Britain was about to escape from the Malthusian trap, thanks to the industrial revolution. The latter has been seen, for good reason, as a unique turning point or a "great discontinuity," the "most important break in the history of mankind since the Neolithic period" (Cipolla 1976). It freed economies from the shackles that had limited their productive powers, enabling them to multiply—fast and endlessly—people, goods, and services. It broke traditional vicious circles, which were superseded by a "virtuous" circle, an ascending spiral, due to which a steady increase in real incomes per capita occurred for a large majority of the population in industrial nations.

The industrial revolution is first—and strictly speaking—a drastic change in the technology and organization of manufacturing industry. Even by itself, this change had consequences for the rest of the economy, notably because the industrial sector grew faster than the others (especially agriculture), which moreover underwent serious transformations. Thus came about structural change, a redistribution of resources; a new type of economy was created that was no longer primarily agrarian and that devoted more and more of its resources to producing nonagricultural goods and services. This is the process of industrialization, which was not only quantitative, but also qualitative, and which dominated the economic history of much of Europe during the "long nineteenth century" (the 1780s to 1914). Except for the United States, where industrialization started in the early nineteenth century, this process was specifically European up to the late nineteenth century.

However, the share of the working population employed in manufacturing industry, though it rose in all progressive countries, never greatly exceeded 50 percent in any national economy (this was the ratio in the United Kingdom in 1910), and the share of tertiary activities greatly increased and changed structurally. Eventually, in the twentieth century, services were to become the largest sector of advanced economies. Nonetheless, the rise of industry (and of closely connected services like transport) was the specific form of economic development in the nineteenth century; it was in industry that technical and organizational change was the most radical, rapid, and spectacular, and thus the major component of overall transformation. There is consequently a broad meaning of "industrial revolution": the whole process of change, including social change, that started in the late eighteenth century, the beginning of modern economic growth through industrialization.[1]

The Industrial Revolution

First, the core characteristics of the industrial revolution: It was a cumulative process of inventions connected by many backward, forward, horizontal, and transversal linkages—plus demonstrative effects. In addition, some inventions (such as the steam engine, first intended to pump water out of mines) made for a specific purpose became adequate for many other uses. A crucial moment—in the 1780s and 1790s—was thus the junction of two major subsystems of technological innovation: in textile machinery on one hand, and in the mining and metal industries on the other; it resulted in the large steam-driven cotton-spinning mills that were erected in the 1790s and achieved large productivity gains. Moreover, progress in the iron industry benefited textile industries in another way, by enabling machines to be built mainly of iron (especially cast iron), rather than wood with only some parts of metal (and mainly brass, not iron). And, needless to say, railroads would not have much developed but for the mutation of the iron industry (coke-smelting, puddling, rolling mills). There is also a causal relationship between mining and steam power, as well as between mining and railroads. Improvements often provided mutual support for each other, and many inventions could not have succeeded without previous or simultaneous progress in other fields. An interrelated succession of changes thus built up a new, coherent, and constantly changing technological system, as a number of limited breakthroughs were gradually transformed into a general advance on a broad front. In late eighteenth-century Britain, mechanical and organizational innovations that had first occurred in textiles were introduced in a wide range of smaller industries such as ceramics and paper, and change was widespread (still, almost two-thirds of the productivity gains achieved from 1780 to 1860 took place in textiles).

The most obvious aspect of change was mechanization, the systematic and generalized use of machinery, which substituted for the efforts and skills of man at all stages of industrial production. The most famous macroinventions of the late eighteenth century were the cotton-spinning machines (with bizarre names: jenny, water-frame, mule) and the steam engine, but there also was a continuous flow of microinventions—small, incremental improvements achieved by small men, by tinkerers—and this flow was quite important. The spread of mechanization was supported by the improvement of machine tools (some of them were derived from appliances that eighteenth-century makers of watches, clocks, and scientific instruments had been using) and gradually by the rise of mechanical engineering.

Second, besides new machinery, there were new processes, particularly in the iron and chemical industries, where machinery played only a secondary role. They were mainly based upon the substitution of new mineral raw materials and fuels (particularly coal and its by-products, metals, and salt) for traditional ones, which had been mainly organic (though cotton, a vegetal, played a crucial role).[2] Whereas traditional materials had been inelastic in supply and relatively expensive, the new materials were more elastic in supply and cheaper. For instance, coke (i.e., coal) was substituted for charcoal in smelting iron ore into pig iron, and a new process —puddling—was developed to decarbonize pig iron and make iron. As a consequence, iron became much cheaper, and its use increased (e.g., in building). The transition from an "organic" to a "mineral" economy, which used the stored energy of millennia, meant that expansion, which previously had been restrained, became virtually unlimited. E. A. Wrigley (1988) has therefore placed this development at the heart of the industrial revolution, which was not merely fueled by coal but was inconceivable without it.

A third aspect was the increasing use of a new form of energy, steam, following the invention of the steam engine. Early models were built by Savery and Newcomen c. 1700, but decisive progress was the achievement of a Scotsman, James Watt, from 1769 onward. The steam engine has been called the "quintessential invention" (Mokyr 1990): by converting heat into power, it opened a new and seemingly unlimited supply of energy; it made possible large-scale mechanization, as it could drive any kind of machinery; and, thanks to overhead iron shafts and leather belts, its power was divisible. Moreover, it also made possible a revolution in transport, both on land and at sea, through the locomotive, the railroad, and the steamship. Nonetheless, waterpower remained widely used at the beginning of the industrial revolution, and the spin-offs from the use of the steam engine in industry were long limited, even in coal-rich Britain. Waterwheels were improved and the first turbines were developed.[3]

Nevertheless, the industrial revolution is not just a matter of technology: it was also characterized by innovations in organization, by the emergence of the factory system. In contrast to the small workshops of traditional industry, a factory gathers in the same premises large numbers of machines and workers, with a central source of power (particularly a steam engine), plus division of labor and a unified production process based upon machinery. The most typical factories were cotton-spinning mills, which proliferated after Richard Arkwright set up his mill at Cromford in 1771.[4] In branches where production was already centralized for technical reasons (like the iron industry), the new processes generated a large increase in the size of the plant. Altogether there was a trend toward larger and larger productive units and a rise of fixed capital, and the investment it required was not unimportant. Some writers have seen a massive and rapid increase in the investment rate and in fixed capital as the keys to faster growth and higher productivity. However, empirical research has shown that the savings rate between the 1760s and the 1790s in Britain only increased from 8 percent to 14 percent, and that it remained stable after 1800; the stock of fixed reproducible capital only increased a little faster than population.[5] Still, capital accumulation remains central to the industrial revolution, as many technological innovations could have an impact only if they were embodied in new capital goods. Moreover, the divorce between labor and ownership of the means of production was completed.

However, the progress of the factory system was relatively irregular and slow, even in Britain. There was for a long time a pluralism of industrial structures, a coexistence and even cooperation of different forms of manufacturing. Small- and medium-scale manufacturers long held the stage; factories were not dominant, and many of them were small; and the domestic and putting-out systems died out only gradually. One can speak of dualism, with a modern and a traditional sector, but the distinction between them was blurred. Roughly, capital and semifinished goods came from capital-intensive, centralized, mechanized firms, while most consumption goods (clothes, shoes, furniture, foodstuffs) were made by domestic workers or in small workshops. A typical example is the garment or ready-made clothing trade, which maintained the protoindustrialization pattern, with control by putters-out and a low-paid labor force of female outworkers; sewing machines brought new life to the system in the late nineteenth century. Around 1860, in Britain and the most advanced "follower" countries, a large majority of industrial workers were in small-scale undertakings. In Germany, concentration into giant firms was restricted to four branches of heavy industry, while swarms of small- and medium-sized but dynamic enterprises flourished; in the Swiss canton of Glarus, the cotton industry was made up of large numbers of tiny but specialized workshops. This was not a cause of stagnation—small firms should by no means be equated with backwardness—and their capacity to innovate was obvious during the industrial revolution, as well as their capacity for "flexible production," which was suited to constant changes in consumption goods demand. In addition, building remained the preserve of small firms (except for large public works, such as railroads), as did distribution; a "revolution" in retailing, with the rise of department stores and multiple branch operations (plus large-scale advertising, branding, etc.), did not start in western Europe before the 1850s, or even the last quarter of the century, and even then the small shop remained ubiquitous.

On the other hand, the loose nebulae of traditional manufacturing gave way to more dense, concentrated, and integrated industrial regions, often sited on or near coalfields. They included a number of urban centers, some of which became regional metropolises (Manchester is the most famous example). This clustering was self-reinforcing because it created innovative and therefore progressive firms, because it favored the rise of industries and services that were ancillary to the major activity, and because of backward and forward linkages between branches. Some regions were specialized, but others had a wide range of industries. Conversely, some traditional regions of manufacturing deindustrialized (e.g., the West of England woolen district). Industrial regions had a dynamic function; Joel Mokyr (1985) has written that "the Industrial Revolution was, above all, a regional affair."

Inventions and innovations were generally labor saving and generated large increases in labor productivity. The most striking came from the spinning machines: c. 1800, one mule spinner made in a day as much cotton yarn as three or four hundred persons had done with spinning wheels forty years earlier. Calculations by C. K. Harley (1998) show that, consequently, the deflated price of a fairly high-count cotton warp (no. 40) fell 88 percent from 1780–1784 to 1825–1827 (prices of coarse weft fell less, those of fine yarn much more). As for calicoes, their prices fell 83 percent between 1780–1784 and 1830–1834, and those of muslins 76 percent.[6] In other cases, new processes resulted in savings of raw materials (e.g., in the iron industry), or of circulating capital, and often time-saving changes were significant. Innovating firms were thus able to produce more cheaply than their traditional competitors (who used spinning wheels or the charcoal-smelting of iron) and drove them out of business. However, the speed of the substitution depended upon the productivity gains that the innovation secured; it was therefore much lower in weaving than in spinning, because the early power looms were imperfect and because hand-loom weavers' wages fell to low levels. Though Edmund Cartwright had patented a power loom in 1785, hand-loom weaving only died out in England during the second quarter of the nineteenth century; in some parts of countries as advanced as Germany or Switzerland, it survived up to the early twentieth century. Handwork also long survived in subsidiary branches of textile industries, such as lace making or embroidery, which used low-paid female workers. Resource endowments also affected the rate of change; for example, the charcoal-iron industry long survived in some areas of the Continent that had extensive forests but no coal.[7]

In a competitive environment, the fall in costs and prices forced entrepreneurs to look unceasingly for new productivity gains, through innovations in techniques or organization. It also widened the market: cotton fabrics had been a luxury in the eighteenth century; in the nineteenth, they were mainly worn by ordinary people. Mass consumption and a mass market were emerging. However, demand was not an independent variable; its increase was the product of technological breakthroughs, of productivity gains, and of subsequent falls in prices. Some demand-led theories have recently stressed the "consumer revolution," which has been mentioned earlier, but it has not been possible to discover any discontinuity in consumers' behavior that would be powerful enough to promote a continuous stream of innovations, even though changes of taste among the middle classes may have shifted demand toward goods such as printed cottons. Actually, the pioneers of the industrial revolution had first concentrated upon making traditional products by new ways, more quickly and more cheaply, but some new artifacts appeared as early as the end of the eighteenth century, and eventually a growing and finally enormous range of novel consumption goods was developed. Moreover, the idea that technical and economic progress was possible, even normal, spread, and a new class of bold and dynamic entrepreneurs emerged.

Altogether, the industrial revolution represents the beginning of what the great economist Simon Kuznets defined as "modern economic growth," that is, a continuous, self-sustaining growth in product per capita, which contrasted with the slow and hesitating progress characteristic of preindustrial economies; it was accompanied by deep structural change.[8]

Fluctuations did not disappear, of course, but they were less sharp than in "old-type" cycles. Once started, moreover, modern growth has no end: it is built into the economy as its normal condition. Indeed, there has been continuity in technological change since the late eighteenth century, with the succession of innovations that started then still progressing without any significant interruption. The industrial revolution is thus not an episode with a beginning and an end: there is no meaning in looking for its end, as its essence is that, from its inception, revolutionary change became the rule for the economies it affected. Thus, the concepts of second and third industrial revolutions are not convincing; the revolution that started in the eighteenth century is continuing in our times. However, technological progress is not linear; some strong clusters of innovations are recognizable over time, and there was also a notable institutionalization of innovation during the nineteenth century, as scientific knowledge and research were increasingly applied to technology.

I am thus proposing an interpretation of the industrial revolution that is from the supply side and technologically driven. It belongs to the "technological school" (Mokyr 1993), for which technology is the crux, the major source of rising productivity. Three-quarters of Britain's increase in wealth between 1760 and 1860, for example, may have resulted from better techniques and equipment. I also think that this view fits with the new theory of growth, which makes technical progress endogenous and puts it at the center of the process, and also with Douglass North's (1981) view that the industrial revolution created an elastic supply curve of new knowledge, which built economic growth into the system.

However, the very concept of an industrial revolution has recently been challenged. "Revolution" implies sudden, rapid, brutal change, while many writers consider that nothing of that kind occurred either in Britain, the pioneer country, or in any other country. Admittedly, a glamour industry like cotton had a fast growth indeed (8 percent per year 1778–1803), but it was an exception (and also at the start a minor branch). Based on recent calculations of aggregate British industrial production, it has been maintained that its growth trend rose steadily from the 1740s to the 1830s, but not dramatically and without any decisive short period of acceleration (e.g., in the 1780s). Technological shocks or "surprises" only had a relatively short and limited effect, while the influence of some macroinventions was long delayed.[9] The full impact of technological developments was only built over time. Moreover, innovation and productivity growth were confined to a few industries and a few regions. The industrial revolution is thus seen as a slow, lengthy, piecemeal process, as a modest affair that extended over several decades in Britain—and longer in follower countries. It has also been said that eighteenth-century inventions had nothing exceptional, that they did not surge suddenly out of the dark, and that they were improvements to existing equipment or processes rather than entirely new departures—having been prepared by much research and trial extending back well into the seventeenth century. The rudimentary character of many new machines or processes has also been mentioned, as well as the "intermediate technologies" that linked traditional and new.

For a long time, therefore, change failed to show up in national statistics, inasmuch as growth was naturally slower for aggregate national product than for industrial output and still slower for product per capita —as population was rising fast (at 1.71 percent per year in the decades after 1800). During the nineteenth century, British GNP grew at 2 or 2.5 percent per year and per capita product at a modest 1–1.5 percent per year.

I am therefore ready to accept a gradualist view of the industrial revolution and to dismiss the idea of cataclysmic change. But I maintain that there was, nonetheless, a revolution, which must be "rehabilitated" (as Berg and Hudson have suggested), and I retain the term "industrial revolution" because it usefully communicates.[10] In fact, the gradualists base their views on estimates that are controlled conjectures; because the foundations of any macroeconomic calculations for the eighteenth and early nineteenth centuries are quite fragile, these can be contradicted by other computations. Moreover, they are myopic to focus upon growth rates. A very sudden acceleration in the rate of growth of national aggregates was simply impossible at those times, and one must not wonder that there are no overwhelming aggregate effects in Britain before the 1820s. Still, there is no incompatibility between recent macroeconomic calculations and the view that there was indeed an "industrial revolution"—even though the latter does not come into play, at the national level, until well into the nineteenth century. Actually, rates of growth were markedly higher in the second quarter of the nineteenth century than during the first half of the eighteenth (admittedly, in the initial stages, growth was more extensive than intensive). Moreover, macroeconomic series definitely show an acceleration between 1750 and 1830, particularly in the 1780s, and a rate of growth that was relatively fast and sustained, even though at lower levels than in earlier estimates.[11] This was unprecedented: something profound, truly revolutionary had happened.

This "something" was qualitative—as well as quantitative: the industrial revolution deserves its name because it was a profound qualitative transformation. Even though their diffusion was often slow, their effects limited for a long time, as teething troubles accompanied the introduction into production of almost all new machines or processes, the eighteenth century macroinventions were revolutionary because they transformed the nature of the economy, because change—and irreversible change—became the norm rather than the exception. Businessmen had to realize this basic fact and then operate and invest on the assumption that change would take place continuously. Technical progress became widespread, even in the rather traditional sector, which was not unable to increase productivity.[12] Despite the dualism, which has been stressed earlier, and the traditional shape that large areas of the economy long preserved, there was an unstoppable, unrelenting advance of mechanized factory industry. The industrial revolution had started as unbalanced growth but it gradually became better balanced. On the other hand, there is no doubt that the industrial revolution had its roots in processes of change that had developed during the preceding centuries. Nonetheless, there was a discontinuity in the eighteenth century, a historically unique breakthrough. As Charles Kindleberger (1978) wrote, "from the perspective of technology . . . the reality of the revolution is clear." Indeed, it is from a multisecular point of view that the word "revolution" is the best justified, as the developments we are considering were unprecedented and had deep long-term consequences; they also were concentrated within a short span of time relative to the preceding centuries of slow change.

A new technical and economic system, deeply different from the one in which Europe had lived since the Middle Ages, was thus born (even though capitalism and the market economy were preexistent). This was an industrial economy, in which, for the first time, a majority of the population in a large state was employed in industry and industry-related services. The industrial revolution meant overall structural change, transfer of labor and other resources from agriculture to the other sectors, which had higher productivity, so that this transfer helped to improve the economy's performance and to accelerate its growth.[13] However, such a transfer—and the increase it involved in the nonagricultural labor force —was only made possible by significant improvements in the productivity of agriculture, which broke the rigid positive relation between population growth and rise of prices (otherwise, subsistence crises would have prevailed, as Malthus predicted).

This precondition, or permissive condition, of industrialization is called the agricultural revolution, an expression that is still more of a misnomer than "industrial revolution," as it was very, very slow. It had started in the late Middle Ages in the Low Countries, spread gradually to England in the seventeenth and eighteenth centuries, and flourished there—on a large scale and over wide areas, not in a kind of market gardening—thanks to original agrarian institutions. The manorial system had disaggregated earlier than on the Continent, and by the seventeenth century few remnants were left. Landowners had to rely upon the economic and not the "feudal" exploitation of their estates, which they were stimulated to "improve," if they wanted to increase their income. On the other hand, large estates, large farms, and the landlord-tenant system dominated (while in France royal courts had given protection to small holders). Inequality in the distribution of landownership and insecurity of landholdings created "a culture of improvement," with many "spirited landlords" wanting to improve their estates and to lease to efficient farmers, while land agents and big farmers were also pioneers of change. In addition, there was the historical legacy of lower population densities and therefore of more favorable land-labor ratios than on the Continent, plus geographical conditions that favored animal-intensive farming.

From England modernized agriculture moved to the Continent in the nineteenth century, but it did not affect many parts of Europe before the twentieth. It involved some improvements of tools—a wider use of iron to make them, better plows, the invention of seed drills and threshing machines—but steam power was not much used, and reaping machines only appeared after 1850. Altogether, there was no large-scale mechanization of agriculture (this only took place after World War II). Change came basically from new crops, partly from potatoes, but mainly from legumes and root crops (clover, alfalfa, sainfoin, turnips), which were used for fodder and which also fixed nitrogen into the soil and so restored its fertility; these crops were used in new and more complex rotations, to the effect that fallow could be abolished. Moreover, larger numbers of animals of improved quality—thanks to selective reproduction—could be fed and therefore produced more manure (from the mid-nineteenth century onward artificial fertilizers were increasingly used). There was also a good deal of land reclamation and land improvement through capital investment (e.g., in drainage of wet soils). At last, the vicious circle of traditional agriculture was broken: major increases were achieved in crop yields per acre (wheat yields more than doubled from 1650 to 1800) and—of greater import—in labor productivity. In England from 1700 to 1800, output per worker in agriculture increased twofold, and from 1700 to 1850, agricultural production rose by a factor of 2.5–3.

With the increase in production, a growing population could be fed —and better fed. The food shortages that had repeatedly stopped economic growth in the past were not to recur. In England the last famine at the national level had happened in 1597. In Europe (Russia excluded) it came in 1868, in Finland (where 8 percent of the population died). But this was an exception, even though some Europe-wide subsistence crises occurred in 1816–1817 and 1845–1847 (the latter turned into real famine in Ireland, where one million died). Large-scale urbanization became possible: the Malthusian trap had been overcome. However, it was on a global rather than on a national scale. In Britain—and some other countries that industrialized—food production, though increasing, grew more slowly than population, for lack of cultivable land; eventually British farmers nourished their countrymen only three days per week! Malthusian traps were avoided through growing imports of foodstuffs—which could be paid for with exports of manufactures and carried cheaply over long distances, because of the revolutions in industry and transport, as railroads and steamships greatly reduced transport costs—and of course through the development of the "new countries," such as the United States and Canada.

This was important for standards of living in Britain as well as in countries that industrialized later. Needless to say, the industrial revolution had a strong impact upon society in general—a problem that diverts us from the central theme of this book but that must be mentioned. It created two new social classes: an industrial bourgeoisie of factory masters on one hand, and an industrial proletariat of factory workers on the other. Though some industrialists became quite rich, most of them were less wealthy than bankers, merchants, and large landowners. If political influence is considered, the industrial bourgeoisie was not the ruling class of the nineteenth century in Britain, and it had still less influence in other countries; almost everywhere, aristocratic large landowners retained a great deal of wealth, prestige, and power.

As for industrial workers and the "lower orders" at large, debates have raged about changes in their standard of living during the industrial revolution. Despite an undoubted rise in average incomes per capita, many historians have maintained that the working classes' standard of living did not improve and even deteriorated. This fits, of course, with the Marxist concept of immiserization of the people under capitalism. There is no doubt, in fact, that working hours were long, that factory discipline was harsh, and that women and young children were employed in large numbers under shocking conditions. Moreover, the environment in which most people lived was unhealthy: in fast-growing industrial towns, most dwellings were slums, sanitation was poor or absent, and pollution was serious. This "pessimist" view has been supported by the work of Jeffrey G. Williamson (1985), who demonstrated that "British capitalism did breed inequality," in accordance with

Kuznets's famous curve, from 1760 until the 1860s (inequality declined modestly afterward). This drift was a product of forces associated with the industrial revolution, especially unbalanced productivity advances and savings on unskilled labor supply. Moreover, the wars in which Britain was engaged, especially from 1793 to 1815, entailed a heavy commitment of resources to military purposes, the crowding out of productive investment by government borrowing, plus sharp rises in the cost of necessities; they tended therefore to inhibit improvements in standards of living. Nonetheless, after 1820, real wages undoubtedly rose, and sharply for unskilled labor, so that the "pessimist" view is not now sustainable; there was no general immiserization, and eventually an improvement. But it is difficult to generalize on such problems. Some groups of workers (especially hand-loom weavers) suffered; there was a large "underclass" of destitute people; periodic downswings during business cycles caused large-scale hardship. Even so, though terrible by present norms, the working classes' standard of living was higher in Britain than in continental countries, as there was a clear positive correlation between degrees of industrialization and real incomes (see table 3.3, below).

Poverty bred discontent and protest. Despite many disturbances between 1811 and 1848, Britain escaped revolution, but a sharp cyclical downturn in 1845–1847 generated revolutions in France, most of Germany, and Austria-Hungary, though their effect upon long-term growth was minimal. However, the later rise of trade unions and socialist parties in industrial countries may have had negative economic effects—though not until the twentieth century.

Why Britain First?

We now have to consider a crucial problem that hitherto has only been mentioned: the industrial revolution started in Britain, which was the only country where it was spontaneous, without outside example or help. The small island of Britain became the first industrial nation and thus played a decisive role in the economic history of Europe and of the world. Almost all the inventions that created the nineteenth-century economy were made, perfected, and introduced into practice in Britain. This can be called the "English miracle," and England's exceptionalism must be stressed.[14] On the other hand, many aspects of Britain's development up to the 1780s were not unique to it, and many changes were shared with one or several continental countries. Britain did not even have a monopoly on inventions: a number were made in France; but the most spectacular of the latter—hot air (and then hydrogen) balloons (1783), which achieved the old dream of flying—had no economic impact! If one takes a long view, the industrial revolution was a west European development (and English technology was not very "English"). Still, Britain was the only starter, the pioneer; what was unique to Britain was the combination of variables that was achieved there but in no other country in the eighteenth century (Mathias 1979).

There have been endless discussions on the question: Why England first?[15] They cannot be even evoked here, but a few basic data will be put forward.

First, the British economy of the mid-eighteenth century was no longer a purely "traditional" economy; one might call it an advanced and prosperous traditional economy, and certainly it was the most advanced in Europe. In the sixteenth century, England was not very different from its neighbors. Like them, it suffered a phase of Malthusian pressure c. 1600, but altogether it escaped the disasters and depression that struck most of Europe during the seventeenth century. Starting at least in the 1660s, it had clearly diverged from the Continent and taken a lead that increased during the century that followed, a long "benign" period during which traditional vicious circles vanished and the balance between population and resources improved along with real incomes. It is to be expected that the industrial revolution, which was a transition to a new stage of development, would start in the most advanced country, a country that was the most commercialized, urbanized, monetized, industrialized, in a word the richest in Europe. This meant that capital was abundant and interest rates were falling, while the capital requirements of the new industry were to be rather modest.[16] There was also an elaborate system of credit and many methods of raising capital, even though the capital market was localized and had a highly personal nature.

The market orientation of the economy had been pushed further than anywhere else but Holland; already in the seventeenth century, all social groups had been deeply embedded in the market economy. Most important was that Britain had a truly national market, the integration of which was progressing, thanks to the absence of internal customs and tolls, to internal transport improvements (these started before the industrial revolution and then accompanied it), and to the impetus of the enormous and fast-growing city of London: 200,000 inhabitants c. 1600, more than 500,000 c. 1700 (over 10 percent of England's total population by this year), one million in 1800. With its unique combination and concentration of functions, it was the largest city in Europe and the biggest port in the world, a major center of consumption, manufacturing, distribution, and finance; within Britain, its influence was widely felt and greatly helped to unify the home market, to prepare the emergence of a mass market, to stimulate and organize local economies. Farmers and manufacturers from all over the country found in London markets, ideas, capital, and credit; conversely, London had a countrywide market for its manufactures and services, plus the many goods it imported from abroad.[17]

Moreover, agriculture had made a good deal of progress. It was capitalist, profit and market oriented, with many large farms that employed wage labor, plus a good deal of regional specialization. Its production and its productivity were increasing; the latter was—and remained during the nineteenth century—markedly higher than on the Continent. Moreover, as mentioned earlier, England's original agrarian institutions were favorable to improvements in farming techniques and also worked toward the extinction of the "peasant" and toward the transfer of resources— especially labor—from agriculture to industry and services; this transfer had already made much progress and was a development unique to Britain. The percentage of English families with incomes of nonagricultural origin rose from 38 percent of the total (an abnormally high figure at the time) in 1688 to 46 percent in 1759; as for the contribution of agriculture to national income, it fell from over 50 percent in the late seventeenth century to over 40 percent c. 1750 or 1770 (this was much less than on the Continent, except Holland). Britain had also overtaken the United Provinces to become the first trading nation, and it had then consolidated its commercial, maritime, and colonial superiority over its rivals. However, it is not possible to designate the progress of either agriculture or foreign trade as the cause of the industrial revolution. Paul Bairoch (1963) maintained that the increased demand for iron by agriculture brought about the diffusion of coke-smelting, and that the growing purchasing power of farmers generated change in the textile industries. Actually, rural demand for manufactures was fairly quiescent in the eighteenth century, and it is difficult to see gains in agricultural productivity as the primary source of expansion for the domestic market of industry. Still, agricultural progress was an enabling factor behind the industrial revolution, just like the transport revolution (road and canal building), which was generated by the needs of industry—and agriculture. The role of foreign trade as an engine of growth at the national level remains a much-debated problem; exports were certainly a principal contributor to growth—especially for the cotton industry from 1783 to the early nineteenth century—but the industrial revolution had started earlier.

Regardless, it is safe to say that Britain had a broad and diversified industrial base, and possibly a wider range of activities than any other country. "British textile production had, by mid-[eighteenth] century, attained a level from which fundamental technological breakthroughs became increasingly likely" (O'Brien, Griffiths, and Hund). Besides, the transfer of industries to the countryside and the putting-out system had developed earlier and farther than on the Continent, so that England had a cost advantage plus a semiproletariat suitable to the future needs of large-scale industry.

Consequently—and this was the decisive factor, and also the link between protoindustrialization and the invention-innovation process—Britain was rich in human capital, of which the new technology was the product. It was a "technologically creative society" (Mokyr 1993), and some manufacturing districts (in the Midlands and in the north) had a truly entrepreneurial culture, an "ethic of improvement" of which there was no equivalent elsewhere in Europe. They had an enterprising middle class (or rather "middle sort") and groups of skilled artisans, especially in mechanical crafts (metalworking, millwork, machine building). It was from their ranks, and also from those of merchant-manufacturers and merchants (who moreover had experience in markets), that many inventors and most of the "first industrialists" rose. Even though inventors came from the whole spectrum of British society, and some (like the Reverend Edmund Cartwright) belonged to the ruling elite, a large majority were from a middle-class background. They were brilliant tinkerers with a willingness to experiment. Their approach was both empirical-intuitive and scientific, as some scientific culture had percolated downward in society (through books, magazines, lectures, and learned societies), even though relations between "science" and industry only became intense in the late nineteenth century (except in the case of the chemical industry). They also had a willingness to innovate and were used to living in a culture of insecurity and risk, in which, at the same time, personal and familial links provided "insurance" for risk-takers. The large numbers of such men in some regions—plus the tools and skilled workmanship that were necessary to carry out their projects—allowed interaction and exchange of ideas, so that a cumulative stream of inventions emerged.

Besides, Britain had a tradition of invention dating to the seventeenth century and including the mastery of "coal fuel technology" (Harris 1992), which demanded innovations each time the use of coal spread to a new industry. Unknown elsewhere in Europe, that technology was of course linked to the abundance of coal in England, which is now seen again as a significant comparative advantage and which created a path dependency—a legacy of history—toward building the first nonorganic economy.[18] Britain had a resources endowment particularly suited to the technological pattern of the time, plus a pervasive potential for inventions.

A second point is that Britain fulfilled most of the conditions for economic growth and innovativeness, conditions set by the neoinstitutionalist school that stress political elements.[19] England had a contractual monarchy, a Parliament controlled by and for an aristocracy for whom security of property was an absolute priority and who had personal interests in promoting economic development; thus, the state was unable to renege upon its financial obligations, and public order was strictly maintained, particularly against those in the lower orders who resisted innovation. Strangely enough, English aristocratic governments followed policies that created the most efficient market economy in Europe. Britain also had a stable legal framework, secure civil liberties, and safe contracts. Property rights were well defined and protected, and the free play of market forces was institutionalized; this allowed the necessary mobility of factors and increased inequality in income distribution.[20] England also stood apart as the country of laissez-faire (with little regulation of industry, a unique degree of freedom for entrepreneurs), though not of laissez-passer (it was staunchly protectionist). And its government, though "small," was strong; it invested heavily in sea power and in aggressive foreign and military policies, which, in the view of Patrick O'Brien (1991), a view I share, contributed to the progress of the economy and also to the weakening and eventual destruction of Britain's rivals; the Royal Navy was a contributor to the industrial revolution!

In this respect, the importance of the financial revolution that started in the 1690s must be stressed again. The major feature was the creation and increase of a massive national debt, which was buttressed by heavy taxation (mostly indirect), so that public creditors knew that their money was safe. The strong fiscal-military state that thus emerged made Britain a great power, one able to finance rather smoothly the "Second Hundred Years' War" against France, which ended in total victory. This system also contributed to the rise of an efficient and prosperous financial sector, and particularly of a capital market.

Therefore, human capital and liberal institutions—plus coal and naval power—are the keys to explaining the industrial revolution, which was more likely to start in England than anywhere else. However, the question of what triggered the revolutionary process remains difficult. The factor scarcity or bottleneck hypothesis was very popular some time ago: the growth of English industry was hampered by deficiencies in the supply of fuel, energy, and labor, which led some ingenious people to search for new techniques—enabling them to overcome those obstacles and to make the macroinventions that have been mentioned earlier. Those new technologies offered great profit opportunities, to which, in the English environment, the response was fast and widespread. However, this hypothesis is now considered inconclusive, except in the case of the iron industry; the supply of labor was not inelastic, and textile innovations emerged in low-wage areas. It is possible that there is no single explanation for all eighteenth-century innovations; it could be that each of them is special, related to a complex interplay of factors. In the crucial case of the cotton industry, for instance, which was an import-substitution manufacture for fabrics that were massively exported from India, it is significant that Britain was more involved with India than other European powers, and that prohibitions against cotton goods were not (because of Parliament's powers) as drastic as in other countries; so a native British cotton industry was able to develop (especially by mixing cotton and flax in fustians) but had to search for better productivity, because of potential Indian competition. There is also an element of randomness in the process of invention—which is stochastic —and especially in the timing of specific inventions. As for individual inventors, they cannot be reduced to the role of representatives of some social groups or to products of economic opportunities. Thus, the "heart of the matter," the crucial inventions of the spinning and carding machines, which emerged from a highly uncertain research process, remains rather enigmatic.

At any rate, by 1750—and even earlier, considering the first cluster of macroinventions around 1700: the early steam engines, coke-smelting— England had a clear lead in technology over the Continent, while it had been an importer of technology in the sixteenth century and part of the seventeenth. Then, from the 1760s to 1800, after half a century of extensive, Smithian growth, there was a new cluster of macroinventions, which had a much stronger and more immediate impact than the earlier ones. A large new industry, machine-spinning of cotton, was created almost at a stroke and had a big role as a model that other textile industries imitated, while the iron industry grew fast and was transformed. By the early nineteenth century, Britain had become "the first industrial nation"—in both meanings of the word "first": it had started first and was the biggest industrial power. By 1831, industry had become the largest sector—as employer (41 percent of the occupied population) and as contributor to GNP (34 percent); it also was the leading sector of the economy. Thanks to this industrial primacy, to naval ascendancy, and to military victories and conquests, Britain had also acquired a very large share of world trade, shipping, and services. By 1815 it was the dominant economy and the only superpower, the "hegemon" to which all nations were tributary. Though this hegemonic system was to generate its own demise through diffusion of its technology, a process Britain could not prevent, it had created, in the early nineteenth century, a serious imbalance in Europe's economy.

Continental Diffusion and Patterns of Industrialization

Nonetheless, the industrial revolution spread on the Continent starting about 1800, first to its northwestern part, later to other regions; yet, by 1914, vast areas had been little affected.[21]

The traditional view is diffusionist: the British industrial revolution was a paradigm, the industrialization of the Continent was an imitative process —by businessmen, and sometimes by governments, of the new technology and forms of organization that the pioneer country had created. This leader-and-followers scheme has been recently criticized, but it remains valid, in my view, with some qualifications.

There was, in fact, a large-scale transfer of British technologies; it is well documented and was achieved through various channels, such as industrial espionage (as several laws—the last of which was only repealed in 1842—prohibited the emigration of skilled workers and the export of most machines from Britain[22]), imports of machinery, and migration to the Continent of British entrepreneurs (like William Cockerill, who built textile machinery in Belgium and France; his son John established large integrated ironworks at Liège), engineers, foremen, and skilled workers. The last were especially important at a time when learning was by doing, by on-the-job training. Britons played a significant, nay indispensable, role in the modernization of Belgian and French industries in the late eighteenth and early nineteenth centuries, but they were only a tiny minority among the mass of entrepreneurs and workers. Yet, it is telling that all continental countries (but Spain and Russia) adopted for their railroads the standard English gauge (4 feet $8\frac{1}{2}$ inches) and left-hand drive of trains.

On the other hand, the early followers—Belgium, France, Switzerland —did soon achieve technological independence, as they already had scientists, engineers, and skilled mechanics, and they increased their numbers by developing scientific and technical education (especially engineering schools[23]); moreover, in several respects, the gap between the traditional and the new technologies was not at first terribly wide. Those countries simultaneously learned to make the high-tech products of the day, such as locomotives, to adapt British technology to local conditions, and to make new inventions.[24] Among continental inventions, one can mention the Leblanc process for soda making, the Jacquard weaving loom, the wet spinning of flax (P. de Girard), the steel-casting process of Friedrich Krupp, and the open-hearth process for steelmaking of E. and P. Martin. Most of these were in turn adopted in Britain, while such inventions as the wool-combing machine and the steam hammer were made simultaneously but independently in England and France. After a time, the early followers helped the industrialization of other countries, particularly Germany (and later Russia); after 1840, Germany became, in its turn, a center that diffused innovation.[25] Still, productivity in follower countries rarely reached British levels.

Diffusion was not imitative but a complex process of creative adaptation. Moreover, recent work has shown that the British pattern of industrialization was unique, atypical, inimitable, nonreproducible, the exception rather than the norm, especially because Britain had an unusually early and pronounced shift of employment from agriculture into industry, because on the Continent there was a large productivity gap between the two sectors, which did not exist in the British economy. Britain can thus be seen as "the odd man out," its industrial revolution as a special case. Its radically different starting basis and its role of pioneer (plus its domination of world trade) made the structure of its economy unique.

Nonetheless, there was a close relationship between developments on the off-shore island and on the Continent, to which the former was threat, example, and help. Undoubtedly, industrialization displayed quite a range of patterns, but we do not have yet a satisfactory typology of European industrialization because of the complexity of the growth process over a continent. It is often maintained that the industrialization of Belgium and Germany (and possibly Bohemia) was close to the British model, and Belgium certainly was the first country that "systematically took over and assimilated the British industrial innovations" (Van der Wee in Teich and Porter). However, textiles were far less important in these two countries than in Britain, while heavy industry (coal, iron, engineering) was the leading sector—largely in connection with railroad building. Moreover, even a small country like Switzerland (at least its northeastern part) displayed a dualist industrialization: capital-intensive, mechanized, factory cotton spinning around Zurich, and labor-intensive, traditional, domestic or workshop manufacture of finished goods in St. Gall and Glarus. Though some common features can be observed in most countries (the most obvious being that cotton spinning was the first branch to be modernized), the variety of experiences is such that Sidney Pollard (1973) has doubted whether there was a single phenomenon of industrialization across Europe. Was each industrial revolution different from all others, or can several distinct patterns be distinguished?

The Gerschenkron thesis on industrialization—that economic backwardness was associated with great spurts in industrial output growth, and that the role of governments and banks in economic development has been proportional to each country's relative backwardness—has few supporters left. Maurice Lévy-Leboyer has countered the notion of "upstream" or "backward" industrialization of the Continent (or rather its northwestern part) with that of a "downstream" or "forward" process in Britain. The English industrial revolution started with the basic industries, making semifinished goods (cotton yarn, pig iron), and later progressed "downstream" to the mechanization of consumption goods production (e.g., of weaving). Because the British had large urban markets and had used technology and war to conquer most colonial and overseas markets, they concentrated on the cheap ends of textiles and other products, which were demanded by those markets and to which the new mass-production methods could be applied (they also fitted with their resource endowment). As productivity improved constantly in Britain, few opportunities were left for rivals in such lines. On the Continent, successful industrial centers took advantage of the cheapness and skill of labor (which actually delayed mechanization, especially of weaving) to first develop the making of labor-intensive consumption goods, especially "luxury" goods in the case of France. Silk was, by value, its first industry, with silks ranked first among its exports; Lyon was the world fashion leader for silks—an exemplary case of product innovation prevailing over the search for new machines and processes; but this choice was made by market forces, according to comparative advantages. Eventually various industries (silk mills, chemical works) developed "upstream" of silk weaving. In other areas later on, continental Europeans were also able to move "upstream" to mechanized spinning and the primary iron industry. However, the perfect symmetry of this model must be qualified. British industrialization had some "upstream" aspects in its early stages and included product differentiation. On the Continent, the upstream process was the most obvious in Germany, during the first half of the nineteenth century, with the growth of consumption-goods industries, based on cheap labor and imports from Britain of semifinished goods (yarn and iron); backward integration came later. Some other continental areas (Alsace, northeastern Switzerland) started with the making of specialized, high-quality finished fabrics. In the small workshops making clocks and watches, in western Switzerland, the emphasis was on product rather than machinery innovation, and on "flexible specialization."

The Scandinavian countries have been described as presenting a different pattern, one of downstream industrialization: first, they exported primary products (e.g., lumber), then they processed them and exported semifinished goods (sawed products, paper pulp), and eventually they created some high-tech "firms of genius" (a Swedish expression) in engineering. This pattern, however, only applies to Sweden—and not very well: that country had a long-established iron industry (which exported semifinished products); from 1830 to 1850, textiles were the leading sector; export-led growth thanks to sawmills was limited to 1850–1880; and after 1890, exports were not only of capital goods, but of iron ore, pulp, and paper.

A different, Latin or Mediterranean pattern of development has been suggested for Italy and Spain (plus Portugal and, possibly, Greece), because of their similar environment—dry summers and mountainous terrain—which was uncongenial to importing northwestern Europe's "agricultural revolution," which made transport expensive, and where energy was costly, due to lack of coal (which was total in Italy). Other common characteristics were that those countries had suffered from economic retardation since the seventeenth century, and that they attained similar levels of per capita real incomes at roughly the same dates (levels which, of course, were markedly inferior to those of northwestern Europe); they also had disorderly public finances and low schooling rates (c. 1900, half of the adult population in Italy and Spain was unable to read). However, there is no common pattern from the viewpoint of structural change. It was profound in Italy starting in c. 1896, so that the country converged toward the European norm. Still, though Italy was an able, flexible, innovative imitator, it did not produce a model to imitate. Spain also had unique features, but they came from its divergence from the European norm and from the country's suffering from relative retardation: income per capita grew, but more slowly than in other countries; agriculture was poor, and there was a low degree of industrialization. Obstacles to modernization were more serious than in Italy, so much that a large traditional agrarian sector remained dominant in Spain up to World War I. Still, industry was not absent from Mediterranean shores, especially in and around large seaports (e.g., Barcelona, Marseilles, Genoa, Piraeus), where imported or local produce was processed and where there was engineering and shipbuilding.

Another qualification is that both a transnational and a regional approach are necessary. Europe's industrialization was a single process that, like an epidemic, took little notice of national borders and crossed them with ease. In several cases, political borders actually cut across industrial districts: the coalfield of Nord and Wallonia was divided between France and Belgium; the large iron-ore deposits of Lorraine, between France,

Germany, and Luxembourg; farther east, Prussia, Austria, and Russia each had a share of Upper Silesia.[26] Needless to say, such situations aroused cupidity and created the potential for conflict. On the other hand, border areas often were the place for fruitful contacts and movements of capital and labor. It is thus a mistake to deal with each country as a plant in a separate flower pot (Pollard 1974). There were mutual interactions among national industrial revolutions of such magnitude as to warrant treating Europe as one single macrodevelopment area and industrialization as a transnational movement: its rise in one given country often had positive effects for its neighbors.

However, a regional approach is also necessary, this because in all countries modern industry first emerged and later was concentrated in one or several regions, with the rest remaining predominantly rural. In short, industrialization occurred within regions, rather than in a nation as a whole.[27] Therefore, backward countries had "advanced" regions (Catalonia, Bohemia), and advanced countries had backward areas (northern Scotland, Valais and other Alpine cantons in Switzerland). Moreover, several areas of traditional industry deindustrialized during the nineteenth century.[28] Unlike the progression of the frontier in North America, European industrialization involved some spatial leapfrogging.

This approach can lead to a typology based on the leading activities of regions; in some (Lancashire, Nord in France[29]), textiles were dominant and had ancillary engineering and chemical industries, while others (the Ruhr is the best example) had mainly heavy industries: coal, iron, and steel, plus again engineering and chemicals. However, within each region, transfers of resources and activities took place over time.

Although the spatial pattern of the European textile industry did not change much between the mid-nineteenth century and 1914, the iron and steel industry underwent a succession of adaptations dependent upon technology and resources. First, it moved from wooded areas to coalfields; then, in the late nineteenth century, after the invention of the Thomas-Gilchrist process of dephosphorization, steelworks mushroomed on phosphorous-ore basins, especially Lorraine, and some others on seaboards, to receive cheaply the rich ores imported by sea from Sweden, Spain, and North Africa.

Coalfields—especially the big ones—attracted a good deal of Europe's industry but not the whole of it. Large capital cities such as London, Paris, Berlin, Vienna, and St. Petersburg also were powerful magnets. Altogether industries concentrated along two major axes: one extended from the Scottish Lowlands to Lombardy (it has been succeeded by today's "blue banana," from London to Milan), the second from Paris and the

English Channel to Saxony, Bohemia, Silesia, and eventually Ukraine. Around the crossing of those two axes was the most industrialized, populous and urbanized part of the Continent, a number of neighboring but distinct regions in northeastern France, the Low Countries, and the Rhineland, with the Ruhr district as the most powerful. This megaregion, at the crossroads of the major trans-European trade routes, had been densely populated since the Middle Ages. It had many large towns, a progressive agriculture, and good transport facilities (particularly by water), and it had protoindustrialized on a large scale, with its abundance of coal easing the transition to modern industry. It was the tragedy of Europe that this rich "Austrasian" or "Lotharingian" region was divided among several nation-states, owing to a sequence of events that went back as far as the Germanic invasions and the Treaty of Verdun (AD 843). At the same time, industrialization was to integrate local, regional, and national economies into an interdependent European, nay global, economy (even though political division slowed down its growth).

Reforms and Industrialization

It was soon known on the Continent that major technological advances had been achieved in Britain, and that they were giving it a competitive edge. In the 1780s and 1790s, some entrepreneurs, with the help of their governments (and of British technicians), tried to "import" British innovations. France was in the forefront: the new cotton-spinning machines were introduced; the making of those machines and of steam engines was started; several cotton mills were built as well as large, coke-smelting ironworks at Le Creusot (coke-smelting was also tried in Prussian Silesia in the 1790s, with little success). However, the French Revolution and the wars that followed slowed the transfers of technology greatly, as did a number of serious hindrances.[30] Nonetheless, obstacles were to be gradually eroded and overcome, a process that will now be sketched.

One obstacle was the long wars that raged from 1792 to 1815. In that period, wars were not as devastating as in the fourteenth or the twentieth centuries (except, possibly, for Spain, which was a battlefield for seven years), but they dislocated international trade relations. In this respect, Holland was the worst sufferer: its export industries were badly hit, and Amsterdam definitively lost its position as Europe's central staple market. In terms of technological transfers, the worst consequence was that relations between Britain and France and its allies and satellites were largely cut off. Thus, the gap between Britain and the Continent widened, even though British growth was slowed by the wars, particularly because of "crowding out" of private investment by heavy government borrowing (though this problem remains under discussion) and disruptions in the export trade, owing to French conquests on the Continent and to the dispute with the United States, which ended with the War of 1812. Despite long and expensive wars and thanks to its powerful and flexible economy, Britain continued its industrial revolution and monopolized overseas markets. Napoléon's "Continental System," on the other hand, was short-lived. Admittedly, he never attempted an economic unification of Europe or a customs union—global or limited—between France and its allies and vassals (indeed, his customs policy was openly selfish, according to his "France first" principle), though some harmonization was imposed in the institutional framework of the economies that France controlled. Nonetheless, wars and blockades caused some serious changes in the Continent's economy. Its Atlantic sector, which had been so dynamic during the eighteenth century, was lastingly weakened and areas on the periphery deindustrialized; on the other hand, there was an upsurge of industrialization in several regions of the European heartland—from Paris to Saxony. However, Napoléon's fall and the 1815 settlement divided and weakened the Continent's economy, which was unable to have an export-led growth and was even threatened with deindustrialization. Not only France but the whole Continent had lost the war. Still, after 1815, Europe was to enjoy a peaceable century without any general and long war, and as a consequence many countries enjoyed monetary stability and low taxes.

Until this time, the Continent had institutions that were more archaic than Britain's—despite some reforms (e.g., Denmark abolished serfdom in 1787). The French Revolution and Napoléon's conquests, however, swept away much of the deadwood in France and other western countries (manorial dues, guilds, internal customs, monopolies, etc.). Moreover, a new institutional and legal framework was introduced, with property as an inviolable right, uniformity of law, equality before the law, and freedom of enterprise, such that it was no longer an impediment to growth but conducive to enterprise and market efficiency. Still, the case of Italy after the French system was introduced is proof that liberal reforms are not a guarantee of development. After its defeat by Napoléon, Prussia from 1807 to 1821 saw an agrarian reform that abolished serfdom, manorial dues, forced labor, common land, and collective constraints and established clear property rights to land, but peasants lost to large landowners a share of the land they had occupied. Elsewhere in central and eastern Europe reforms came later, but they came: serfdom was abolished in Austria-Hungary in 1848, in Russia in 1861, and in Romania in 1864; guilds were abolished in Prussia in the 1860s; freedom of enterprise was proclaimed in Austria in 1859 and in northern Germany in 1866.[31] There was also a gradual but important liberalization of laws pertaining to joint-stock companies and limited liability, which started in Britain in 1825 and spread to most countries. On the other hand, complete laissez-faire never existed, even in Britain, and governments often played a positive role in getting rid of obsolete institutions.

In 1815, most European countries had narrow domestic markets because they were small and poor and because transport was inadequate. However, the *Zollverein* or Customs Union of 1834 created a large national market in Germany, among most German states, which stimulated industry and railroad building. This arrangement had started in 1818 with a customs union, mainly motivated by fiscal concerns, among the several parts of Prussia. However, the Prussian tariff (and later the common external tariff of the *Zollverein*) was not high because top Prussian civil servants were influenced by British free-trade views. This customs union was a great success in the matter of revenue, so that most smaller German states were ready to join it in 1834 and later to renew treaties that were of limited duration.[32] Austria remained outside; its statesmen's project of a central European common market, of 70 million people, failed and was limited to a customs union with Hungary (1851). Before 1848, each Swiss canton had its own customs, currency, and the like; the constitution of that year abolished those peculiarities and thus created a national market. Italy was unified politically and economically in 1861, but this did not have the same beneficial effect as the *Zollverein:* indeed, regional disparities between northern and southern Italy widened after unification. In addition, the *Zollverein* soon imposed monetary integration (as fixed parities were needed for revenue sharing) by treaties of 1837, 1838, and 1857. The Prussian bank of issue became the de facto regulator of the *Zollverein*'s money supply, the Prussian taler the most used currency, and in 1857 it became legal tender in the whole union. After the foundation of the Second Reich in 1871, a single currency, the mark, was created. In Italy, the Sardinian lira became the national currency in 1862; and in 1867 Austria and Hungary unified their currency. Both from a tariff and from a monetary point of view, the map of Europe had been significantly simplified.

Moreover, protectionism had prevailed in Europe after 1815 and often had been counterproductive.[33] But Britain converted to free trade in the 1840s (duties were retained on some items for revenue purposes); then, in 1860, a trade treaty was concluded between Britain and France, and it was followed by a network of treaties with most-favored-nation clauses.[34] This opened a period not of complete free trade, but of freer trade and low duties. Admittedly, this period was short, as from 1879 onward the main continental states (Germany was the first) raised their tariffs, though not to very high levels; and those tariffs were mitigated by bilateral treaties with most-favored-nation clauses. However Britain continued to adhere to free trade, and transport costs were falling. Up to 1914, intra-European trade enjoyed a freedom and expansion that only returned after World War II, particularly when the Common Market was formed.

Railroads

The increase in trade was greatly helped by spectacular improvements in transports—which by 1815 had been inadequate almost everywhere—especially railroads, though the improvement of roads and rivers and the building of canals must not be neglected.[35] Unlike in Britain, water transportation retained an important role in northwestern Europe, especially for carrying bulk goods like coal; the Seine, Scheldt, Elbe, and above all the Rhine, plus the canals connecting them, were the major traffic arteries.[36] Railroads were another revolutionary English invention, and the first major line opened in England in 1830, between Liverpool and Manchester. The Continent followed, slowly at first, with governments (generally in partnership with private companies[37]) playing a significant role in the planning and financing of railroads, while in Britain private enterprise and capital raising through share issues prevailed. Massive building took place in the 1850s and 1860s, when 50,000 miles of track were laid down in twenty years. The first major line in Russia, connecting St. Petersburg and Moscow, opened in 1854. Building went on until 1914, for branch lines in the west and main lines in the east, especially Russia; by 1914, Europe had 180,000 miles of rail track, 70 percent of the amount in the United States, but its network was more dense, even sometimes overdeveloped.[38] Long tunnels had been dug through the Alps (Mont Cenis, 1871; St. Gotthard, 1882; etc.[39]), and transcontinental luxury trains, like the Orient Express to Istanbul (which was connected with the European network in 1889), were running. Railway building and other large public works were an international, pan-European achievement on an unprecedented scale, in which foreign capital, contractors, and workers often played a leading part.

There has been no Robert Fogel to quantify the aggregate contribution of railroads to European growth, but the cliometrics approach has been applied to a few European countries (England, Italy, Russia), and O'Brien (1977) has written a synthesis that takes into account both this research and the well-known works on the United States. When social savings are expressed as percentages of national income, the benefits derived from the operation of railroads in Europe appear almost as "small" as in America: 4 percent in England in 1865, 4.6 percent in Russia in 1907 as far as freight transport is concerned; but they would be larger if other—perfectly valid—ratios were used. Still, O'Brien considers that it has become difficult to regard railroads as indispensable for European countries' attaining the levels of income they had in the second half of the nineteenth century. On the other hand, estimates of social savings convey limited information about the importance of railroads relative to other major innovations, and they are not very helpful for quantifying the contribution of railroads to the long-term transformation of European economies in the nineteenth century. Nonetheless, O'Brien contends that cliometric research has invalidated the large claims that used to be made, in the matter of backward linkages, for the effects of demand from railroads upon industrialization. In England, the highest share of crude-iron output absorbed by railroads was 16 percent in 1846–1850 (it was only 6 percent in 1856–1860). In Italy before 1914, admittedly, railroads regularly absorbed a third of the country's steel output, but the latter was small in size and had been created mainly to supply railroads and the armaments industry, and there was no strong impact upon technical progress in metallurgy and engineering. As for forward linkages that flowed from cheaper transport, they elude measurement, but that there was a sharp fall in transport costs cannot be disputed. In England c. 1865, average charges for minerals per ton mile by rail were 16 percent of those by canal and 2 percent of those by road. And more generally, it is often said that costs per ton mile fell by one-half as soon as a railroad line was opened. The large increase in the speed of transport, and in comfort for passengers, must also be taken into account. Altogether, the new economic history has not offered a definite answer to the question of how much railroads contributed to economic development in Europe, but O'Brien concludes that this contribution must not be overestimated, that railroads were not more of a "leading sector" than any other single innovation, as nineteenth-century growth was multifactoral and complex.

However, some European historians have been less restrictive, especially in the matter of railroads' forward linkages, which, as just mentioned, elude measurement. They have stressed the dynamic effects that railroads had, the external economies they generated, and the pervasive influence they had upon all economic activities and upon society at large, as they were, to nineteenth-century people, the very embodiment of modernity. Thanks to railroads, some productive activity relocated in order to be more efficient, and some natural resources were opened. In Russia, there was no feasible alternative to railroads for linking Donets Basin coal with Krivoy Rog iron-ore deposits and thus creating the Ukraine steel industry. In France, Languedoc was able to flood the Paris market with bad but inexpensive wine, carried in tank wagons. Regional specialization was thus stimulated, markets widened and integrated, and stronger competition benefited the modern sector. Moreover, because the building of railroads involved large sums of capital, it did much to stimulate the rise of banking systems, capital markets, and stock exchanges (and the nationwide drainage of savings).

These views are supported by several nations' experiences. In the case of France, François Caron (1997) concludes that orders from railroad companies had a "decisive" role in industrialization during the third quarter of the nineteenth century (but later the railroads' impact was far less strong). In Germany, according to experts' views, railroad building was from the 1840s to the 1870s the main driving force of the country's fast progress; a railroad-heavy industry complex developed and played a leading role. Business cycles were largely dominated by fluctuations in railroad investment, which became a "cycle-maker." The large and modern ironworks of the 1860s were firms that had grown thanks to railroads' orders; the development of powerful industrial regions was also stimulated. Things may have been different in poorer countries, for which railroads may have been too expensive to build and to operate. In Italy, railroads did not work efficiently, and their contribution to the creation of a national market was limited. In the case of Spain, Gabriel Tortella (1977) has maintained that too much capital was diverted to railroad construction, to the detriment of industry. This view has been criticized by A. Gómez Mendoza, who suggests that the completion of the railroad network gave rise, in a country that has practically no river or canal transportation, to very substantial social savings (11 percent of national income in 1878, 19 to 24 percent in 1911). On the other hand, Ivan Berend (in Teich and Porter) writes about Hungary: "It is hardly possible to overestimate its [railroad's] impact on industrialization"; a solid connection was created with Austria, so that agriculture boomed and became the prime mover of industrialization. The making of locomotives was central to the emergence of an engineering industry (likewise in Italy).

Europe's seaborne trade, meanwhile, also benefited from a sharp fall in freight rates, which was practically continuous from 1815 to 1914. The cause was technological change, and especially the substitution of iron (and later steel) for wood in building ships, and of steam for sail in propelling them. Admittedly, those substitutions were gradual and came rather late. By 1850, the British merchant marine—which was the most advanced—had a steamers-to-sailing-ships ratio of 1 to 20; not until 1883 did the tonnage of British steamships exceed that of sailing ships—thanks to the introduction in the 1870s of the compound steam engine, which drastically reduced the coal consumption of marine engines and thereby made steamers much more competitive. The victory of steam over sail strengthened the primacy of the British merchant marine, which from c. 1850 onward made up a third of the world merchant fleet (and 40 percent of steam tonnage in 1913). By 1900, the real cost of shipping goods across the Atlantic was just a seventh of what it had been in 1800. This fall in freight rates, which had started before steam triumphed, as sailing ships had benefited from many technical improvements, created some new currents of trade that otherwise would not have been profitable, especially in bulk goods over long distances. Europe's supply of raw materials and foodstuffs was made much easier and cheaper, but its agriculture was to suffer.[40]

Banks

Another handicap of early nineteenth-century Europe was its shortage of capital and credit, and a banking system far less developed than in Britain, which also had an integrated capital market and widespread banknotes circulation.[41] Still, banking grew stronger; small private banks dominated (the first half of the nineteenth century was indeed the golden age of private banking), but a number of large banks organized as corporations were established, first in Belgium, then, after 1850, in France, Germany, and elsewhere.[42] Unlike in Britain, many of those banks engaged in corporate or investment banking. This has been called the "banking revolution," though the contrast between "old" and "new" banking must not be overestimated: some of the major "new" banks were actually established by "old" private banks or with their help; but they were much bigger. Still, Europe's banking structure was largely established in the third quarter of the nineteenth century, but with each national system having specific characteristics, as its structure was determined not only by the market but also by legislation and experiences unique to each respective country.

There was, of course, an English model; it had clearly emerged by the 1830s and displayed a marked specialization of activities.[43] The commercial joint-stock banks, which had been authorized in 1826 (except in London, where the ban against them was abolished in 1833), and which greatly expanded to the detriment of the country banks and private banks, did deal in short-term credit. London had bill brokers, discount houses, and private merchant banks that were outward-looking: they financed international trade and issued foreign securities.[44] It also had colonial and foreign banks, with their headquarters in the City but their activities abroad.

Quite different was the system in several continental countries of the mixed or universal bank, which is often called the "German model," though, actually, it had emerged first in Belgium (rather accidentally) and then in France. The Revolution of 1830 against Dutch rule in Belgium and the economic crisis that resulted forced the Société Générale (a large bank that had been established in 1822) to take up shares in a number of coal-mining and iron-making firms. Eventually, this policy became a strategy, and it was completed by the Générale's direct intervention in the management of firms in which it was a shareholder; links between banks and industry became increasingly close in Belgium and typical of that country. During the 1830s and 1840s in both France and western Germany, meanwhile, private banks had been involved in the financing of railroads and heavy industry. Then, in 1852, the Crédit Mobilier was founded in Paris by the Pereire brothers; it was a mixed bank that both received deposits and made long-term investments. It played a leading role in the development of railroads, banks, and industry, in France and in several other countries, up to its failure in 1867. After this unfortunate experience—and some others—France gave up mixed banking and established a separation between "deposit" banks (like British commercial banks) and investment banks (*banques d'affaires;* Paribas, the best known, was established in 1872), which took shares in industrial firms and also arranged loans to foreign governments. They often had connections with complex international business networks.

Eventually, central Europe became the major field for mixed banking. It started with the 1853 founding of the joint-stock Darmstädter Bank, by a group of financiers who realized that private banks were not able to finance railroads and industry. Several similar institutions followed, and, after 1871, most German joint-stock banks became universal or "maids of all work" banks; they had large shareholdings in industrial companies and supervised their management through directors who were their nominees, a system still prevalent in Germany. In the late nineteenth century it spread to neighboring countries, particularly to Austria-Hungary in the 1890s, and—to a lesser degree—Italy, Spain, and Sweden. In Russia, the large banks of St. Petersburg were also involved in industrial investment, but under the pressure of government, which wanted to develop some strategic industries.

There was certainly a relationship between the specificities of each banking system and the respective country's economic structure. In

Britain, long-term finance for industry came either from the plowing back of profits or from the capital market; banks supplied what industrialists wanted: short-term credit. On the other hand, universal banking dominated in continental countries where the capital market was undeveloped but which were faced with demand for large investment—essentially in railroads. This was the case in Austria-Hungary, which had very few great capitalists and only a small affluent middle class, so that there were few buyers other than banks for industrial firms' stock, and in Italy, where private wealth was reluctant to invest in industry.

The degree of impact that banking systems—the British and the German ones, mainly—had upon economic growth has been much debated. It has often been maintained that the differences between the two systems explain the unequal performances of Britain and Germany both before 1914 and since 1945. A recent view, however, is that industrial investment by German banks—especially the four *D* giants—was relatively unimportant (likewise their control of companies as creditors and shareholders). Besides, only joint-stock companies could be affected, and they made up only a small sector of industry. Conversely, the abstention from mixed banking by British banks has been considered a strength; it gave them a much more liquid position and a greater degree of stability, which benefited the whole economy; they also were evenhanded and not discriminatory in supporting their customers. According to this view, investment banking only reflected market deficiencies in the countries where it prevailed. However, it cannot be denied that German banks had some positive and entrepreneurial role. In many episodes, they helped or forced industrial firms to develop in certain directions; for example, from the 1880s, they mobilized a lot of capital to support the expansion of the electrical-engineering industry. (British banks abstained from such an intervention.) They also initiated many large-scale mergers and takeovers, especially in the chemical and electrical industries. This role was unique in industrial countries.[45]

Another important development in banking during the nineteenth century, particularly its last decades, was concentration. Banks of issue became concerned when governments, for obvious reasons, tried to reduce their number. In England, where there had been up to a thousand tiny and often fragile note-issuing country banks, the Bank Charter Act of 1844 forbade the opening of any new bank of issue, and existing ones gradually died out. In 1848, the Bank of France was granted a monopoly over issuing notes. In federal states, such a monopoly came later, as in 1907 in Switzerland. Europe eventually saw a national bank of issue become an attribute of every independent state; the two different models, the Bank of England and the Bank of France, were widely imitated. Gradually, the major banks of issue also assumed the function of a central bank—lender of last resort, "bank of banks," regulator of the banking system, guarantor of monetary stability; conversely, they gave up the role of commercial banks. The Bank of England was playing such a central role in the late eighteenth century, and the Bank of France took it under the Second Empire, but the Bank of Italy only assumed it in the 1890s. Most central banks were privately owned establishments, but they were not fully independent from their respective governments.

Another aspect of concentration was the emergence in each major country of a small number of giant banks that took over smaller banks, opened hundreds of branches, and operated nationwide (an evolution quite different from what happened in the United States). England, Germany, France, and Hungary each had its "big five" or "big four."[46] However, they coexisted with numerous smaller—and often specialized—institutions, particularly those that had been established to give credit to small and medium firms, to cultivators, and to individuals with modest incomes, constituencies to which most banks did not cater. There was a great variety of them (and each country had its peculiarities); they often were encouraged by governments or even state owned—like the Post Office savings bank in Britain (1861). There were savings banks, land banks (which lent on mortgage), credit cooperatives (which emerged in Germany), and so on. Altogether, they helped mobilize the necessary savings for railroad building and other large-scale enterprises.

Stages of Industrialization

The preceding remarks suggest that there were changes in the pace and nature of industrialization (though the drama of takeoffs, big growth spurts, etc. is out of fashion) as well as disparities in its extension (see table 3.1, below).[47] The first followers were the countries of northwestern Europe, which had much in common with Britain, being its close neighbors, and were relatively rich.

The industrial revolution on the Continent started around 1800, when many mechanized cotton-spinning mills, on the English pattern, were established in some parts of Belgium, France, Switzerland, and Germany. They came about thanks to war, which is the best form of protection. The new industry suffered after the peace but survived and continued to develop nonetheless; the new technologies were also introduced in other branches of textiles and in the iron industry. Meanwhile, obstacles to further progress, including resistance to change, particularly by vested interests, were being reduced. Roughly speaking, like in Britain, the modernization of textile industries started earlier and was faster in cotton (which was the fastest-growing branch) than in wool, and faster in wool than in linen (silk being a special case); it also was much earlier and faster in spinning than in weaving. By 1850, many hand-loom weavers survived, even though the depression of 1846–1851 had destroyed a good deal of traditional—especially rural—manufactures. In the iron industry, where transport costs along with endowments in and localization of coal and ore resources had a strong impact, the puddling process for refining iron spread faster than the use of coke-fired blast furnaces (particularly in Germany). Anyway, some English innovations that had not been introduced during the wars were taken up shortly after the peace: puddling furnaces were built in France in 1817, in Belgium in 1823, and in Germany in 1824; and coke-fired blast furnaces in 1818 in France, in 1821 in Belgium. Later inventions were adopted after reasonable time lags, though the self-acting mule, which was invented in 1825, only appeared on the Continent in 1836. But diffusion was another matter: by 1850, coke-smelting of iron was dominant in Belgium, on par with charcoal in France, but rare elsewhere (by 1857, the Russian-ruled kingdom of Poland had only one coke-fired blast furnace). Altogether, up to the 1830s and even the 1840s, industrialization was not massive (except in Belgium and, of course, in Britain), economies remained largely traditional, growth was moderate (though substantial by previous standards), the industrial revolution was incomplete on the Continent (and limited in its extension), and dualism prevailed.

The 1850s, on the other hand, witnessed the "great mid-Victorian boom," which was particularly strong in France and Germany; it was

_____ Table 3.1 _____
Rates of growth of Europe's real product, 1800–1913
(percentage per year)

	Aggregate	Per capita
1800 to 1842–1844	1.2–1.3	0.5–0.7
1842–1844 to 1866–1869	2.0	1.2
1866–1869 to 1889–1891	1.0	0.0
1889–1891 to 1913	2.4	1.5

Source: Bairoch 1976, pp. 277–78.

somewhat helped by the inflow of gold from California and Australia. This was the time of massive railroad building, the banking revolution, and large-scale mechanization in industry. The exploitation and generalization of the industrial revolution's major innovations—self-acting mule, power loom, coal-using ironworks, steam engines—reached their final stage, while traditional industries contracted or even died out, and textiles began to lose its role of leading sector to metal making and engineering.[48] This was true at least in the more advanced countries of the west; elsewhere in Europe, the latecomers were only taking the first steps toward modern economic growth (notably, the building of railroads).[49]

Then, from 1873 onward, after a violent boom that ended in a stock-market crash (especially in Vienna), came the misnamed "great depression," which was far less serious than the slump of the 1930s. Still, prices and profits fell. Agriculture suffered the most due to the competition of cheap foodstuffs from the "New World" and from Russia, which flowed in thanks to lower transport costs on railroads and steamships. The cultivation of wheat declined, particularly in Britain; even there, however, the total level of agricultural output was roughly constant, but the agricultural workforce fell by a quarter and the balance of production changed markedly, to the detriment of grain and to the benefit of animal produce. In France, gross agricultural product fell by 20 percent in value from 1869–1873 to 1884–1888 and did not return to its 1869 level before 1907.[50] On the other hand, the fall in food prices clearly improved real wages and the working-class standard of living. In industry, growth slowed down, mainly in Britain, France (which was deeply depressed after 1882), and Austria. Germany had bad years in the 1870s but strongly recovered afterward, and Switzerland—where the number of factory workers doubled from 1880 to 1890—became in the 1880s a truly industrial nation. Moreover, industrialization spread during the 1880s and 1890s to the European periphery, or, more precisely, became pronounced in some countries where it had hitherto been modest: Russia, Hungary, northern Italy, and Sweden. Swedish industrial production, which had grown at a rate of 3 percent per year from 1830 to 1880, accelerated to 6 percent per year for the period 1880–1910 (and 10 percent for the most dynamic industries). This was the time of the Swedish industrial revolution, with many technological innovations, widespread mechanization (and thus increasing productivity of capital and labor), creation of "firms of genius," and introduction of modern business organization.

Moreover, technological progress went on—and possibly accelerated. The "revolution of steel"—that is, the substitution of steel for iron, which the Bessemer process (1856) had started—was accomplished (though the

Eiffel Tower of 1889 was built of iron!).[51] And new, largely science-based technologies and industries, depending on or inspired by scientific advances, were emerging, not only in advanced countries, but also in the newcomers (like Italy). The "second industrial revolution"—as it is often called—had started. The production and use of electricity spread in the 1880s, as did the connected branches of electrical engineering, electrometallurgy, and electrochemistry. Following discoveries in the 1850s and 1860s, organic chemicals were extracted from coal-tar distillates and coke ovens' waste gases, to make synthetic dyes and drugs; the modern pharmaceutical industry was born. Thanks to the internal combustion engine (a German invention by Gottlieb Daimler), the making of automobiles was started in France by Panhard and by Peugeot (1890–1891). Also developed and produced were several new materials, such as aluminum, plastics, and artificial textiles, and many durable consumption goods (from cameras to typewriters).

Finally, in the last two decades before World War I, a general economic boom again developed in Europe (and in the rest of the world as well). The French call it *la belle époque,* or golden age, in contrast to the hard times that followed. The new industries, which have just been mentioned, grew fast, even though some of them were still relatively small by 1914; the armaments race, which developed during those years, partly stimulated some industries and had some technological fallouts, especially in the follower countries. And the extension of industrialization went on. Italy is a striking example: from 1896 to 1914, it had a very swift expansion that might be the only case of a Gerschenkronian "big spurt." In Austria, real GNP per capita grew at 2.5 percent per year between 1896 and 1911, against 1.5 percent between 1873 and 1896. Even Spain started a recovery from 1900 onward—if not earlier.[52]

It was a prosperous and fast-growing Europe that was struck by the guns of August 1914.

National Disparities

Behind the aggregates shown in table 3.1 (above), there were serious disparities among countries and groups of countries. There was a rough correlation between levels of industrialization and GDP per capita (see table 3.2, below), and by 1913 the industrial heartland of Europe, northwestern and west-central Europe, was in both respects in the lead.

First, of course, was Britain, which had been the pioneer. Moreover, it was, because of its navy and empire, which made it the only global superpower, the "hegemon"; this status gave advantages to its firms. It also had (as was stressed earlier) an economic structure of its own—with low and falling agricultural employment, large incomes from services, and the like. As a result it long enjoyed an overwhelming superiority, the peak of which came at midcentury: in 1840, its share of worldwide modern production of manufactured goods was 40 percent, and it made more iron than the rest of the world.[53] Indeed, up to 1850, the gap between Britain and the most advanced continental countries was increasing both quantitatively and qualitatively. Britain played such a unifying and integrating role in the economy of Europe and of the world that it is often seen as the guarantor of their economic and political stability, and as the creator of a world market economy. Thanks to free trade, it provided large markets for many products of continental countries, from French and Portuguese wines to Swiss watches, German toys, Dutch butter, and Danish cheese, while imports of British coal were indispensable to several countries. The City of London was the heart of the world economy, the leader of the world monetary system, with unrivaled money and capital markets. Its insurance and shipping markets and its role in trade finance were also unrivaled, and it was directly involved in commodities trade through entrepôt, office, and futures trades. Its merchant fleet had a dominant share in world transport, and the country long remained the major center of new-technology diffusion.

However, at the century's end, British leadership was challenged by the faster growth of the United States and of Germany, which overcame it as far as GNP and industrial output were concerned. Still, Britain remained the foremost trading and financial power, the first exporter of manufactured goods, and the leader for all kinds of intermediation, with the largest merchant fleet and the biggest foreign investments, plus more large companies than Germany.[54] By 1913, the British still enjoyed the highest standard of living in Europe, and in this respect Germany had definitely not caught up; indeed, it was far behind, with a real income per capita that was only three-quarters that of the British. It has even been maintained that the first industrial nation had become, with the United States, the first mass-consumption society, where services had outgrown manufacturing, meaning that its relative industrial decline was proof that it in fact remained far ahead. Nonetheless, it is notable that by 1913, Britain had 27 percent of Europe's manufacturing capacity, versus 32 percent for Germany; that it was responsible for 10 percent of world steel production, against 24 percent for Germany and 42 percent for the United States; and that Germany was ahead in the new "high-tech" industries—chemicals, electrical engineering, and machinery making— even though it fell short of overtaking Britain in various other fields.[55]

Moreover, the productivity situation was definitely worrying: according to Steve Broadberry (1997a, 1997b, 1998), from 1871 to 1911, Germany had been catching up; the aggregate Germany-U.K. labor-productivity ratio had risen from 60 to 76 percent. In some sectors (especially agriculture and services), Britain retained the lead—and kept it up to the mid-1960s—but in manufacturing German labor productivity was 115 percent of the British, which had stopped growing c. 1900.

There are numerous theories about this decline and its causes: the handicap of having an early start, path dependency on traditional industries and neglect of new ones, failure of entrepreneurs, archaic managerial structures, bank conservatism, excessive capital exports, shortcomings in education, the gentleman's ethos, the cult of amateurism, the class system of a segregated society, institutional rigidities in labor relations, overcommitment overseas, and overdependence upon imperial markets are among the proposed explanations. Ascertaining the real impact—or even the existence—of several of these supposed deficiencies is problematic, particularly the so-called entrepreneurs' failure. Cliometricians have supposedly demonstrated the rationality of most decisions made by British industrialists, given the constraints within which they operated. For example, the British did not fall behind in steelmaking technologies; it was just that German firms' strategies, helped by protection, cartelization, and tight organization, were more successful. Likewise, the British environment was certainly less conducive than the U.S. to the formation of Chandlerian-style firms—which internalize the market's function—but the Chandler model was not relevant in some British industries.[56] As for the "cultural thesis," it is not taken seriously by economic historians. Antibusiness, anti-industry attitudes existed in nineteenth-century Britain, but they did not grow worse in the late Victorian period, and they were certainly far less widespread and influential than on the Continent, especially in Germany. Though education had deficiencies, it is also untrue that British universities were unable to train the scientists and technicians that industry needed; the teaching of sciences and of engineering made much progress after 1870. Several—but not all—recent writers have therefore dismissed the idea that there was a failure of late Victorian and Edwardian Britain and played down the decline, which, of course, was relative, but the existence of some sort of decline remains indisputable. In fact, it was the inevitable counterpart of the equally inevitable (except if Britain had opposed it by force) diffusion of technology and industrialization on the Continent and in America. For a long time, Britain had been first, because alone, but this was an artificial position for a small island and it could not be maintained. Even so, by 1914 the British position remained quite strong, but the two world wars were to undermine it.

The British did not concern themselves much with American achievements, but after 1880 they became anxious about the progress of Germany, even though the latter was their second-largest customer and supplier (and the United Kingdom was Germany's best customer). Germany had lagged behind its western neighbors in the early nineteenth century; it had a good deal of protoindustrialization but was the last country in the west to acquire a modern iron industry. However, growth accelerated starting c. 1840—thanks to the *Zollverein* and to railroad building. Industrialization was well under way before the foundation of the Second Reich (1871), and German GNP was overcoming that of France. The rate of GNP growth rose from 2.1 percent per year from 1850 to 1869, to 2.9 percent from 1871 to 1913 (i.e., an increase by a factor of 3.5). However, because of the fast growth in population, income per capita increased far less (especially before 1850) and remained inferior to that in Britain. Industrial production, meanwhile, saw its index grow at a rate of 3.6 percent per year from 1872 to 1913—and more than quadrupled. Still, a large share of the labor force remained in agriculture.

The magnitude and suddenness of Germany's growth are striking. It built up the largest steel, engineering, and chemical industries in Europe and took the lead in science and technology.[57] Starting in the 1880s, it exported on a large scale and became a serious competitor to Britain, even in the latter's home market. From 1870 to 1913, German exports grew in volume at a rate of 4.1 percent per year, British exports at 2.8 percent; the latter, however, remained ahead in the aggregate and in markets like Latin America. Moreover, on the eve of World War I, Germany was making satellites of its neighbors: in 1913, out of eighteen European countries, ten had Germany as their largest supplier, and seven as their best customer.[58] John Maynard Keynes wrote a brilliant though biased account of this situation at the beginning of his *Economic Consequences of the Peace* (1919). If Germany had not made the mistake of starting war, it would have soon dominated Europe's economy. That it does so today shows that defeat in two major wars did not durably reduce its primacy.

A major factor behind Germany's rise was a fast and long demographic growth at a rate greater than 1 percent per year: population increased from 25 million in 1817 to 41 million in 1871 and 67 million in 1913, making it the largest in Europe save Russia.[59] Indeed, up to the 1880s, the country suffered from population pressure, underemployment, and poverty (which caused emigration). It had a labor-supply economy that could make goods at competitive prices and where the share of income going to capital increased and the investment rate was high and rising. Cheap labor was an advantage, but the high quality of some of the labor force may have been more important. Prussia was the first European country to introduce compulsory schooling, and literacy was high, even in the early nineteenth century; moreover, an effective system of technical education and training, both by on-the-job apprenticeship and in specially created schools, was established. Higher education in technology, engineering, and scientific research was also developed. An "education revolution" had preceded the industrial revolution, and when the latter started, Germany had a training potential more powerful than other nations at the same stage of industrialization. This accumulation of human capital was certainly crucial for its progress. After 1871, new organizational methods and technologies spread from the leading sector to a wider spectrum of activities, making Germany the only European country to modernize its management in the late nineteenth century. Large-scale undertakings emerged in coal, steel, heavy engineering, and chemicals. Alfred Chandler has stressed the role of organizational capabilities in the giant firms, or *Konzerne;* concentration (and cartelization) may have encouraged investment and technical progress, as in the steel industry. However, as mentioned earlier, there was also a network of dynamic medium-sized enterprises. Finally, it would be silly to overlook such natural resources as the abundance of coal; the Ruhr coalfield was not mined before the 1840s, but it was the largest in Europe: by 1913, it supplied 59 percent of the Continent's coal output.

The performance of the French economy in the nineteenth century has also been much discussed. It was long thought to have stagnated; indeed, the growth of its GNP was slower than in most countries, but this was mainly because French population stabilized after midcentury, which means that the growth of product per capita was actually close to the rates of some other advanced countries, especially Britain.[60] The relative income gap with the latter was probably constant in the long run (but it was rather large: France was 15 to 25 percent below British levels), and this stability means that France did not "catch up"; moreover, some countries did markedly better. Labor productivity in industry and services also kept well below British levels. Bairoch (1982) also found that in terms of level of industrialization per capita, the position of France relative to the rest of Europe was roughly constant during the nineteenth century, and the productivity of agriculture close to the European average (Russia excluded). In addition, the French industrial revolution was slow and incomplete: in the 1860s, France was an industrial power—the second in the world, in fact—but not an industrial nation: half the labor force remained in agriculture. (By 1913, the figure was still 41 percent, but

Germany was at the same level.) The modern sector of French industry can be considered as artificial, as owing its existence to protection from British competition, and also as a rather mediocre imitation of British models. Moreover, recent research has stressed the seriousness of the structural depression that struck France in the late nineteenth century; this was in many ways a consequence of its pattern of industrialization, which has been analyzed earlier, as the traditional sector of the French dual economy partly collapsed. On the other hand, the fast growth of *la belle époque*—which was cut short by World War I—has also been emphasized, and especially the flowering of such new industries as automobiles and aircraft. These have been said to have made the suburbs of Paris the Silicon Valley of the time (Caron 1995) thanks to dynamic entrepreneurs, inventive craftsmen, and a cross-fertilization process, while the capital itself was creating twentieth-century patterns of consumption. At the same time, some regions and some sectors remained quite backward.

Obviously, some "hyperrevisionist" writers have gone too far. George Grantham has written that "the 'problem' of French economic backwardness . . . is largely an artifact of non-economic concerns" and that France was "as economically successful as England." Actually, the French performance, though "substantially better than was once thought" (Crafts 1984a), was close to the European average, creditable, honorable, and respectable, but certainly not brilliant.

On the other hand, revisionist writers and cliometricians have shown that several traditional explanations of French economic backwardness were wrong: including the immobility of the labor force because of the prevalence of peasant landownership, entrepreneurial failure resulting from an irrational bias toward small family enterprise (in fact, French firms were not markedly smaller than the British), and excessive protectionism. The essential rationality of French economic agents has been stressed, but geographical constraints and the legacy of history slowed down structural change.

"Brilliant," however, is the word for the performance of several small countries located, with one exception, in northern Europe: Belgium, Switzerland, the Scandinavian countries, and, to a lesser degree, the Netherlands. Still, they suffered from various handicaps, the first being their geographic smallness: their home markets were narrow, and they were unlikely to be endowed with many mineral resources. Belgium alone had coal (and in plenty), but Switzerland, Sweden, and Norway had a rich waterpower potential, so that the former was a leader in the application of electricity to industry from the 1870s onward. In the latter three countries, much of the territory was mountainous or arctic in

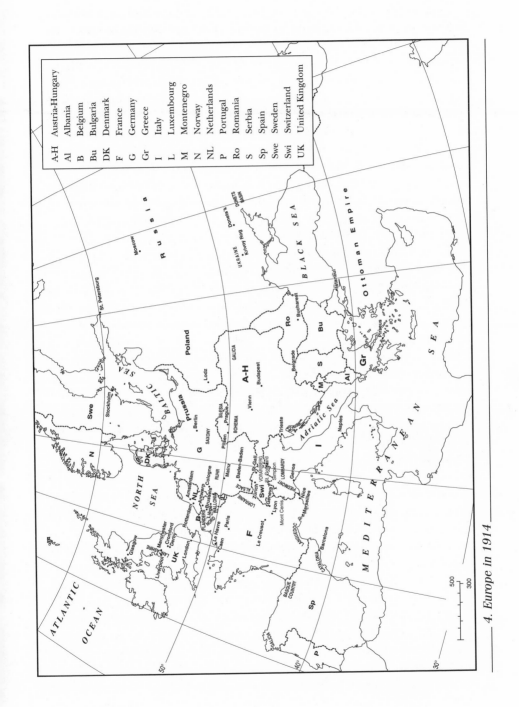

A-H	Austria-Hungary
Al	Albania
B	Belgium
Bu	Bulgaria
DK	Denmark
F	France
G	Germany
Gr	Greece
I	Italy
L	Luxembourg
M	Montenegro
N	Norway
NL	Netherlands
P	Portugal
Ro	Romania
S	Serbia
Sp	Spain
Swe	Sweden
Swi	Switzerland
UK	United Kingdom

4. Europe in 1914

climate and therefore scarcely populated. In the early nineteenth century, some of these countries were quite poor, including Sweden, the capital of which, Stockholm, had been a stagnating backwater for a century. The Netherlands, meanwhile, despite French occupation from 1795 to 1813, retained high per capita incomes but suffered from path dependency toward its seventeenth-century golden age; the transition from commercial to industrial capitalism was difficult, inasmuch as commodities and labor markets were rigid and infrastructure was deficient.

On the other hand, those small countries developed their educational systems early, and their workforces were literate and skilled, while wages (except in the Netherlands) were low. Thanks to accumulation of human capital, abundance of either local or foreign capital, and other advantages, such as a quiet political life—with only one short war for each country, except Sweden, which had none—they succeeded in overcoming the obstacles to industrialization (a challenge and answer process is appropriate). Most of them had an industrial tradition, but any growth of industry had to be export driven, and actually they became heavily involved in international trade. This was particularly true in the case of Switzerland, even though it was landlocked and surrounded by protectionist neighbors; up to 1914, it was the world leader in exports of manufactured goods per capita.[61] These countries benefited, in this respect, from the demand by the large advanced countries—especially Britain—for their manufactures and primary products, but they also exported to distant markets like Latin America. The adoption of free trade by Britain and the general liberalization of trade after 1860 were also beneficial. However, in order to export, these countries needed to be competitive, and they achieved efficiency by a strategy of niches, of specialization adapted to their factors' endowments.

Belgium, as already mentioned, experienced the most complete industrial revolution on the Continent, with an emphasis on heavy industry and large exports of coal and semifinished and finished metal products. Its industrial structure was peculiar: its universal banks created holding companies that controlled a large share of industry.

In Switzerland, on the other hand, there were mainly light industries making high-quality goods: luxury cottons, watches, machinery (at first for the textile industries, with the manufacture of electrical equipment becoming important later), fine synthetic chemicals such as dyes and drugs (for which the Swiss held second rank, far behind Germany), and processed foods.[62]

Sweden was rather a latecomer, as mentioned earlier, and for a long time its exports were mainly of primary and semifinished products—bar iron, cut timber, paper pulp, and iron ore. However, from the 1880s onward, it developed a high-tech engineering industry, often on the base of Swedish inventions, and became a large-scale exporter of some specialized products such as ball bearings, telephones, cream separators, and other capital goods. Its GNP more than tripled from 1870 to 1913.

Norway (which only became independent from Sweden in 1905) specialized in exports of fish, lumber, pulp, and paper, and in shipping services. Its industry was small, but electrochemistry was introduced in the 1900s with the help of French and Swedish capital.

Denmark's main export was initially grain, but when competition from "new countries" became acute, farmers reconverted to animal products: bacon, butter, cheese, and eggs—mainly for British breakfast tables. Danish agricultural productivity became the highest in Europe, making the country proof that industrialization is not the only road to wealth.

The Netherlands also benefited from high-productivity agriculture and from its exports. Industry there, which had suffered from the Napoleonic wars, had a slow but steady recovery, with large-scale industry emerging in the late nineteenth century.

Each country thus had its product niches, as well as some in services: Belgium and the Netherlands greatly benefited from their land encompassing the estuaries or deltas of the Scheldt, Meuse (Maas), and Rhine, such that Antwerp and Rotterdam were the seaports for Europe's industrial heartland; Norway and the Netherlands had large merchant fleets; and Switzerland attracted many tourists, especially thanks to railroads after 1860. Altogether this group was very successful and its growth fast. From 1870 to 1913, the Scandinavian countries outperformed the rest of Europe in per capita growth rates and achieved a spectacular convergence with the richest countries, especially in standards of living. As for Belgium and Switzerland, they had been "rich" for some time.[63]

Small, however, is not always beautiful, and the group of successful northern countries was matched by the poor and backward countries of southeastern Europe, the Balkans.[64] The feature that set them apart was more than three centuries under the rule of Ottoman Turks, a reign that was sometimes tolerant, sometimes murderous, but always predatory. The best land, which was in the plains, belonged to Turkish landowners; Christians were sharecroppers there or smallholders in the mountains. Through taxes, the Ottoman regime siphoned off agricultural surpluses. During the nineteenth century, the Balkan nations were freed, in stages, and established independent states—Greece being first in 1830, Albania last in 1912. But liberation from the Turks only came after long, bloody, destructive struggles; moreover, it had its drawbacks. Independent Greece, for example, lost access to the large "common market" of the Ottoman Empire, the trade of which had been largely in the hands of Greeks. In addition, there were more wars with the Turks, many domestic disturbances, heavy military expenditures, and dependence upon great powers (Britain or Russia); governments were inefficient and often corrupt, and finances were chaotic. Michael Palairet has therefore maintained that the framework of order and property rights imposed by the Ottoman Empire was more conducive to economic growth than the nation-states that succeeded it.

At any rate, those countries' new independent life started in a state of backwardness (with, e.g., high illiteracy rates). Additional handicaps were small population (2.8 million in Greece in 1912) and the corresponding narrow markets, mediocre natural resources (except in Romania), the absence of modern transportation (Belgrade and Bucharest were only linked to Austro-Hungarian railroads in 1883–1884[65]) and of a credit system (but for usurers). A national bank was founded in Greece in 1841, but in Bulgaria banks did not really develop before 1905. There were imports of foreign capital, for example for modernizing the banking system, but some of them were wasted.

Agriculture therefore remained the dominant sector. In Bulgaria in 1913, 80 to 85 percent of the labor force worked the land—the highest rate in Europe. Small owner-occupiers were very numerous in Bulgaria and Serbia, but in Romania, most of the land belonged to large estate owners, and a system of quasi-forced labor survived the abolition of serfdom. Farming methods were traditional, and productivity very low (admittedly, in many areas natural conditions were uncongenial). Still, agriculture supplied most exports: currants and wines from Greece, grain from Bulgaria and Romania, pigs and prunes from Serbia.

Developments in "industry" came late and were limited; they hardly deserve to be called industrialization. At the start, the Balkan countries had handicrafts—rural or urban—that supplied the limited needs of poor populations. During the nineteenth century, this sector declined, not because of the rise of local factory production, but due to competition from cheaper and better articles imported from western and central Europe, though high transport costs afforded some protection to local craftsmen. Nonetheless, a number of modern undertakings were established in various locations at the end of the century, but by 1914 their total labor force remained much smaller than that engaged in handicrafts. Bulgaria had some woolen industry, and flour milling and food processing were rather widespread, but engineering was practically absent, and all capital goods were imported.[66]

Romania, with fertile plains and oil resources, did somewhat better than the other countries. By 1913, GNP per capita was about the same in Bulgaria, Greece, Serbia, and Albania—and the lowest in Europe.[67]

Between the "big three" (Britain, Germany, and France) and the small countries—successful or poor—there were, on the periphery, three large countries and one very large one, which were, at various degrees, cases of "demi-industrialization," or "partial-modernization" (Matis, in Teich and Porter). Worth considering first is Austria-Hungary, the Hapsburg empire. It was a mosaic of nationalities, a fact that contributed to its economic heterogeneity, and, from 1867 onward, it was made up of two autonomous states: Austria and Hungary (although they had a customs union and a single currency). It was also marked by social and political backwardness: the traditional landowning aristocracy remained the ruling class, and it was not keen on modernization, which was likely to undermine its power.[68] Only in Bohemia and Moravia were noble landowners much involved in industrial enterprise. The slowly emerging middle class was quite weak for a long time, and it lost capital and talent because of gentrification; in Hungary, it was made up mainly of non-Magyars, particularly Jews. The population purchasing power was very low.

A basic economic fact was heterogeneity, the starkly different levels of development between neighboring areas. Some regions had industrial growth and change—an industrial revolution of sorts—rather early (roughly the second quarter of the nineteenth century). These were mainly Bohemia and northern Moravia, where the cotton industry grew fast and mechanized, and where heavy industry developed thanks to coal resources; lower Austria and some Alpine lands also industrialized (cotton and iron), as did Vienna. Those regions shared an industrial tradition with a good deal of protoindustrialization during the eighteenth century. Moreover, they were generally close to industrializing regions to the west. Bohemia, for example, can be considered part of the large manufacturing area that included Saxony and Silesia, and the textile industry of Vorarlberg was a spillover from Switzerland.

The rest of the empire, that is, its largest area, retained traditional agrarian forms of life. By 1913 there was an income gap of 1 to 3 between Galicia and the Alpine lands, which was wider than those between regions in western Europe and Germany. However, during the second half of the nineteenth century, a new pole of innovation and industrialization emerged in Hungary (mainly in the capital, Budapest), which had previously been very backward. The customs union of 1851 with Austria and the building of railroads (thanks to Austrian capital) created wider markets for Hungarian agriculture, and its products were increasingly shipped in processed form (this was rather unique in Europe). Sugar refining and then flour milling grew fast, helped in the latter case by the invention of roller mills. Budapest became the second-largest center of flour milling in the world, after Minneapolis. Engineering emerged, to supply mills and railroads, and the firm of Ganz became one of Europe's largest makers of electrical equipment. After 1890, consumption-goods industries also progressed.

The Hapsburg empire, which was economically backward relative to western Europe in the eighteenth century, had lost further ground until the 1860s, but after 1870, and even more so after 1896, its growth accelerated; after 1896 it may have been one of the fastest-growing regions in Europe: "In its final four decades, the empire began to catch up" (Good).[69] Though industries made mainly consumer goods, Austria had a strong and fast-growing machine-building sector and was the world's fourth producer in this respect in 1913. The firm of Skoda, in Pilsen, supplied heavy guns to the German army.

However this progress must not be overestimated. By 1913, Austria-Hungary only supplied 6 percent of Europe's industrial output; traditional ways, like the domestic putting-out system, remained widespread. And on both sides of the Leitha, agriculture employed far more people than industry. The empire was an "industrialized agricultural state" (Matis, in Teich and Porter). Even Bohemia was not really industrial, and Hungary was, according to Berend (in Teich and Porter), a case of semisuccessful, moderate, follow-up industrialization. Moreover, economic progress did not solve conflicts between nationalities and did not prevent the empire's disintegration—at the end of a world war for which its rulers had heavy responsibility.

Italy had both a past and a future of economic brilliance, but its performance during the nineteenth century was mediocre, except at the very end. It suffered from fragmentation into several states (up to 1861), bad transports (especially in the south), and the poverty of its people. On the other hand, there was a good deal of protoindustry, especially in the north, where peasant families completed farming with sericulture. This created an entrepreneurial spirit and gave birth to small but dynamic family firms, which established many mills for throwing silk or spinning cotton. Still, for two decades after Italian unification, there was no significant progress except a lot of railroad building. Then came an upswing from 1879 to 1887, a severe depression, and, starting in 1895–1896, swift expansion: industrial production more than doubled from 1896 to 1914, while GDP was growing at 3 percent per year—versus less than 1 percent during the preceding decades. This spurt benefited not only the textile and food industries (which remained the largest) and a small military-industrial complex, in steel and engineering, which was supported by the state in order to produce armaments (like in Russia), but also new technologically advanced sectors: hydroelectricity and its derivatives, artificial textiles, automobiles (Fiat was founded in 1899), and others. There was a cluster of process and product innovations. The structure of industry also changed: the number of industrial limited companies rose from 316 in 1898 to 1,988 in 1914. Italy had moved from the periphery to the core and had become an industrialized nation, though clearly below the leaders, especially in terms of income per capita. According to Carlo Poni and Giorgio Mori (in Teich and Porter), this was the true "Italian miracle"—rather than the period after World War II. Moreover, though in 1913 agriculture retained 57 percent of the working population, it was market oriented and efficient, at least in the north, which diverged increasingly from a stagnant south that had neither enterprise nor capital.

It has been stressed earlier that, despite their similarities as Mediterranean peninsulas, Italy and Spain had quite different experiences. Obstacles to modernization were more serious in Spain than in Italy, and the former had no (or very little) protoindustrialization base. As for government policies, they were ineffective in such important matters as transport, irrigation, and schooling. During the first half of the nineteenth century, output and population grew at the same pace, so that the income per capita gap with western Europe became wider. Then, from 1850 to 1913, came a period of steady (but not fast) growth in income per capita, and Spain almost held its own or even, possibly, somewhat caught up, especially after the 1890s. Industry was, of course, a party to this growth, and two rather large and modern branches developed: textiles (particularly cotton) in Catalonia, where there were eighteenth-century antecedents, and mining, as Spain is rich in various metallic ores. Mines, however, were mainly worked by foreign companies, and exports were mostly of ores, though a small steel industry developed in the Basque country. If the whole period from 1815 to 1914 is considered, incomes per capita grew slowly but failed to converge with those of advanced countries, and Spain suffered from progressive retardation. In addition, there was no transfer of labor from agriculture to industry before the 1890s when competition from cheap imported wheat created a shock. Altogether, the Spanish economy diverged from the European pattern and had unique features.

Russia is another unique case, but in different ways. A common view has it that its industrialization came late but fast and dramatically, being forced by the czarist state in the absence of an entrepreneurial class. This view must, however, be severely qualified. First, industrialization did not start suddenly in the 1880s. From the 1830s onward, many cotton-spinning and -printing mills, beet-sugar factories, and distilleries had been established, and rural domestic manufacturing by *kustars* (both peasants and artisans) had widely spread. In Russian-occupied Poland, a large textile (mainly cotton) center emerged in and around Lodz; its first large, steam-powered spinning mill opened in 1835. From 1850 to 1880, industrial output may have increased threefold. Nonetheless, there was very fast growth of industrial production (8 percent per year, possibly) in the 1880s and 1890s, and—after some years of stagnation—from 1907 to 1914. New steel and engineering industries, which were largely railroad related, emerged and grew fast.[70] A modern and large steel industry was created in the Donets coalfield of Ukraine, which became the Ruhr equivalent for Russia. Pig-iron output rose from 350,000 tons in 1870 to 2,700,000 in 1899. The oil industry in the Caucasus made great progress.[71] By 1914, Russia had become a major industrial power—the third or fourth in Europe. But it was not an industrial nation; the level of industrialization was very low. Industry was concentrated in a few regions and cities (especially St. Petersburg and Moscow), its productivity was low, and it was not internationally competitive. It included giant firms but also a multitude of small, *kustar* enterprises, which served a large share of consumers' demand.[72] Moreover, a large majority (three-quarters) of the labor force remained in agriculture. Still, immense changes had taken place since the emancipation of serfs in 1861.

As for the part played by the state in this industrialization process, though it was certainly much more significant than in other European countries, it still was mostly indirect and through the market, except for railroads, which for strategic reasons were largely built by government, and for armaments industries. In order to maintain Russia's status as a great power, the state intervened through protectionist tariffs, stabilization of the currency and adoption of the gold standard (1894–1897), subsidies, orders to industry, and other measures. Those policies had mostly financial and political objectives, and they were not deliberately intended to foster industrialization, but they had the indirect effect of accelerating it, particularly by attracting to Russia foreign capital and expertise.[73] There was thus some Gerschenkronian substitution of factors: through the budget, through the banks, and through imports of capital, the state mobilized large funds. However, government did not have exclusive—or even prime—responsibility for industrialization. There was a great deal of spontaneous development by autonomous forces that had grown since the eighteenth century—despite the persistence of conservative mentalities: Russia had a business bourgeoisie of its own and a lot of native entrepreneurship. On the other hand, the important role of foreign capital, especially in heavy industries—which were largely foreign owned and even foreign managed—is unique to Russia. Still, the heavy industry's development was basically capitalist in character, just like in the rest of Europe. Another autonomous phenomenon was the long-term rise of production and labor productivity in agriculture, which succeeded in feeding a fast-growing population (at a rate of 1.5 percent per year) while also exporting food, particularly wheat, on a massive scale. Peasants became increasingly involved in the market, and a new class of "improving peasants" began to emerge in the early twentieth century. Admittedly, incomes per capita were low (and dire poverty was widespread), but they were also rising (at a rate of 1.7 percent per year from 1883 to 1913, according to P. R. Gregory).

Industrialization was thus achieved neither by depressing the living standard of the masses nor by exploiting the peasantry (despite high taxes on vodka!), meaning that Russia was less a case of forced industrialization than has often been said. Indeed, recent work downplays the role of state-promoted heavy industry and stresses autonomous, market-induced, balanced growth. The uniqueness of Russia was perhaps that it all ended in disaster.

In general, proximity to the industrial heartland of northwestern and north-central Europe was important to the regions of the periphery (if Russia is excluded), or the initial periphery, that industrialized: Catalonia, Sweden, Lombardy and Piedmont, Bohemia (so that c. 1900 Italy and Austria-Hungary had typically dualist economies). But the farther one looked east and south, the lower were the levels of industrialization and of incomes per capita (table 3.2). The periphery remained basically agrarian, with a backward agriculture; only a few enclaves of modernity (such as Budapest, some Russian cities—especially the two capitals—and the steel industry of Ukraine) emerged. Admittedly, even the most advanced countries also had backward and poor regions.

One wonders, of course, whether the gap between poor and rich countries, or the rich heartland and the poor periphery, narrowed or widened during the nineteenth century. The inadequacy of statistical data, particularly for the period before 1850 or 1870, makes a definitive answer difficult. However, from Angus Maddison's (1995) calculations (see table 3.3, below), it seems that eastern Europe's relative performance was not bad as far as aggregate GDP was concerned, especially after 1870; but its population increased faster than in the west, so that GDP per capita grew more slowly than in the core countries.[74] As a consequence, the gap between the core and the periphery widened, but not terribly, as

_____ Table 3.2_____

Relative GDP per capita (column A) and relative levels of
industrialization (column B) in 1913

Country	A	B	Country	A	B
Britain	100	100	Ireland	60	—
Belgium	83	77	Italy	52	23
France	81	51	Spain	48	19
Switzerland	81	75	Finland	46	18
Denmark	80	29	Hungary	41	—
Germany	77	74	Greece	38	9
Netherlands	75	23	Portugal	35	12
Sweden	71	58	Bulgaria	32	9
Norway	68	26	Russia	29	17
Austria	62	29			

Sources: For column A, Prados and Sanz, pp. 43–44, table 3. These two authors give three alternate estimates (one by Maddison) of which this series is the arithmetic average (the three estimates have been
recalculated on the basis of Britain = 100). The convergence among the richest countries is closer than
in previous calculations, and the difference between them and the poorer countries is also smaller.
France is in a better position than in some other series. For column B, Bairoch 1997, vol. 3, p. 282.
The level of industrialization is calculated on the basis of manufacturing production per inhabitant.
It has been recalculated based on Britain in 1913 = 100.

_____ Table 3.3_____

Rates of growth by major regions, 1820–1913 (percentage per year)

	Year	Western Europe[a]	Southern Europe	Eastern Europe
GDP	1820–1870	1.7	1.0	1.6
	1870–1913	2.1	1.5	2.4
Population	1820–1870	0.7	0.3	0.9
	1870–1913	0.7	0.4	1.3
GDP per capita	1820–1870	1.0	0.6	0.7
	1870–1913	1.3	1.1	1.0

a. Italy is included among the twelve countries of "western Europe," and not among the four of
"southern Europe."

Source: Maddison 1995, p. 62, table 3.1.

the difference in growth rates per year is a matter of decimal fractions. The ratio in product or incomes per capita between the richest nation (Britain) and the poorest ones may have risen from 3 to 1 to 4 to 1.

On the other hand, the enrichment of Germany and Scandinavia and the concurrent poverty of the Balkans, southern Italy, and even Iberia created a growing contrast between northern and southern Europe, replacing the earlier distinction between northwestern Europe and the rest.

In northern Europe, actually, there was convergence in incomes per capita and labor productivity in manufacturing, which from the 1880s (or 1870s) was narrowing the gap between Britain, which had the highest levels, and several other states: the Scandinavian countries, Belgium, Switzerland, Germany, even France and Austria. A "convergence club" of "rich" nations emerged (see table 3.2, above), and its membership would not change much during the century that followed (but there was no leapfrogging before World War I). Convergence resulted from a slowdown in the growth of the leader (Britain), from acceleration in the growth of some countries (Denmark, Sweden, Germany), and also from mass emigration (Scandinavia). Market integration and international trade also played a role.[75]

Convergence, however, did not much reduce the relative economic power of the core. By 1913, Britain, France, and Germany, with half the population of Europe, concentrated 70 percent of its industry, supplied 60 percent of its exports, and owned 80 percent of its foreign investments.

Reasons Why

How can we account for the disparities in the diffusion of new technologies, industrialization, and growth?

An old explanation was based upon the skewed distribution of natural resources in Europe, especially that of coal, the basic fuel in the nineteenth century. According to this reasoning, Britain, Belgium, and Germany were in a better position than France and the Mediterranean countries. Although this view has been dismissed by most recent writers, it is valid as far as heavy industries are concerned: being fuel intensive, they developed mostly on coalfields (with some exceptions, particularly Lorraine, which had large deposits of iron ore).

Indeed, transfers of technology succeeded only where there existed a matrix of related capacities receptive to change.[76] Such a matrix existed only in western Europe (in a broad sense), which was ready to receive and adapt British innovations; it did not exist in eastern and southern Europe. Moreover, the former had been relatively "rich" and advanced in the eighteenth century, while the latter regions were poor. This fact is the basic reason for disparities. Russia and the Balkans show how difficult it is to overcome the burden of centuries of backwardness, a cumulative burden, as its components interact to reinforce each other. Protoindustrialization also mattered: most industrial regions of the nineteenth century (Bohemia included) had undergone protoindustrialization in the eighteenth century or earlier; however, some regions that had been "industrial" in the eighteenth century deindustrialized in the nineteenth century, because of such factors as shortage of energy, failure to adapt to technological change, and poor entrepreneurship. On the other hand, there was a second generation of new industrial regions based upon natural resources, which technical innovation (or an inflow of capital) valorized; examples are Lorraine, Donets, and some Alpine areas.

I am thus stressing path dependency, or heritage, or the legacy of history, of which human capital is a crucial component.[77] Nineteenth-century industrialization was the work of the middle class, of the bourgeoisie. This explains the superiority of western Europe, where conditions going back to the Middle Ages had created a large and rich middle class, over the periphery, where the bourgeoisie was small and weak. Moreover, where the middle classes were powerful—in Britain, in France after the Revolution —they succeeded earlier than elsewhere in getting rid of institutional obstacles to economic growth. Still, entrepreneurship was not of the same quality in all segments of Europe's middle classes; some of them were attracted by investment in land, or by careers in government bureaucracy (e.g., in Austria), leading to some disparities in development.

Human capital also includes the labor force and its quality, which partly depends upon education.[78] Indeed, there is a strong correlation between literacy levels (which are a proxy for the quality of human resources) and the timing and scope of industrialization, and in the long run between expansion of educational opportunities and incomes per capita. This was yet another reason for the West's superiority. The ranking of European countries according to literacy rates in 1850 is about the same as their ranking by incomes per capita in 1950. The correlation is improved by taking into account the gender gap: the narrower the gap between male and female literacy rates, the stronger the positive impact of literacy upon growth. Moreover, the advance of Germany in scientific and technical education contributed to its rise to become the leading industrial nation. It was also ahead in research as well as in cooperation between universities and industry at the time when the potential of such links for technological progress was increasing.

Economic policies and institutional change (which may have accounted for half of the explained variance in growth rates) must also be stressed. Again, western Europe, with its liberal parliamentarian regimes, its relatively free factor markets, and its legal system that supported their effective functioning, had an obvious advantage over other regions, which often had authoritarian and inefficient governments and lingering aspects of feudalism. Thus, the institutional reforms of the early nineteenth century were important for the progress of Germany, while in Spain, the failure of governments to reform contributed to economic backwardness, which was concomitant with a state of latent or open civil war.

Still, in the west, degrees of openness varied; many economists consider that commitment to free trade—or at least low tariffs (and to the gold standard)—is associated with better performances, including high productivity in agriculture, which led to balanced growth. Thanks to gains in efficiency through specialization, free trade had a quantitatively large positive effect on income. Doubts over the universal validity of this assumption are raised, however, by the fact that Germany performed better than Britain from the 1870s to 1914, despite having returned to protectionism in 1879 and its somewhat authoritarian regime, while Britain kept firmly to free trade. Admittedly, the protection of German agriculture (especially of wheat and rye production) tended to slow down industry's growth, but the protection of the latter helped cartels to be effective, to practice dumping abroad and stabilization at home; eventually, there was more investment, more innovations, and better productivity. In other cases, however, the "dead hand" of protectionism is undoubtedly visible. For instance, it was strong and persistent in Spain, except from 1860 to 1890 (which has been seen as a period of steady growth), leading to a strengthening of traditional agriculture and to an inefficient industry, which grew almost exclusively on the basis of the home market.[79] There is also a case to be made for protection being neither very harmful to welfare nor helpful to industry, as has been said about Italy. Kevin O'Rourke and Jeffrey Williamson (1999) consider that tariff policy had a small impact on globalization and convergence. In most cases, protectionism may have been only a small handicap, of which free-traders make too much. Some writers have also seen as a factor behind poverty the complementarity with—and therefore dependence on—Britain, which developed in the case of several "small" countries (they exported mainly agricultural produce or minerals). Nonetheless, the Scandinavian countries became quite "rich." Indeed, attempts to correlate late-nineteenth-century growth rates with tariff levels give weak and inconclusive results. In all, it seems that protectionism neither enhanced growth performance nor did much harm to it.

Another much-debated problem is that concerning the relationship between industrialization and the situation of agriculture. Improvements in farming techniques, in pace with those of industry, certainly worked to increase rates of incomes per capita growth; likewise, stagnation of agricultural productivity (especially when a high share of labor was engaged in agriculture) slowed down overall growth and reduced domestic incomes, savings, and rural demand for manufactured goods. It also reduced the migration of labor from the land to industry and the latter's expansion. The role of the agricultural factor—an increase in the productivity of land, labor, and capital employed in agriculture—may have been the most important at the beginning of industrialization. It certainly facilitated the industrial revolution in Britain; and it is noteworthy that the first follower, Belgium, included Flanders, the cradle of improvements in farming techniques.

In Sweden, enclosure of land started in the eighteenth century and went on in the nineteenth. This brought prosperity to better-off peasants, who improved their methods and markedly increased production. It also created a landless proletariat that was available for nonagricultural work. Therefore, due to the increased purchasing power of certain peasants and to the need for jobs for the poor, the textile industry rose in the period 1830–1850. In Germany, there was an agricultural revolution during the first half of the nineteenth century: fodder crops expanded while cereal yields, labor productivity, and total output increased. At the same time, agrarian reforms created surplus labor on the land and a landless proletariat, which moved from agriculture to industry. Later, in Hungary, thanks to the abolition of serfdom, to railroad building—which opened large markets in Austria—and to better farming, agricultural output grew at 2 percent per year from 1867 to 1913. This rural prosperity had spin-off effects: Hungary processed its agricultural produce before exporting it, sugar factories and flour mills were built, and an engineering industry emerged to serve them and to supply farmers with machinery.

On the other hand, countries where agriculture remained backward did not really industrialize; this applies to Mediterranean countries, particularly Spain, Portugal, and southern Italy, and to the Balkans. Agrarian reform did not result in many changes in Spain, except in landownership (but the new owners were conservative in outlook). Even so, output rose, and Spanish agriculture was able to feed an increasing population, but this was accomplished by extending cultivation in the countryside, which had been underpopulated in the eighteenth century; the output mix—basically of wheat, olive oil, and wine—did not change, labor productivity did not improve, and there was a retention in agriculture of a large but largely redundant workforce (72 percent of the total in 1910). Admittedly, there was not much demand for labor or produce by the urban sector. Agriculture has therefore been seen as the major source of Spanish backwardness. In Italy, conditions were better—at least in the north, where agriculture was capitalist and progressive; it contributed to industrialization, particularly through the involvement of peasant families in protoindustries (especially silk).

O'Brien and Leandro Prados de la Escosura (1992) have rightly seen environmental constraints as a major factor behind the deficiencies in Mediterranean agriculture. Indeed, the innovations of the agricultural revolution were adapted to conditions in northwestern Europe, where they had emerged. They were irrelevant to Mediterranean countries (except northern Italy), mainly because these areas experience a long summer drought, which is inimical to fodder crops and legumes, and therefore to an intensive livestock farming system. Southern agriculture was never in a position to lend the kind and scale of support to industry that Britain and its immediate followers enjoyed.

A last problem to consider concerns the consequences for agricultural progress of the different systems of landownership and tenure. It is generally admitted that the British system—of large, well-managed estates and big farms in the hands of "capitalist" farmers who employed landless laborers—was the most propitious to agricultural improvements. It is also generally admitted that the early-nineteenth-century agrarian reforms in Prussia and some other parts of Germany introduced there a system akin to the British, as they transferred to the lords, in exchange for the abolition of labor services and manorial dues, one-third to one-half of the land previously held by peasants. Estates were consolidated, farming became capitalist, and many landless proletarians moved to nonagricultural employment. Hungary had the same pattern of reform: the abolition of serfdom gave half the land to 1 percent of landowners. This "Prussian way" is considered more congenial to agricultural progress and to economic growth generally than the "French way," in which most of the land was held by small owner-occupiers—a system that the French Revolution had consolidated and that also existed in western and southern Germany and in the Low Countries.

These views need some qualifications. First, continental estates were not all (even in Prussia) as well managed and well cultivated as in Britain.[80] They often were divided into small farms leased to peasants; and many regions of large estates did not industrialize. On the other hand, in several parts of Germany where small owner-occupiers were dominant due to partible inheritance, peasants often turned to skilled artisanal activities. This was the base on which an important sector of German industry emerged; it was made of small, specialized firms that resorted to outsourcing and subcontracting.

Regarding France, several cliometric studies have not confirmed the traditional view that its industrialization in the nineteenth century was significantly retarded by its agrarian structure. The rural-urban wage gap was narrow, and its size does not support the idea that retention of labor in agriculture seriously inhibited industrial development. Besides, Grantham has found that labor productivity in agriculture grew at the same rate in France as in Britain during the nineteenth century (of course, France started from lower levels). Peasant farming and small farms did not hinder agricultural improvement.

Altogether, agriculture remained a large sector of the European economy: in the early twentieth century, it employed half of the working population (Russia is excluded), with ratios varying from 8 percent in England to 82 percent in Bulgaria. It was also a sector that had greatly changed—despite persistent backwardness in many areas. Where climatic conditions permitted, mixed farming had been widely introduced, with new—and often complex—rotations, in which fodder crops had replaced fallow. Potatoes and sugar beets had greatly expanded, the latter in central and northwestern Europe, except Britain. Research and industry had some impact, too—such as the use of artificial fertilizers, improvement in tools, and some mechanization.

Specialization also made much progress due to transport improvements —especially railroads—and to trade liberalization; agriculture became increasingly market oriented. Animal farming much increased, particularly the raising of dairy and beef cattle in the cool and wet areas of northwestern Europe.[81] But even in southern regions, specialization in producing wine, fruits, and flowers had developed. Nonetheless, and despite competition from overseas and from Russia, cereals still occupied in 1914 about half of cultivated land, with average yields for Europe (Russia excluded) that had doubled since the eighteenth century. Countries like France and Germany had almost caught up with Britain in terms of labor productivity, and they obtained higher returns per acre because of more intensive cultivation.

Traditional rural societies of Europe may have reached their zenith in the mid-nineteenth century, when they had escaped poverty, thanks to better farming, but had retained many old manners and customs. The "great depression" of the 1870s and 1880s hit them hard, and many old ways declined, but even by 1914 they had not disappeared.

Altogether, a kind of ambiguity or neutrality of factors is obvious. No variable had a universal, predetermined, and thus predictable impact upon the process of economic change in the various parts of Europe. Thus railway building stimulated the growth of industry in France, Germany, and Russia, but it may have slowed it down in Spain and other countries; and it accelerated the deindustrialization of several regions. The various factors are made positive or negative by their context, their interaction, and their combination within a broad historical context (which includes culture and values, as Landes, 1998, has stressed).

Global Views

After stressing the diversity in Europe's nineteenth-century development, we shall now try to consider it as a whole, starting with its economic growth.

According to Bairoch (1976), Europe's real GNP (Russia included) grew from 1800 to 1913 at a mean rate of 1.7 percent per year and thus increased more than fivefold. For industrial output, the rate from 1830 to 1913 would be 2.6 percent, compared to 1 percent for agricultural production—which shows that industry was the leading sector. Bairoch (1982) has also calculated an index of the level of industrialization (i.e., manufacturing output per capita; see table 3.3, above) on the basis of the United Kingdom in 1900 as 100; for Europe as a whole, it rises from 8 in 1800 to 11 in 1830 and 45 in 1913. At the latest date, six countries are above this average: the United Kingdom, Belgium, Switzerland, Germany, Sweden, and France.[82]

On the other hand, Europe's population (European Russia included) increased by a factor of 2.5: from 180 million in 1800, to 265 million in 1850, to 390 million in 1900, to 450 million in 1914. Its share of world population rose from 19 percent c. 1800 to 25 percent—its historical peak—in 1914, as it grew faster than other continents, except North America and Australia. The rate of growth of 0.8 percent per year in Europe was well below current rates in the Third World but clearly above eighteenth-century figures (0.5 percent in the second half of the latter), and of unprecedented magnitude.

This growth resulted mainly from falling death rates, due to both improved standards of living and the disappearance of the most deadly epidemics, such as the plague and smallpox (new ones, like cholera, were less devastating). Fertility rates, however, began to decline in advanced countries, but rather late (except in France, where population did not increase much after 1850). Therefore, the demographic transition from the traditional demographic system of high fertility and high mortality to a modern one where both are low, which is a major aspect of the late nineteenth and early twentieth centuries, did not prevent population growth from accelerating slightly up to 1914, as the numbers indicate. Moreover, there was much diversity in the demographic patterns of European countries (and even regions). Though the populations of Britain and Germany showed a strong rise, the fastest growth took place in eastern Europe; by 1900, Russia, with 133 million inhabitants, up from 30 million in 1800, had become by far the most populous state.

Europe's population would have increased more but for emigration overseas—mainly to the Americas, and mainly to the United States—of 50 to 60 million Europeans, an unprecedented mass movement that was not repeated after 1914. This movement, which was stimulated by income gaps between Europe and countries "of recent settlement," gathered momentum as the nineteenth century went on: 300,000 persons per year migrated at midcentury, and it was more than one million after 1900. The United Kingdom sent overseas the largest contingent (18 million from 1850 to 1914, including more than 5 million from Ireland), mainly urban, unskilled workers. Migration from Germany peaked in the 1840s and 1850s, and departures from Italy, Scandinavia, Austria-Hungary, and Russia took place mainly after 1880. The annual gross migration rate was on average 0.2 percent of Europe's population, but it reached 1 percent in some countries after 1880, and 4 percent during the 1890s in Ireland, Spain, Italy, Norway, and Sweden. By 1910, the population of Norway was 19 percent below what it would have been if there had been no emigration since 1870; if the labor force alone is considered, it was 39 percent below the no-emigration level in Italy and 45 percent in Ireland. Emigration, which absorbed roughly a quarter of population's natural increase, was thus a useful safety valve. It also contributed to the development of "new countries," of which Europe benefited. Moreover, recent research has seen emigration from Europe as a major aspect of globalization in the late nineteenth and early twentieth centuries, and as a main force for convergence—especially in labor productivity and real wages—in the Scandinavian countries, Ireland, and Italy.[83]

Europe thus escaped the Malthusian trap (with some exceptions, particularly the great famine in Ireland), as product grew faster than population, and GNP per capita more than doubled, with a mean rate of growth of nearly 1 percent per year (1.3 or 1.4 percent for advanced countries, 0.5 for backward ones). This is modest by some recent standards, but at the time it was far better than anything previously achieved.

Needless to say, growth was not linear, and the nineteenth century was a golden age of a sort for "Juglar" (short-run) business cycles, which were largely international: Europe was a close enough community for major events—especially credit crunches—to affect simultaneously its different parts (particularly those under the gold standard). Over time, fluctuations were increasingly prone to move over borders—and across oceans.[84] But they may also have become less violent: during the first half of the nineteenth century, grain harvests continued to have a significant impact, so that crises of "old" and "new" (i.e., of industrial overproduction) types might intermingle and create serious depressions, such as the one in 1846–1849. In major slumps, GDP per capita might fall 5–7 percent.

However, because of the rise of nationalism and the existence of recurrent tensions in international affairs starting in the 1860s, some historians have wondered whether there was indeed a European economy, and not just competing nation-states.[85] From 1879 onward, many of them increased their customs barriers, ending the short-lived age of free trade, which had begun in 1860. Some tariff wars broke out: one of them, between France and Italy, started in 1888 and lasted eight years. However, this "return to protectionism" must not be overestimated: customs duties remained moderate (except in Russia and Spain), effective protection rates were much lower than nominal rates, and a network of trade treaties preserved openness. In fact, during the nineteenth century the mobility of factors greatly increased at the international level; moreover, intra-European trade greatly expanded. The transport and banking revolutions made much easier and cheaper the movements of humans, goods, and capital, of course, so that specialization and productivity increased.

In the nineteenth century, Europe was "the world's banker," according to the title of the classic book by Herbert Feis, but it was first its own banker, as the richer countries invested in the poorer ones (where yields on capital were higher), that is, roughly, the west in the east and south.[86] In 1913, 31 percent of total world foreign investment (portfolio—which was by far the largest—and direct) had been made in Europe.[87] With almost complete freedom for capital movement, Europe had become a single international capital market, which was more integrated a century ago than it is today. The average amount of capital flow in and out of several countries was often as high as 4–5 percent (or even more) of national income (actually higher than today); in some years, Britain invested abroad more than half its total savings, and France over 30 percent. For both countries, cumulative foreign investment was eventually equivalent to more than their GDP for one year. Exports of capital were made possible by surpluses on current account in European countries' balances of payments (in fact, they were largely reinvestment of income from previous foreign investment). On the other hand, thanks to the openness of most European countries, they imported growing quantities of primary produce from their debtors, which could thus service their loans, while capital imports made them able to buy more European goods. There was a circular, cumulative process. Movements of short-term capital were also large, money markets were interdependent, and their short-term rates fluctuated in unison (though asymmetrically, as the London rate was the world leader).

Investment abroad started right after 1815 but was rather modest up to 1850 (and mainly in government bonds); then it grew by leaps and bounds, to reach enormous sums (hundreds of millions of dollars each year) on the eve of World War I.[88] It was helped by specialized financial institutions (such as the London merchant banks) and by the rise of multinational banking. Many large banks established branches or affiliates abroad; foreign bankers settled early in Paris and Brussels, and later in London. At the end of the nineteenth century, a number of German financiers set up in London and had close connections with the great German banks, which had branches in the City, where French banks also had branches. There was thus an internationalization of banking activities, which encouraged foreign investment.

Still, there were some obstacles: in France and Germany, governments could, for political reasons, ban the issue of loans to unfriendly powers.[89] Conflicts occurred between such policies and bankers, who were rather cosmopolitan and had a strategy of cooperation and sharing with foreign banks; they often organized international syndicates to float a loan on several financial centers or to invest in some industrial enterprise.[90]

Exports of capital were started by Britain, but after 1850 its investment in Europe became marginal and its capital exports went overseas—mainly to the United States and other countries of European settlement (but it also provided much short-term credit to sustain trade, by "bills on London"). So France became the main lender to European governments, as well as investing heavily in railroads, banks, and various industries, especially in Spain, Italy, and eventually (from 1888 onward) Russia, which had become the largest importer of capital in Europe.[91] Owing to the Russian Revolution, this ended in disaster for French investors. Germany, Belgium, the Netherlands, and Switzerland were also active in investment abroad.[92] Foreign investment often acted as pump-primer or trigger in countries that were starting their industrialization, especially when it was associated with transfers of technology and expertise; in the less developed regions, it helped to establish a basic infrastructure, including railroads. Foreign capital thus played a significant role in the development of Norway, Sweden, Italy, Spain, and, of course, Russia; after 1897, a high percentage of investment in the steel, engineering, electricity, chemical, and oil industries of Russia came from foreign sources, and foreign companies introduced some new branches of manufacturing.

By 1914, the aggregate gross nominal value of foreign investment was 44 billion current dollars, and their distribution by country of origin was: Britain, 42 percent; France, 20 percent; Germany, 13 percent; Belgium, Netherlands, and Switzerland (together), 13 percent; United States, 8 percent; others, 4 percent.

There was also increasing mobility of labor, with rather complex patterns.[93] Intra-European migrations were mainly within national borders, from the countryside to cities, that is, to industry and services—including domestic service, which attracted many migrating women. Such moves were mostly over short distances, but sometimes over long distances, for example, from Russia to its "frontier" in Siberia. Meanwhile, traditional seasonal or temporary migrations, for agricultural or nonagricultural work, persisted and even increased. Altogether, there was a continuous outflow from the countryside and a relative rural population decline; in a number of regions the decline was absolute, though only some mountainous and very poor areas suffered desertion. On the other hand, the population of towns greatly increased, thanks to immigration, but also to natural increase, as they had ceased to be *mouroirs,* with a surplus of deaths over births. In London and other large British cities, a third of the increase in population from 1841 to 1911 came from net migration. Industrialization was the major engine of urbanization, which became faster and more widespread after the mid-nineteenth century. It created large numbers of industrial towns—a new type of town—and enlarged many existing cities. Around 1800, 12 percent of Europeans had lived in towns with more than 5,000 inhabitants; by 1913, this ratio had risen to 34 percent—Russia included—and 39 percent if the latter is excluded; Europe then had 226 towns with more than 100,000 inhabitants, including 12 with over one million.

Movement of people at the international level was also significant. Unlike capital, people moved from poor countries to more advanced ones. France and Germany were the main poles of immigration, while Italy, Poland, and Russia were those of emigration.[94] Of special significance was the migration of Jews from western Russia and Poland to central and then western Europe, including Britain, which received 120,000 of them before 1914 (many also emigrated to the United States). For instance, in the late nineteenth century, there was a massive movement from Polish Galicia into Hungary. In the villages and small towns of the "pale," Jews had been craftsmen and petty traders, but their westward move allowed many of them to enter upscale activities.[95] In Hungary again, they made up half of the emerging middle class and were dominant in trade, banking, and industry. Farther west, they created the diamond-cutting industry of Antwerp.

Migration, in transferring labor from sectors with low growth potential to those with better ones, contributed to overall growth and, like overseas emigration, to convergence.

A quite different kind of seasonal migration was tourism. This was one more English invention, with roots in the "grand tour" by eighteenth-century young aristocrats, but it greatly expanded in the nineteenth century, though only among the upper and middle classes, thanks to railroads and rising incomes.[96] The British were again pioneers: they invented sea-bathing and mountaineering, and they discovered the French and Italian Rivieras. Visiting spas, to drink thermal waters (and to gamble), was another traditional practice that greatly increased, to the benefit mainly of German and Austrian resorts; in the mid-nineteenth century, Baden-Baden was called the summer capital of Europe. Switzerland, France, and Italy obtained from tourism significant invisible earnings.[97]

Among other factors contributing to European integration, the gold standard is generally given prominence. Britain had used it in the eighteenth century and made it official in 1819, but most continental countries retained the silver standard (like the German states) or were bimetallist (France). Nonetheless, these different currency areas were integrated, and Europe had an effective fixed-exchange-rate system and a solidarity of financial centers, largely thanks to France, which had a large metallic stock and played a pivotal role in the system of international settlements. It provided the instruments necessary to clear balances in the international credit system, so that exchange-rate movements were dampened. The country's bimetallism was a critical component of the international monetary system: France had the leading role in the world specie system, while Britain dominated the credit system.[98] It is often said that bimetallism was thrown into chaos by the sharp increase in gold production from 1849 onward (and later in silver production), but actually France, which took in almost half the increase in the world gold stock from 1850 to 1870, acted as a shock absorber during the disturbances that resulted from that increase. The world price of metals was thus stabilized at the French mint ratio, and the exchange rates between the gold and silver currency areas were also stabilized.

The heyday of this French-operated international bimetallism was in the 1850s and 1860s, when, moreover, Paris threatened London's monopoly over the finance of international trade—thanks to the rise in multinational trade and capital inflows. In 1865, the "Latin" monetary union was set up by France, Belgium, Switzerland, and Italy (a few other countries joined later), on a bimetallist base, with the French franc as the unit of coinage. Coins of the same fineness and weight circulated in all member countries, which thus had a commitment to maintain their currencies at par.[99] However, the position of France was seriously weakened by its defeat in 1870–1871 and by suspension of specie payments from 1870 to 1879, so that Britain recovered for twenty years an unchallenged dominance. Germany, on the other hand, took advantage of its victory, its unification, and the French war indemnity to unify its currency and move to gold, by creating the mark (1871). Marc Flandreau (1995) therefore considers that the gold standard did not emerge from the contradictions of bimetallism (which, despite some tensions, could have survived), but from historical and political circumstances, especially from the failure of coordination between the French and German governments during the crisis of 1873. In 1876, France suspended the minting of silver, and its Latin monetary union allies also adopted the gold standard in 1878. The emergence of monometallism was thus uncoordinated and mainly intended to protect exchange rate stability. Adhesion to the gold standard was also a signal of financial rectitude, which made it easier for peripheral countries to attract foreign capital. By 1900, all important trading nations (including Russia in 1897) had adopted it.[100]

Thus a single criterion of value underlaid both home and foreign trade. The resulting simplification and confidence were beneficial to international trade and to the integration of capital markets. The gold standard was based on the London money market, where sterling was freely exchangeable into gold and where many international transactions were settled, so that it has been called a sterling standard. Paper assets denominated in sterling replaced metals for international settlements; businessmen everywhere were ready to settle debts and to hold balances in sterling. Some central banks (mainly of countries closely linked with Britain) were encouraged to keep part of their reserves as sterling balances in London. So London—with Britain's strong balance of payments, its open economy, and the City's efficiency in its favor—was the financial capital of Europe and of the world, and apparently it ran the international monetary system. Still, its old rival Paris revived, and a new one emerged in Berlin, so that the gold-standard system was trilateral, with three key currencies: pound, franc, and mark (a good deal of German trade was mark denominated). It has therefore been maintained that financial integration led to some measure of regionalism, to the construction of "imperial" monetary areas, while the rise of central banks and their interaction with governments created wedges between national money markets.

The appearance of a globalized system was superficial, and the gold standard was decentralized and cooperative rather than a British-dominated hegemonic system; the role of the Bank of England as "orchestra conductor" has often been overestimated. On the other hand, cooperation among central banks, especially the Bank of England and the Bank of France, in matters of discount rates and pooling reserves in times of crisis, was exceptional, pragmatic, and unilateral, and it happened on an ad hoc base; it never was reciprocal, institutionalized, or unselfish (banks helped others when it provided a direct benefit). Moreover, there was no trend toward greater cooperation, and conflict prevailed at some periods. Though the Bank of France's large gold reserves were seen as the world gold reserve and buttressed the system in contingencies, cooperation among central banks was not the keystone of the international gold standard (Flandreau 1997).

Altogether, before as after the victory of the gold standard, the century from 1815 to 1914 was a long period of monetary stability, both at the national and international levels. However, Barry Eichengreen (1992) has stressed that this success was historically specific, that it implied capital and labor mobility, plus price flexibility and financial rectitude by governments, and that it was fragile and did not need a world war to be destroyed. James Foreman-Peck, on the other hand, sees no reason why this order would have collapsed but for World War I.

In considering other factors of integration, brief mention must be made of the progress of telecommunications, by electric telegraph—an American invention that was soon taken up in England (1837) and the rest of Europe. The first cable from London to Paris started transmitting in 1851, and the first transatlantic one in 1866. Instant communication by telegraph greatly reduced uncertainty and risk; it created national financial markets, made arbitrage cheaper and easier, and also strengthened the central position of London.[101] International conventions simplified and made uniform arrangements for relations by railroads, postal services, telegraph, and also customs formalities. International produce exchanges helped to create a single European and world market for many commodities.

Quite different were the international cartels, to "organize" markets and limit competition, which emerged starting in the 1880s.[102] Still, their number was not large (the interwar period was to be their golden age), and they concerned mainly intermediate goods (e.g., aluminum and plate glass). Much more significant were national cartels, for which Germany was the favorite ground, as the strong concentration of some branches of German industry made market-sharing agreements easier.[103] Some international cartels resulted from German initiatives.

As for multinational manufacturing (i.e., by corporations that had a base of operations in several countries), it started in the 1850s and 1860s but progressed mostly from the 1880s onward (there was some connection with the renewal of protectionism).[104] In many cases, it was developed by large firms of small countries, which found their domestic markets too narrow (especially for new, specialized products) and created branches abroad to avoid tariffs. Ericsson and SKF from Sweden, Nestlé from Switzerland, and Philips from the Netherlands are good examples. But there were also large German firms, making electrical equipment, that established factories in other countries (or had joint ventures with local firms).[105] The arrival in Europe of American firms was also significant: in 1867 Singer established a factory in Glasgow (this was typical, as the United States was dominant in mass production of light machinery). American corporations—especially Standard Oil—also dominated world markets for oil and established distribution networks in Europe; they competed successfully with the Nobel and Rothschild companies, which distributed oil from Russia (in 1907, however, a merger created Royal Dutch-Shell, the first European oil giant). Altogether, by 1914, 349 foreign manufacturing subsidiary firms had been established or acquired by parent companies: 122 were American owned, 60 British owned, and 167 belonged to continental firms. Many European multinational enterprises operated in the United States as well.[106]

Finally, the growth of an international (or cosmopolitan) bourgeoisie must be mentioned. It was nothing new, as colonies of foreign merchants since the Middle Ages had played a major role in international trade, but it greatly increased in the nineteenth century. In the eighteenth century, Huguenots had made up the major transnational financial network, but during the century that followed, Jewish—mostly German Jewish—bankers came to the forefront.[107] In Germany and Austria-Hungary, 70–80 percent of banking elites, both in private banking and in the corporate leadership of joint-stock banks, were Jewish. As for western countries—Britain, France, Belgium—their small Jewish communities were greatly reinforced by a diaspora, mainly from Germany, that started during the Napoleonic wars. A number of highly successful dynasties, such as the Bischoffsheims from Mainz, the Oppenheims from Cologne, and the Warburgs from Hamburg, built up strong banking networks. The most famous were the Rothschilds, from Frankfurt, who settled also in London, Paris, Vienna, and, for a time, Naples. Their fortune was built at the end of the Napoleonic wars by transferring funds from London to Britain's armies and allies, and then by "inventing" the modern international market for government bonds. Thanks to their "network of brothers," they could transmit information and money across Europe faster than any rival. For most of the century, they were the world's biggest bankers and its richest family (one might say a "family multinational"). The combined capital of their four houses gave them huge resources; for a long time, they completely dominated international government finance and the issue and guarantee of government bonds. Still, in the City of London they were an exception, as other Jewish banking firms were not many and did not enjoy a dominant position.[108] On the other hand, the Haute Banque of Paris was more cosmopolitan, as it included strong Protestant (often Swiss) and Jewish elements. In 1872, the Paribas bank was founded by a group of French, Belgian, Dutch, Swiss, and German bankers under the auspices of the Bischoffsheim group. Despite their common faith, Jewish bankers were not infrequently torn by sharp rivalries, but generally top European bankers were more inclined to cooperate than to fight; they tried, during the pre-1914 years, to defuse international tensions.

I now come to the international trade of Europe. After a setback during the Napoleonic wars, it greatly increased during the nineteenth century, much faster even than output. From 1860 to 1910, the volume of Europe's exports grew at a rate of 3.4 percent per year.[109] Needless to say, the liberalization of trade at midcentury and the transport revolution of railroads and steamships reduced transaction costs and stimulated growth.

Europe dominated world trade: it consistently accounted for 60 percent or more of world exports plus imports.[110] France exported more than the United States; Britain, three times more. But the bulk of European trade—more than two-thirds of it—was conducted within Europe throughout the period. This was particularly true on the Continent, because Britain had a large and expanding trade with overseas countries, while its exports, which had flooded the Continent after 1815, lost ground after 1850 because of the latter's industrialization. By 1910, only 35 percent of British exports went to the Continent. On the other hand, the share of European imports that came from Europe was about 60 percent. There was a decline in the entrepôt trade of colonial powers, which had been dominant in the eighteenth century, as the new industrial countries of Europe opened direct trade relations with the other continents (nonetheless, Britain retained a large entrepôt traffic). The new trading pattern was based on imports of primary products by industrial countries and exports of manufactures by the latter. It promoted seaports that were mainly engaged in those activities, like Liverpool, Rotterdam (which had a large industrial hinterland along the Rhine), Antwerp, and Le Havre (which imported cotton and sent out emigrants).

As earlier on, intra-European trade was based upon differences in resources and levels of development, upon a shifting system of complementarities. The three main powers (Britain, Germany, and France) had a range of industries that was almost complete, and domestic markets that were large enough to support them (inasmuch as mass production progressed slowly). For most of the century, therefore, their exchanges of manufactured goods were mainly in specialties where they had a clear superiority (like French silks). However, as time went on, they increasingly exchanged manufactures (textiles included, particularly semifinished articles) and capital goods; they also exported them to the periphery, from which they bought primary products such as minerals and foodstuffs. The small advanced countries depended upon the big three for most of the manufactures they consumed; they paid them—and also their imports of raw materials and overseas produce—by exporting to the big three (mainly to Britain) foodstuffs, raw materials (timber, mineral ores), and the manufactures in which they had specialized and excelled (like Swiss watches). A special case, resulting from the unequal endowment in coal, was the large exports of this primary product from advanced countries— Britain, Belgium, and Germany—to France, Scandinavia, and the Mediterranean countries. After 1880, however, France and Sweden exported iron ore, mainly to Germany.

There was a trilateral network of trade and payments among Britain, the Continent, and overseas countries: continental Europe had a trade surplus with Britain, which was used to pay its deficit with overseas countries, with which Britain, meanwhile, had a surplus. This network was finely balanced, with the City of London as its axis, and rather vulnerable, as later events were to show. Indeed, Europe's industrialization cannot be considered in purely European terms: the relationship with the whole overseas world must be kept in mind. Because of its growing population and expanding industry, Europe became increasingly dependent upon that world for food, raw materials, markets, investment, gold supplies, and space to absorb some of its population increment.[111] Without that contribution, according to some writers, Europe might have run into a Malthusian or a demand-shortage trap. On the other hand, the development of overseas countries was only made possible by massive imports from Europe of immigrants, capital, and technologies, but it helped to maintain the momentum of industrialization.

However, the enrichment of Europe was not at the expense of what we now call the Third World, through colonialism and exploitation. In the pre-1914 liberal economic order, colonies were neither necessary nor sufficient for development, as demonstrated by the cases of Belgium (which acquired Congo when its industrialization was very far advanced) and Germany on one hand, and Spain and Portugal on the other. By 1900, European empires (the Russian not included) covered 20 million square miles, about 35 percent of the earth's land surface. Nonetheless, "hypo-thetical but plausible estimates of the net benefits derived by the British and other economies from trade with empires suggest that after mid-[nineteenth] century they could not have been other than 'small,' pos-sibly below 2 percent of GNP" (O'Brien and Prados de la Escosura 1998). The last figure applies to Britain; for other powers, including France and the Netherlands, benefits were smaller, sometimes negligible. The sig-nificance of empires for economic growth was not large, and they were not particularly favored destinations for emigrants or capital—or exports, with some exceptions, like British cotton goods. Trade with the new colonies acquired in the age of imperialism (1871–1914) was actually unimportant for European powers, and these lands were not a source of abnormally high returns on investment. Indeed, because of defense and administration costs, they were an expensive hobby. In Britain, this bur-den fell upon middle-class taxpayers, while benefits accrued for some busi-ness interests and for the traditional British elite. One thing the rush for colonies surely created, however, was international tensions and crises, which played a part in the origins of World War I—which had disastrous consequences for Europe's economy.

At any rate, the growth of foreign trade made it increasingly impor-tant for national economies; the ratio of Europe's exports to its GNP had risen from 4 percent c. 1830 to 14 percent in 1913; it was higher for the small, advanced, and specialized economies of northwestern Europe. This increased openness—though lower than today's—lends credence to the notion of an increased integration.

Indeed, growth in trade created growing interpenetration and inter-dependence among European countries, especially after the mid-nineteenth century. There was globalization at the European level as well as in the world at large, which contributed, of course, to the convergence among European countries that has been stressed earlier. Pollard (1981) has written: "Everywhere it became increasingly clear that, economically speaking, there existed only a single European community"; and Foreman-Peck maintains that in 1913 Europe was more integrated than presently and that this integration had been spontaneously achieved. Moreover, both national economies and international commerce were de-veloping without the disturbances—such as inflation, balance-of-payments crises, and the like—that later affected even the richest countries during the "golden age" of the twentieth century's third quarter; this smoothness and stability were the product of structural conditions, which disappeared with World War I. One can thus understand why the pacifist Norman An-gell, in his famous book *The Great Illusion* (1909), stated that economic and financial interdependence would make war unfeasible; and also the nostalgia for the pre-1914 lost paradise that Keynes expressed in his *Economic Consequences*.

The European economy of 1913 was a capitalist economy where free enterprise prevailed and which the market's invisible hand was regulating, conditions that were thought to lead to optimal allocation of resources, so that governments did not follow activist policies to promote growth. Altogether, state intervention was limited, state-owned (or -run) undertakings rather rare (consisting mainly of dockyards, some railroad networks, mail, and telecommunications). There was little social spending other than primary education. Government expenditures and taxes were therefore low: by 1913 (despite the armaments race), total government expenditure in France, Germany, the United Kingdom, and the Netherlands was, on average, 12 percent of GDP. On the other hand, Europe had not entered the stage of monopoly capitalism, as Marxists contended: the system remained highly competitive—except for some cartels and a few monopolies; the family firm was everywhere dominant. The concept of financial capitalism, that is, the dominance of the economy by a handful of giant banks, was also inappropriate, even in Germany and Austria, which had inspired it. This system was working efficiently, but its equilibrium was nicely balanced and therefore fragile. World War I was to destroy the balance—and the European dominance over the world's economy. Admittedly, Marxist writers maintain that capitalism was responsible for the war, because of rivalries among capitalist powers, which contended for markets for their industries and investment opportunities for their surplus capital, and especially because of the conflict between Britain, the established hegemon, and Germany, which wanted to supersede it or at least to reach parity. Actually, however, things were much more complex. War resulted mainly from precapitalist survivals in Germany, Austria-Hungary, and Russia, plus an unreasonable British quest for absolute security, and the weakness of France relative to Germany.

In 1913, western Europe alone had twice as many inhabitants as the United States and a bigger economy.[112] It remained "the workshop of the world," as it supplied 60 percent of world exports of manufactured goods. Europe (including Russia) mined 50 percent of the world's coal output, made 57 percent of its steel, had two-thirds of its cotton-spinning capacity, and was responsible for 40 percent of its industrial production. It also was the world's banker—the United States being then a net debtor—and had a quasi-monopoly in services (shipping, insurance, etc.).[113] Europe was the hub and engine of the world economy; it exercised an influence and even a domination over economic developments in other continents.

Moreover, the ratio between average real GNP per capita in Europe and in the rest of the world (new countries excluded), which may have been 2 to 1 c. 1800, had widened to 4 to 1 c. 1900, and it was probably 6 or 7 to 1 if only the richest European countries are considered.

On the other hand, a new pole of economic power and of wealth had emerged. America had long been ahead for labor productivity in manufacturing, which since 1870, and possibly since 1850, was about twice that in Britain. For aggregate productivity of labor, however, the United States overtook Britain later—around 1880 or even 1890, and the gap between the two countries was not large: by 1910, America was at 118 percent of the British level (according to Broadberry 1998). This was because Britain long retained a better productivity in agriculture and in services. The way the United States (and also Germany) finally overtook Britain was by shifting resources out of agriculture and improving comparative productivity in services, rather than by increasing comparative productivity in manufacturing. As for GDP per capita, America passed ahead during the 1880s, but some writers see the gap with Britain by 1913 as small (America at 105 percent of the British level, according to Maddison 1995), while others put the United States a third above Britain. But certainly, by 1900 at the latest, the United States and other new countries of recent European settlement (e.g., Canada, Australia, New Zealand) had achieved higher standards of living than Britain and, a fortiori, than the continental countries. As early as 1870, GDP per hour worked in the twelve core countries of Europe had only been 69 percent of the U.S. level; by 1913, it had fallen back to 59 percent.[114]

William Parker has written that western Europe and the eastern United States had the same innovative, competitive, capitalist culture. However, the very fast growth in territory, population, and wealth of the United States has no equivalent on the other side of the Atlantic. This raises two questions, the two faces of the same problem.[115] Why was the United States so successful in developing a technical lead over Europe and in reaching a higher GDP per capita? Why did the advanced industrial countries of northwestern Europe—Britain, Germany, Belgium, Sweden, and others—fail to do as well as America, particularly in product (or income) per capita? This is not the place to attempt a full answer, and we shall just mention the unique combination in the United States of enormous resources endowments (which, moreover, were adapted to the mineral-resource intensive technology of the nineteenth century), large and fast-expanding integrated markets (c. 1900, the American market was equivalent to those of Britain plus France plus Germany), liberal institutional arrangements in a country that was "born free," generous imports of capital, and cheapness of capital goods. The interaction of these factors created a lead in manufacturing techniques and in capital intensity as well as the emergence of mass-production technology, while Europe retained a system of flexible production, relying on skilled labor. On the other hand, some retarding forces were still at work, even in the most advanced European countries, and the political division of Europe had a negative influence, even in a period of relatively free trade. Still, a world war was needed to widen decisively the gap between the Old World and the New.

Four

Disasters, Renaissance, Decline, 1914–2000

It has been maintained that Europe's division into many states contributed to its dynamism by stimulating competition and also by always allowing dissidents to find refuge. Still, it may have slowed down economic growth, and eventually, Europe nearly died from its divisions, from antagonisms between nation-states to which technological progress and industrialization had given the means to wage war on a much more bloody and devastating scale than in the past. Nationalism prevailed over economic solidarity, and during the Second Thirty Years' War, from 1914 to 1945, Europe attempted suicide and almost succeeded. Its liberties were only saved, particularly in World War II, by a non-European power, the United States—and this was a proof of Europe's decline. Weakening was also obvious in the economic sphere: Europe's share in world production and trade fell, and the position of dominant economy passed to America.[1] By 1925 (when reconstruction in Europe was almost completed), the GNP of the United States was 80 percent of the product of Europe (the USSR not included), while in 1913, it had been 62 percent; U.S. industrial capacity was 97 percent of Europe's, and its GNP per capita 247 percent. The last figure reflects the large margin in productivity leadership that the United States had established by 1913 and that was to widen up to the 1950s, thanks to massive and systematic research and development, to the institutionalization of industrial research, and to the diffusion of mass-production methods, which even the major industrial countries of Europe found difficult to absorb. American labor productivity in manufacturing was 203 percent of the U.K. level in 1909–1911, 250 percent in 1929, and 263 percent in 1950. On the other hand, though the United

States had become a large creditor nation, prior to World War II it was not ready to accept responsibility for world economic stability, and there was a long interregnum, of damaging uncertainty, while currency hegemony passed from the pound to the dollar.

Admittedly, it has been maintained that those disastrous wars had their roots in the capitalist industrialization of the nineteenth century, which exacerbated rivalries between imperialist powers. But only die-hard Marxists would now stick to this Leninist view, and the two world wars were actually exogenous shocks.[2]

Regardless, World War I caused a breakup of the intricate system of European integration and division of labor that had grown in the preceding century. During the twenty-year truce that followed, this system was not restored and indeed suffered new blows. World War II, which was the almost inevitable consequence of its predecessor (especially considering that World War I generated Nazism), crowned the self-destructive process, but it was followed by an amazing recovery and by large-scale integration—at least in the West. Only recently has the future of Europe again become cloudy. Altogether, disasters and massive losses of life were concentrated within the three decades 1914–1945, for Western Europe, anyway, where after 1950 life became gradually more secure and comfortable for most people. So twentieth-century Europe would not be such a dark continent, as it is often said, were it not for the unatonable sin of the Shoah.

The Economic Consequences of World War I

World War I had powerful disruptive consequences for the European economy, though it is not easy to isolate them. In 1920, the population of Europe (Russia excluded) was 22 million less than it would have been had there been no war: 11 million had been killed or had died from war-induced causes, and another 11 million had not been born. France was the worst sufferer, with almost 1.5 million men killed, 14 percent of the prewar male population of military age (fifteen to fifty years old); it has never recovered. For other countries, war losses were only a small share of the total labor force (except for Serbia, which lost a quarter of its population).[3]

Direct monetary costs of the war were about 200 billion 1914 dollars for military purposes; damages to property plus output sacrificed exceeded $150 billion. Still, the devastation was concentrated in a narrow zone, mainly in northeastern France—where 810,000 buildings had been wholly or partly destroyed—and Belgium, and was made good in a rather brief period. But there also was much depletion of equipment, and the fall in productivity widened the gap with the United States. On the other hand, production in some sectors was stimulated, so that they suffered after the war from excess capacity (e.g., in shipbuilding). It has been estimated that the war cost the belligerents the equivalent of four to five times their production for 1913, or even more, and also that, but for the war, the level of industrial production of 1929 would have been reached in 1921 (so eight years were wasted). Actually, it was at 77 percent of its 1913 level in 1920, 82 percent in 1923, and 100 percent in 1924.

However, others suggest that the direct but temporary effects of the war—destruction and depreciation of human and physical capital, massive reallocation of resources—however painful, were less costly in the long run than "the damage inflicted to the liberal international economic order that had sustained development down to 1914" (O'Brien 1995). Because of the loss of potential gains from international commerce and competition, this damage had deep and lasting influences and constrained the growth of almost all national economies.

Moreover, the 1919 peace settlement had economic consequences. John Maynard Keynes immediately denounced these, and although he overstated his case, a good deal of it was valid. The peacemakers did not pay enough attention to Europe's economic problems, and indeed they exacerbated them unwillingly instead of devising a program of reconstruction, so that recovery was hampered and obstructed.

A first criticism is that Europe was balkanized by the creation of small new states. Actually, there were only six more states, but the breakup of Austria-Hungary can certainly be deplored, as it had been a large and balanced free-trade area; its division, however, was inevitable, as its component nations refused to go on living together. Still, the new borders often either broke up economic regions (e.g., the coalfield of Silesia) or separated areas that had been complementary. Vienna, which had been the capital of a large empire, became that of a small—and impoverished—republic. Attempts at establishing a customs union among the new states failed, and they soon protected and artificially stimulated their agriculture and industry, even though their home markets were quite narrow. In the 1920s trade among them was reduced to less than half its former level. This hindered recovery in the Danubian region and added to its instability. Eventually those states became authoritarian and tried to achieve self-sufficiency; they attracted some western capital but misused it, failing to bring about development. Czechoslovakia, alone in having a democratic regime, and with the most industrialized regions of the former Austria-Hungary, still had a disappointing performance—and a deep depression in the 1930s, largely because of the protectionist policies of the other "successor states," its neighbors. However, the new states were created according to the people's right of self-determination; solving this conflict between economics and politics is a matter of personal choice. Besides, it was not unusual in pre-1914 Europe for political borders to cut across geographic and economic units, such as the Franco-Belgian coalfield, or the complex that was made up of Lorraine, Luxembourg, and the Saarland. Such divisions contributed to Europe's tragedy, but it is wrong to believe that they were all created at Versailles (moreover, in the 1920s, some restrictions on trade were abolished, and tariff levels stabilized). In addition, Russia, which had become the Soviet Union, had "left" Europe and was no longer an important trading partner for European countries (especially as a supplier of grain).

However, the worst problem that resulted from the peace settlement was that of reparations. Frenchmen and Belgians wanted indemnities for the massive damage their territories had suffered, a good deal of which had been deliberately done by the retreating German armies; but the British, who had only lost merchant ships, insisted that pensions to war victims be included, in order to get something. So the total sums demanded from Germany were astronomical—equivalent to three times its 1913 GNP. It soon became obvious that they were far beyond Germany's capacity to pay, and also that there was a transfer problem: in order to pay, Germany would have to export on such a scale that the victors' economies would suffer. As the German government was dragging its feet in meeting its commitments, France and Belgium tried, unsuccessfully, to enforce payment by occupying the Ruhr in 1923. In 1924, the Dawes plan significantly reduced the sums Germany would have to pay, and they were again reduced by the Young plan of 1929 (nonetheless, it provided for German payments up to 1988!). The matter was aggravated by war debts among allies and by the American government's insistence on strict repayment of the wartime loans to its allies (to the tune of $10 billion), while it refused to admit any relationship between reparations and debts: "They hired the money, didn't they?," was President Calvin Coolidge's famous saying. At the same time, the United States was raising its tariff walls and imposing drastic restrictions upon immigration. Yet France and other countries could only repay the United States if they received at least an equivalent amount in reparations. Recriminations between former allies about debts and reparations hampered the reconstruction of the international economic system.

The reparations and debts issue poisoned the 1920s; in Germany it left a heritage of bitterness that weakened the fragile Weimar Republic and helped the rise of Hitler. This issue also was at the heart of postwar international financial and monetary disorders, but it was not their only cause. During the war all belligerents had printed money and borrowed on a massive scale, and then suffered from different degrees of inflation. After the peace, they had to service enormously increased national debts (by a factor of 12 in Britain, of 30 in Germany), while raising taxes and cutting expenditures were politically difficult. Most governments just continued borrowing and printing money, and in some countries hyperinflation developed. The most spectacular case was in Germany in 1922–1923.

During the war, large budget deficits had resulted in suppressed inflation; deficits became worse afterward, because, inter alia, of political instability. The prospect of heavy reparations payments caused a loss of confidence in the currency and a search for liquidity, while the Reichsbank was willing to monetize vast quantities of debt. It has been wrongly maintained that there was no alternative policy. The authorities could have reduced the budget deficit, but they made the mistake of allowing inflation to accelerate, through massive money-printing, in the hope that the mark's fall would prove Germany's incapacity to pay reparations. When political tensions over the latter became worse and the French occupied the Ruhr, there was a collapse into hyperinflation—at 1000 percent per month. At its peak, in November 1923, one dollar was worth more than four trillion paper marks. Inflation also raged in the successor states of Austria-Hungary and in the Balkans. In France, expectations for reparations for financing reconstruction were too high, and finances were not strictly managed; thus, the franc fell after more than a century of stability, much upsetting the people. By 1926 it had fallen to a tenth of its legal parity, hyperinflation was threatening, and capital was fleeing the country. However, a new government under Raymond Poincaré restored confidence, and the franc appreciated and was in 1926 stabilized at a fifth of its prewar parity.[4] It was certainly undervalued (but not deliberately), which attracted a lot of gold to France, with destabilizing effects on the international monetary system. Only proud Britain managed to restore sterling to its prewar parity in 1925, though at some cost for the real economy, as a moderate devaluation would have somewhat reduced unemployment but not solved the British staple industries' structural problems. Neutral countries also retained prewar parities.

These disorders and the division between stable and fluctuating, convertible and nonconvertible, currencies created uncertainty and disparities in prices, which made the recovery of trade difficult. Inflation may have preserved employment, helped reconversion and reconstruction and—sometimes—stimulated investment, but it certainly caused a misallocation of resources, a destruction of savings, and a weakening of many banks. Another delayed but unfortunate consequence was that the countries that had experienced the worst inflation—especially Germany (but also France)—were frightened by expansionary policies after 1929 and chose deflation. Political and monetary insecurity in the postwar years resulted in brutal and destabilizing international movements of capital, the so-called hot money, which often made crises worse. For the first time, national currencies had become the focus of speculative attacks. It was at that time that Swiss banks became a favorite refuge for frightened capital, and Switzerland a first-class international financial center, a turntable for capital, with the specific role of managing wealth.

Because the distribution of gold stocks had become very unequal (most of them were in the United States, and in France after 1928), gold could not continue to fulfill its prewar function, and the general determination to return to the gold standard and to prewar parities was met with frustration. Thus, the gold exchange standard emerged at the Conference of Genoa in 1922. Central banks' reserves were to be made up not only of gold, but also of foreign currencies (mainly the leading ones) and of claims on other central banks. The circulation of gold coins, which had ceased during the war, was not resumed, and gold became an international asset, for external settlements only. Governments hoped to enhance world liquidity and to restore de facto the prewar international monetary order. This aim appeared to be achieved when Britain returned to gold in 1925, and by the late 1920s all European currencies had been drawn into this system. However, the new arrangement had the disadvantage of all fixed-exchange-rate regimes (inasmuch as prices and wages were less flexible than before 1914, which made adjustments more difficult) and was more vulnerable to shocks than its predecessor, particularly because Britain had lost its ability to manage the world money order as it had done before 1914. Its balance of payments had deteriorated, and its gold reserves were low; when confidence would vacillate, the claims on its reserves would become very great, and it would be forced into deflationary policies. Moreover, many countries had overvalued exchange rates and unsound finances; when they had little gold, they also had difficulties accumulating dollars or pounds, so their position was precarious and balance-of-payments crises were frequent—which again imposed deflationary policies. And policy techniques that had developed under the pre-1914 convertible regime proved to be inadequate to deal with the new problems that emerged after World War I. Though the role of central banks had greatly increased, their apprenticeship of new practices was often slow.

Some other consequences of World War I also deserve brief mention. The industrial countries of Europe had lost many of their traditional overseas markets for manufactures, which they had been unable to supply during the war, so their former customers (like India or Brazil) had started to make the goods they had imported or to buy them from the United States and Japan. This change would have come anyway, but much more slowly, if there had been no war. The United States, which had been the fourth-largest exporter of manufactures before 1914, was second in the 1920s, while the share of Europe in world exports fell from 55 percent in 1913 to 49 percent in 1929. The large British textile industry was to contract sharply because of the rise of local industries in many of its former markets and competition from Japan, which in the 1930s became the largest exporter of cotton goods, while British exports of cottons were by 1938 only a quarter of their 1913 level. This is the classic case of Europe's loss of dominance over world markets. The case of primary produce, on the other hand, is different. Production of such produce had greatly increased overseas both during and after the war, to supply Europe, where agriculture had suffered from hostilities. In the 1920s, however, European farm output recovered, and the growth of demand for primary goods was slow because of low population growth in industrial countries (owing to war losses and to birth control). As a consequence, prices of those goods fell (and eventually collapsed), so that the purchasing power of primary-goods-producing countries—and markets there for European manufactures—was restricted. There was also the sale or loss of foreign investment, to finance essential imports during the war or because of debt repudiation by the Soviet Union and others. Britain lost a quarter of its foreign investment, France one-half (including everything invested in Russia), Germany 100 percent. The United States, meanwhile, had moved from the position of net debtor to become a large net creditor. Whereas the prewar gold standard had been based on one strong center, London, the new system had two poles: New York and London. But, unlike free-trade Britain, the United States was highly protectionist, and London had become too weak to bear the burden of sterling as a major reserve currency.

The consequences of the war and then the peace—including the drastic change in the relationship between Europe and overseas countries—made necessary large-scale change in European production and trade, particularly some transfers of resources, if Europe was not to suffer stagnation and unemployment. The drama of the interwar period is that this task—admittedly, an enormous one—was not accomplished. The problems that had arisen had been unknown to previous generations, while the price mechanism and profit differentials were less efficient as agents of change and resource allocation than before 1914. Moreover, they challenged governments as well as the business world, as both international and domestic politics intruded on European (and world) economic affairs with more intensity than before; indeed, they often dictated trends in the international economy.

The Interwar Years: Chronology

The interwar period is generally divided into four subperiods. First, the years 1919–1924; they were dominated by the havoc caused by the war: at its end, Europe's real GNP was 20 percent less than in 1913. The fear of revolution was also widespread—and revolutions were indeed attempted, though unsuccessfully, in Germany and Hungary. After a brief speculative boom in 1919–1920, a serious slump occurred in 1920–1921, and recovery was slow and difficult, inasmuch as productivity had fallen, particularly in farming and coal mining. Only in 1924 did Europe's industrial production return to its 1913 level.[5]

Then came a few years, from 1925 to 1929, of "prosperity." The same word is used in the United States, but its upswing was sharper: in 1929, industrial production in Europe was 30 percent above its 1913 level, and in the United States it was up by 80 percent. Europe's GNP per capita (the USSR excluded) grew at a rate of 2.8 percent per year between 1922 and 1929 but in the last year was only 6 percent above its 1913 level. Nonetheless, most difficulties that had prevailed appeared to have been solved or on the way to being solved. Détente progressed in international affairs, as symbolized by the Treaty of Locarno (1925). Reconstruction had been completed, much old capital equipment was replaced, and successful financial reorganizations were achieved in several countries, particularly Germany (the new reichsmark was created in 1924). The latter also made reparations payments, according to the Dawes plan, which enabled its creditors to meet their obligations in turn. But this was because American capital poured into Europe, especially into Germany (partly thanks to the international connections of its private banks), which received far more in loans than it paid out in reparations. Actually, there was a danger inherent in dependence on continued investment by the United States, inasmuch as Germany had borrowed short-term and invested some of the money long-term, to modernize and rationalize its industry. However, one could believe that the long-hoped-for return to "normalcy"—the pre-1914 lost paradise—had at last happened, though a major country, Britain, did not much partake of prosperity. It depended more than other countries on a high level of exports, which was not achieved, and retained a solid core of unemployment. According to Keynesian received wisdom, the restrictive monetary policy, which was followed to support sterling at its prewar parity, was responsible for high un-employment and slow growth. Some other countries (in Scandinavia, e.g.) also suffered from deflationary policies, in order to stay on the gold stan-dard. Altogether, the European economy failed to grow fast as a result of mistaken policies. It was both more unstable and more rigid than before 1914, and also less synchronized, as national performances greatly depended upon economic—and especially monetary—policies. Still, "prosperity," though not unmitigated, did not encourage European countries to carry on the restructuring and adaptations that were necessary.

Needless to say, the third period, starting in 1929, was dominated by crisis and depression. When lending by the United States began to tail off in 1928, and when American capital was repatriated after the stock-market crash, Europe (and especially heavily indebted central Europe) soon felt the effect, though panic came only in 1931. It started in May in Vienna with the failure of the Credit Anstalt, the largest Austrian bank, which was basically unstable because of the breakup of Austria-Hungary and of the early 1920s hyperinflation. It spread to other Austrian banks, to the Danubian countries, and to Poland and Germany, where it was es-pecially severe. It was exacerbated by panicked recalls of foreign credits, capital flight, and runs on the banks, which were not too solid (and uni-versal banks are, regardless, sensitive to recessions). Foreign emergency-bridging loans were unable to ward off the collapse of banks, and the world crisis greatly limited the assistance that Germany could expect from outside—even though it brought a de facto end to the payment of repa-rations and of interally debts. Then, because Britain had lent heavily to Germany, there was suddenly, in the summer of 1931, a question of its abil-ity to defend the gold value of the pound, inasmuch as its Labor govern-ment was mistrusted by the markets. After heavy losses of gold, it had to leave the gold standard on 21 September 1931.

The depression of the 1930s was the most severe, universal, and protracted that Europe had yet known. From 1929 to 1932, industrial out-put fell 27 percent (41 percent in Germany) and was back to its 1913 level, and GNP by 12 percent (15 percent in industrial countries).[6] Still, though Europe was much more dependent upon international trade, which col-lapsed, the depression was not as bad as in the United States, where GNP fell 31 percent from 1929 to 1933, and industrial output 45 percent. The dates of the nadir (generally 1932 or 1933) and the degree of recession (and recovery) varied from country to country. Germany was the worst hit at first, but in France the depression lasted longer.

Still, many countries—including Britain and Germany—managed to pull out of the depression rather early and so went through a fourth period, recovery. In 1935, Europe's GNP was back at its 1929 level, and in 1937–1938 it exceeded it by 10 percent; for the twelve countries of western Europe, GDP rose by 26 percent from 1932 to 1938 and GDP per capita by 23 percent. However, foreign trade, including intra-European trade, which had fallen sharply, did not recover as well: in 1937–1938, it was 20 percent under its 1913 and 1929 levels.

This is not the place for an interpretation of the depression and its long duration. There is a consensus that it originated in the disruptions and imbalances of the international economic system that World War I and the peace settlement had caused, and in the mistaken policies that were followed in the 1920s. The fragility of the international system that had been reconstructed in that decade (the gold exchange standard), and to which most countries were committed, and the fragility of the banking system were crucial if not decisive.[7] "Golden fetters" (Eichengreen 1992) transformed a cyclical downturn—which occurred first—into a world disaster by constraining the policies that governments could pursue; they greatly contributed to the diffusion and severity of deflationary shocks and of the depression; the gold standard "mentality" or ideology, which was pervasive among central bankers and political leaders, prevented adaptation to change during the 1920s and then led to actions that accentuated economic distress, such as the deflationary policy followed in Germany in 1929–1932. On the other hand, the collapse of the gold exchange standard did deepen and prolong the depression. Maladjustments interacted and accumulated until the system could not bear the strain and collapsed. There also was the war-induced disruption of trade, which was never fully restored, and the structural change in the relationship between Europe and overseas countries. Owing to Europe's central position in the world economy, there was a vicious downward spiral involving Europe's exports of manufactured goods, its imports of primary products from overseas, the depression of agriculture and of intra-European trade. The fall in world prices of primary produce—slow at first, precipitous after October 1929 —and the deterioration in the terms of trade of primary-producing countries had negative consequences for European industries.

Then again, it bears consideration that crisis and depression were imported from the United States and had their direct causes in their internal *konjunktur*. Moreover, U.S. tariff and immigration policies, plus its attitudes toward international cooperation and its unwillingness to act as leader and to replace Britain as lender of last resort, played a negative role, while the country, with its massive gold reserves, was not constrained by "golden fetters." Even before Wall Street crashed, exports of American capital to Europe (which were necessary to the working of the gold exchange standard) had dried up in 1928, so that the position of debtor countries (especially Germany) had been weakened. After the crash, the fall in American imports of both primary produce and European manufactures was badly felt abroad. On the other hand, some monetarist writers are wrong to see the 1929 crisis as a purely American domestic affair; it had some deep-rooted causes in the imbalances that World War I had created in Europe and overseas.

Answers to the depression were purely national and unilateral; attempts at international cooperation failed. The rivalries and disputes of the 1920s (especially those about reparations and debts) had left a bitter inheritance of distrust and suspicion, which was made worse by depression. For instance, Francophobia prevailed among British politicians, civil servants, and businessmen. Cooperation among central banks was deficient: the Bank of England and the Bank of France disagreed on monetary policy and were, several times, at intense strife. This jeopardized the efforts by Montagu Norman, the Bank of England's governor, to promote a regional European system coordinated by London. In order to improve cooperation, the Bank for International Settlements was established in Basel in 1930, but it was ineffective owing to the ill will of central banks and governments. As customs barriers were often seen as the main obstacle to economic growth and peace, the idea of a European customs union had been put forward in the late 1920s, most notably by some French and German industrialists (and the steel magnate Emile Mayrish, from Luxembourg). In May 1930, the French foreign minister Aristide Briand proposed a plan for a European Federal Union, mainly in the economic field, but the British said no. In 1932, the Lausanne Conference ended de facto reparations payments by Germany, but the United States refused to cancel its former allies' debts (actually, its debtors—except small Finland— defaulted). In 1933 in London, the World Monetary and Economic Conference failed, mainly because of President Franklin D. Roosevelt's hostility. However, in September 1936, a kind of monetary agreement was reached among the United States, Britain, and France, which declared their intention to avoid disturbances in exchange rates and to work toward more stability in international economic relations. This was in fact a fig leaf for the devaluation of the French franc (which a disastrous economic situation imposed); it did not lead to stabilized exchange rates, and it established definitively the dollar as the leading currency.

After this brief periodization, I shall try to stress the unity of the interwar period, as the four subperiods I have outlined are obviously linked together, dominated by the same problems, especially by the adaptation —or rather lack of adaptation—of Europe to post–World War I conditions. Economic growth was slower than before 1914—and after 1945; de-globalization and disintegration prevailed.

The Interwar Years: Overall Views

The economic picture of the period between the wars must not be painted too black, however; there were some positive aspects, mostly owing to developments that had started before 1914, as there were not many new technological breakthroughs.

The diffusion of new technologies from the "second industrial revolution" continued rather quickly, and some new industries that had been relatively small in 1913 grew to be quite large, particularly the production of electricity and electrical equipment, artificial textiles, cement, the automobile and aircraft industries, and the making of many kinds of cheap, standardized, durable consumer goods, such as domestic appliances and radio sets. Although Europe—even in its most advanced regions—was a generation behind the United States in the area of these new products, a trend toward mass consumption can be noticed. Still, the real explosion of such goods would not come until the 1950s.

Some attention must be paid to the development of electricity and automobiles. The use of electricity and of the internal combustion engine brought such advantages, in convenience, flexibility, and prices, that it made great strides in all countries. Indeed, the production of electricity progressed so fast (at a mean rate of growth of 7.1 percent per year from 1920 to 1937) that it is a striking exception to the gloom of the interwar period; moreover, it was relatively independent from the overall *konjunktur* thanks to technical progress (in production and transport) and to concentration, which brought about a sharp fall in prices and thus encouraged consumption. The manufacture of motor vehicles, which benefited from the European innovation of the small car, cheap to build and to run, also grew fast: the total number of such vehicles in Europe increased at a rate of 12 percent per year from 1920 to 1937. Though concentrated in four countries, production actually grew markedly faster than in the United States, so that the "motorization gap" between America and Europe narrowed.[8] Still, by 1938, Britain and France only had 40 cars per 1,000 inhabitants, versus 200 in the United States, and the other European countries were far behind.

Meanwhile, productivity continued increasing from 1913 to 1938, at a rate of 1.9 percent per year for productivity per man-hour in manufacturing (GDP per hour worked in twelve west European countries grew at a rate of 1.2 percent per year).[9] Still, it grew more slowly than in the United States, which had become the locus of the technological frontier. New methods for organizing work were imported from the United States and given American names, such as Taylorism and Fordism, and the conveyor belt was introduced as well. In the 1920s, there was a widespread rationalization movement, based on American methods, in France and Germany (where some firms adopted the multidivisional structure). American direct investment also helped: for example, the two largest U.S. carmakers, Ford and General Motors, established plants in Europe. Still, neither in Britain nor in France did mass-production methods make large inroads. Overall industrial output (the USSR excluded) grew at a rate of 1.6 percent per year from 1913 to 1938 (i.e., an increase of 50 percent), clearly less than the 3-percent growth from 1880 to 1913. Some countries, of course, had a faster industrial growth, particularly Scandinavia and Italy (and, outside Europe proper, the Soviet Union's growth was 10 percent per year from 1928 to 1940). The level of industrialization progressed in almost all countries and, for Europe as a whole (the USSR excluded), Paul Bairoch's industrialization index (1982) rises from 45 in 1913 to 63 in 1938. Concentration also progressed, and giant firms such as I. G. Farben, Imperial Chemical Industries, and Unilever were established. On the other hand, beginning in the early 1920s agriculture sunk into a state of depression, even during the supposed prosperity; nonetheless, its output slowly increased.

As for Europe's (the USSR excluded) real GNP, it increased by 40 percent from 1913 to 1938, at a rate of 1.4 percent per year. Since population grew at 0.5 percent, per capita product's growth rate was 1 percent (while real wages grew faster), which was not much lower than before 1913. The effects of a big cut in the working week during the 1920s plus improvements in welfare institutions must also be kept in mind.[10] Thus, by 1938, the standard of living in most countries was higher than in 1913 and even 1929, and the dispersion among countries' growth rates was not large, because some of the underperformers from the 1920s (like Britain and Germany) did better in the 1930s, while the converse was true for some others (especially France). Still, serious disparities among incomes per capita persisted, as most of industry remained concentrated in northwestern and central Europe, while the modest industrialization of the eastern and southern periphery was not enough to employ populations that were growing faster than those of the industrial core, because the demographic transition came later to them; the gap with the West was not narrowed.[11] The spatial expansion of industrialization—which took place before 1914 and increased the number of advanced countries—was checked.

Meanwhile, the large agricultural sector of geographically peripheral countries, which often made the biggest contribution to their national product and supplied most of their exports, was badly depressed, and their terms of trade deteriorated. Those countries also suffered from the end of out-migration to the United States (following the U.S. quota laws of 1921 and 1924) and from the sharp decrease in foreign investment: the lending capacity of the "rich" countries had been reduced, and investors were often frightened by political instability.[12] For political reasons, France did invest in the east European countries that were its allies, but it did not offer markets for their agricultural exports (in fact, their economies were more complementary to Germany's than France's).[13] Because the industrial heartland was slow to solve its structural problems, because its population did not increase much, and because it generated most of its "national" product, its sluggish growth was shared by Europe as a whole. Only some small northern countries—the Netherlands and Scandinavia (which now included Finland, as it had been freed from Russian rule)—had an increase in population, substantial investment, improvement in their terms of trade (especially for those that exported wood products), and therefore the fastest economic growth in Europe; Switzerland also did relatively well, except during the early 1930s.

On the other hand, the negative reputation of the interwar period is not undeserved. The main reason is that insecurity prevailed except for the prosperous years from 1925 to 1929. This insecurity was both economic and political, with close links between the two fields: the threats of war, disturbances, and revolution were liable to upset the economy, while crises and depressions threatened political stability. One consequence was sudden migrations of hot money, which destabilized economies, as they caused dramatic exchange-rate crises and extensive banking failures; another was a reluctance to invest and a shortage of risk capital—despite Keynes's view that excessive savings were at the root of the troubles. So this was a period of instability, of sharp fluctuations, particularly in prices.

However, the most spectacular aspect of this period was the new phenomenon of mass unemployment: to cyclical, short-term unemployment was added a long-term unemployment, which hit hard in the declining, "old" industries (such as coal, steel, shipbuilding, and textiles). Demographic changes in the population of industrial countries tended to make unemployment worse: the 15–65 age-group increased faster than total population—and with it the number of entrants on the labor market.

Before World War I, in developed countries, coal had been almost the only source of primary energy. Afterward, it suffered from competition by hydroelectricity and petroleum (especially as fuel for ships); nonetheless, its share of total energy consumption fell by only a few percentage points. More serious to the coal industry were the savings in the use of coal, especially in electric power stations; the depression of industries that were big consumers of coal, especially the steel industry; and the slow overall economic growth. The extraction of coal in Europe stagnated in the long run: by 1937, it was not higher than in 1913. Britain, however, was the country where coal mining suffered most; the German coal industry was completely reorganized in the 1920s and withstood better the later depression.

The steel industry, meanwhile, suffered from overcapacity, because of a large expansion during World War I and after (mainly in Germany to make good the losses resulting from border changes). Prices and output sharply fluctuated, and remedies were sought in market regulation and cartelization. One factor behind steel's difficulties was the depression in shipbuilding. Though Europe retained a quasi-monopoly over this industry (and two-thirds of the world's merchant marine), the demand for new ships was reduced by the stagnation of international trade and there was again excess capacity. The tonnage of ships launched never reached its 1913 level, and actually was only two-thirds as high in 1937. However, some small builders (e.g., the Netherlands, Denmark, Sweden, and Italy) enlarged their market shares at the expense of Britain, which again was the major sufferer.

Likewise, the crisis in the cotton industry was the worst in Britain, because of its dependence upon Asian markets (continental cotton manufacturers, who did not export much to Asia, fared better). One-third of British capacity was dismantled, and, owing to the primacy of Britain, Europe's cotton consumption in 1937 was only 80 percent of its 1913 level.

The depression of traditional industries created contrasts in Britain (and elsewhere) between the depressed areas of old industries in the north, where permanent unemployment was massive, and the prosperous regions of new industries, working mainly for the home market, around London and Birmingham. However, the expansion of the new industries and of services was not fast enough to absorb the workers who had been made redundant by the depression in the old staples.

Still, the most depressed sector of the European economy was agriculture, which employed more people than industry (over 60 percent of the labor force in the most economically backward countries). Moreover, its difficulties predated 1929, owing to worldwide surpluses of primacy produce and falling prices; and the agrarian regimes in countries on the periphery—either latifundia or microfundia—were uncongenial to progress. On the other hand, no sector of the economy received so much protection, but government policies in favor of agriculture were generally ill conceived. When they had some success in the short term (farm prices in France and Germany were maintained above world levels), it was at the detriment of efficiency and of the whole population's standard of living. Archaic structures (e.g., small farms) were preserved, but productivity was not promoted, and the condition of the rural population was not at all improved. By 1925, the agricultural output of Europe was back at its prewar level; then it grew slowly and in the late 1930s was 20 to 30 percent above that level. Productivity had risen by the same ratio, but few innovations had been introduced, and mechanization was quite slow (except, to some degree, in Britain and Germany in the 1930s). In that respect, Europe was, of course, far behind the United States. Altogether, agriculture did not make any significant contribution to Europe's economic growth, and it hoarded much labor that might have been employed more productively in other sectors. Indeed, there was much underemployment and concealed unemployment in agriculture, especially in eastern and southern Europe, but it was less obvious there than in industrial regions.

Unemployment rates were constantly and abnormally high in all countries, even in good years (like the late 1920s in Britain and Germany), and, of course, reached their peak during the depression. In 1932, Europe (the USSR excluded) had a seasonal peak of 15 million adults (mainly males) in industry and trade who were unemployed—about 15 percent of the labor force; for the industrial labor force of Germany, the level reached 44 percent. The average for the two decades was 7 million, or 7 percent of the total labor force in urban occupations. In the late 1930s, Britain, despite its recovery, retained an "untractable" million people unemployed. Moreover, taking into account underemployment and concealed unemployment in the agricultural sector and in some services like the retail trade, unemployment may have affected a quarter of Europe's labor force.[14] It slowed down, of course, the adoption of new processes and equipment. Population stagnated in many large towns—especially the great capital cities—and housing improvements leveled off (except in Scandinavia and the Netherlands).

A last aspect worth stressing is the stagnation and decline of international trade, which made clear the disintegration of the economic system that had been built up in the nineteenth century, and which was based upon international division of labor. Before 1914, international trade had been rising at the same rate as production of tradable goods, but by 1928, intra-European trade was only back at its 1913 level while commodity production had increased 15 percent. The depression hit both trade and production, but by 1938 the latter was 15 percent higher than in 1928, while intra-European trade had fallen by 10 percent. Consequently, the ratio of foreign trade to national income fell sharply: the average ratio for Britain, Germany, France, Italy, and Sweden was 46 percent in 1913, 23 percent in 1938. The countries where it had been the highest were the worst hit by unemployment; exporters of luxury goods, like France and Switzerland, badly suffered. All countries restricted their imports as much as they could, but the three main industrial powers were in the best position to cut them down. In the 1930s, therefore, trade in manufactures among Germany, Britain, and France fell to less than 50 percent of its prewar volume, and in 1937 the per capita value of their exports, at constant prices, was lower than in 1913. The trade in motor vehicles among the four carmaking countries was very low, and their exports went to third markets. As for steel, home markets became almost completely isolated, reserved to national steelworks; intra-European trade in steel was very small. At the world level, however, the 1920s trend of decline in the market share of Europe—to the benefit of the United States —was reversed in the 1930s (despite a fall in the volume of Europe's exports) due to imperial-preference systems and bilateral trade agreements.

Though our view of the 1920s and the 1930s may be too colored by the terrible war that closed the period, it undoubtedly was a time of slow growth and of disintegration—or deglobalization, a reversal of the movement toward integration and specialization that had marked the pre-1914 period. This change also concerned the international capital market; capital mobility survived World War I and lasted right up to 1929. But the depression was a watershed: exchange controls and other impediments put an end to intra-European foreign investment—except as an instrument of power politics.

The interwar years saw transition between liberalism and interventionism by the state, which greatly increased. During World War I, governments had intervened in their economies to an unprecedented extent, in order to mobilize resources, organize, and enhance the production of armaments; controls such as the rationing of basic foodstuffs and the freezing of prices and rents were established. In the 1920s, however, a return to the prewar liberal order prevailed, and most wartime controls were soon dismantled. The depression brought a complete change: liberalism was discredited, the anarchy of the market was denounced, and the apparent failure of capitalism and free enterprise raised loud demands for dirigisme and planning. State intervention progressed in almost all countries, including democracies, but it was the most extensive under authoritarian regimes. Fascist Italy, which before the depression had followed classical economic policies, became in the 1930s the most interventionist country outside the USSR. The government nationalized bankrupt banks and became an entrepreneur by creating in 1933 an institute for industrial reconstruction that controlled a large share of industry.

Generally, however, intervention was more protective than directive (with the exception of Germany, to which we shall return): it aimed at preserving existing activities (e.g., small shops as opposed to chain stores) while preventing bankruptcies (some large firms, especially banks, were rescued) and more unemployment.[15] It looked for stability rather than efficiency and growth and had a trend toward corporatism, or self-regulation of industries, to restrain competition. In all, there was an effort to isolate individual economies from the world economy, to promote exports, and to reduce imports and dependence upon foreign trade. A kind of neomercantilism prevailed.

Thus protectionism became the rage, especially after Britain renounced free trade in 1931–1932 (following its abandoning the gold standard).[16] Tariffs were raised, and an armory of new and more prohibitive weapons was also widely used: quotas, licenses for importing and exporting, preferential duties in trade with imperial partners. Britain (through the Ottawa agreements of 1932) and also France tried to build up self-sufficient imperial blocs. Nazi Germany went further with barter and clearing agreements, to avoid the use of gold and scarce currencies. Thus, the free flow of multilateral trade was broken up and constrained within narrow, bilateral channels, and there was a trend toward autarky, especially in Germany and Italy. It is difficult to disentangle the effects of protectionism from other changes that were taking place, but the loss of income from trade restrictions must have been substantial, inasmuch as there was a vicious circle: protection reduced trade, thus creating demands for more protection. Subsidies to agriculture and price support for its products also warrant mention, as do subsidies to destroy excess capacity (e.g., in British shipyards and cotton mills). Moreover, many national and international cartels existed before the depression, but cartelization became general, with the encouragement and support of governments; it aimed, of course, at preserving the status quo, by reducing competition. The International Steel Cartel had been founded in 1926; it faded away in 1930–1932 but was restored in 1933, with more member countries and more power.

A second major aspect was the final disintegration of the international monetary system. Here also, the decisive turning point was when Britain, on 21 September 1931, went off the gold standard and devalued the pound. Other European powers that traded extensively with Britain, like the Scandinavian countries, Greece, and Portugal, imitated it and linked their currency to sterling; and all Commonwealth countries except Canada joined the "sterling area." France, its neighbors, and some eastern countries tried to retain the gold standard at all costs, but their currencies were overvalued, and they became locked into a deflationary spiral and were the slowest to recover from depression.[17] Eventually, Belgium defected in 1935, France had to devalue in 1936, and the "gold bloc" disintegrated. The retreat from gold permitted all kinds of methods for manipulating currencies; everywhere governments increased their control in this field, but Nazi Germany, again, went the furthest, by imposing strict exchange control.[18] Britain, meanwhile, discouraged exports of capital outside the sterling area.

The transition to floating exchange rates was not in itself a disaster, but the result of competitive devaluations was that, by 1939, most currencies had roughly the same mutual exchange rates as in 1929, so that no country—except Britain, with its policy of managed rates—gained a durable competitive advantage. Moreover, the volatility that resulted from successive unilateral devaluations was disrupting to trade, and most countries responded to devaluations by their competitors with tariff wars and strengthened protection. On the other hand, devaluation freed domestic monetary policy, which could be changed from deflationary (with cuts in public spending, tax hikes, lower wages) to expansionist. By 1935, industrial output was 21 percent below its 1929 level in gold-bloc countries, 18 percent higher in the sterling area.[19] Still, it has been argued that generally the effects of lower levels of foreign trade on incomes swamped the stimulus to domestic activity. Moreover, recovery was hampered by the formation of currency blocs: the dollar bloc (to which no European country belonged), the sterling bloc, the group of countries which remained on the gold standard to a greater or less extent, plus another group around Germany. The latter had an inconvertible currency, but it satellitized most countries of eastern and southeastern Europe through a system of bilateral trade agreements, and it became isolated from the rest of Europe.

Such policies went directly against the trend that had prevailed up to 1914. They have been condemned as beggar-my-neighbor policies that exported unemployment and were mutually self-defeating; moreover, they were an obstacle to change and to adaptation. They largely explain why international trade did not recover after the worst of the depression had passed.

Nonetheless, there was a recovery in the late 1930s. It started in countries that adopted new economic policies that had similarities with the New Deal, though they were not inspired by it or by Keynes, whose influence was then limited. They were based on devaluation, on pump-priming, on increasing domestic demand by budget deficit and cheap money, and on partial or complete isolation from the world economy. Still, they greatly varied from country to country in both content and success. In Britain and Sweden, expansion under protection, within a mainly laissez-faire framework, was achieved. Most writers consider that the renunciation of gold and free trade gave to the British economy a substantial stimulus (protection may have raised Britain's national income of 1938 by 2.3 percent); it encouraged import substitution, but the protected sector improved its performance. Still, a housing boom, fueled by cheap money, was also a major factor behind expansion, and Britain's terms of trade markedly improved. From 1932 to 1938, British GNP per capita increased at a rate of 3 percent per year, or 20 percent total. Nonetheless, a hard core of unemployment persisted. In France, the "reflation" by the Popular Front government of 1936 failed utterly, particularly for having reduced the working week to forty hours. On the other hand, social-democrat Sweden was a success: by 1938 its industrial production was 50 percent above its 1929 level.

Nazi Germany was a special case; sad to say it was the first large industrial country to achieve complete recovery.[20] The index of industrial production (1929 = 100) rose from 59 in 1932 to 107 in 1936 and 127 in 1938—115 percent above 1932. By 1936, unemployment had almost disappeared, and the standard of living had improved. However, the economy was government-directed according to a primacy of politics, which severed the connection between its goals and economic rationality. Actually, the Nazis did not have an original, new economic order, and their anticapitalist rhetoric was all on the surface. The means of production remained private property (except those belonging to Jews, which were "Aryanized"), but under restrictions, as government decided what was to be produced: bureaucratic command replaced the price mechanism. Moreover, when it was deemed necessary, state-owned or state-controlled firms were set up—for instance for making the "people's car," the Volkswagen, which was a propaganda trick—but German business leaders were willing to go along. The Nazis had inherited from their predecessors an elaborate system of controls over the economy, but they greatly extended it—over foreign trade, prices, wages, raw materials supplies, investment, and the like. This apparatus was used to expand demand and to channel investment into such "vital" activities as Aryanization, import substitution, and military production.

At first, recovery was based upon large-scale public works (the building of a network of autobahns, land reclamation, inter alia), plus housing and increased production of consumption goods. Preparations for war only started seriously with the four-year plan of 1936; armaments production increased but was not massive (military expenditure rose from 3 percent of GNP in 1933 to 28 percent in 1938). In order to make the country self-sufficient in wartime, the production of *ersätze* (substitute materials) was developed as much as possible: synthetic fuel (from brown coal; its output was to rise from 1.8 million tons in 1936 to 6.3 million tons in 1942), synthetic rubber, synthetic wool, for example. The Nazis boasted that they preferred guns to butter, but up to 1944 Germans had both guns and butter. Financing came mainly from short-term borrowing, through the banking system (savings banks included), which channeled private savings into state debts, and from the issue of nonrediscountable instruments.

A serious problem was the shortage of gold, foreign-currency reserves, and foreign credits. Moreover, German competitiveness in foreign markets suffered from autarky (which often meant poor-quality and/or expensive raw materials) and from the devaluation of the pound. Overall, Germany's foreign trade did not recover (the closure of its markets was harmful to some of its neighbors, like the Netherlands), but trade was developed with the primary producing countries of southeastern and eastern Europe (and also with Latin America) through a network of bilateral barter and clearing agreements.[21] This involved some advantages for those countries: their exports were bought above world prices by Germany, which also offered credit for the goods it sold. But payments for German imports were in inconvertible "blocked marks" and their counterpart in goods came after long delays and was often made in articles (like cameras) that were not useful to poor countries or were never delivered. Some of Germany's partners (Bulgaria, e.g.) benefited, nonetheless, from an expanded money supply, but altogether they made de facto loans to their powerful partner, which had regained its dominance over *Mittel-Europa*. But, as we know, Hitler wanted more.

In a parallel with Nazi Germany, another totalitarian state, the Soviet Union, became during the 1930s a great industrial power. This was a big change, as the Soviet economy had remained backward during the decade that followed the Bolsheviks' seizure of power in the "Great October Revolution"—actually a putsch in November 1917. Three years of bitter civil war ensued, during which the Bolsheviks enforced a system called "war communism." Industrial firms (except very small ones) and banks were nationalized; firms belonging entirely or partly to foreigners were included, and Russia's foreign debt was repudiated. Landowners were expropriated and peasants were given free use of the land they occupied. As food supplies to the Red Army and the towns were insufficient, compulsory acquisition of grain and other foodstuffs by the state and its agencies was imposed, with the use of armed force when necessary and very little payment to peasants in return. Food was distributed to the urban population through an elaborate rationing system; but there was much illegal private trade and barter.

When the civil war came to its end, the economy was devastated. From 1914 to 1922, 16 million "excess deaths" had occurred—from violence, disease, and hunger—and the birth deficit had been 10 million; population within the Soviet Union's frontiers had fallen by 6 to 9 million. Agricultural production had declined by a third, and industrial output by 1920 was not more than 20 percent of its prewar level. Foreign trade was practically nil.

A disastrous fuel, transport, and food crisis early in 1921 obliged the Communists to adopt the "New Economic Policy" (NEP), which was a limited (and temporary) retreat from a socialist to a mixed economy.[22] Its main feature was an effort to conciliate the peasantry: requisitions were replaced by a rather moderate food tax, and peasants, after paying it, were allowed to sell freely any surplus they had left. Most retail trade and some small industrial firms were "privatized." However, the private sector was not large, market forces were restricted, the state retained the economy's commanding heights, and the "dictatorship of the proletariat" (i.e., the Communist Party) was not at all mitigated.

The NEP was a success: production in both agriculture and industry recovered, and by 1928 real GDP was back at its prewar level (though GDP per capita was 18 percent lower). On the other hand, this was largely the same economy as in 1914 (except for some progress in electrification): old factories had been restarted, the technological gap with the West had widened, the traditional peasant economy was roughly intact, and the problem of adequate food supplies for the urban sector was not solved, as a grain crisis proved in late 1927. There was also much unemployment due to migrations from the countryside to the towns.

For both doctrinal and empirical reasons, however, Communists considered it necessary and urgent to develop industry on a large scale, in order, inter alia, to be able to resist an attack by capitalist powers. They were also worried by the rise in the countryside of a bourgeoisie of well-to-do peasants (kulaks), while they generally thought that industrialization could only be achieved by "exploiting" the peasantry (which, indeed, had to make heavy sacrifices to industrialization during the 1930s).[23]

"Now we are fifty or a hundred years behind the advanced countries," Joseph Stalin proclaimed. "We must make good this lag in ten years. Either we accomplish this or we will be crushed." Therefore, the NEP was replaced by a policy of forced and fast industrialization, through a succession of ambitious five-year plans, the first of which was started in 1928. Henceforth, the USSR had a planned, or rather administrative, "command" economy, in which investment and production were regulated through physical controls from the center. Nonetheless, horizontal relations between enterprises existed, as well as important market or quasi-market features: this was a money economy, as well as a physically planned one. Its main lines were to remain unchanged for sixty years, though with fluctuations in detail. Results are difficult to assess, as Soviet statistics were established according to peculiar methods, suffer from many biases, and often were deliberately falsified so that growth is much overstated.[24] The table below (table 4.1) presents one of the recalculations made by western (and recently Russian) scholars; although the new figures still overestimate Soviet economic growth, at best they give a realistic upper limit.

According to this calculation, from 1928 to 1940, Soviet industrial production tripled and GDP almost doubled, which means average rates of growth of about 10 percent per year for the former, 5 percent for the latter. The investment ratio was 30 percent of GDP, and top priority was given to the development of heavy, capital-goods industries: coal, oil, electricity,

_____ *Table 4.1*_____
Index of the USSR's real GDP, 1913–1989

Year	GDP	Year	GDP
1913	100	1950	220
1928	100	1965	460
1940	181	1973	651
1946	143	1989	887

_____
Source: Maddison 1995, pp. 166–67, table B-10c. Maddison has used the work of R. Moorsten and R. P. Powell, *The Soviet Capital Stock, 1928–1962* (Homewood, Ill., 1966) for the period up to 1950, and for 1950–1989, publications by the Joint Economic Committee of Congress, based on CIA data.

steel, and engineering. Some branches of the latter were completely new, such as tractors and other farm machinery, machine tools, plus a modern and very large armaments industry.[25] Most new factories were very big, nay giant, units. Moreover, there was an effort to change the location of industry—mainly for defense reasons—and large "complexes" were set up in the Urals (Magnitogorsk), Siberia, and central Asia.

The performance of agriculture was much poorer, largely because of the massive collectivization and "dekulakization" that started at the end of 1929 and were carried out ruthlessly. More than 2 million members of kulak families were deported to distant regions, and many kulaks were shot. By the end of 1932, over 60 percent of the 25 million peasant households had joined the 250,000 collective farms (kolkhozy) that had been set up.[26] This was a massive and unprecedented social upheaval, and it caused a fall in output, the slaughter of many animals, and a major famine in 1932–1933, during which 6 million people died. Recovery was slow, despite some concessions to members of kolkhozy (each household was allowed its plot of land and a cow, with the right to sell produce on markets) and large-scale mechanization of farming. By the end of the decade, agricultural production was 10 percent or more above its 1928 level, but population had increased, and output per capita was slightly lower than in 1928.

Industrialization and collectivization generated large-scale migrations: from 1926 to 1939, 23 million persons moved from the countryside to the towns. The latter's share of total population increased from 16 to 33 percent, but only as late as 1961 would it overcome rural population; in 1939, 54 percent of the working population was employed in agriculture.

Still, by 1939, the USSR had become the third industrial power in the world, second in Europe after Germany. This had been achieved at a high human cost. The number of excess deaths in the 1930s was about 10 million. This includes 682,000 persons—mainly Communist Party members, army officers, and other cadres—who were executed for political crimes in 1937–1938. As for the prisoners in the forced labor system (gulag), their number rose from 2.5 million in 1933 to 3.3 million in 1941 (1.5 million were in concentration camps). Slave labor was important for capital construction in remote areas of Siberia and the far east. Though inefficient, the gulag was also useful for instilling fear and zeal among workers and managers. The bulk of the people suffered much hardship and misery: real wages fell and total personal consumption per capita was 9 percent lower in 1940 than in 1928. This was despite the increase of GDP, as a large and growing share was devoted to investment and defense.[27] And the effectiveness of the forced industrialization system was not remarkable: the rise in total factor productivity and its share in GDP growth were relatively small. After all, economic and social upheaval is not conducive to efficiency. Up to its end, the Soviet economy had higher ratios of capital to output and of energy–raw material inputs to output than the West.

A last point is that the Soviet Union—though it received some foreign aid, mainly from Germany and America—was economically isolated from capitalist Europe: in 1913, Russia had been responsible for 7 percent of Europe's foreign trade; by 1938, the Soviet Union's share of the latter was 2.5 percent. On the other hand, it had a considerable political and intellectual influence abroad. Fear of bolshevism was a major factor in the rise of fascism and Nazism. In western democracies, many workers and intellectuals were attracted by the emergence of an economic and social system that was radically different from capitalism, where the exploitation of man by man and the curse of unemployment (the scourge of the 1930s in many countries) had been abolished. Mass executions and deportations, meanwhile, were either ignored, denounced as reactionary lies, or said to be the just punishment of traitors and saboteurs. The attraction of the Soviet mirage and of the "new civilization" that socialism had created was, of course, to become more influential (in some countries, like France and Italy, at least) after World War II had given to the USSR glory and respectability—and also justified a posteriori the terribly expensive forced industrialization of the previous decade. Soviet planning also had some influence on the mixed economies and dirigiste policies that emerged in the West after the war.

Bairoch has rightly stressed that the idea of a general depression during the 1930s is wrong: out of nineteen European countries, twelve had, in 1938, a GNP per capita that was higher than in 1929. Unemployment had retreated and was lower than in the United States. Obviously, by 1939, Europe had progressed toward adapting to the new economic environment: old industries had contracted, new ones had expanded—though basically to supply home markets (yet some ground had been regained on overseas markets). Still, much fixed capital was obsolescent (its average age was higher than in 1914), productivity was often low, there was a great deal of rigidity or even arteriosclerosis, and there were too many depressed areas. Moreover, Europe had economically disintegrated. The free movement of people, goods, and capital that had been achieved before 1914 had ceased (by the late 1930s, the average ratio of capital outflows to national income, for twelve countries, was 1.5 percent, versus 4–5 percent before 1914). Economic nationalism was increasingly turning into isolationism, as each country tried to live an independent existence. Even Britain had turned away from Europe and toward its empire. Economists deplore this development, but this setback was of small import in relation to the new war that broke out.

World War II and Its Aftermath

World War II was even more destructive than World War I. The whole Continent, except four countries that managed to stay neutral, was occupied by the Nazis. For the first time its economies were unified under a single yoke. Indeed, Hitler and the Nazis spoke of a new order that went far beyond the large customs union that imperial Germany had planned to impose upon most of the Continent if it had won World War I; it would achieve a total economic and political reconstruction of Europe on antiliberal lines, to make it self-sufficient, under the domination and to the benefit of the *Herrenvolk*. Despite their prewar efforts at autarky, they had not succeeded in making Germany truly independent; this goal could only be reached by war and the domination of a large economic area (through a *Grossraumwirtschaft*).

Actually, the new order was a propaganda slogan, as Hitler, because of the hazards of war and of short-term needs, never defined it with precision. So it is not known whether a victorious Germany would have annexed the Netherlands, Belgium, and a large slice of northern and eastern France, or would have been less greedy. On the other hand, Germany certainly would have had a monopoly over heavy industry, while its vassals would have been restricted to primary production and consumption-goods industries. Countries that retained their independence would have been included within a customs union with Germany. However, the crucial part of Nazi plans concerned eastern Europe, where Germany would find its indispensable "living space." Most Poles and Russians would be either killed or transported to Siberia, but about a quarter of them would stay as helots, working for German settlers (plus some members of the "Nordic" race, like Dutchmen and Scandinavians); 100 million of those colonists would populate the east, over several generations, and supply Europe with food and raw materials. There would be no place for sentimentality toward the helots. Those plans were not implemented, of course, except the mass murder of Jews, but in Poland, in the occupied parts of the USSR, and even in Czechoslovakia, many entrepreneurs and specialists were killed or deported and many firms were taken over or bought up by the German authorities or by German companies. Even in countries of southeastern Europe, which were Hitler's allies, there was a significant penetration of German capital (but far less in the west and in Italy).

Germany's failure to invade England in the summer of 1940 and to decisively defeat the USSR at the end of 1941 made many of those grand plans pies in the sky and caused a drastic change in Nazi economic policy. Within two years Germany had conquered most of Europe by a succession of blitzkriegs, short campaigns that were inexpensive in terms of lives and material. Therefore, there had been no need for Germany to fully mobilize resources and to impose sacrifices upon civilians, while business did not want to invest too much in plant that would be unusable in peacetime. But the prospect of a long war on two fronts obliged it to set up a total war economy, to switch German industry to mass production of armaments, and also to intensify the exploitation of German conquests.

Despite deficiencies in Nazi economic planning and the polycratic nature of the Reich's structure, Albert Speer, the armaments minister, introduced much rationalization and managed to improve productivity. He also deconcentrated industry to the benefit of the Reich's southern regions, a move that was very valuable to postwar Germany. German armaments production increased threefold from February 1942 to September 1944, when it reached its peak (over five times its 1938 level), while total industrial production was 38 percent higher in 1943 than in 1938. This was achieved despite massive Allied bombing—which destroyed houses, not factories; it only became effective starting in the summer of 1944, when synthetic-fuel plants and railroads were targeted.

A more serious problem was a shortage of manpower, but it was largely corrected by resorting to forced and slave labor. By mid-1944, more than 7 million foreign workers (including prisoners of war) were employed in Germany; they comprised 20 percent of the total labor force. Forced labor was drafted from occupied countries, and slave labor was leased from concentration camps by firms such as I. G. Farben, Volkswagen, and Mercedes-Benz. On the other hand, the Nazis—with typical incoherence—murdered millions of Jews and let deportees and Russian prisoners of war starve.

The exploitation of occupied countries—which had started with their conquest—was increasingly harshened. Yet some experts consider that Germany failed, not only to rule and reorganize Europe as an integrated economic unit, but also to exploit it rationally and systematically; it only lived off its conquests, through a gigantic but piecemeal looting operation, in an act of sheer vampirism.

Plunder was achieved by many means, including arbitrary fixing of exchange rates with the reichsmark, enormous indemnities for maintaining troops of occupation (those obtained from France were ten times the actual costs), nonpayment for "imports" under clearing agreements, and commandeering of workers for labor in Germany. Over a quarter of Germany's war expenditures from June 1940 to September 1944 was financed by the conquered countries. As France was the biggest economy among them, it paid 42 percent of the total "special income from abroad" received by Germany; for the whole occupation period, the equivalent of a fourth or even a third of the French national income of 1938 was transferred to Germany on average each year (the Netherlands fared worst, with 38 percent, and also Norway, on a per capita base); the share of the actual income of the war years was higher, reaching almost half at its peak in 1943. On the other hand, total payments extracted from France in 1943 amounted to perhaps 8 or 9 percent of Germany's GNP in that year and were therefore an important source of war finance, and the total value of goods and services obtained from France by Germany from 1940 to 1944 was roughly equivalent to a quarter of German prewar GNP.

Gains from eastern Europe were much smaller, despite a harsher occupation regime, because of the scorched-earth policy of the retreating Red Army and also the region's poverty. An exception was the protectorate of Bohemia and Moravia; Hitler had plans to Germanize it, but they had to be postponed because the crucial importance of Czech heavy industry to the German war effort limited mass terror and killings. Some western countries, on the other hand, did not suffer much, especially Denmark, where German occupation brought full employment and drew agriculture from a depressed situation. After a fall, Danish GDP climbed back in 1944 to its level of 1939. In the Netherlands too, large German orders to industry restored full employment and prosperity—up to 1944, when the northern, highly urban parts of the country were not liberated; in these areas the population, hitherto well fed, starved during the last months of the war. Still, in 1945, Dutch industrial capacity was higher than in 1940, and a fast recovery was possible.[28]

Altogether, the Nazi "new order" was just a system of economic exploitation of conquered countries; if it unified the Continent, it was under the banner of force, loot, racism, and massacre. It was nonetheless effective: German armaments production soared, and the German standard of living was quite good, while hunger and even starvation prevailed in many occupied countries, which had been bled white when at last they were liberated. In those areas, standards of living had fallen much more than during World War I. In France, the reduction in food consumption per capita—about one-third—was more drastic than in other western occupied countries.

As for the few European neutrals, they were in some respects integrated into the "new order" and harnessed to the German war machine. Sweden supplied Germany with a quarter of the iron ore it consumed and with special steels; it extended credits to its dangerous neighbor. Switzerland, which from June 1940 was encircled by the Axis powers, became a "turntable" for gold transactions. The Reichsbank sold gold in Switzerland—mainly to the Swiss National Bank—to the tune of more than $400 million (as of 1945). Much of this gold was used to pay neutral countries (e.g., Portugal, Spain, Sweden, and Turkey) for their exports to Germany of strategic raw materials (iron ore, chrome, manganese, tungsten, and wolframite). Smaller sums paid for weapons and machine tools that Swiss industry supplied to Germany. Most of this gold had been stolen, mainly from central banks in occupied countries, but also from individuals; a small share was taken from persons whom the Nazis murdered. The criminal origin of the gold was known starting in 1941 in Switzerland, but, under the pressure of some business groups, gold from Germany was accepted up to April 1945. Meanwhile, the Swiss National Bank bought even larger quantities of gold from the Allies, who used proceeds to pay for imports from Switzerland (clockworks sent by parcel post) and for war-related and humanitarian purposes.

Among the consequences of the war, property damage was far more serious and widespread than in World War I, because it mainly resulted from aerial bombardment. Carpet bombing flattened all large German cities, but many towns in occupied countries also suffered—as well as London and many other British cities. In France, the whole province of Normandy was devastated, and in August 1944, the longest segment of railroad track in working order was under ten miles long, as communications had been a prime target of the Allies. Overall, damage was equivalent to one year of French national income. In the USSR, a quarter of prewar capital assets had been destroyed. The worst was the cost in human lives: 35 to 40 or 45 million people (including Russians) had lost their lives.[29] They included more than 6 million Jews; and eastern European Jewry, which had been a reservoir of talents in arts, science, and business, had been destroyed.[30] There were other changes in the ethnographic map of central and eastern Europe. The most significant was the expulsion of over 10 million Germans from eastern Europe after the war had ended, mainly from Czechoslovakia and Poland; the latter's border was moved westward to the Oder-Neisse line, while it lost territory in the east to the USSR. The boundary between Germans and Slavs was thus shifted westward and the medieval *Drang Nach Osten* was reversed.

Economically, when the war ended, the Continent lay prostrate, almost paralyzed, a pile of ruins at first sight (actually, in Germany, only

20 percent of buildings had been destroyed). Normal economic relations had often broken down, money being replaced by barter exchange or the use of cigarettes as currency. War and postwar needs generated inflation, which became hyperinflation in a few countries (Germany up to 1948, Hungary, Romania), and which, in more fortunate ones, took a long time to bring under control. In France prices increased twenty-fivefold from 1938 to 1952—including a sixfold rise between 1944 and 1948.

Europe's GDP (the USSR excluded) in 1946 was 19 percent below its 1939 level.[31] In some countries, production in 1945 had fallen to half its 1938 level—or less—and was back to its levels of the early 1900s, or even the late 1800s (1891 for France, 1908 for Germany). Restarting production was made difficult by shortages—of coal, raw materials, fertilizers, and so forth—by transport problems, and by worn out equipment. Only Britain, which had been undefeated, neutral Sweden, and Switzerland were over prewar levels. One or two generations of work and accumulation had been lost, and the productivity gap with the United States had become enormous (the latter also had almost half of world manufacturing capacity).

There was a dwarfing of Europe in a world that was dominated by two giants—the United States and the USSR. Admittedly, in 1945, Britain was one of the new "big three," but it was the smallest among them despite its brilliant war record. Britain's war effort had been the most intense among belligerent countries: in 1944, 55 percent of the labor force was either in the armed services or in war-related employment. Yet it had only held out thanks to massive help by the United States, and its enfeebled economy was to be beset by terrible difficulties in the postwar years.

Moreover, postwar prospects were gloomy. The Great Alliance soon broke down and was succeeded by the Cold War, and the Soviet Union imposed Communist regimes all over Eastern Europe, including East Germany. Europe was divided in two by an Iron Curtain, or rather "Europe" stopped at the Iron Curtain: it had been pushed back to the borders of Charlemagne's empire. The Soviet bloc will be discussed later, but it must be mentioned here that it isolated itself from the capitalist world. Western Europe, meanwhile, was under a double threat: external, because a Soviet invasion looked possible, even likely; internal, because, at least in France and Italy, powerful Communist parties and unions flourished on the hardships and shortages that prevailed. Actually, Stalin had no plan to take over Western Europe, which, in the half-century after 1945, was to enjoy the longest period of peace it had ever known. But nobody knew this, and the fear of war and of communism might have crippled recovery and investment.

Besides, partly in order to contain communism, and partly to modern- ize (and industrialize) their economies, most West European governments —often left-of-center, social-democrat leaning—followed economic and social policies in the line of wartime ones: widespread state intervention and controls; extensive nationalization of key industries; attempts at some form of planning; cooperation between the two sides of industry; wider roles for unions; expansion of welfare institutions, such as na- tional health services; and heavy taxation and transfer payments to re- distribute income. A majority of public—and expert—opinions favored such policies on the grounds of the failure of liberalism during the in- terwar period, of the successful management (in Britain) of the econ- omy during the war, plus a theoretical framework that Keynes had sup- plied. State intervention looked necessary to achieve full employment and to solve difficult problems of reconstruction, inflation, and balance- of-payments deficits. It aimed both at structural modernizing and at reg- ulating demand during business cycles, through budget and monetary policies. "Mixed economies"—the expression of the time—or "managed capitalism" prevailed almost everywhere up to the 1960s under a variety of shapes, from the neocollectivist formula of France to the "social mar- ket economy" of West Germany, which adopted competition and free markets but rejected pure laissez-faire and gave to the state a significant role. Postwar "Keynesian" policies are often nowadays considered as ne- farious, but Herman Van der Wee (1986) thinks that they contributed to fast economic growth, and studies of economic controls in postwar Britain suggest that they improved the balance of payments and caused the rise of several new industries.

Another important development for Britain, France, the Netherlands, and Belgium was the loss of their colonial empires, sometimes after ex- pensive wars (this loss was actually a blessing, but it was not perceived as such at the time!). Despite such uncongenial circumstances, the decades that followed 1945, unlike the 1920s and 1930s, were to be marked in Western Europe by a fast recovery and then an unprecedented economic growth.

The speed of Western Europe's recovery surprised everybody. Within five or six years after the war, reconstruction of damaged property was almost completed, the losses in output and capital stock were made good, and between 1948 and 1950, Western (and Eastern) European countries, but for very few, returned to their prewar output and income per capita levels; some exceeded them. By 1950, Maddison's "capitalist Europe" had higher levels of GDP per capita than in 1913, by 58 per- cent for his twelve core countries and by 26 percent for countries of the periphery. Altogether, despite two terrible wars, those sixteen countries had a rate of per capita growth of 1.7 percent annually from 1913 to 1950. In addition, most European countries proved their resilience with a baby boom (while the death rate was falling); the birthrate jumped in France from 14.6 per thousand in 1938 to 21 per thousand in 1947, in Britain from 15.2 per thousand in 1939 to 20.8 per thousand in 1947. Then, from 1950 onward, came an amazing growth.

How are we to explain this achievement? Of great importance were the European people's great efforts to get out of the dreadful poverty into which they had fallen, and their acceptance of necessary sacrifices. Second, some of the mistakes that had been made after 1918 were not repeated. The Western powers did not impose reparations upon Germany, they gave up some plans to weaken permanently its economic power (as it was realized that the rest of Europe was dependent upon it), and in 1949 they admitted the new Federal Republic into the family of democratic countries; the Russians, meanwhile, thoroughly plundered East Germany. The United States, for its part, canceled the enormous debts its Allies owed it. Third, the strident economic nationalism of the 1930s did not survive the war: international cooperation was established in the West, and —this was decisive—the United States granted massive aid to Western European countries (while the nuclear umbrella, under the North Atlantic Treaty of 1949, gave security against Soviet aggression).

After the war's end, Europe needed substantial imports of food, raw materials, and capital goods, but it was unable to pay for them, as its industries were not yet in a position to export on a large scale, its invisible incomes from services (including those from foreign investment) had been lost, and its terms of trade were deteriorating. This so-called dollar gap (as most necessary imports could only be obtained from the United States) impeded recovery and the restoration of free trade, to which the United States was committed. Even Britain, the strongest of the European economies, was in such dire straits that it failed in July–August 1947 to fulfill its promise to the United States that it would reestablish sterling convertibility. At first, America granted aid piecemeal, country by country.[32] But on 5 June 1947, after a terrible winter that augured a bad European harvest in 1947, U.S. secretary of state George Marshall announced that the American government was ready to help European countries, on the condition that they would cooperate to apply for help and distribute it, according to a coherent program of recovery. This was the origin of the European Recovery Program, which was voted by Congress in April 1948, and of the Organisation for European Economic Co-operation (OEEC), which was established to distribute U.S. aid and facilitate trade and payments among member countries.[33] The latter only included Western nations: Marshall's offer had been extended to the Eastern ones, but they had refused it under Soviet orders. The aim was to make Western Europe self-supporting within a period of four years (but it was prolonged, because of the Korean War, in order to help Europe to rearm).

The Marshall Plan, as it is generally known, was both extremely generous (on the part of American taxpayers) and highly successful, though some recent writings warn against overestimating its role—the sums involved were only about 4 percent of Europe's GNP per year, and their effects may have been mainly political and psychological.[34] When it came to its end in 1953, U.S. aid to Europe had passed $23 billion ($88 billion in 1997 dollars, most of it as gifts), $16 billion of it for economic aid; it had covered 25 percent of Europe's imports. Food, raw materials, and equipment flowed into Europe, a minimum standard of living was guaranteed, domestic tranquillity and stability were promoted, confidence revived, controls were relaxed, and investment was stimulated. Western Germany was integrated into "Europe" and made its pivot. After its recovery, which the United States had sparked, Europe was put on the way to its equilibrium growth path. Both Barry Eichengreen (1995) and Van der Wee (1986) have therefore rightly seen the Marshall Plan as a decisive contribution, as the keystone to European recovery, a critical catalyst to growth.

Moreover, as the dollar gap was bridged, despite expert predictions of its permanence, restrictions on trade and payments among Western countries could be gradually lifted, and the Bretton Woods international monetary system could work. Some monetary unbalances were reduced when, in September 1949, many countries followed Britain's lead to devalue their currencies and establish new and realistic exchange rates with the dollar. Then the useful European Payments Union (EPU) was created in 1950; thanks to multilateral clearing, it facilitated trade among OEEC countries. During the 1950s, Western Europe retained a large trade deficit with the United States, but with invisible incomes it had a positive balance of payments and benefited from a gold and dollars inflow, so that its monetary reserves doubled from 1949 to 1956. OEEC countries were thus able, in 1958, to restore free convertibility of their currencies, for current international payments, and full multilateral trade. This was the end of the trade wars that had raged during the interwar period, and a more relaxed, pre-1914-like system was restored, with the exception of capital movements; up to the 1960s (and even later), most countries maintained exchange controls to prevent capital flights.

Still, the OEEC and EPU only provided for intergovernmental cooperation, not for integration or federation. Many people who had been through the experiences of war, defeat, and occupation, meanwhile, thought that the union of European countries was the only way to avoid a new European civil war and to create durable prosperity.[35] This "European idea," with its interlinked political and economic aspects, was common among the social democrats and still more so among the Christian Democrats who ruled continental countries in the postwar decades—politicians like the German Konrad Adenauer, the Italian Alcide de Gasperi, the Frenchman Robert Schuman, and the Belgian Paul-Henri Charles Spaak—but it was completely foreign to the British. The pillar of European union was to be a firm reconciliation between France and Germany. Right after the war, France asked for a policy punishing toward Germany, but there was a complete change after the blockade of Berlin, and Franco-German friendship became the order of the day. Advance toward union was achieved step by step, along the tactics of Jean Monnet, who hoped to gradually refashion Western Europe into a smaller version of the integrated single market that existed in the United States. In retrospect, however, it was a mistake not to establish a federal Europe, a United States of Europe, and not to destroy nation-states (especially France) at a stroke, in the dramatic circumstances of the early Cold War—a policy that the U.S. government ought to have imposed upon Europeans.

The first major steps were the Schuman Plan of May 1950 and the establishment of the European Coal and Steel Community in 1951 (ECSC). Its inspiration was both economic and political. France, lacking good cooking coal, needed secure access to German coal. The ECSC created a free market in coal and steel among the six member countries, under the supervision of a supranational "High Authority" that would prevent any discrimination. At the same time, it was hoped that economic conflicts among the six could be eliminated, especially between France and Germany. In fact, this political aspect was the most important, and the ECSC had little economic impact. It thus appeared necessary to go further, toward trade disarmament, inasmuch as intra-European trade much increased during the 1950s, with Germany as its neighbors' main partner. Thus, in 1957, the Treaty of Rome was signed and established the European Economic Community (EEC)—commonly called the Common Market—of six countries: Belgium, France, (West) Germany, Italy, Luxembourg, and the Netherlands (which included the old industrial heartland of the Continent). From 1959 to 1968, all tariffs among the six were gradually abolished, and a complete customs union with a moderate external tariff was created, while free movement of labor, services, and capital was to be gradually achieved. In order to implement these changes; to harmonize legislation; to take measures against cartels, monopolies, and government subsidies; and to encourage competition, supranational institutions were established in Brussels.[36] Though it could have played a leading role, Britain kept out at first and created in 1960 a European Free Trade Area (EFTA), of seven members, as a rival. It soon wanted, however, to join the EEC, but its entry was vetoed by the French president Charles de Gaulle, who suspected the British of planning to sabotage the community in order to work for a one-world free trade system; Britain achieved entry only in 1973. More countries joined, and in 1995 the European Union (EU; its name since 1993) had fifteen members, all the "Western" European countries except Norway and Switzerland. The EU also has "associated members" (mainly former European colonies, with mutual preferential treatment); this is a form of aid to the Third World.

The Golden Age

After this digression, we shall return to economics and to Europe in the years 1950 to 1973. This time is often called the golden age, a period of supergrowth, of unparalleled prosperity, of "miracles" (a somewhat misleading word, and one not to be reserved for Germany: there was certainly an Italian *miracolo*[37]); the French speak of "years of glory." Indeed, this was an exceptional, unique episode in the economic history of modern Europe, one that contrasts with both the period 1913–1950 and the years since 1973. After underperforming, economies overperformed; the Soviet Union and its satellites also did well (see below; in this section, only "capitalist" Europe will be considered), but high growth was a distinctly European phenomenon, as North America grew more slowly, and the Pacific Rim was only starting to develop.

Rates of growth were high, as table 4.2 (below) shows for the twelve Western European core countries. With the higher growth rates of the four countries of the periphery (Ireland, Portugal, Spain, and Greece; 5.7 percent per year for aggregate GDP and 5.2 percent for GDP per capita), in the whole of "capitalist Europe," GDP grew at 4.8 percent per year and product per capita at 4.1 percent; it more than doubled (as much as from 1870 to 1950, 80 years!). Moreover, some experts consider that those rates underestimate progress in the standard of living.

Cyclical fluctuations, when they occurred, were very mild, milder than in the United States, and were mostly in rates of growth; the combined GNP of Western Europe did not fall once between 1948 and 1973; several countries had small setbacks, but others had none. Unemployment fell to its lowest secular level: 2.4 percent of the labor force in the twelve core countries, on average, for 1950–1973 (3.6 percent in the periphery).

Inflation was kept at socially acceptable rates (4.1 percent per year, on average, for sixteen countries, but with a significant dispersion among them).

According to E. F. Denison, the national income of eight West European countries grew from 1948 to 1962 at a rate of 4.78 percent per year, with 1.69 percent resulting from increases in total factor input, and 3.07 percent—roughly two-thirds—from better productivity. The central fact was thus productivity growth and its trend toward conditional convergence. Unlike in the nineteenth century and the first half of the twentieth, the countries that were the poorest in 1950 (e.g., Greece and Spain) progressed faster than the richer ones; consequently, in the early 1970s, dispersion among European countries in levels of GDP per hour worked was far less pronounced than in 1950. The real GDP per capita ratio between the poorest and the richest West European countries was 1 to 5.7 in 1950, 1 to 2.9 in 1973; there was also some convergence among the provinces of certain countries, such as Italy. Thus, a core of countries with roughly similar and high standards of living emerged.[38] Moreover, after the sharp divergence of the period 1913–1950, there was a dramatic and unprecedented catch-up by Europe relative to the United States, as the latter's total factor productivity and GDP per capita grew more slowly, though the gap was far from being closed: in 1950, GDP per hour worked in twelve advanced European countries was only 46 percent of the Amer-

_____ Table 4.2 _____

Economic growth of twelve Western European countries,[a] 1913–1996 (percentage per year)

	1913–1950	1950–1973	1973–1996
Real GDP	1.4	4.6	1.9
Population	0.5	0.7	0.3[b]
Real GDP per capita	1.0	3.8	1.7
Real GDP per hour worked	1.9	4.7	2.3[b]

a. Austria, Belgium, Denmark, Finland, France, Germany, Italy, the Netherlands, Norway, Sweden, Switzerland, and the United Kingdom. Figures for the fifteen EU members and for "capitalist Europe" (sixteen countries) would be quite similar.

b. 1973–1992.

Sources: Maddison 1995, pp. 64, 80, 85, tables 3.2, 3.13a, and 3.18; Crafts and Toniolo, p. 2, table 1, using Maddison's data.

ican level; in 1973, it had risen to 70 percent (and in 1992, it was 87 percent).[39] There was also a convergence of real wage rates starting in the mid-1960s, so that, roughly, the core of Western Europe at the end of the golden age reached two-thirds of the U.S. standard of living; it had become an "affluent society," where only a minority still suffered from poverty, and it had adopted some American ways—such as the importance of the automobile (see table 4.3, below). Actually, the automobile industry —and the whole consumer durables industry—was one leading sector of high growth.

On the other hand, the gap in incomes and standards of living between Europe and the Third World had greatly widened.

Needless to say, many explanations of the golden age have been put forward, but they leave many loose ends, as it is demonstrated in an important book edited by Nicholas Crafts and Gianni Toniolo. First, there was a massive transfer of technology from the United States to Europe, which was reflected in rapid total productivity growth.[40] Such a transfer was easier after 1945 for various reasons, including the reduced importance of natural resources and market size (though both still play a role), plus lower freights for bulk materials; these changes also reduced the relative advantages that the United States had enjoyed. Moreover, circumstances created by the two world wars and the intervening depression had built up a backlog of technological innovations—particularly in mass-production techniques, which matched new demand patterns—that only waited to be used, a backlog of opportunities for swift catch-up. The poor economic performance of Europe from 1914 to 1945, its backwardness in relation to the United States, partly explains the high growth of the 1950s and 1960s. There was also a major increase in industrial research in Europe, but the United States retained a clear technological leadership (especially in the most research-intensive and high-tech sectors), thanks, particularly, to a higher ratio of research-and-development expenditure to

Table 4.3
Private automobiles per 1,000 inhabitants, 1950–1990

	1950	*1970*	*1990*
United States	264	436	504
Western Europe	20	182	377[a]

a. Germany had the highest individual number at 485 per 1,000.

GDP (though the gap would be smaller for nonmilitary R and D). Still, if the United Kingdom, France, Germany, and Italy received from the United States half of the technology they acquired through patents and licenses, they received as much from one another. Eventually, Europeans were not too far from the technological frontier, in some fields at least: nuclear power stations went into operation in Britain in 1956, in France in 1959; the first (and last) supersonic airliner to fly was the Franco-British Concorde, in 1970, but this technological feat led to commercial defeat because of American ill will and the oil crisis. Moreover, Europeans understood that this large potential for growth existed, and a new ideology of productivity spread; a new, progressive generation of business leaders and managers emerged and made a managerial revolution, which included the introduction in the 1960s of the multidivisional system of business organization.[41] Finally, there was a social basis for productivity-enhancing policies.

Transfers of technology need investment, and indeed there was a large increase in capital formation (because of the backlog of new technology, high rates of return were ensured), which reached unprecedented high levels of broad capital, both physical and human.[42] Actually, despite the losses of World War II, Europe had an adequate stock of human capital, of skilled and knowledgeable people, such that its social capability for growth had not been destroyed; it was only hibernating. In the golden age, meanwhile, the capability for catch-up was enhanced by the spread of education at both high school and university levels. Thus, the acceleration in growth during this time period came partly from greater accumulation of broad capital, which has constant returns so that growth is endogenous. Thanks to full employment, this capital was fully used.

Economic policies and institutional structures (both national and international) also played a role; many economists see them as of paramount importance, and at any rate they affect the investment process. The so-called German miracle emerged from the liberal institutional changes of the late 1940s, particularly the currency reform (which invalidated nine-tenths of the money in circulation) and the liberation of prices in June 1948.[43] There was political and social stability and a good deal of general consensus, which was not unconnected with full employment and the welfare state, a reasonable level of government expenditure, and altogether enhanced social capability for growth. Moreover, some obstacles to growth that had existed during the interwar period were eliminated: there was increased openness to international trade, and tariffs were lowered. In some countries (e.g., France, Spain, Ireland), there was an acceleration in the pace of growth in the late 1950s, as a result of moves away from interventionist and protectionist policies. The volume of exports by the twelve European core countries increased sevenfold between 1950 and 1973, at a rate of 8.6 percent per year (versus 3.2 percent from 1870 to 1913). Now freer trade has the potential to disseminate knowledge, the fruits of research and development, the technological advances by leading countries. Mancur Olson has also argued that many special-interest groups were broken down as a consequence of the war (especially in Germany), but his views have been disputed.

Then the EEC created free trade within a market of almost 200 million people, and its establishment coincided with a most prosperous period for the six member countries; nonetheless, some writers maintain that a causal connection is not proven, and that the six economies were growing quickly and integrating before the Treaty of Rome was enforced. Their fast growth in the early years of the EEC did not in fact result from their rising intertrade, which was mainly in similar manufactures (like motor vehicles), so that gains from trade were small. However, exchanges of manufactured goods between industrial countries can be seen as one of the most dynamic factors behind growth. In addition, expectations of freer trade and of a steady decline of barriers were liable at least to stimulate growth. Indeed, trade among the six increased sixfold from 1958 to 1970 (when it was 28 percent of world exports), from 30 percent of their total trade to 52 percent (1972). And, thanks to the widening of the market, trade creation, in relations among the six, outweighed trade diversion. Lastly, while little income convergence among the six had taken place from 1870 to World War II, trade liberalization under the EEC was accompanied by a marked reduction in income disparity among its members, due to a movement to new, higher-growth paths by each country.

The fairly liberal trade and monetary regimes that prevailed at the world level also played a role. Like the gold standard before 1914, they were conducive to technology transfers, and there was a clear correlation between globalization and convergence.

Another development that worked toward globalization was the progress of multinational companies (MNCs) and of foreign direct investment (FDI)—even though the size of international capital flows, relatively to world product, had fallen to an all-time low. In the post–World War II period, MNCs were mainly large American corporations that wanted to bypass tariff barriers in Europe and then to take advantage of the huge market that the EEC had created. By 1966, almost 9,000 subsidiaries of American companies operated in Western Europe—particularly in manufacturing, as in petrochemicals and automobiles. For European companies, the Common Market rather reduced the incentive to set up plants in other European countries, but there was a good deal of such investment nonetheless. On the other hand, many British—and continental—companies retained and developed their overseas FDI, particularly in the British Commonwealth and in former colonies. Altogether, by 1973, Britain, West Germany, Switzerland, France, and the Netherlands had 4,607 MNCs—49 percent of the world total (but only 101 of the 260 largest MNCs). In 1997, 39 of the 100 biggest MNCs were based in the EU, and 5 more in Switzerland, compared to 30 in the United States and 18 in Japan. Conversely, to take just one example, in 1970 there were 200 foreign-owned manufacturing companies operating in Sweden (by 1993, their number was to rise to 651, and they employed 16 percent of persons working in Swedish industry). MNCs are generally efficient firms, technical leaders, and innovators; they have played a significant role in transfers of technology and of management methods.

The increasing activity of MNCs was one factor in the emergence and expansion of the Eurodollar and Eurocurrency market (nothing to do with the euro—the new single European currency, which was launched in 1999), which specializes in borrowing and lending currencies outside their country of origin. It started in earnest at the time of the Cuban missile crisis (1962), when the state bank of the USSR, fearing that its U.S. accounts would be frozen, shifted its foreign-currency reserves to London banks while retaining them in dollars. The Soviet satellites followed suit, and the Eurodollar was born: a transnational currency denominated in dollars but domiciled in London. Shortly afterward, the American government established a heavy tax on payment of interest to foreigners; this drove from New York to London the flourishing foreign-bond market and produced the Eurobond, again denominated in dollars but domiciled in London. This international capital market greatly expanded in the 1960s, as most foreign-exchange transactions were gradually freed in Europe and it was more profitable for American funds to be deposited in European banks or in European subsidiaries of American banks than to be left at home. At first Eurodollars dominated, but the German mark and the Swiss franc also became Eurocurrencies. After the oil crisis of 1973, the Eurocurrency market was a major channel for recycling petro-dollars from OPEC states to oil-buying states. The amount of transactions on the Eurocurrency market was thus to become enormous, but the system was highly volatile. Still, it was a sign that Europe (or at least London, Luxembourg, and Zurich) had again become a major financial center.

A last factor that favored growth, in some countries at least, must be mentioned: an elastic labor supply resulting from the inflow of refugees from the East (mainly in Germany), from substantial immigration of Mediterranean origin, and from the reallocation of resources from low-productivity agriculture to other sectors.[44] European agriculture underwent a revolution after World War II: it was mechanized and industrialized; the use of high-yield crop varieties, herbicides, pesticides, and artificial fertilizers was generalized; and farms became much larger; "peasants" almost died out, to be replaced by "farmers" in the American sense. This had unfortunate consequences for the environment, as hedgerows and trees were felled and rivers and underground waters were polluted by chemicals. But yields per acre increased over 50 percent for all grains, and productivity per worker rose faster than in any other sector: at a rate over 5 percent per year in French agriculture after 1960; from that year to 1990, French output of cereals increased threefold (much more than in the preceding 150 years). Driven out by low incomes and mechanization, labor left agriculture on a massive scale. In six Western European countries (including the four large ones), male agricultural employment fell from 15 million in 1950 to 4 million in 1980. In the twelve core countries, employment in agriculture (plus fishing and forestry) fell from 24.7 percent of total employment in 1950 to 9.7 percent in 1973 (and 4.5 percent in 1995). The fall was especially steep in France and Italy, which had retained 30 to 40 percent of their labor force in agriculture, and steeper in the four countries of the periphery, where agricultural employment fell from 50 percent of total employment in 1950 to 27 percent in 1973 and 11 percent in 1995. Nonetheless, Western Europe was more or less self-sufficient in farm produce. There was convergence in productivity among European countries (though the Mediterranean countries remained behind) but not with the United States, which actually widened its lead, thanks, inter alia, to a lower labor-to-land ratio. A 1975 index of gross added value per person employed in agriculture, with the United States at 100, put Britain at 55, France at 40, and Germany at 30. "European farmers face an almost insuperable natural disadvantage in comparison with that land abundant continent" (O'Brien and Prados de la Escosura 1992).

However, the shift of labor from the land and increased productivity in agriculture contributed to total productivity growth and to overall catch-up. This was one reason why Germany and France, which had large reserves of agricultural labor, outperformed Britain, which had none. An elastic labor supply also contributed to wage moderation, and thus to reasonable inflation.

Actually, despite the overall trend toward convergence, there were significant differences in the performances of individual countries. The most important was that Britain had a rate of growth that, though fast and unprecedented by its own historical standards, was slower than all other core countries (2.5 percent per year for GDP per capita, from 1951 to 1973, versus 4 percent and more for the large continental states) and was overtaken in income per capita, first by Germany, then by France in the 1960s, and eventually by Italy around 1980, not to mention by small but rich countries, like Austria and Norway. By 1975, Britain was seventeenth in the world in GDP per capita (and at the same rank in 1995), whereas it had been first or second a century earlier.[45]

This relative decline of Britain—like the earlier one before 1914, although the United Kingdom had remained ahead in income per capita at that time—has produced a huge literature. Recently, Charles Feinstein (in Floud and McCloskey) proposed a "backward convergence hypothesis": in 1945, countries like Germany, France, and Italy started from a much greater degree of backwardness than Britain and so had the scope for achieving high rates of growth, especially in productivity, which were simply not attainable in Britain; the latter's relative decline was therefore inevitable, and neither the British people nor their leaders had much responsibility for it.[46] This last point is questionable. In the 1950s and 1960s, the investment ratio and therefore productivity gains were lower in Britain than on the Continent.[47] A major factor was the "stop and go" policies that all governments followed and that repeatedly checked investment. Admittedly, the stops were imposed to fight recurrent balance-of-payments crises, because governments—and the Bank of England—gave priority to the defense of sterling's exchange-rate parity. Now deficits in the balance of payments resulted mainly from heavy military expenditures abroad, or, namely, from the British leaders' determination to preserve their country's world role. This was a clear case of a declining empire being weakened by "overstretching."[48] Supply-side weaknesses in management, industrial relations, and training also cannot be dismissed. Some other writers have stressed that the deterioration of Britain's position was only obvious during the golden age and that, since 1979, thanks to the "Thatcher revolution," supply-side reforms have improved the country's social capability, and that it has been able to maintain a broadly constant relative position with other European countries. It is correct that Britain's relative decline has been arrested (something in which mistaken policies by some rival countries have also played a part).

Still, to some Britons, the word "decline" is unpalatable, and they have maintained that GDP per capita is not a good summary of economic performance or of well-being and that a human development index gives to Britain a leading position. They also point out that, in the 1960s, the City of London was engaged in a process of reinternationalization, even though world-trade finance moved largely out of sterling after the 1967 devaluation; British banks seized the opportunity offered by the fast emergence of Euromarkets. And in the 1960s and 1970s, the City, as the world's foremost financial-knowledge center, attracted many financial "immigrants."

There is no doubt, on the other hand, that Germany soon became the biggest European economy—a position that reunification (1991) only made stronger—and the dominant country. However, the often-used expression the "German miracle" is somewhat misleading in that it ignores much hard work, well-conceived economic policies, and other advantages —such as Germany's central position, which makes it a large natural trading partner of continental countries, or the fact that its industrial potential had been modernized under the Nazi regime and had not much suffered from the war.[49] Monetary and wage policies were more stability oriented than in most other countries, largely due to the Bundesbank, which had acquired its autonomy in the 1950s. The deutsche mark was a hard currency, but without loss of export competitiveness. Indeed, German prosperity was export driven: the ratio of exports to GDP rose from 10 percent in 1950 to 30 percent in 1989, and Germany's world market share from 2 percent to over 10 percent. In this respect, its specialization in capital goods (machinery, transport equipment, chemicals, and the like) was a key asset in the 1950s and 1960s, when there was an investment boom in its main trading partners.

As for France, its performances were remarkable relative to both the majority of Western countries and its own economic growth in the past, which had been "moderate." Moreover, one must take into account the dreadful human and material losses it had suffered during the two world wars, the burden of colonial wars in Vietnam and Algeria, the power of the Communist Party and the unions it controlled, and clumsy interventions by the bureaucracy. Nonetheless, from 1950 to 1973 real GDP grew at an average rate of 5 percent per year, GDP per hour worked (e.g., labor productivity) at the same rate, and GDP per capita at 4 percent. The economy was markedly modernized and the standard of living greatly increased.

The southern European countries, for their part, achieved much progress, as the periphery grew faster than the core during the golden age (and also after 1973). Italy effectively became an industrial nation —and a major exporter, thanks to a thick network of small and medium-sized, export-oriented, light-manufacturing firms in its northern and central regions. But substantial government intervention did not heal the relative underdevelopment of the south. Spain had stagnated under the Franco regime, as it followed, up to 1959, an irrational autarkic policy that resulted in a static agriculture and an inefficient industry. Nonetheless, growth started in the 1950s and accelerated during the 1960s, when the process of convergence with the rest of Europe began. Structural change also took place, with an "agricultural revolution" and industry overcoming agriculture from an employment point of view. Though southern countries—except northern Italy—remained poorer than those to the north, the gap between the two regions, which had been an enduring aspect of Europe's economic structure since the seventeenth century, was markedly narrowed during the second half of the twentieth century. A case of late industrialization (it started in the 1960s) is that of Ireland, the "emerald tiger"; its GDP has grown at 4 percent per year since 1960 (except for some years in the 1980s), and its GDP per capita, which was 63 percent of Britain's in 1987, overtook the latter in the late 1990s. Large FDI and help from Brussels have played a significant role in this "Asiatic" growth.

Altogether, the golden age did see the reemergence of Western Europe as a major economic power, in international trade (its share of world exports was over 40 percent) and also in monetary affairs. During the 1960s, the dollar weakened while the deutsche mark, the Swiss franc, and the Dutch guilder became hard currencies. The dollar gap was forgotten as the U.S. balance of payments went into large deficits. Faced with the success of the EEC, President John F. Kennedy wanted to integrate it within the orbit of the United States; he proposed an "Atlantic Partnership" between America and an enlarged EEC, and a sharp reduction of barriers. This project, however, was stopped by de Gaulle's veto to the admission of Britain into the EEC and by Kennedy's assassination. On the other hand, an informal collaboration developed between Europe's central banks and the U.S. Federal Reserve Board, with regular meetings in Basel, the seat of the Bank for International Settlements, which had been the official agency for intra-European payments within the EPU framework. And yet a few years earlier, European leaders had come to Washington to beg for money.

The Eastern Bloc

There was also a golden age for the USSR and its Eastern European satellites. As mentioned earlier, the Soviet Union suffered dreadful human and material losses during World War II—the "Second Great Patriotic War." Despite serious defeats during the summer of 1941, the Soviet system did not collapse and the economy displayed much resilience. The Nazis and their allies had occupied large territories; over 20 percent of Soviet industrial capacity had been lost; and in 1942 the country's GNP was only two-thirds of its 1940 level. Nonetheless, owing to evacuation eastward of key factories, and to strenuous efforts by workers (and consequent productivity rises), munitions production in 1942 was three times higher than in 1940, and by 1944 it was four times larger. The USSR actually succeeded in outproducing richer Germany in the things that mattered—battlefront weapons—and it won the war thanks to masses of men and equipment. For military purposes, it managed to mobilize a share (over 50 percent at its peak) of a reduced national product that was almost as great as Britain's; this was, of course, at the expense of production for civilian purposes and of living standards, which had already been low before the war. In addition, aid by the western Allies (i.e., the United States) was significant: it was equivalent to 5 percent of Soviet GNP in 1942, 10 percent in 1943–1944.

Postwar recovery was fast (see table 4.4): by 1950, GDP, which in 1946 had been 21 percent below its 1940 level, exceeded it by 22 percent. Until the death of Stalin (1953), the same economic policies as before the war were enforced, especially top priority for capital-goods industries, and the use of forced labor was even extended.[50] However, the gulag was largely dismantled under Stalin's successors, especially Nikita Khrushchev (general secretary of the Communist Party, 1953–1964), who also tried to introduce significant economic reforms.[51] Still, de-Stalinization was to fail—even though the worst Stalinist excesses disappeared; but it had irreversible consequences: sacrificing consumption to accumulation was never to be as absolute as under Stalin.

Agriculture, which was lagging far behind industry—with low productivity (15 percent of the U.S. level in 1952) and low yields, benefited from a sharp increase in investment, particularly to put into cultivation

_____ *Table 4.4* _____

Economic growth of the USSR, 1928–1989 (percentage per year)

	1928–1940	*1946–1950*	*1950–1973*	*1973–1989*
Real GDP	5.1	11.4	4.8	1.9[a]
Real GDP per capita	3.8	10.3	3.4	0.9
Real GDP per hour worked	—	—	3.4	–0.8[b]

a. 1.3 for 1971–1985, according to a recent calculation.

b. 1973–1992.

Source: Calculated from Maddison 1995, pp. 198–99, 212, 267, tables C-16c, D-1c, and J-5.

extensive virgin lands to the southeast of the Urals.[52] Prices paid by the state to collective farms were much increased. There was also a relative and absolute, but irregular, progress in resources devoted to consumer goods (especially durables, such as radio sets) and to urban housing construction.

Economic growth from 1950 to 1965 was thus rather fast and better balanced—at least apparently—than earlier. During this period, production increased by 79 percent in agriculture and by 230 percent in industry (by 1965 it was fourteen times bigger than in 1928), and GDP doubled.[53] Moreover, the USSR showed itself capable of remarkable technological achievements: it had exploded an A-bomb in 1949, and an H-bomb in 1953, and it was first in the world to launch a satellite (*Sputnik*, 1957) and a manned spacecraft (1961), thus creating much alarm in the West.[54] Meanwhile, the standard of living for the mass of the population increased substantially from 1956 to 1962, for the first time since the 1920s—though it remained far below American and even West European standards, and shortages were frequent. Still, the USSR had caught up to some degree with the West, as far as the levels of industrialization and technology were concerned (but not in labor productivity, while—as seen earlier—Western Europe was greatly narrowing the productivity gap with the United States). Thus, Khrushchev could tell the capitalist world: "We will bury you"; and many people, including anticommunists, believed around 1960 that the USSR was catching up with the United States.

Actually, the Soviet leader was conscious of the command economy's shortcomings (to which we shall return later), and he made serious reform efforts. Planning in volumes was given up, and targets were fixed in monetary terms; the profit criterion was introduced in the management of firms; and a decentralization of decisions and, then, a project of regionalization were adopted. And, as mentioned earlier, more attention was paid to agriculture and to consumer-goods industries, but in a discontinuous way, and actually agriculture was to suffer—under Khrushchev and later—from brutal alternations between concessions and hardening. Only a reduction in military expenditures could have given some leeway, particularly in arbitration between consumption and investment, but after being lowered from 1955 to 1960, they were increased again from 1961 onward. Moreover, Khrushchev was erratic, his supposed reforms lacked coherence and, anyway, were fiercely opposed by the bureaucracy, especially the central planning agencies and ministries in Moscow. After a disastrous harvest in 1963, he was ousted from power. In the years that followed, Prime Minister Aleksey Kosygin tried some more reforms (e.g., of the price system), but to little effect. In the 1970s, the clock was to be turned back to "recentralization" and compulsory planning. Indeed, under elderly, sick, and inert general secretaries of the Communist Party —Leonid Brezhnev (1964–1982) and his two successors—the USSR entered "the era of stagnation."

One reason for the "we will bury you" was that socialism was no longer confined within one country, but had expanded, particularly in Eastern Europe (and also, of course, to China, Vietnam, Cuba, etc.).

Thanks to the Red Army's victories in the later stages of World War II, the Soviet Union was by 1945 in control of Europe eastward of a line from Lübeck to Trieste (with the exception of Greece), a boundary that soon became an "Iron Curtain." Indeed, at the Yalta Conference, the United States and Britain had accepted that the USSR would play a major role in that vast area. However, Stalin was intent on imposing a complete Sovietization. There was first a transition period, during which power was somewhat shared between the Communists and other political parties and a mixed economy was established; only large estates and large firms were nationalized, and a substantial private sector survived. But after a couple of years, the Communist parties imposed their dictatorship (e.g., by the coup of Prague in February 1948) and introduced uniformly the Soviet-Stalinist model. The countries of east-central Europe (ECE) became "people's democracies"—their regimes were actually undemocratic and unpopular—and nonmarket, centrally planned economies that were "building socialism"; to many observers, they seemed "satellites" of the Soviet Union (though Yugoslavia, as early as 1948, and Albania and Romania later, escaped from direct Soviet control while retaining socialist regimes). For those "ferryboat countries" of Eastern Europe, which have moved alternately eastward and westward, this represented their most drastic separation from the West, while Sovietization imposed an apparent unity to regions that had varied historical and cultural traditions and different economies at the start (though most of them were backward).

Industry and banking were fully nationalized, and the bulk of the land was collectivized, though not to the same extent as in the Soviet Union —especially in Poland. Peasants, who just after World War II had benefited from an agrarian reform that distributed among small owner-occupiers the land of large estates, were now forced to join collective ("cooperative") or state farms. For instance, in Hungary, within fifteen months in 1959–1961, the peasantry was liquidated. At short intervals, there were two abrupt and contradictory changes, and every plot of land changed hands—and farming systems—twice. Moreover, crash programs of industrialization under five-year plans (as in the USSR) were introduced, with the stress, of course, on heavy industry (Bulgaria created its own steel industry). Capacity was greatly increased, but consumer-goods industries were neglected. Productivity, though rising (see table 4.5), remained much lower than in the West, despite the catch-up potential that the people's democracies had due to their backwardness at the start. This failure to narrow the productivity gap persisted up to the fall of communism; economic growth was extensive, based on new labor and capital inputs. Agriculture, for its part, suffered from collectivization, and grain output grew more slowly than in the USSR, while yields were one-half to three-quarters of West European ones.

Nonetheless, an industrial base was built up or enlarged, and the peasant societies of most of ECE were transformed into industrial (or at least semi-industrial) and urban ones, and a fast rate of growth was attained: 4.8 percent per year for the aggregate GDP of six people's democracies, from 1950 to 1973, and 3.9 percent for their GDP per capita. Strangely enough, these rates are close to those for the twelve capitalist Western European countries during the same period (see tables 4.2 and 4.5 for comparison) and, apparently, they made the Soviet satellites one of the most successful regions of the periphery, but, it must be emphasized, they are overestimates. Based on more realistic data, the level of personal consumption per capita in those countries deteriorated relative to Western Europe and was lower than before World War II. Still, growth was faster in the most backward countries (Bulgaria, Romania) than in Poland and Czechoslovakia, especially the latter, where rigid centralized planning

_____ Table 4.5_____

Economic growth of six socialist countries,
1950–1989 (percentage per year)[a]

	1950–1973	1973–1989
Real GDP	4.8	1.7
Real GDP per capita	3.9	1.2
Real GDP per hour worked	4.3	0.4[b]

———————

a. Bulgaria, Hungary, Poland, Romania, Czechoslovakia, and Yugoslavia (except for GDP per hour). As mentioned earlier, these Western recalculations of Soviet and socialist countries' growth remain overestimates, at best a possible upper limit.

b. Three countries only and for 1973–1992.

Source: Calculated from Maddison 1995, pp. 198–99, 212–13, 267.

was inappropriate for a relatively advanced economy and led to stagnation in the 1960s.

Foreign trade was, of course, a state monopoly, but the most interesting development was the effort of economic integration within the Soviet bloc. In 1949, the Council of Mutual Economic Assistance (commonly called COMECON) was set up by the USSR and its satellites. An answer to the Marshall Plan and to the OEEC, and ostensibly intended to coordinate the development of socialist countries and to promote socialist division of labor among them, it was more compelling and comprehensive than Western institutions for cooperation.[55] Actually, the USSR, which had already extracted substantial "reparations" from Eastern Germany, Hungary, and Romania (as former enemies in World War II), at first used the COMECON to exploit its satellites (e.g., through barter transactions at arbitrary prices) and to make them more dependent. However, from 1953–1956 onward, it granted better conditions: it sold raw materials to its partners at very low prices and accepted unfavorable terms of trade. There was thus a paradox in the Soviet bloc: the leader supplied its satellites (some of them with more advanced economies) with cheap primary products and bought from them, at high prices, manufactured goods of poor quality. The United States and its allies, meanwhile, had imposed an embargo upon exports to the Soviet bloc of a number of strategic materials and products (still, it did not prevent Eastern countries from importing a good deal of Western technology). As a consequence there was a complete reorientation of ECE's foreign trade: before World War II, it had been mainly with Germany and Western Europe; now it became mainly an intra–Eastern bloc trade, in which most satellites' trade was with the USSR.[56] From 1950 to 1978, the growth of intra-COMECON trade was rather fast, but it remained a small share (even a decreasing one) of world trade, while the foreign trade–GNP ratio of its members was low. After all, their development model was autarkic and their foreign trade was managed by bureaucrats and mainly based on bilateral agreements. The division of Europe into two blocs, with limited contacts, was both political and economic.

Altogether the people's democracies' economies suffered from the same defects as the USSR's; the standard of living remained low or even fell (except for the highly privileged *nomenklatura*), particularly because of heavy investment and military expenditure, and economic discontent was fueled by national resentment against foreign (Soviet) domination. Repeatedly, therefore, Communist rule was threatened by popular movements, but each time they were crushed by force (though only Hungary, in 1956, suffered much bloodshed). Nonetheless, in some countries, the

Communist leadership concluded that reforms, including some liberalization, were necessary. In 1956, the forced collectivization of agriculture
was stopped in Poland. In Hungary, there was a change of agricultural policy in 1964–1965 that provided for a relatively free market in farm produce
and thanks to which food supplies became plentiful. This success led to
more comprehensive reforms in 1968, the "New Economic Mechanism,"
which mitigated planning, abolished compulsory targets, and gave some autonomy to firms. There was henceforth a distinctly Hungarian socialist
economy, which was rather prosperous, but this was an exception; in other
countries half-baked reforms were useless, while alternation between liberalization and hardening was destabilizing. On the other hand, any serious reform involved unforeseeable risks. In Czechoslovakia, the fifth plan
(1966–1970) provided for decentralizing the planning mechanism, freeing
some prices, using profits for guiding resource allocation. But it was soon
realized that economic decentralization was not compatible with single-
party, bureaucratic rule. This led to calls for democracy, for "socialism with
a human face," and to invasion by the Warsaw Pact armies in August 1968.
Therefore, in both the Soviet Union and its satellites (except Hungary),
the centrally planned economic system remained substantially intact when
its "golden age" ended, and it contained germs of decomposition.

Slowing Down and Not Working

"Will the European miracle continue?" This question posed by
Sidney Pollard in his 1974 book had indeed just been answered. The oil
shock of 1973 is generally considered the end of the golden age: OPEC,
the cartel of oil-exporting countries, decided to raise the price of oil by
a factor of four. Petroleum by now had largely displaced coal in Europe,
but the latter had little oil and was dependent on imports from the Middle East.[57] It therefore had to pay a heavy tribute to Arab potentates, even
though balance-of-payments problems were not terribly serious, as most
petro-dollars found their way back to the West by means of OPEC deposits
in the Eurocurrency market, where Western countries borrowed to finance their trade deficits. France alone decided to go all nuclear.[58] The
rise in the price of oil—which other primary produce followed—fueled
inflation and caused other disturbances, including a braking effect on
consumption in Europe. In 1979–1980, there was a second and sharp
price hike—with similar consequences.[59] However, before the oil shock
of 1973, the late 1960s and the early 1970s had already seen some major
departures from the main trends of previous decades, especially the breakdown of the Bretton Woods system in August 1971.

By this point, the golden age was over, succeeded by a period of slow-down that continues for Europe presently, one that also affected the so-cialist countries. Production and productivity growth rates for the period 1973–1994 were only half those of the golden age (see table 4.2, above): "capitalist Europe's" (consisting of sixteen countries) real GDP grew in the aggregate at 2.1 percent per year (compared to 4.8 percent in 1950–1973), per capita at 1.8 percent (versus 3.6 percent). The slowdown continued in the 1990s (especially in the big countries); from 1991 to 1998 the GDP of the EU fifteen only grew at 1.7 percent per year. However, the growth of productivity also slowed down in the United States, up to the mid-1990s, so that the catching-up process continued for some time.[60] Consequently, unemployment increased fast: in the fifteen OECD Euro-pean countries, it rose from 2.8 percent of the working-age population in 1960–1967 to 5.1 percent in 1970–1979 and then 9.2 percent in 1986–1990; the four countries of the periphery had the highest rates (12.2 percent in 1984–1993). Altogether, in the 1980s unemployment was three times higher than in the 1960s and it became worse in the 1990s. Cyclical volatility also increased: in the downturns, several countries had negative rates of growth for their GDP (e.g., in 1975, 1981, and 1993), but they were low and, unlike in the 1930s, there was no sharp fall of pro-duction and incomes, which went on increasing, but more slowly. More-over, in another departure from the 1930s, there was no strong protec-tionist response to recession, even though the EEC imposed antidumping duties in 1978 and took steps to limit imports of Japanese automobiles, and international trade did not collapse. In fact, it went on growing, but not as fast as in the golden age: the rate of growth of exports (volume) from twelve European core countries fell from 8.6 percent per year in 1950–1973 to 4.2 percent in 1973–1992, but it increased for the countries of the periphery. Interdependence among European countries went on rising; the ratio of foreign trade to GDP in the core countries was to reach 30 percent by 1992 (it had been 9 percent in 1950).

There was also inflation, as a result of rises in the prices of oil and other raw materials, of a wage explosion after workers' strikes (this had started at the end of the golden age, c. 1968), and of floating exchange rates. Be-tween 1974 and 1983, the twelve core countries had double-digit inflation for most years (with a peak at 13.4 percent in one year) and an average rate of price growth of 9.4 percent per year. Then the inflation rate fell to 3.8 percent annually for 1983–1995 and lower during the late 1990s. There were marked differences between countries in inflation rates—and there-fore a number of monetary adjustments—but later a convergence toward stabilization prevailed. Economists thus forged the ugly word "stagflation."

Indeed, recent studies have shown that inflation had a negative short-term impact upon growth rates and created unemployment: sharp rises in wage rates per unit produced led firms to make savings in the use of labor.

Finally, the process of convergence also slowed down, the inverse correlation between initial income level and subsequent growth became much weaker, and a kind of stability prevailed, so that presently one can observe a core of fourteen European countries fairly consistent across different convergence indicators, which had 1999 GDP per capita between $21,800 and $27,600 at purchasing-power parity (PPP); they also show a convergence of macroeconomic indicators and productive structure.[61] Down the scale come three catching-up Mediterranean countries that are by no means poor and that receive generous aid from the EU (Spain made much progress after entering it in 1986); and then the newly liberated economies of eastern Europe.

On the other hand, though income disparities among EU members have fallen, inequalities among regions within countries have often risen; in Italy after 1970, the convergence between north and south came to a stop. A concentration of industry and wealth has developed within the "blue banana," which extends from Florence to London, across northern Italy, Switzerland, Alsace, southern Germany, the Rhineland, the Netherlands, Flanders, and southeastern England, with outposts in Île-de-France (which generates 5 percent of the EU's GDP), around Lyon, and in Austria. This large area, reminiscent of medieval Lotharingia, and where the EU's capitals—Brussels, Luxembourg, and Frankfurt—are located, flourishes, while many outlying areas are withering away.

However, this dismal picture must be qualified: rates of growth since 1973 appear uncomfortably low because of the high expectations that the golden age had created, but they are not unsatisfactory if the secular trend is taken into account. Growth per capita (which has taken place in all western countries) is higher than in the interwar period, equal to that of the *belle époque,* and much better than before 1890.[62]

Indeed, the case can be made that the high growth rates of the golden age were not sustainable in the long run, inasmuch as they were based upon the simultaneous—but unrepeatable—occurrence of favorable circumstances. And the golden age has been described as an accidental, particular, transitory historical episode, the catching up for the ground lost because of two world wars and the economic collapse of the 1930s. It was a one-time opportunity, which had been seized. As for trade liberalization, it had greatly progressed during the golden age, and there was not too much scope left—except in the matter of services. Moreover, from the late 1960s, some threatening clouds had gathered, so that the oil shock was not the sole factor of the new and darker *konjunktur.* The Bretton Woods system had become unstable, as it increasingly postulated both American deficits and willingness of Europeans to hold dollar-denominated reserves rather than gold, and it finally broke down. In May 1971, the West German government decided to abstain from further intervention to maintain the existing parity of the dollar; the deutsche mark and the Dutch guilder were let to float. As a result, there was a flight from the dollar and on 15 August, President Richard Nixon suspended its convertibility into gold. Discussions about a new international monetary system did not lead anywhere because the United States was not interested. Though the dollar was inconvertible and devalued, America retained a hegemonic position and a de facto dollar standard prevailed, with a "benign neglect" of the floating dollar's rate of exchange. This was to the disadvantage of the rest of the world and especially of Europeans, who had to go on accepting massive quantities of dollars. Moreover, floating exchange rates created uncertainty, enormous speculative flows of capital (controls on capital transfers were abolished in one country after another), and a vicious circle of inflation for the weaker economies. The establishment in 1979 of the European Monetary System was not an adequate remedy.

On the other hand, returns from high investment and from transfers of technology began to diminish. Wage explosions (in 1968–1969) and higher taxation squeezed profit rates to a level that was incompatible with the boom's continuance, inasmuch as rates of productivity growth shrank relative to wages, and investment therefore declined. There also was a shift from manufacturing to services, where productivity growth is generally slower, and the gap for catching up with the United States had narrowed. In all, there was a deterioration of the delicate balance, national and international, of the golden age, and the latter's end is not surprising in a long-run view.

What is more surprising is that as of 2000 the slowdown had lasted for more than twenty years (with fluctuations, of course, and national differences: some periods were better for a number of countries, worse for others), and that for a long time the situation grew gradually worse, especially in the area of employment. In 1996, the EU had 18 million unemployed, almost 11 percent of the total labor force—a level at which it had been stuck for several years. Subsequently, there was an improvement: in December 1999, the EU had 15 million unemployed, 8.8 percent of the labor force (but 9.6 percent in the Eurozone of eleven countries). Of course, unemployment rates greatly vary among countries, from 2.6 percent in Luxembourg and the Netherlands to 10.4 percent in France and

15 percent in Spain. The EU is roughly divided between two halves: in one the unemployment rate is under 6 percent; in the other, it is higher.[63] What a contrast with the 13 million jobs created in the United States from 1990 to 1998 and its 4 percent unemployment rate in January 2000! Indeed, from 1985 to 1997, employment grew at a rate of 0.3 percent in the EU, 1.7 percent in the United States.[64] The arsenal of measures (admittedly piecemeal and small-scale) that European governments have taken to reduce unemployment have had little effect.

"Deindustrialization" is often seen as a major reason for the unemployment that devastates Europe, but some qualifications are necessary.[65] Undoubtedly, there has been a relative decline of industrial employment to the benefit of services, so that, in the very long run, and as far as employment is concerned, the decline of agriculture and the rise of services are the only permanent trends: the progress of industry was only temporary. Industrial employment as a share of total employment was 38.5 percent in 1965 in Western Europe and then fell gradually to 27 percent in 1995—one worker out of four (viz. one of six in the United States).[66] As for the share of services, it increased in all countries from the 1960s, and in the 1990s it has passed 50 percent everywhere and two-thirds in the "core countries." The contribution of manufacturing to GNP has also fallen markedly: in the fifteen EU members, it was 32 percent in 1996, compared to 3 percent for agriculture and 65 percent for services.[67]

Moreover, there also was an absolute decline in industrial employment, especially in the "old" industrialized countries—Britain, Belgium, France, Switzerland, Germany, and Sweden—which lost more than 9 million industrial jobs (a third of the total) between 1965 and 1995; the loss for the whole of western Europe was 11 million. From 1990 to 1996, industrial employment fell by 22 percent in the EU countries.

Still, deindustrialization took place mainly at the regional level. This was nothing new: since the industrial revolution—and even before—many industrial districts had declined and even died out. During the golden age, the difficulties that some areas underwent were camouflaged by overall prosperity. After 1973, however, deep depression struck many regions, especially the "black countries"—the industrial areas based on coal and steel. They had already been in trouble in the interwar period, but, starting in the 1960s, many went into terminal decline—despite ineffective and often counterproductive rescue attempts by governments. A journey along the Sambre and Meuse valleys in northern France and

Belgium, a region that was one of the cradles of the industrial revolution on the Continent but that is now a long rust belt, is very depressing.

Indeed, the industries that were crucial in the coalfields were among the worst sufferers in the late 1900s. Coal is, of course, the most spectacular disaster. In 1950, 2 million miners extracted 434 million tons in Western Europe; by 1995, 150,000 miners were left and the output was 135 million tons. Coal mining has ceased in Belgium; the last French coalfield will close in 2005. The peak British production in 1913 was 287 million tons; by 1995, it had fallen to 55 million (by 20,000 miners, down from 1.2 million in 1924). In 1998, only 15 percent of the EU's total primary energy supply came from coal. Competition by oil was the main cause of this collapse, but the noncompetitiveness of European coal mines played a part: much of the coal burned by the European steel industry is now imported by sea from far-off coalfields—in the United States, South Africa, Australia—and steelworks are now sited on the seaboard, not on the coalfields. Despite such moves as well as much rationalization and modernization, the European steel industry is in a fragile position, with a permanent excess capacity and a weak financial performance. Since the 1970s, its workforce has fallen from 900,000 to 300,000, and it has suffered from the emergence of such large overseas competitors as Japan, South Korea, and Brazil. However, the EU as a whole is the largest steel producer in the world—well ahead of China and the United States—and has become more competitive.

In the interwar period, the British cotton industry badly suffered from Asian competition. Still, this was only a harbinger of worse to come for almost all European textile industries. In Britain, the terminal crisis of the cotton industry started during the golden age, and by the 1980s most of it was gone; worsteds, woolens, and artificial textiles were struck later, but hard. By 1998, British textile industries were shedding five hundred jobs per day, while in France the number of workers in textiles and clothing fell by 60 percent from 1980 to 1999, leaving Italy the only European country among the ten top textile producers in the world. Altogether, from 1990 to 1996 in the EU countries, production of the textiles, clothing, and leather industries fell by 13 percent and employment by 37 percent.

Shipbuilding is also not far from extinction in Europe, especially in Britain, which before World War I produced half the world's new tonnage. This, moreover, is an aspect of the maritime decline of Europe. Few merchant ships sail today under European flags—except the Greek—though, if corporate control is considered, Greece is number one among the world merchant fleets, Norway fifth, and Britain sixth. The fishing industry is also in decline in most European countries because of overfishing and depletion of fish resources. The many small seaports of Cornwall and Brittany, which used to swarm with fishing boats, are nowadays almost exclusively used by pleasure boats.

This may not be the end of the story. The automobile industry suffers from persistent and profit-crushing overcapacity; the French and Italian automakers are threatened by more powerful competitors. The aerospace industry has some achievements to its credit, as Airbus has conquered about half the world market for airliners, almost on a par with Boeing, but it has thus incurred hostility in the United States.

In identifying the causes of deindustrialization, the main problem is determining their relative importance. Somewhat paradoxically, one of them has been the rise in the productivity of European industry, due to concentration, rationalization, automation, and robotization, which have made it possible to produce more goods with a smaller workforce. This is the case for industries like steel or automobiles, and also for explaining why prosperous branches have not absorbed the labor shed by dying ones (in the EU chemical industry, output increased by 12 percent from 1990 to 1996, yet employment fell by 18 percent).

On the other hand, deindustrialization is also the result of competition —by oil in the case of coal (inasmuch as there was a depletion of coal reserves, which pushed prices upward) and by emergent countries with low wages for many manufacturing industries. Thanks to globalization and free trade under GATT, the EU has been invaded by cheap foreign goods, and some of its industries have been delocalized to eastern Asia, North Africa, or even eastern Europe. Although the share of manufactured imports from developing countries (including the former Soviet bloc) in the EU's consumption has been small (2.7 percent in 1981, 3.2 percent in 1990), these imports have been concentrated in labor-intensive products (e.g., textiles, footwear, and electronics) and they have had a strong impact on firms, jobs, and wages in the relevant branches. Moreover, delocalization, or mass migration of investment to low-wage countries—which has only started—might become much worse. Admittedly, both higher productivity and foreign competition have mainly destroyed unskilled jobs, while skilled labor has rather benefited; globalization has thus caused a redistribution of incomes inside nations, to the detriment of unskilled labor.

To free traders, there is no reason to fear such changes. "It's wise to deindustrialise," claimed the *Economist* (26 Apr. 1997), as it is a natural consequence of economic progress, and eventually the effects upon rich countries of the Third World's growth will be beneficial. Manufacturing has become a genuinely international affair; Europe (and the United

States) are losing and will lose only its simpler, lowest-value-added parts, and will retain the sophisticated, higher-value sectors of the global chain —where new jobs will be created. Moreover, the old dichotomy between industry and services has been blurred, and the development in the old industrial countries of specialized, knowledge-based services will be beneficial to manufacturing.

Still, despite the rhetoric about the postindustrial service society, one cannot help but be sad that nowadays no cottons are made in Manchester, little steel in Lorraine, and no big guns in Essen. Likewise, the "desertification" of large tracts of the European countryside is depressing: in thousands of villages most houses are falling into ruins, and no shopkeepers or craftsmen are left.[68]

However, the major trouble is not the depression or even the dying out of traditional industries, but the brute fact that Europe has not created enough new jobs, in new branches of activity, to make good for those that have been lost. Services have expanded, as in the case of tourism: the number of foreign visitors to European countries has risen from 200 million in 1980 to 400 million in 1996. The EU has four of the five top tourism destinations in the world, the first being France, which received 71 million foreign tourists in 1999; nonetheless, like Spain, Italy, and Greece—other receivers of crowds of tourists—it has a high rate of unemployment. As for industry, Europe has not kept pace with the acceleration of technological progress and inventions since the early 1970s, especially in electronics and information and biotechnologies, and it has not invested enough in these new activities. Indeed, the United States has retained and even increased its ascendancy as a source of innovations (and in some areas, Japan has also beaten Europe). There are exceptions in the high-tech sector: compact discs and CD-ROMs were introduced by Philips of the Netherlands, while in the pharmaceutical industry, Europe has managed to maintain a strong position in the world markets.[69] Still, despite the financing of many projects by the EU, the United States continues to devote to research and development a larger share of its GDP than Europe (40 percent more in 1996) and to have more scientists and engineers doing research per thousand inhabitants than the EU; it is miles ahead in the use of information technology.

The creativity of Europeans—especially in technology—has been in the past their strength, their "lever of riches" (Mokyr 1990). This creativity now seems exhausted: most EU countries have a deficit in their technology balance of payments. Europeans invented economic modernity, but they were and remain unable to push it as far as the United States. Indeed, the Continent has become a laggard in technology; it does not have enough knowledge-based high-tech industries. For example, efforts in the field of both computers and software have largely failed, and Europe has no Silicon Valley equivalent (except some small areas). Moreover, its corporate governance is deficient.

In 1991, the French businessman Michel Albert contrasted two types of capitalism. The American—or Anglo-Saxon, as it also prevails in Britain—is individualist, competitive, short-termist, and focused on quick and high profits for shareholders; relations between sources of finance (the stock exchange, mainly, not banks) and companies are kept at arm's length; and predatory behavior is not restricted, so that hostile takeovers and mergers are epidemic. The other model, which Albert called "Alpine," or "Rhenish" (because of its prevalence in Switzerland, Germany, and the Netherlands) or also "Nippo-Germanic" (as Japan has a similar pattern), is a regulated market economy with a comprehensive system of social security; it is built on consultation and close ties among employers, trade unions, banks, and government; it is long-termist, consensus-seeking, and mindful of the interests of stakeholders (including banks and workers) rather than of shareholders.[70] Albert believed that the second model was giving better performances—especially stable and continuous growth—and pressed all Europeans to adopt it. This was also the time when the "declinist" school was most influential and forecast—wrongly—the worst for the United States. In fact, as Albert was writing, the Rhenish model had been crumbling for some time and, in the 1990s, its failure became obvious; if it was sheltering the poor, it was at the cost of stifling economic growth, and therefore of mass unemployment; on the other hand, German firms were starting to adopt "American" ways. It has also become obvious that countries that lead are those where the environment is favorable to entrepreneurs, and that Europe's culture is less entrepreneurial than that of the libertarian United States; its business management is inferior.

"The European system is no longer producing the goods," wrote the *Economist* (4 May 1997); it was failing to generate decent returns on investment. It suffered from low profitability and from close ties among government, banks, and corporations. Though intimate and long-term relationships between companies and capital suppliers can be useful (when banks exercise a constructive form of control), cross-shareholdings (especially when they are consolidated by membership of a closed elite) may create collusive complacency, allowing bad decisions to remain unchecked and managerial failures not to be penalized—while, under the Anglo-Saxon model, poorly performing managers are liable to be soon dismissed. Moreover, on the Continent, the venture-capital sector was underdeveloped, and this was a cause of the high-technology industries' weakness. "Measured against American standards, European firms have a long way to go" (ibid.).

Actually, some of this way was covered in the 1990s. Globalization, European integration (including regulations from Brussels), the creation of the euro, plus the impact of multinational companies have eroded the particularities of national capitalisms; a new, transnational form of continental capitalism has been gradually emerging.

The relationship between banks and companies is unraveling. The most dynamic banks have become international, global operators, and their traditional links with industry will loosen; they are pulling out of corporate lending, which offers mediocre returns.[71] In corporate governance, the balance of power between stakeholders (particularly banks) and shareholders has shifted in favor of the latter, who increasingly include institutional investors—many of them international and swift to discipline wayward firms. Those investors demand more profitability and also more transparency; the closed, back-room conduct of corporate affairs is under siege. Shareholder value has become a fashionable objective, and managers may be held to account for their companies' performances. Moreover, they are better educated, have been through business schools —not infrequently in the United States—and share something of American business culture. In some countries, the balance of power in industrial relations between management and unions has also shifted—to the latter's detriment.

Though change is and will be slow, much progress has been achieved since the 1980s in privatization of state-owned companies and deregulation, not only in Thatcherite Britain but even in socialist France (where the banking system has been largely freed from government control); in the late 1990s, state-owned telecommunications were privatized in several countries. A good deal of restructuring, cost-cutting, and refocusing has also been achieved. Some conglomerates have been slimmed down or even dismantled. Many mergers and takeovers have been arranged, including hostile takeovers, which were once taboo in Germany; no firm is safe from predators, and some famous ones have thus disappeared. In fact, a mergers boom that started late in 1998 exploded in 1999. Among the major operations that were achieved (or at least announced) are: Banque Nationale de Paris and Paribas, Deutsche Bank and Bankers' Trust in banking; Daimler-Benz and Chrysler, Ford and Volvo, and Renault, Dacia, and Nissan in the automobile industry; British Petroleum and Amoco and Total, Petrofina, and Elf-Aquitaine in oil; Vodafone, AirTouch, and Mannesmann in mobile telephones; Rhône-Poulenc and Hoechst, Zeneca and Astra in pharmaceuticals; British Aerospace and GEC-Marconi in defense, plus the Franco-Italo-Germano-Spanish EDAS (European Defense Aeronautic and Space Company). These operations have taken place sometimes within one country, sometimes across borders, and sometimes across the Atlantic, and behind them are many other mergers between smaller firms. Concentration is expected to improve efficiency and profitability (often at the cost of job losses), but some previous mergers have been expensive failures. Moreover, venture capital is booming, to the benefit of many start-up firms, especially in the high-tech sector.

Altogether, European business is not in the hopeless state that is often described, and many EU countries have moved up in the classification of the business environment—as theirs is of higher quality than in emerging countries and has sophisticated financial and legal systems. Nonetheless, early in 2000, the *Economist* (12 Feb. 2000) warned again that "despite all this, Europe [i.e., the Continent] has a long way to go. By most measures, its firms remain laggards." Their profit margins are only half those of U.S. companies; there is not enough concentration (e.g., the Continent is "overbanked"); and restructuring is yet at an early stage. "The revolution in European business has just begun," but the famous weekly concluded that it will happen, leading to a more transparent, more efficient capitalism, "and, yes, redder in teeth and claw" (like American business). Still, this process could be delayed by governments and trade unions.

This brings us to a last and major cause of slow growth and of unemployment—on which, besides, there have been sharp disagreements: economic policy, in a broad sense. During the golden age of the 1950s and 1960s, the mixed economy—or managed capitalism—prevailed and was apparently successful. In the 1970s, however, serious doubts were raised about its efficiency; Keynesian policies failed utterly to cure stagflation and became discredited. A complete change in the establishment view of macroeconomic policies took place, dictated partly by circumstances, partly by an ideological switch among economists. Priority was henceforth given not to full employment and fast growth (as in the golden age), but to stability of prices and exchange rates and to restoring a free-market economy. From this so-called conservative revolution, a neoliberal and monetarist orthodoxy emerged, at least in some countries, particularly Britain, where under Thatcher's rule the switch was the most dramatic; her government went much further than any other in promarket activism and was the only one to enforce structural microeconomic reforms. Still, in 1983, the French socialist government turned to a policy of currency stability.

Since the 1980s, most European governments have followed anti-inflationary policies; in the 1990s, the new orthodoxy was strengthened by the adoption of monetary union as an objective and by the necessity of meeting the Maastricht criteria—especially reducing budget deficits. These policies have been quite successful in defeating inflation, which in twelve core countries fell below 2 percent in the late 1990s. On the other hand, those restrictive policies have often been blamed for the rise in unemployment.

The free marketeers' answer is that "the bulk of continental Europe's 11 percent unemployment rate . . . is not due to insufficient demand caused by high interest rates. Rather it results from structural rigidities in Europe's labor and product markets" (*Economist,* 5 June 1999). In this view, Europe needs to use labor more flexibly. Except for Britain, where trade union power was broken by Thatcher, Europe is far from the American pattern of a "ruthless economy" (Samuelson). There has been some but not enough freeing of labor markets, and strict job-protection laws discourage firms from hiring, because firing is so difficult and expensive. Indeed, they are job-killing laws, while a strong correlation between high flexibility of the labor market and low unemployment has been demonstrated. Moreover, a significant share of the labor force works in the public sector and thereby enjoys the complete security of life employment, a security that creates unemployment among the rest. Part-time work is one potential solution, but only in a few countries (especially the Netherlands) has it been widely accepted (and successful). Indeed, workers and unions are not ready to accept more flexibility. Likewise, they are hostile to any dismantling of the welfare state, though its counterproductive economic effects are obvious.[72] As of 2000, left-of-center or leftist governments are in power in all west European countries but two; they remain so frightened by the "ruthlessness" of the American model that one can wonder whether any serious reform either of labor markets or of the welfare state can be expected from them.

To many economists, slow growth and unemployment result from excessive money creation by government and the financial sector, and particularly from structural budget deficits caused by welfare states, which Europeans have inherited from the golden age, but which they can no longer afford. Social-protection expenditures such as unemployment benefits have made the largest contribution to the continuous rise in government outlay relatively to GDP, which has been characteristic of the last decades (and even of the twentieth century!), in all European countries; in this respect there has been a striking, but unfortunate, convergence. When unemployment increases, transfer payments rise automatically, and there is also a steady buildup of pensions for an aging population (the expression "pensions time bomb" has been used); in 1996, 28.3 percent of GDP of the EU countries was devoted to social protection (twice the American or Japanese level). Before 1914, total government expenditure was on average about 10 percent of GDP. At first, its rise was related to the financial necessities of the two world wars, and its ratio to GNP (which had been over 50 percent in some countries in wartime) fell back after 1918 and 1945—to 20–30 percent in Western Europe in the 1950s and 1960s—but later it rose again. In 1998, it was 48 percent of GDP in the fifteen countries of the EU. Total tax receipts were a somewhat lower percentage of GDP: 41.5 percent in the EU (1997, unweighted average).[73] Many experts see diminishing returns to public spending beyond a certain level—and the present level in Europe as growth retarding and job destroying.

Moreover, unemployment benefits are often too high and paid for long periods, so that people are not stimulated to look for jobs. High minimum wages ($6.50 per hour in France in 1997) reduce job opportunities for the low-skilled and for young persons (for whom also they reduce job training). Unlike in America, where people accept modest wages rather than stay unemployed, Europeans have preferred high unemployment to the widening of wage differentials. Still, the worst might be high employment taxes and other nonwage costs (especially contributions to social protection), which push up labor costs. In some European countries, the latter are the highest in the world. In 1996, for example, the average manufacturer in western Germany paid $31.77 per hour for an employee ($17.75 for wages, and $14.02 for other costs), against $19 in the United States, so that in 1998, American workers were the cheapest in the OECD except those of Spain, Italy, and Canada. This has led to questions about the future of *Standort Deutschland* (Germany as a location for industry) and to temptations (that also exist in France and Sweden) to delocalize to eastern Europe, Asia, and even Britain.

The European social model is thus based upon the maintenance of a high degree of both labor-market rigidities and social protection. In an environment of sharpening competition, this model becomes increasingly costly in terms of employment (especially for low-skilled workers), and it threatens the sustainability of the social-protection system, especially with an aging population.

Finally, Europe suffers from too much "big government," from excessive regulation, from constant state meddling. This creates a hostile environment for business, discourages the creation of new firms, and pushes entrepreneurs to create jobs abroad rather than at home. On the other hand, there is a crisis of the state: governments can no longer be engines of modernization; their autonomy is reduced by international constraints; their economies have become hostages to financial markets; and they are under pressure to adopt a leaner brand of social protection. However, views about the retreat of the state, to the benefit of markets and multinational companies, must not be pushed too far: the gross product of foreign affiliates in Europe in 1994 was about 6 percent of GDP, while the fiscal rapacity of most governments has just been stressed. On the other hand, to many people, this "retreat" has torn societies apart and substituted the brutality of markets for the state's helpful hand, and they cling to a system that they see as guaranteeing security—which they prize first and foremost. Indeed, one must admit that the welfare state, whatever its drawbacks, has prevented fragile and sick countries like France from succumbing to revolution and falling into chaos. On the other hand, one must remember Olson's "distributive coalitions," which were weakened in the post–World War II period but have again become very strong: those vested interests—especially trade unions—protect their privileges with ferocity; they block decisions and have contributed to "Eurosclerosis." After fifty years of welfare state, the continental economies suffer from "fundamental weaknesses" (*Times*, 3 Mar. 1999).

Europe and Euro

A more cheerful vista is opened by further progress in the "building of Europe," which had been for years at a quasi-standstill, amid wrangling between the EU's members, but had a new start after the mid-1980s. The Single European Market Act of 1986 provided for the abolition of all significant barriers, particularly nontariff ones, such as controls of goods at borders within the EU, among the twelve members (later fifteen)—an abolition that actually took place on 1 January 1993 (controls on movements of capital had come to an end in 1990). The single market extends to networks industries (e.g., telecommunications, electricity, transports), to banking and other services, and to public procurement. A good deal was achieved in the 1990s in terms of deregulating and promoting competition in those sectors, where previously monopolies often dominated; the Brussels bureaucracy has indeed been an agent of liberalization. The single market harmonized 100,000 national regulations and abolished 60 million customs formalities per year; it has thus helped to increase intra-EU trade, to stimulate restructuring, and to enhance growth. Meanwhile, the EU also adopted "structural policies" of aid to its poorer countries and regions.[74]

However, the most spectacular developments have been in monetary affairs. Their direct origins went back to the tensions and turbulence that preceded and followed the collapse of the Bretton Woods system. In 1969 the six founding members of the EEC decided to start work on monetary union. In an important 1970 report, P. Werner (from Luxembourg) proposed the establishment of a common currency that would coexist with national currencies, but this plan was vetoed by France as too federalist. Nonetheless, Europeans were worried by monetary instability and by the danger of contagious currency crises coming from outside, and keen on fixed parities. In 1972, therefore, the six adopted a compromise, the "snake in the tunnel" system—or just "the snake": the fluctuations band of their mutual exchange rates would be limited to ±2.25 percent from the central parity. If a central bank was unable to maintain its currency within the tunnel, this currency would be devalued (or revalued). Macroeconomic convergence was the objective, but, because of the fast inflation that prevailed during the 1970s, the "snake" did not work properly and had failed as early as 1973.

Even so, the idea of a stable monetary zone, facing the vagaries of American monetary policy, remained strong, and in 1979 the European Monetary System (EMS) was adopted by eight countries (Britain did not join). It again pegged member currencies within bands that allowed 2.25 percent deviations from the central rate, but the mechanism of adjustment was more flexible and easier than in the early system, and very short-term credit could be provided (actually by the German Bundesbank or Buba) to support weakening currencies. Moreover, a European accounting unit—a synthetic basket currency known as the European currency unit or ECU—was created; exchange rates would be measured against it, and it acquired an existence of its own in the bond market. Still, stability was not achieved at first: several currencies (most notably the French franc) were devalued or revalued during the early 1980s; but the EMS was a reasonable success from 1985 to 1992. Britain joined in 1990. However, on 16 September 1992 (Black Wednesday), a major crisis occurred: the pound and the Italian lira, which were overvalued, were attacked by speculators, forced from the EMS, and in fact devalued. After a second crisis, in the summer of 1993, the margins of fluctuation were extended to ±15 percent, and this was the de facto end of the EMS.

Meanwhile, however, another and much more ambitious project had emerged: to solve the problem of stabilization at a stroke, by full monetary union.

On the suggestion of the French and German governments, Jacques Delors, the president of the European Commission, had presented in April 1989 a plan to achieve in three stages economic and monetary union (EMU) among EEC members. In December 1991, European leaders met at Maastricht and adopted this objective. The plan was embodied into a treaty that was signed on 7 February 1992, according to which a single European currency would be created by 1 January 1999; it also fixed the convergence criteria that would-be members of EMU would have to satisfy before admission: a budget deficit under 3 percent of GNP, a national debt under 60 percent of GNP, plus low inflation and stability of exchange rates. Due to the EMS's crises in 1992 and 1993 as well as nationalist resistance, particularly the reluctance of Germans to sacrifice the deutsche mark, which was both strong and a symbol of the country's postwar prosperous and democratic condition, ratification was not easy. Still, the process went on. In 1994, a European Monetary Institute was established in Frankfurt to prepare the way for a European Central Bank (ECB), which would be independent and free from intervention by governments; price stability would be its primary objective. In 1995, the name "euro" was selected for the single currency, and the next year a "pact of stability and growth" was drawn up to prevent budgetary laxity by future EMU members. On 2 May 1998, European leaders found out that eleven countries had met the Maastricht criteria (not without some dodging); Greece did not qualify, and Denmark, Sweden, and Britain did not want to join. On 31 December 1998, the exchange rates between the euro and eleven currencies were definitively fixed; and the next day, 1 January 1999, the EMU came into effect and the euro became the official currency of "Euroland's" eleven members; and on 4 January, quotations on the Eurozone's stock exchanges were given in euros. A transitional period of three years began, during which the use of the euro and of the national currencies is neither forbidden nor compulsory. On 1 January 2002, the issue of euro notes and coins will start, and on 30 June 2002 the old currencies will cease to be legal tender.

The *Economist* (2 Jan. 1999) stressed the "genuinely historic nature" of the euro's birth: "It is the first time that countries of anything like this number, size or global economic weight have gathered together to share a currency. . . . All should hope that it will be a success." Actually, the creation of EMU was a political decision (like, previously, those behind the ECSC and the EEC) imposed by President François Mitterrand and Chancellor Helmut Kohl; it had been for Germany the price of reunification: it had accepted letting the other ten members have a say in monetary policy, which previously had been all but dictated by the Buba.

It would be foolish to make forecasts about the euro's future, and one can only summarize the pros and cons. "Euroskeptics" have contended that the costs and risks involved in a common currency have been overlooked. Euroland, unlike the United States, is not an optimal currency area; wages are rigid, markets not flexible enough, and the mobility of labor very low because of cultural and linguistic barriers.[75] It is therefore vulnerable to asymmetrical shocks, specific to some regions or countries, because of cyclical and structural differences among economies. National governments will be less able to react than before 1999, as monetary policy and exchange rates will be no longer available to them as tools of adjustment to such shocks. They will retain fiscal policy, but its use will be severely constrained by the stability pact—which provides for sanctions (i.e., fines) against delinquents. And changes in interest rates by the ECB will have different effects among member countries.

Another Euroskeptic argument was that all member countries would have to converge toward German standards of price and exchange-rate stability, to the detriment of growth and employment.[76] By itself, the official endorsement of the Maastricht criteria had strengthened the deflationary bias in policies and contributed to the high levels of unemployment on the Continent in the 1990s.[77] Now, the ECB would have to build up its credibility, through an ultraorthodox and austere policy that would result in more slowing down of European economies; moreover, the euro might thus become overvalued relative to the dollar, and Europe's competitiveness would suffer.

The pessimists' forecast, therefore, is: deep regional recessions, rioting in the streets, disharmony among governments, defections by some members (the "Club Med" countries, as northern racists call them), and eventually war. "For the downtrodden of Europe, individuals or nations, the euro is bad news" (Alan Milward, *Times Literary Supplement,* 25 Sept. 1998).

In point of fact, the fear of a "strong" euro soon vanished. Within one year, it depreciated 16 percent against the dollar, and early in 2000 it fell under par with the latter. The major cause was the widening of the cyclical disparity between the United States and the Eurozone; the "new economy" had been booming in America, while continental economies were sluggish—especially in Germany (indeed, the euro's price depends upon the performance of Germany). The markets were also disappointed by the lack in Germany and elsewhere of the reforms that free marketeers deem necessary. However, the very weakness of the euro was a boon for continental countries—as their exports became more competitive—and it was a major factor behind the recovery they had in 1999. The ECB, which is the most independent central bank in the world, had a pragmatic, not dogmatic, policy and lowered interest rates. Moreover, EMU protected its members from currency crises, and in the view of its supporters it will lower transaction costs by eliminating those resulting from currency conversions and exchange-rate risks. It is indispensable for achieving a genuine single market, which instability and competitive devaluations put at risk, but which will become more competitive and transparent. It will also create a pressure for structural reforms while helping to reduce rigidity in labor markets (and thus unemployment), to improve corporate governance, and to harmonize legislation and taxes. EMU has already had a substantial effect in integrating Europe's hitherto fragmented financial markets; a market in euro-denominated bonds is fast growing; and eventually, EMU may make Europe's capital markets as deep and as liquid as those of America. Mergers of banks and other companies will be stimulated, and business cycles will be more synchronized. In time, the euro "will encourage the formation of a single European economy as the corollary of a single European currency" (*Economist,* 23 Oct. 1999).

On the other hand, though the euro is the world's second currency, it is unlikely that it might soon challenge the dollar's rule of the world financial system (even though some countries have indexed their currency on the euro or one of its components). It has also been observed that no monetary union based upon agreement among autonomous states has ever been successful and lasting; an economic government of Europe, nay a close political union, would thus be necessary, but this is unlikely to be achieved. However, Michael Bordo and Lars Jonung have drawn different conclusions from the historical record of monetary unions. In their view, the economic shortcomings of EMU will be overcome as long as the political will to maintain the union is present; once it disappears, EMU may break apart, but such an outcome is likely only under extreme circumstances. Moreover, though EMU is a multinational monetary union, it will function as a national union, with one central bank, one currency in circulation. Altogether, EMU is the only way for European states to retain influence over their own future in an age of globalization.

An age in which Europe faces threatening challenges. "Now much of the world sees Europe as chronically sick." This statement by the *Economist* (31 May 1997) may seem excessive or malicious: from some simple figures, Europe looks an impressive economic aggregate, even though its share of world output and trade is lower than it was, not only in 1913, but also by 1950 and 1973 (and so is the U.S. share).

As shown in table 4.6, the EU has a larger population than the United States, a GDP of the same order of magnitude, and therefore a lower product per capita. Only Luxembourg has succeeded in overcoming America from this point of view, and in the EU the average income of 1999 is only two-thirds of the American level. After half a century of "catching up," Europeans (excluding, of course, the former Eastern bloc) have not fully succeeded, possibly because they do not work enough and, unlike Americans, they do not live to work![78] On the other hand, they must be considered as "rich": the EU's GDP per capita is three times the world average. It is also clear that Europe retains a large share of world trade (in 1999, it had five of the ten leading merchandise exporters in the world, which were responsible for 27 percent of world exports). And in exports of commercial services, Europe enjoys the largest share—ten European countries are responsible for 40 percent of the world total, against 19 percent for the United States.

In addition, Europe has once more become a large net exporter of capital thanks to a growing surplus on current account (it exceeded $100 billion in 1997 and 1998). It is therefore a large net creditor, while the United States, with its deficit twice the size of Europe's surplus (and an

_____ Table 4.6_____

Europe and the world economy, 1995–1997
(percentages of the world total)

	Europe (excluding Russia)	European Union (15 countries)	Eurozone (11 countries)	United States
GNP, 1995[a]	31	28	—	25
GDP, 1997[a]	—	27[b]	22	27
Exports 1997	—	40	32[c]	12
Imports 1997	—	41	33	16
Population, in millions, mid-1997	582	374[d]	291	268
GDP per capita, 1999, as % of the U.S. level[e]	—	65	65	100

_____

a. At current prices and rates of exchange. At PPP in 1997, 21 percent of world GDP came from the EU (16 percent from the Eurozone), 23 percent from North America.

b. If Norway and Switzerland are added, the percentage of "capitalist Europe" (i.e., Europe excluding the former Soviet bloc) is 28.8 percent.

c. If intra-Eurozone trade is excluded, the Eurozone is responsible for 19 percent of world trade (United States: 17 percent).

d. 376 on 1 January 2000.

e. At PPP.

Sources: Various, particularly OECD in Figures. 2000 Edition. Statistics on the Member Countries (Paris, 2000).

investment-income deficit since 1998), is the world's largest net debtor. Britain gave the lead but was followed by the Netherlands, Germany, Switzerland, France, and others, so that by 1996 the gross outward stock of FDI from the EU was larger than the American. However, the ratio of the outward stock of FDI by western European countries to their GDP, though it doubled from 1980 to 1995 (rising from 7 to 14 percent), remains smaller than in 1913, so that financial markets were more integrated in the early twentieth century than at its end.

Another difference is that recently European capital has been exported to other rich nations—especially the United States—rather than to "emerging" countries. Capital moves across the Atlantic both westward and eastward: in 1998, European firms invested twice more in the United States (for making acquisitions) than American firms in Europe. European countries also attracted capital from other sources: the oil kingdoms of the Middle East, and the new Asian industrial giants—Japan and South Korea (Japanese investment in Europe more than doubled from 1983 to 1993); indeed, Asian investment in Europe—which started roughly c. 1970—has been an outstanding development of the late twentieth century. Thanks to the English language, low taxes, and low wages, Britain has been very popular with both American and Asian investors.

Europe has thus become both a large exporter and a large importer of capital. This position worries some observers for conflicting reasons. On one hand, Europe is becoming a rentier continent, as its surplus capital is invested in America and not at home. On the other hand, foreign capital—and especially Anglo-Saxon institutional investors, such as pension funds—now own a substantial share of large European companies' capital, so that they can dictate their strategies in order to get high returns on their investment. The large American investment banks have also made dramatic inroads in Europe, while the automobile industry of Britain is entirely foreign owned.

Meanwhile, the City of London has succeeded, within the last thirty or forty years, in rebuilding its position as a world financial center: together with New York, it is the only global financial center, especially since the 1997 crash destroyed Tokyo's ambitions; it is the biggest net exporter of financial services and is also first for global foreign-exchange business (and Eurocurrency transactions); and it has the biggest stock market in Europe, the second in the world. Thus, as of early 2000, it remains top among Europe's financial centers, but plans for an alliance among the stock exchanges of London and Frankfurt have been announced. Moreover, the City has regained its nineteenth-century position as headquarters for financial institutions from all over the world: no other center has so many foreign banks, but most famous London merchant banks are now controlled by large foreign commercial banks—American, Swiss, Dutch, and German. However, some experts think that London's primacy might not last unless Britain joins the Eurozone; others believe that the euro will benefit London anyway, as it has the most dynamic and freest financial industry.

The point can also be made that a European economic space does exist, consisting of a bloc of economies that have become increasingly similar. And their integration has progressed: the percentage of intracommunity trade in the total trade of twelve EU members rose from 40 percent in 1960 to 60 percent in 1990, and by trade creation more than by trade diversion. For the fifteen current EU members, this percentage is over 50 percent. Roughly speaking, foreign trade is equivalent to a third or more of their GDP, but within the Eurozone, the ratio of external trade (with non-Eurozone countries) to GDP will fall to 10 percent, as its members do the bulk of their trade with each other, and the Eurozone will be as relatively closed as the United States and Japan. The growing importance of intra-EU trade in intermediate goods—which actually move among factories belonging to multinationals and sited in different EU countries—is one more indication of integration.

On the other hand, it bears repeating that economic growth in the EU has been markedly slower than in the United States during the years 1992–1999 (though the difference narrows if growth is measured over the decade 1989–1998, to adjust for the business cycle). Admittedly, a recovery started in 1999 and took shape in 2000; there has been a tangible fall in unemployment; prospects are considered as better than at any time since the 1970s. But it has not been long enough to erase the contrast between American sustained growth, falling and low unemployment (4 percent in January 2000), and low inflation, compared to the "moroseness," high unemployment, and sluggish growth that prevailed in Europe (with exceptions); between the slowing down of capital formation in almost all European countries during the 1990s and its acceleration in the United States; between the massive creation of new jobs in the United States and the inability of Europe to do the same; between American flexibility and Euro-sclerosis, American innovative capacity and European inertia.

The combination of fast growth, low unemployment, and low inflation created in America a "new economy" largely based upon the information-technology revolution (ITR), which transformed the way companies are run, and which is supposed to sustain (indefinitely?) faster and inflation-free growth (say 4 percent per year). This resulted from an acceleration in productivity growth that started in 1995 and raised it to 4 percent per year.

For Europe, the trouble is that it is not "guaranteed to enjoy the benefits of the 'new economy'" (*Economist*, 5 Feb. 2000) by following the American example; its recent spurt of growth may be mainly cyclical. Indeed, Europe is far behind the United States in information technology, and the number of European companies that have capability in the high-tech sector is very low in comparison with America, which also has much better universities than Europe (with the exception of Britain). In the Eurozone, total spending on information technology is 5 percent of GDP, against 8 percent in the United States and 7.5 percent in Britain. The relative number of Internet hosts in 1999 was three times greater in the United States than in the Eurozone (which, moreover, does not manufacture much hardware). So there are not yet any signs of the acceleration in productivity growth that would support a faster progress of GDP in Euroland.

Moreover, according to free marketeers, the ITR can only develop and lead into the "new economy" after some structural reforms, which were achieved in the United States in the 1970s and 1980s: rigidities in labor and products markets, which discourage investment, must be eliminated, and labor costs and taxes must be cut. As observed earlier, such reforms are not too likely under the governments that most continental countries have, and there are notorious counterexamples, like the French thirty-five-hour working week. So the *Economist* repeats once more: "There is still a long way to go in Europe" (5 Feb. 2000).

Thus, for the first time since the 1950s, divergence has replaced convergence between the United States and western Europe. From 1995 to 1999, real GDP grew at a rate of 2.2 percent per year in the EU and 4.1 percent in the United States. As a consequence, U.S. GDP per capita (at PPP) in 1996 was 40 percent higher than the EU average (to which Britain, France, Italy, Sweden are quite close) and 54 percent higher in 1999, even though the latter had risen by 50 percent since 1970 in real terms (see table 4.7, below).[79]

Then there is the consideration that cooperation among the fifteen EU members—and even the eleven Eurozone countries—is far from harmonious. Some large-scale projects have been successful, such as Airbus, Arianespace (world leader for launching civilian satellites), Eurotunnel (opened in 1994, between England and France), and the bridge-cum-tunnel between Denmark and Sweden (opened in 2000). On the other hand, plans for a pan-European network of high-speed trains have been discussed for years, without much progress but for the Brussels-London-Paris triangle. Many transnational mergers or alliances between large companies have run into difficulties or collapsed altogether. And there are serious disagreements among EU members about its budget and especially the financing of the CAP, which many dislike, but which is vital for France.

Moreover, since the German elections of 1998, all EU members except Ireland and Spain have left-wing governments run by social democrats, and some of them (especially in Germany and France) include "green" ministers. The irrational ideology of "green terrorism," which is akin to Nazism, is hostile to modern technology and might be one of the worst dangers for Europe (e.g., it might ruin its automobile industry).

It is therefore no surprise that in the rating of global competitiveness (i.e., aptitude for long-term sustained growth) for 1999, only four European countries—Britain, the Netherlands, Sweden, and Switzerland—had an honorable rank, while France (twenty-fourth), Germany (twenty-fifth), and Spain and Italy (tied for thirty-fifth) were far below, lower than several Asian countries.[80]

This brings us to the point that in the 1980s and in the early 1990s, European stagnation was contrasted with the dynamism and fast growth not so much of the United States as of eastern Asia. Indeed, by 1998, at PPP, China's GDP had overcome Japan's, and India's GDP had passed

_____ Table 4.7_____

Relative GDP per capita of European countries at PPP, 1999 (USA = 100)

Luxembourg	116	France	65
Norway	81	**EU 15 and Eurozone**	**65**
Switzerland	81	Italy	64
Denmark	78	Spain	53
Ireland	74	Portugal	49
Netherlands	74	Greece	44
Austria	73		
Belgium	72	Czech Republic	39
Germany	70	Hungary	32
Sweden	67	Poland	24
Finland	67	Japan	72
United Kingdom	66	S. Korea	44

_____

Source: OECD in Figures. 2000 Edition. Statistics on the Member Countries (Paris, 2000), pp. 12–13, 79.

France's and Germany's, so that Germany fell from third to fifth place among the big economies and France from fourth to sixth. The forecast, by extrapolating current trends from 1980, is that by 2020, China will have passed the United States, India and Indonesia will be bigger than Germany (which will fall to sixth rank), South Korea and Thailand bigger than France (which will be ninth), and Taiwan bigger than Italy (twelfth) and Britain (fourteenth). Seven of the ten largest economies will be in Asia. Moreover, it is not sure that Germany and France will retain GDP per capita higher than those of South Korea and Taiwan (though, presently, only Japan and the city-states of Singapore and Hong Kong have become "rich" countries). A return to the economic ascendancy of Asia in the Middle Ages will have been achieved.

Admittedly, the crisis that has devastated Asia since the summer of 1997 gives us pause over these prophecies, but the "tigers" had a spectacular recovery in 1999 and some experts believe they will enjoy a very fast growth in forthcoming years. Still, some pundits have observed that North America and western Europe have been an area of tranquillity—while Asia was in depression, Russia collapsed, and Brazil was tottering—and are converging to form a "new economy." However, the view that the twenty-first century will be the "Atlantic century" may be as ephemeral as the idea that it would belong to Asia.

"The European Union has been one of the great political success stories of the post-war world," and the *Economist* (23 Oct. 1999) sees the prospect of a stronger Europe for decades to come. Still, it is often said that the EU is an economic giant, a political dwarf, and a military larva. Indeed, Europe does not exist as far as defense and foreign policy are concerned; from the economic point of view, its union is imperfect, incomplete, and disturbed by frequent bickering and quarrels. The dream of a United States of Europe has not been realized and now looks a pipe dream, inasmuch as a federal "superstate" will always be opposed by Britain. And many people, apparently, do not wish the "ever closer union" among European peoples that the Treaty of Rome had contemplated. As for the question of eventual consequences of the euro, "the answer is that monetary union will push the EU toward political union, but not guarantee it" (ibid.).

For years, several visions of Europe's future have competed. The idea —somewhat protectionist and mercantilist—of "Fortress Europe" is now dead (to this writer's regrets). On the other hand, doctrinaire and fanatic free-traders favor European integration only as far as it leads to freer markets; they want to use the EU as an instrument to extend free trade, an instrument that would eventually be dissolved into an Atlantic or global free market.[81] Actually, one can wonder whether liberalization and globalization at the world level have not already made (or are on the verge of making) European integration obsolete, whether the loss of sovereignty, which European nation-states have accepted, has not been to the benefit of markets and MNCs rather than of European institutions. In this perspective, any European economic identity would disappear. There is, however, a third strategy, the one embodied in the Maastricht and Amsterdam treaties and in the EMU. It is in favor of free markets and flexibility, but within a European regulatory framework, and with economic security plus social consensus as one of its aims. The power of the markets is softened by European legislation from Brussels and by the survival of traditional institutions and networks.[82] After all, national differences are far from having been erased by integration, and it is necessary to mention some of the special traits that national economies have retained, as they will affect their prospects within the EU.

Britain is often considered to be the only one of the large European economies that has good prospects. Thanks to the Thatcher revolution, which broke trade unions, deregulated, and privatized, "Britain's century-long relative economic decline has been arrested," and its economy "is in its best shape for several decades" (*Economist*, 12 Apr. 1997). Unemployment is much lower than on the Continent, and foreign capital flows in. Services are Britain's forte; the City of London is a crucial asset that generates jobs and wealth. Still, labor productivity and (to a slightly lesser degree) total factor productivity remain far below the U.S. level, lower than in Germany and France (even though the gap has narrowed); GDP per capita is just above the EU average. To some observers, economic and social structures are nowadays completely different from the Continent. Britain, when the conservatives return to power, might leave the EU.

Germany, for its part, is a giant. Reunification and the fall of communism have made it more than ever before the center of the European economy, over which it enjoys an informal (and peaceful) economic empire, from the Atlantic to the Urals, after having twice failed to establish domination by force. Presently, German big business is "Europeanized," while having worldwide strategies.[83] On the other hand, to many people who adulated the "German miracle," the giant now has feet of clay. Reunification has not been an economic blessing: western Germany had to spend huge sums to try to revive the former German Democratic Republic, and those transfers have caused budget deficits, inflation, tight monetary policies, and then unemployment.[84] Nonetheless, productivity remains low and unemployment high in the east, and Germany has been endowed with a large depressed region, a *mezzogiorno* of the north.

The German welfare system is strongly criticized as bloated and ter-ribly expensive: Germans work too short hours and have too many holi-days. Labor costs are crushing; the cost of one hour of work in German industry is the highest in the world. As a consequence, the viability of Ger-many as a productive location for industry has been questioned, and there has been some delocalization. However, as productivity goes on in-creasing, unit labor costs in Germany (and also in France) are lower than in Britain and Japan. It is also said that German entrepreneurial culture is less vigorous than it was, that investment in technology as well as in re-search and development has been inadequate. But it is also maintained that Germany retains a competitive edge for high quality and sophisti-cated goods. Curiously, within a few months of 1999, a respected maga-zine wrote first that German industry was not as sclerotic as it is often de-scribed and that, likewise, in many other fields, things were not as bad as they looked; then that Germany was a "blocked society," "the sick man of the euro"; and later that it was the only country that could "lead Europe in the future," and that "its ascendancy will make Europe a better place" than if France were the leader.[85]

Among Benelux countries, there has been a change of positions since the golden age, when Belgium was ahead; later on, despite the rise of new industries in Flanders, it was handicapped by the depressed or dying heavy industries of Wallonia. On the other hand, the "Dutch disease" of the 1970s (resulting from the windfall of North Sea oil and gas) has been succeeded by a "Dutch miracle"consisting of low unemployment based on social consensus and generalized part-time work, after reforms of a lux-urious and corporatist welfare state. The Nordic countries have also made less generous their egalitarian welfare system, but they "still live extraor-dinarily well and happily" (*Economist,* 13 Jan. 1999). Sweden, however, which alone has a broad industrial base and many world-class companies, slipped badly during the 1980s and 1990s in the classification for income per capita. Norway—which has refused to join the EU—has, thanks to its oil and gas, a high GDP per capita. But a great success is Finland, despite the loss of the Russian market, which used to be its largest; high-tech elec-tronics have become the chief export. As for Ireland, one can also speak of a miracle there, one that has made it richer than Britain.[86]

The "Club Med" countries, considered by Anglo-Saxon racists as no more than "banana republics" (even though Spain has a king), has actu-ally had good recent performances as far as productivity and exports are concerned; on the basis of finances, inflation, and employment, they have done worse than the north, but progress has been achieved. And the vitality of Italian industry—which, besides its luxury sector, is the fourth in the world for production of machine tools—remains amazing, with its many clusters of small but dynamic firms in the north and the center of the peninsula.

France is generally seen as the "sick man" of Europe. It has a strange variety of capitalism—with few capitalists (as most big firms are run by a narrow oligarchy recruited from the top civil service), few entrepreneurs (as overregulation and taxes drive out talent and capital), and low profitability. The public sector is far too large: one active French person out of every four works in it, a much higher ratio than in other western countries; it includes state-owned firms, which are generally money losers, and an enormous but inefficient civil service. As a consequence, government spending is greater than 50 percent of GDP. Nonetheless, the welfare system, which confiscated most benefits of golden age growth, is in serious trouble. Workers in the protected public sector—generally with jobs for life—defend ferociously their vested interests and privileges, and the price is more unemployment and less enterprise. High productivity is offset by a low participation rate. Some optimists consider that European integration and membership in Euroland will impose modernization and the emergence of a genuine capitalism. But public opinion, imbued with a toxic culture, the media, the ruling parties, and the intelligentsia oppose change. France looks like a last relic in Europe of old-fashioned, Soviet-style socialism. Foreign observers see French economic policies as execrable and incomprehensible: they cannot understand how an economy can revive if people are forbidden by law to work (the working week was reduced in 1998 to thirty-five hours).

On the other hand, France has changed a great deal within the last fifteen years. Several problems that had plagued it for years have been solved; dirigisme has lost some of its prestige. Since 1994, economic growth has been faster than in Germany; 650,000 jobs were created in the private sector in two years, and since its peak in 1997, unemployment has fallen by 10 percent. According to the *Economist* (23 Oct. 1999), "the French economy is showing much more vitality and adaptability than its critics outside France often allow."

Upheaval in the East

The sickest man of Europe will, however, be found much farther east. Capitalist Europe since 1973 has slowed down and suffered from various ailments, but its ills are nothing compared to those of socialist Europe, where stagnation led eventually to collapse of the political and economic systems the Communists had built.

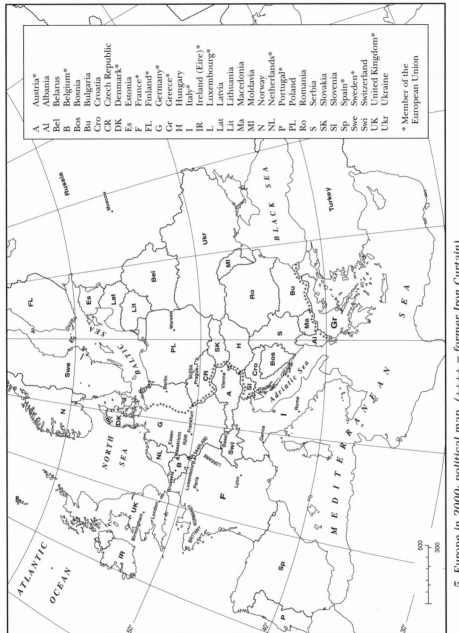

A	Austria*
Al	Albania
Bel	Belarus
B	Belgium*
Bos	Bosnia
Bu	Bulgaria
Cro	Croatia
CR	Czech Republic
DK	Denmark*
Es	Estonia
F	France*
FL	Finland*
G	Germany*
Gr	Greece*
H	Hungary
I	Italy*
IR	Ireland (Eire)*
L	Luxembourg*
Lat	Latvia
Lit	Lithuania
Ma	Macedonia
Ml	Moldavia
N	Norway
NL	Netherlands*
P	Portugal*
PL	Poland
Ro	Romania
S	Serbia
SK	Slovakia
Sl	Slovenia
Sp	Spain*
Swe	Sweden*
Swi	Switzerland
UK	United Kingdom*
Ukr	Ukraine
*	Member of the European Union

5. Europe in 2000: political map. (++++ = former Iron Curtain)

While Khrushchev was showing off his triumphalism, he had been conscious of shortcomings in the Soviet economy and had tried to make reforms. But the problems were much more serious than he could realize and were inherent in the whole system.

Central planning was able to enforce the allocation of a large share of GNP to investment, and in particular to investment in heavy industries and armaments production. This gave superpower status to the Soviet Union, but only to the detriment of the standard of living. Moreover, it is better to have guns than butter only when guns are used to lay hands on other people's butter (as Nazi Germany had done for a brief period). The Soviet mistake was to accumulate, to hoard guns (plus tanks, rockets, nuclear weapons, etc.), but not to use them—though it was wise not to do so, in the nuclear age of mutual assured destruction! Large resources were thus immobilized. "We have made guns," was the simple but excellent explanation of his country's crisis that a Soviet scholar suggested to this writer in 1990.

Central control of investment and production was supposed to ensure a perfect allocation of resources and a rapid diffusion of the best technology, but the giant and heavy bureaucracy had no institutions to ensure that resources were wisely used, and many mistakes were made, with a heavy cost, as wrong choices (e.g., in technology) had an impact over large sectors of the economy. As a consequence, the waste of resources was terrific—and included the devastation of the environment in many areas (e.g., the Aral Sea almost dried up). Investment was inefficient: in industry, its marginal productivity was only half its level in Western Europe; production was also over three times more energy intensive. The USSR became first or second in the world in production of a number of basic goods, such as coal, oil, electricity, steel, and cement, but this was not reflected in the output of final goods, while the government was obliged, because of the danger of shortages, to go on investing massively in heavy industries.[87] Moreover, full employment (which, it has to be recognized, was achieved), shortages, and a seller's market resulted in slack control and poor quality for nonmilitary goods.

"Socialist emulation" was expected to induce workers and managers to enthusiastic efforts to fulfill the plans. But, as terror subsided, there was much apathy and low morale, much disorder behind the facade of despotism. From the 1960s alcoholism greatly spread among the population, with bad effects upon productivity. Moreover, the command system was unable to encourage technological innovation from below and actually prevented initiative at factory level. It had been able to industrialize a backward economy and to win a rather old-fashioned war, but it proved inadequate when a relatively advanced stage of development had been reached, where sophisticated signals and personal liberties are necessary. It also proved unable to fill in the technological gap with the West —except in armaments and space research, which had a quasi-monopoly over research and development; productivity remained much lower than in the West.[88] Similar dysfunctions were, of course, present in the Soviet Union's satellites.

The deceleration of Soviet economic growth started in the 1960s, if not earlier: GDP grew at 5.1 percent per year from 1950 to 1960, and at 4.6 percent from 1960 to 1973. There were also some sharp cyclical fluctuations. As for TFP growth, after high rates in the early 1950s, it decelerated afterward and became negative after 1967. Then GDP growth fell to 1.9 percent for 1973–1989 and GDP per capita to 0.9 percent (see table 4.4, above).

As usual, the worst performance was in agriculture, for lack of fertilizers, machinery, and incentives to work for peasants; moreover, lack of storage and transport facilities caused serious losses. Production failed to keep pace with the increase in population, so that from 1972 onward the Soviet Union became a chronic importer of grain (mainly from the United States and Canada), on an increasing scale.

On the other hand, the world was changing. The United States was developing new advanced technologies (in electronics and telecommunications) that had important military applications, but which Soviet planners had neglected. The Soviet government made the fatal decision to embark on a huge effort to secure military parity with (or even superiority over) the United States. This imposed a dangerous strain upon a smaller, poorer, less advanced economy and caused a fall in the standard of living.[89] Despite imports of Western machinery, the high-tech gap was not reduced. And the decrepitude of much Soviet physical capital was made clear to the world by an accident in the Chernobyl nuclear power plant in 1986.

After slowing down and even stagnating in the 1970s and early 1980s, the Soviet economy disintegrated in the late 1980s and collapsed in the early 1990s—a development that hardly anyone had anticipated, but an outcome that is not rare when attempts are made to reform a decaying system. After too much inertia under Brezhnev, there was perhaps too much zeal under Mikhail Gorbachev, who became general secretary in 1985 and who was convinced that radical reforms were needed if the Soviet Union was to retain its military power and improve the standard of living of its people ("everything is rotten through and through," he said). But he made hasty—and often incoherent—decisions and procrastinated in important matters, such as reforming the price system and the military sector. On the other hand, one can wonder whether serious economic reforms were possible without changing the whole political fabric of the Soviet Union, and especially abolishing the concentration of power in the hands of a narrow oligarchy of highly privileged apparatchiks, as well as censorship and the police state, which prevented the emergence and discussion of innovative ideas.

Anyhow, reforms were rather modest: the development of a semiprivate sector was authorized; planning ceased to be imperative and was de facto abolished, as firms were given a wide degree of autonomy. As several times earlier in Russian history, reform was being imposed from above, but the power of the center was crumbling and reform was opposed by the *nomenklatura* and the managers of the command economy. On the other hand, inflation had developed during the 1980s and the state had to increase its subsidies to maintain the low prices of basic goods and services—and also to service a growing foreign debt. By 1989, the budget deficit was 14 percent of GDP. The economy was exhausted and disaster started in 1990, when GDP fell by 2.5 percent.

In August 1991, die-hard Communists launched a putsch against Gorbachev, but failed. Eventually, however, the latter had to resign and was replaced by the president of Russia, Boris Yeltsin. The Communist system was dismantled, and the USSR disintegrated into fifteen independent republics, loosely associated within a "Commonwealth of Independent States," while the three Baltic republics became fully independent.

Russia—the biggest state, with 147 million inhabitants (1999), of whom 117 million live in Europe—thus started its "transition" from a socialist to a market or capitalist economy. Hitherto, this transition has been far from smooth (to say the least!), inasmuch as political instability has prevailed and the state has largely collapsed. The terribly heavy inheritance from seventy years of command economy has not been easily shaken off. There has been privatization on a large scale (by 1999, the private sector was responsible for 70 percent of GDP), but in a rather chaotic way, and often to the benefit of buccaneers (many are former apparatchiks); the term "robber capitalism" has been used for such a system, inasmuch as massive corruption, extortion, fraud, and mafia activities have greatly progressed and perverted the economy. Moreover, those "oligarchs" often export their ill-gotten gains. The budget deficit has grown worse, as taxes remain unpaid; so inflation—and even hyperinflation—has become rampant. Industry has suffered because armaments orders and government-financed investment have stopped, because of competition by better-quality foreign goods, and also because of the people's immiserization. Factories—

often run by the same managers as earlier—have closed or are overstaffed and kept artificially alive despite huge losses; equipment becomes worn out. In the realm of agriculture, there has been little privatization of land, production has fallen, and much food has to be imported. Altogether, Russia's GDP has been falling every year since 1989 except in 1997; by 1992, it was 33 percent lower than in 1989, by 1998, 45 percent; however, there is a large black, "virtual" economy and a great deal of barter, even between large firms. Indeed, statistics for both Russia and the former satellites (which during the Soviet period, as we know, overestimated the USSR's product and growth) have recently had an inverse bias and give too bleak a picture, as the informal economy is not taken into account and as many fictitious productions have been eliminated.[90]

Russian government policy in the face of such terrible difficulties has been wavering and fluctuating (and advice by foreign experts was not always wise). Though it has benefited from generous help by western governments and by the IMF (foreign direct investment has not been large), it borrowed abroad on a large scale. Eventually, on 17 August 1998, Russia defaulted partly on its debt; banks failed, inflation soared, and the ruble, which was overvalued, collapsed. However, the catastrophe that was widely expected did not materialize, and the effects of the 1998 crisis were less damaging than had been feared. Early in 2000, Russia seemed to be on a path of recovery, especially in industry. Still, some basic and thorny problems will have to be solved; the banking and fiscal systems and other institutions need rebuilding; and a majority of the people live in poverty.[91] Russia, however, has immense resources—both physical and human; its case is not hopeless.

The domination over Eastern Europe that the USSR established after World War II seemed to much increase its power, but this glacis of satellites was actually the source of recurrent and eventually insuperable problems. Admittedly, the process of disintegration of the Soviet bloc started in the Soviet Union under Gorbachev, but decisive consequences of *glasnost* emerged first in the satellites, where the system's implosion occurred two years before the end of the Soviet regime. The Eastern bloc disaggregated at its margins, which were more fragile and vulnerable than the core (Asselain). On the other hand, since the fall of communism, things have turned out better for most of the former satellites than for Russia. Like the USSR under Brezhnev, they had their era of stagnation and decline, their great depression (Berend, 1999a). In all of them, though at different rates, there was a marked slowing down of growth during the 1970s and 1980s. In the six countries mentioned earlier, GDP grew at 1.7 percent per year from 1973 to 1989, versus 4.8 percent from 1950 to

1973, and GDP per capita at 1.2 percent, against 1.7 percent in the earlier period. The slowdown was therefore more marked than in the capitalist West, and the gap in standards of living, which had somewhat narrowed between the 1950s and the 1970s, widened, just as more information became available about Western ways of life, which many people found most attractive; this created feelings of frustration. Unlike in the West, admittedly, there was no mass unemployment, but much underemployment was camouflaged in jobs with very low productivity. By the late 1980s, all the satellite economies were in trouble (like the USSR), and this strengthened the alienation of popular sentiment from the Communist regimes.[92] Economic factors contributed to their overthrow, though other causes also played their part. Even within the "ruling class," the feeling had spread that the command economy was not working and that minor reforms of the old system could not be effective.

By 1989–1990, after four decades of Communist rule, the eastern countries had achieved an average growth per year of 3 percent for their GDP, which was not bad (even if it is an overestimate), but they had failed to catch up with the West and were overtaken by Mediterranean Europe. The levels of their real GDP per capita as percentages of the United States in 1990 are presented in table 4.8.[93] As for the German Democratic Republic, which had been praised as the most advanced socialist country, its labor productivity was only 25 percent of West Germany's.

From 1989 onward, Communist regimes collapsed in Eastern Europe, one after the other, after "velvet," bloodless revolutions (except in Romania); the most spectacular episode being the fall of the Berlin Wall on 9 October 1990. Much credit is due to Gorbachev, who refused to use force or to allow his vassals to use it, and who agreed to withdraw Soviet troops from Eastern Europe. The political map was seriously altered (see map 5, above): the German Democratic Republic disappeared, absorbed by West Germany; the three small Baltic states became independent from Russia; the Czech Republic and Slovakia separated; and Yugoslavia broke into five states and into bloody warfare. Altogether, twenty-eight different countries have emerged from the eight that once made up the Soviet bloc, and those of ECE generally have democratic regimes. On the economic front, transition was started and has been carried out, in the 1990s, with many differences from country to country in the extent of change and the degree of success.

Broadly, the trend has been to privatize, to liberalize (including prices and foreign trade), to deregulate, and to restructure.[94] But some governments have resorted to "shock therapy" (i.e., speedy reforms), while others have chosen gradualism, either because more or less reconstructed

Communists have retained or regained influence or power, or because some consequences of reform (especially growing unemployment) looked unpalatable to the electorate. Most economists consider that shock therapy delivers the best results, in terms of faster growth, declining inflation, and the like, but it can also cause great hardships that are counterproductive. Altogether, in the heady days of 1989–1991, the difficulties of the transition had certainly been underestimated (particularly by foreign experts and advisers). Privatization of an economy involves very tricky microeconomic problems, and even then privatization plus liberalization is not sufficient to create a successful market economy in countries that lack its superstructure—such as private-property rights, the professions that support them, and the know-how that is so common in capitalist countries—and where banking and financial structures are fragile.

In fact, in the early years after the "systemic shock," production fell in east European countries, but not as sharply as in the former USSR, and then a recovery took place in most of them. The fact that Communist rule lasted seventy-four years in the Soviet Union and about forty in its former satellites (where some autonomous forces, such as the Catholic Church

_____ Table 4.8 _____

Relative GDP per capita of eastern European countries, 1990 and 1998; United States = 100 (in each year)

	1990	*1998*
Czechoslovakia	39	41[a]
USSR[b]	31	—
Hungary	29	34
Bulgaria	26	16
Yugoslavia[b]	25	—
Poland	23	27
Romania	16	19

_____

a. Czech Republic only

b. Relative GDP per capita in 1999 for selected successor states of the USSR and Yugoslavia (United States = 100) was Russia, 21; Ukraine, 10; Estonia, 25; Lithuania, 20; Latvia, 19; Slovenia, 47; Croatia, 21; Slovakia, 32.

in Poland, had survived) is certainly important, as is these countries' orientation toward the West before they fell under Communist rule. Moreover, in some countries, economic policy has been less incoherent and erratic than in Russia. From 1989 to 1992, the GDP of six eastern countries fell by 25 percent, but from the latter year onward growth became positive, first in Poland, then in the Czech Republic, then in Hungary. For central and eastern Europe countries plus the Baltic states, as a whole, growth has been positive since 1994; in 1998, GDP was only slightly under its 1989 level, though three economies—Poland (often described as the tiger of the region, as it grew very fast in the 1990s—at 5.3 percent per year, 1995–1999), Slovenia, and Slovakia—exceeded their levels of output of 1989. The Czech Republic and Hungary were not far below.

These countries (and also the Baltic states) have reasonably functioning markets and economic institutions; most means of production have been privatized (except land in some cases); and they enjoy robust growth, though with occasional hiccups, and with high—possibly too high—levels of deficits, inflation, and unemployment, plus some disaster sectors similar to those in the West: coal, steel, shipbuilding. The other countries, especially Romania, Bulgaria, and Serbia, are far behind, both for reforms and for living standards. GDP per capita varies within a range of 1 to 3 between the poorest and the richest countries but remains well below EU levels; Slovenia is at two-thirds of the average GDP per capita in the EU, Hungary at one-half, and Bulgaria at just under one-fourth. Interestingly, the dividing line between successful and failed transitions is roughly the old one between Catholic and Greek Orthodox countries. Altogether during the 1990s, many people in ECE had a hard time, but most countries, though not yet functioning completely normally, are seeing improvements in economic conditions and in standards of living.

Like in Russia, industry suffered at first from the interruption of investment by the state and from market losses, both abroad (because of the Soviet bloc's dislocation) and at home (owing to massive imports from the west). Moreover, privatized firms, which lacked capital and managers, did not perform well in many cases; there were failures and redundancies. On the other hand, subsidiaries of western companies and new undertakings that had emerged ex nihilo after 1990 enjoyed fast growth (the latter are one base of Poland's success). Agriculture accounts for 9 percent of the GDP and employs 22 percent of the labor force (against 2.4 percent and 5 percent in the EU); "reprivatization" of land has been a difficult and slow process, particularly because there was no more "peasantry," strictly speaking. Still, as early as 1993 in Hungary, 1.5 million households were engaged again in small-scale agricultural production. From 1989 to 1995, production fell by a third, and large food imports became necessary. But in later years, output went up and some modernization was achieved.

In foreign trade, there was a setback in the early 1990s, as exports to Russia and other former socialist countries collapsed, but there was also a reorientation toward the west, a reintegration within the European market, and presently most of the central and eastern European countries' (CEEC) trade is with the EU (two-thirds for exports); Germany has replaced the USSR as first customer and supplier. This has been helped by the Europe agreements, which gave to CEEC free access to EU markets, except for agricultural produce and for so-called sensitive articles (steel, textiles, etc.).[95] Moreover, western countries, particularly Germany, have given bilateral public aid; the London-based Bank for European Reconstruction and Development (BERD) was established in 1991 to grant long-term credit to transition countries; and there have been private flows of capital—including delocalization of Austrian and German firms—of which Hungary and later Poland have been the major recipients. FDI has helped to upgrade technology and to restructure firms, but it also has been destabilizing. Still, the contribution by the West to the consolidation of capitalism and democracy in the East has been criticized as insufficient (on the other hand, it has not always been well used), and western investors as too cautious.

Moreover, most CEECs want to join the EU—and even the Eurozone, but several of the latter's members have been slow or even reluctant to welcome the applicants. They fear the sharp rise in EU spending that CEEC's entry would make necessary as well as eventual competition by cheap labor producers, though some experts maintain that the net cost of "eastern enlargement" would be tiny for the EU. At any rate, in 1998 the EU decided that negotiation would start in 1999 for entry of five best-qualified eastern countries—the Czech Republic, Hungary, Poland, Slovenia, and Estonia (plus Cyprus); the first three were also admitted into NATO in 1999. Then, on 15 February 2000, negotiations started with the five less-advanced eastern countries (plus Malta). It is hoped that the first adhesions could take place in 2003—or rather 2005. Undoubtedly, discussions will be difficult and protracted, maneuvering on all sides intricate. The EU has enlarged before, but never on such a scale, and never to include new members with an economic and cultural history so special, which includes four major shocks in the twentieth century: World War I, German conquest, communism, and liberation. Several candidates are well below the level of wealth and governance that Portugal and Greece had reached when they were admitted into the EU. If all candidates entered in 2000, the EU's population would rise from 373 million to 480 million, but its GDP would only increase by 11 percent, and its GDP per capita would fall by 14 percent. Moreover, two especially difficult problems are the free circulation of people (some EU countries fear massive immigration from the east) and agriculture: extending the CAP eastward would be terribly expensive. On the other hand, Polish farmers (in a country where agriculture employs 27 percent of the working population and methods are archaic) are frightened by western competition. The ferryboat countries are impatient to join the West and to anchor firmly to it, but, according to Ivan Berend (1999b), it is not sure that all will succeed: "Sailing toward the West will continue for a long time in rough waters and a gusty wind."

For over four decades, Europe was divided into two hostile blocs—ideologically, politically, militarily, and also economically. By 2000 this division was gone, but the economic contrast between the rich west and the poor east is still with us—and possibly worse than a century ago.[96] It makes difficult the "widening" of the EU. On the other hand, widening will greatly complicate its working while hampering its "deepening" and its progress toward federalism. One can wonder whether a "variable geometry" Europe of twenty-seven members, or an EU that would be just a huge free-trade area, could be a genuine community and union.

Conclusion

On 14 August 1999, the *Economist* wrote that one month earlier, "many pundits doubted that Europe's economy has much life left in it. Overtaxed, overregulated, resistant to change, Europe—they said—was bound to stagnate. . . . That view was always misguided," and anyway, despite some worrying signs, a recovery had started. Some months later, early in 2000, some other pundits were stressing that Europe was in the same situation that the United States had been in 1992, and that by developing information and communication technologies, and thanks to the euro, the Continent would have a long period of balanced and fast growth.

Economic forecasting is a notoriously dangerous exercise. However, there is one social science—demography—that is a far better prophet than economics, and its worrying prophecy is that Europe is facing depopulation. Since the mid-1960s, birthrates and fertility rates have dropped sharply—even collapsed—in all European countries, the birthrate roughly falling from 20 to 10 per thousand. The death rate has also fallen, but more slowly, because the population has aged. Therefore, the rate of natural increase has been greatly reduced: from 8 to 1 per thousand, in the countries of the EU between the 1960s and the 1980s. Immigration has become the major contributor to population's increase (over three-quarters of it for the period 1957–1997), inasmuch as immigrants retain for at least one generation their traditional behavior and often have large families. But this increase has been slow—0.3 percent per year in the last two decades, against 1.0 percent in the 1950s. Indeed, in 1993, deaths exceeded births, and in 1996, for the first time (except during wars), the population of Europe did not increase (however, eastern Europe and Russia were responsible, as they had an excess of deaths).[97] Still, if there was no immigration, the populations of Germany and Italy would decrease. As for fertility rates (average number of children per woman of childbearing age), they have fallen well below the fatidical minimum of 2 (or rather 2.1), which is the equilibrium figure for a stable population. The rate for the present EU in 1965 was 2.7; in 1996, it was 1.4. There has also been a reversal of positions between north and south. Northern Europe has the highest rate: 1.8 (and Iceland is the only European country slightly above 2), while southern Europe (plus Germany) has the worst position: 1.4 (and 1.19 for Italy—where the birthrate is 9 per thousand); western and eastern Europe are in between (France: 1.7). Moreover, the number of women of childbearing age has started to decrease because the absolute number of births has fallen since 1974.

"The levels that have been reached are so low that the problem of the demographic continuation of the west has been set."[98] It is estimated that the population of Europe will fall by a few million between 1997 and 2025, and then more markedly between the latter date and the middle of the twenty-first century, and altogether between 13 and 24 percent from 2000 to 2050 (see table 4.9). About 40 percent of the present cultivated acreage of the EU will become superfluous (except for reforestation, which would restore many regions to their appearance in the seventh century!).[99] The weight of Europe in the world would thus be greatly reduced, as population would continue to increase on other continents. By 1900, Europe had 25 percent of the planet's population, and by 1950, 22 percent; by 1995, this ratio had fallen to 13 percent (6 percent for the EU); by 2025, it will only be 9 percent, and 7 percent by 2050; Africa might then have three times more inhabitants.

Moreover, Europe's population will be old, and it already has aged markedly in all European countries, as life expectancy has risen. Pyramids of age structure have narrowed at the base and widened at the top. The median age of Europe's population has risen from 30 years in 1955 to 36 in 1995. From 2005 onward, Europeans over 60 will be more numerous than those under 20. The percentage of the population of working age (15–65) will peak c. 2000 at 67 percent and fall below 60 percent after 2030.[100] Around 2050, the ratio of people of working age to retired people will be 2 to 1, while it was 4 to 1 in 1960. This is the pension and social-protection time bomb that has been mentioned earlier: there will be soon a tremendous and increasing burden of taxation and/or debt upon a dwindling proportion of young people, to the benefit of a rising number of old ones. Moreover, an aging population might drag economies and societies into a vicious downward spiral. Another danger is the demographic inequilibrium with the poor countries to the south, where population keeps on increasing fast.

The hopes raised by the end of the Cold War, of a united, pacified, prosperous Europe, might have been fanciful. The British historian T. C. W. Blanning wondered, in 1996, whether developments in Europe since 1990 did not "herald a return visit from the four horsemen of the Apocalypse."[101] Perhaps Europe is expiating the deadly sins of two world wars, of begetting communism and Nazism, and of the Shoah. Common sense would suggest that remedies to the European disease are to work more (and longer) and to have more children. And also to display creativity again, to achieve, after the American example, more inventions and innovations; to imagine new products, services, and technologies; to invest

_____ Table 4.9 _____
The population of Europe, 1950–2050 (in millions)

	Western Europe	Eastern Europe[a]	Europe
1950	303	241	544
2000	388	338	726
Total increase, 1950–2000	+85	+97	+182
Projected total for 2050		from 550 to 628[b]	
Total projected decrease, 2000–2050		from –102 to –176	

_____

a. Including Russia, Belarus, and the Ukraine.

b. Low and medium estimates according to changes in fertility, which would bring it in 2050 either to 1.3 or to 1.8. In both cases, deaths will exceed births in the twenty-first century. A high estimate, resulting from a recovery of fertility, is considered unrealistic. It is assumed that the fall of the death rate will continue and immigration will be stable.

Source: Population et Sociétés (published by the National Institute for Demographic Studies [INED] of France), no. 353 (January 2000).

in research and development. After all, from 1820 to 1995, western Europe increased its GDP per capita at an average rate of 1.5 percent per year, which is not as high as North America's (1.68 percent) and Japan's increases, but much better than the rest of the world. As for eastern Europe, it has suffered—with much courage—terrible ordeals, but it is now on the way to renaissance. Liberty and creativity were the springs behind the development of Europe in the past, behind the primacy it enjoyed over the world for a time, behind the economic growth that, contrary to claims by false prophets, is the only way to reduce poverty. Is it naive to think that Europeans will remain devoted to liberty and that their creativity will bloom again?

Notes

Introduction and Abbreviations

1. M. Mazower, in *The Times*, 21 May 1998.
2. "Do you know the land where lemons bloom? / In the dark foliage, golden oranges gleam."
3. It is not a rigorously scholarly book either, in the sense that detailed references are not provided. When an author is mentioned or quoted, documentation for his or her work is given in the bibliography; dates are given parenthetically in text when more than one work by the author is listed in the bibliography. A few items that only concern one passage in the text are in the notes rather than in the bibliography.
4. PPPs are the rates of currency conversion that eliminate the differences in price levels between countries. They are the best instrument to compare the GDPs of different countries.
5. TFP is the ratio of all output to a composite of all inputs—or "factors"—taken together. It is called "total" because it is not merely output per unit of labor or any one input alone.

One   The Emergence of a European Economy

1. See table 1.1; c. 600, Europe had about 10 percent of the world's total population; after rising up to 25 percent c. 1900, this ratio returned to little more than 10 percent in the 1990s.
2. There was urban decline in the Balkans and an overall fall in population; in the countryside, changes were roughly the same as in the west: large estates extended, peasants were brought into subjection.

3. Some towns—and some rural settlements—were abandoned, but almost all eighty-two Roman cities in what is now France survived; there was continuity, rather than discontinuity, of settlement. But it is wise not to generalize, as the situation was complex and varied.
4. Technological progress will be examined again later in the chapter.
5. Amid anarchy in the ninth to the eleventh centuries, local lords usurped the royal power to mint money; Charlemagne's unified system broke down and *denarii* depreciated.
6. The use of the expression "feudalism" to characterize this economic (and social) system is discussed below.
7. In the twelfth century, expansion also took place in the Byzantine Empire.
8. Still, leprosy was a serious problem; in the thirteenth century, there were two thousand leper hospitals in France.
9. See table 1.1. The series that excludes Russia gives 28 million c. 900, 30 million c. 1000, and 70 million c. 1300.
10. In England, however, labor services survived later than elsewhere. In southern Europe, where they always had been rather light, they practically disappeared.
11. Some vacant manors were bought by rich burghers—a process that went on during the early modern period. In England, shortage of labor led to the development of sheep raising, to the detriment of grain cultivation.
12. Sicily also had to be partly repopulated, after its Muslim inhabitants revolted and were massacred in the thirteenth century.
13. Yet the new plow was used on the heavy soils of the Po plains. Its use reached Poland in the twelfth century.
14. This includes the change from a rotative to a reciprocating movement. Moreover, setting up a mill involved deviating a brook or river, arranging a weir and waterfall.
15. Windmills were horizontal in the Middle East; in Europe they were made vertical.
16. During the "Dark Ages," Jews had settled in northern Europe as long-distance traders. This role—never dominant—declined in the Mediterranean as early as the eleventh century, and the twelfth in northern Europe, but Jews remained prominent in minting, money changing, and credit operations. Many were massacred in the Rhineland at the beginning of the First Crusade. Jews were expelled from England in 1290 and from France in 1306.
17. The Rhineland and northern France also were fairly urbanized.
18. Excavations at Gdansk have shown that cloth was imported there

from the west in the late eleventh century. However, in the fourteenth century, Poland exported cheap woolens to its neighbors.

19. From the eleventh and twelfth centuries, Italians also imported cotton wool and yarn from Sicily (where the Arabs had introduced it), Malta, Crete, and the Levant, mainly to mix it with flax in fustians. They also made linen, an industry that was important in southern Germany (where fustians were also made) and other places.

20. The number of religious houses in England and Wales rose from sixty-one in 1066 to six hundred in 1216.

21. Merchants had earlier started their own guilds, with security as their main purpose.

22. The nature of the coastline, currents, and prevailing winds gives an advantage to powers that control the Mediterranean northern coasts.

23. Since the eleventh century, goods from Asia came through the Red Sea and Egypt, rather than the Persian Gulf, Iraq, and Constantinople. Some writers consider the Mediterranean world only a subsystem of a global economic system that had its center in the Indian Ocean.

24. Pepper was an appreciated accompaniment to the strong taste that venison and other meats often had, owing to the lack of refrigeration.

25. This trade growth took place in the Mediterranean, to start with; for example, there were exports of grain from Sicily to supply the large Italian cities.

26. Bridges had been rare c. 1000, but there was a wave of building—in stone—in the twelfth century; this network adequately met traffic demands well into the early modern period.

27. Maritime laws also emerged, with two different codes—one for the Mediterranean, one for the Atlantic and the northern seas.

28. The exported salt was known as "bay salt," as it was collected along the coasts of the Bay of Biscay, in southern Brittany and between the estuaries of the Loire and the Gironde. Salt, a biological necessity for humans and animals, was difficult to produce on northerly coasts, but Germany and Poland had mines of rock salt.

29. The towns were Troyes, Provins (each with two fairs per year), Bar-sur-Aube, and Lagny. The fairs rotated almost throughout the year.

30. This explanation is not accepted by some writers: they stress the rise in the late thirteenth century of trade in bulk goods (especially alum for the textile industries of Flanders and England), which could only be shipped by sea. An increase in taxation, after the annexation of Champagne to the French kingdom (1285), has also been held responsible.

31. The journey from Genoa to England lasted about three months.

32. Around 1300, Italian merchants had superseded the Flemish as exporters of most English wool.
33. The drafting of customs (common laws) in northern Europe and the revival of Roman law in the south must also be mentioned.
34. See chap. 2. This usual view has been disputed.

Two   Change and Continuity in the European Economy

1. English coal output increased from about 200,000 tons c. 1550 to 3 million c. 1700. On the Continent, the district of Liège was the only important coalfield.
2. Shorter canals were opened in Lombardy in the thirteenth century, and then in the Low Countries. In France, the first important canal, one that joined the Seine to the Loire, was built between 1605 and 1640.
3. "Multinational" is an equivocal term. The phenomenon of businesses having bases of operations in more than one country started very early and concerned many merchants involved in foreign trade —Italians, Hansards, Dutch, and others. In the sixteenth century, the house of Fugger, from Augsburg, in southern Germany, had many bases and operated extensively in most of Europe.
4. Their liquidity depended upon the banking system, as they were increasingly endorsed by bankers or "merchant-bankers." Thus, the widespread use of bills of exchange is connected with the rise of banking.
5. From the eleventh and twelfth centuries on, Jews and later Lombards did much pawnbroking, at high interest rates (despite bans by the church), first in Italy and then north of the Alps. But the link between those pawn offices and proper banks is not direct. In the thirteenth century, any town of some importance had several money changers.
6. The Casa di San Giorgio was not the oldest public bank; the Spanish cities of Barcelona and Valencia had established such banks in 1401 and 1407, respectively. Moreover, the Casa stopped operating in 1444, to be revived in 1586.
7. Again, the earliest *monte* was in Spain, in 1431; the first one in Italy was established in 1461.
8. See n. 24. An early but special (and transitory) "international banker" was the Order of the Knights Templar; thanks to its network of *commanderies,* it acted as a deposit and giro bank, made loans, and transferred large sums, but it was dissolved in the early fourteenth century—for usury and heresy.

9. Transactions with King Edward III of England are often considered responsible for the banking disasters of the 1340s, but this has been recently denied. The Medici bank declined after 1450 and closed as a consequence of the French invasion of Italy in 1494, but the Medicis became great dukes of Tuscany.

10. The Swedish diet salvaged the debris to found the Bank of Estates (1668), which became the Bank of Sweden in 1866, the oldest of the present-day central banks.

11. After the "Glorious Revolution" of 1688, Parliament had more control over public finances; this inspired confidence among rich people who supported the new regime and its fight against Louis XIV —like those who founded the bank.

12. They also settled in ports like Bayonne, Bordeaux, and Hamburg. Amsterdam had about eight hundred Portuguese Jews in 1626, twelve hundred in 1655.

13. Farther east, in Poland, to where many Jews had migrated to escape persecution in Germany starting in the fourteenth century, their consistories became banks of a sort in the seventeenth century, and those banks flourished in the next century.

14. An early but significant projection of Europe in the Atlantic was the rise of cod fisheries on the Great Banks, off Newfoundland. The banks were "discovered" in the late fifteenth century (possibly before Columbus's first voyage) by seafarers from Bristol and Brittany, who were soon joined by fishermen from Normandy, French Atlantic ports, the Basque coast, and Portugal. In the sixteenth century, several hundred fishing boats visited the Banks every year, and a triangular trade developed: cod-fishing ships went first to France or Portugal to load salt, then to the Banks, from which they returned directly to ports in southern Europe, where demand for fish during Lent was large. The Basques and Portuguese dropped out, and the fisheries were monopolized by the French and the British (later joined by New Englanders). In the late 1700s, about fifteen hundred boats went to the Great Banks each year.

15. In some countries, including England, prices continued rising until the mid-seventeenth century. An index of English wheat prices rose from 100 in 1450–1499 to 717 in 1640–1649.

16. It has been maintained, however, that this movement resulted from silver-market disequilibrium and not from European trade deficits: silver went to Asia because it had its highest-value use there and was in demand as a real commodity.

17. Total trade of the two countries increased far less (in volume) dur-

ing the same periods: by a factor of 2.8 in the case of France, and 2.3 for England. As a consequence, there was an "Americanization" of their trade; British exports to America rose from 10 percent of total exports in 1700–1702 to 37 percent in 1772–1774. The contribution of trade outside Europe to total trade has been estimated, for 1752–1754, at 20–25 percent for the United Provinces, 33 percent for France, and 50 percent for England.

18. Denmark also acquired the Virgin Islands, in the Caribbean.

19. Still, in the sixteenth century, the city of Ragusa (now Dubrovnik), on the eastern coast of the Adriatic, had many large ships for bulk cargoes. It also played an important role in the Balkans' trade.

20. The large number of coastal ships—carrying such products as grain from Brittany to Bordeaux (and coming back with wine), or coal from Newcastle to London—must not be overlooked.

21. Some light goods exported to the Baltic traveled overland from Hamburg to Lübeck, but the sea route became increasingly important after 1600. From 1553, the English, followed by the Dutch, opened direct relations with Russia through the White Sea, where the port of Arkhangel'sk was created in 1584, but this was not a serious competition for the Baltic trade.

22. There was some revival in the eighteenth century: colonial produce from the West Indies was imported in Marseilles and shipped to Geneva, Switzerland, and southern Germany.

23. Switzerland also exported dry and salted meat plus hard cheese, which kept well and—like Dutch cheese—was used for provisioning ships.

24. Already in the fifteenth to the seventeenth centuries one can perceive an "international republic of money" or financial "superstate," i.e., a network of international bankers and merchants who were lending to governments and helping their financial dealings.

25. In Bohemia, production of woolens rose from 39,000 pieces in 1731 to 142,000 in 1780. Still, the linen industry was larger, and some other industries also developed. A special trait was that industry was mainly on aristocratic estates, at the initiative of their owners, and used serfs' labor. In Poland also, magnates developed manufactures on their estates, for producing vodka, beer, textiles, glass, and the like.

26. However, fustians, in which cotton and flax were mixed, had been made since the Middle Ages (see above); calico printing was started in Marseilles in 1648 and in London and Amsterdam in 1678.

27. The prohibition came about due to lobbying by manufacturers of

traditional fabrics. In some countries (like France up to 1759) the making and printing of cottons were also prohibited, so that the rise of the cotton industry was delayed.

28. Another case of import-substitution of Asiatic goods is the porcelain industry. The secret to making china was discovered in 1709 in Saxony, by J. F. Böttger. Manufactures—often state owned or state protected—were established in various places: Meissen, Copenhagen, Sèvres, Derby, Worcester, Capodimonte, etc.

29. In central Europe, production peaked in the sixteenth century and then declined. In England, Cornwall and Devon produced copper and tin. Sweden also had copper mines.

30. However, towns retained a great deal of industrial work, for example, the finishing of textile fabrics; silk weaving was mainly urban as well. Actually, there was a symbiosis between towns, which supplied capital, commercial, and service functions, and countryside.

31. In fifteenth-century England, more than half the wool cloths made were woven in country cottages. In Italy, on the other hand, city authorities, who controlled the countryside, succeeded in impeding the process. Landes (1998) sees this difference as crucial for the rise of industry in England and its decline in Italy.

32. Examples of atrophying areas: the wool-industry districts of East Anglia and the West Country in England and of Languedoc in France, and the linen areas of Brittany, Westphalia, upper Austria, and Galicia.

33. However, many Italian engineers, craftsmen, and artists went to work in central and eastern Europe.

34. Portugal persecuted its "new Christians," i.e., converted Jews, who handled a large share of its trade; many emigrated, and English merchants replaced them. Spain also suffered from having expelled its Jews in 1492.

35. A consequence was that the regions between the two former poles (e.g., southern Germany) suffered. The relative share of Mediterranean countries in Europe's total population fell.

36. Antwerp's trade recovered during the twelve-year truce, and the money market was active during the Thirty Years' War, in which Spain took part.

37. Holland's position, roughly midway between the Baltic and the Iberian Peninsula, was an advantage, especially for supplying the latter with grain.

38. The ribbon loom (see above) was a Dutch invention, like the "hollander" (in paper-making) and the microscope.

39. The VOK ruled the Dutch possessions in the East. Around 1670, it owned two hundred ships, employed eighty thousand men (civilians and soldiers), and paid a 40 percent yearly dividend on its shares.

40. Thanks to its sales of textiles and Baltic goods to Spain, Holland had a favorable balance with the latter, so that it received a lot of silver —which was necessary for the East India and the Baltic trades.

41. Borrowing by foreign states was arranged by Amsterdam private bankers—and their agents in London, in the case of English loans; both groups included a number of Jews of Portuguese and Spanish origin. This kind of operation had antecedents in the seventeenth century, and even in sixteenth-century Antwerp.

42. Except with the lower Volga area and central Asia; relations with Byzantium had been severed by the Mongol invasion. In the seventeenth and eighteenth centuries a caravan trade with China, across Siberia, developed.

43. The trade that southern Poland had been carrying on with the East was destroyed.

44. The population of Hungary and much of the Balkans had markedly decreased because of the wars of conquest (and reconquest) by the Turks, but it grew sharply after those countries had been freed.

45. ECE also includes Hungary—after it had been freed from the Turks —and other parts of the Hapsburg empire.

46. Lithuania had been a great dukedom, much larger than the present state of the same name.

47. The last king of Poland, Stanisłas II August Poniatowski (1764–1795), his family, and some magnates had an interest in economic problems. But Poland had no state structure and no middle class (except within the Jewish community); it was partitioned among its three powerful neighbors and disappeared from the map in 1795.

48. Serfdom was the product of abundance of land and scarcity of labor; when Hungary was recovered from the Turks, it was so depopulated that surviving peasants were tied to the land.

49. The received wisdom that the alternating of good and bad crops determined prosperity and depression for the economy as a whole has been recently qualified (see below). Nonetheless, economies were greatly subject to the impact of natural forces, especially the weather.

50. However, in Zeeland, yields and productivity did not increase from 1600 to 1870 because early progress in the Middle Ages had made advances later on difficult.

51. Hoffmann considers that "agricultural productivity turned upon

what happened outside agriculture," i.e., peace or war, taxes, urbanization, and transport conditions. He sees the main sources of higher productivity in the exploitation of comparative advantages, which depended upon transport costs and trading opportunities. The lack of transport improvements in France was a serious drawback. In England productivity gains would have resulted rather from capital investment in land reclamation, drainage, improvement of farm roads, and storage facilities, and the increase in number of farm animals.

52. Rice was brought to Sicily by the Muslims and was introduced in northern Italy in the fifteenth century. Thirsk has drawn attention to "alternative agriculture": when grain prices were low (1650–1750), English farmers developed some crops that had been grown as luxuries or rarities for a wider market, e.g., hops, madder, woad, rape, tobacco, and salad greens; they also bred rabbits, turkeys, and other small animals. Some new plants were first introduced in gardens by immigrants from the Low Countries (in the mid-sixteenth century), and then spread more widely.

53. Poor communications—few roads could be used by wheeled vehicles —have been seen as a major cause of the kingdom of Naples's underdevelopment.

54. The conclusion of Cipolla (1976), that "the productivity of the economic system as a whole made only very limited progress," has already been quoted.

55. During the War of Spanish Succession (1702–1713), Louis XIV had half a million men under arms. It is worth mentioning, however, that improvements in the administrative and fiscal apparatus helped to make the "military revolution" possible.

56. Likewise, most "national manufactures" that were started in eighteenth-century Poland, before the country's partition, failed: they had a very cheap but inefficient labor force of serfs, and no skilled cadres.

57. Venice was the first state to pass, in 1474, a law about industrial patents.

58. Grantham has disputed this view, arguing that reclaimable land was only a tiny share of France's cultivable area. The views of Hoffmann, that the real obstacles to agricultural growth were outside agriculture —in politics, institutions, taxation, and the rest of the economy— have been mentioned earlier.

59. In France, some difficulties have been observed as early as c. 1270, but imbalances worsened after 1300.

60. Some recent writers have been more optimistic about conditions before the plague and therefore stressed the latter's role. An extreme view has even been put forward by Goldsmith: in the early fourteenth century, France was not overpopulated but underpopulated; there was no fundamental imbalance between food supply and population; the agrarian system had not reached an unsurpassable ceiling of production; there was no preplague economic and demographic crisis, no Malthusian-Ricardian trap, but limitless expanses of unfarmed land. On the other hand, Bailey is pessimistic about peasant welfare in England in the late thirteenth century and afterward: they were exposed to volatile markets and to a greater degree of economic risk than formerly.

61. This was the view of David Herlihy, in his posthumously published book: *The Black Death and the Transformation of the West* (Cambridge, Mass., 1998).

62. The London incidence killed some 100,000 people, i.e., one-fifth to one-fourth of the population.

63. A midcentury decrease of imports of American silver is often said to have contributed to the recession.

64. Though economic recovery was slow, German population (within the borders of Germany in 1871) more than doubled between 1700 and 1800.

65. There was no single factor determinant of that decline, and no close relationship with economic growth. But a spontaneous fall in the aggressiveness of smallpox (the great eighteenth-century killer) may have started the decline. Improvements in nourishment and in mothers' and children's care also played a role—though the diet of lower classes may have deteriorated after 1760.

66. Some writers stress the fluctuating food supply, according to harvests, which at intervals dipped below the population requirements, rather than the two episodes when a growing population ran into the ceiling of inelastic food supplies. According to M. Morineau, "retro-Malthusianism has failed."

67. Still, there were deviations from the Malthusian model, notably in the southern Netherlands in both the thirteenth and the sixteenth centuries: thanks to increased productivity in farming and to grain imports, both population and real wages rose (Van der Wee 1999).

68. Even the kingdom of Naples underwent profound changes from the sixteenth to the eighteenth century.

69. *Wall Street Journal Europe*, 1 Nov. 1999.

<u>*Three*   The Age of Industrialization</u>

1. To define the threshold beyond which a country has become in-dustrial (or industrialized) is subjective. A decisive stage is, however, when employment in agriculture falls below 50 percent of the work-ing population and/or when its contribution to GDP becomes smaller than that of industry.
2. This was a case of delocalization of textile-fibers production, which provided a cheap raw material, thanks to slave labor on cotton plan-tations in the United States and to the invention of the cotton gin by Eli Whitney (1793). The production of other fibers (wool, flax, silk) was also largely delocalized to nonindustrial countries during the nineteenth century. On the other hand, though some organic raw materials were replaced by mineral ones (e.g., madder, by ani-line dyes), new ones emerged, like rubber, and paper was increas-ingly made from wood.
3. Waterpower revived in the late nineteenth century, with the devel-opment of hydroelectricity. It was a boon for the Scandinavian and Alpine areas.
4. Actually, the "first" factories in England were silk-throwing mills (the earliest was built in Derby in 1719), but their number remained small and their impact marginal. Some "embryo" or "protofactories" had also been established.
5. The savings-rate figures are Feinstein's (in Mathias and Postan, vol. 1); Crafts (1985) has found a rise from 6 percent of national income in 1760 to 8 percent in 1800.
6. The price of bar iron in Britain fell from £18 per ton in 1750 to £8 in 1820.
7. Even in England, coke-smelting, which had been invented in 1709, did not prevail over the charcoal process before the mid-eighteenth century, for quite simple reasons of cost.
8. See below for some social consequences of the industrial revolution.
9. Moreover, even in Britain, there was a good deal of resistance—by the "Luddites" and their like—to the introduction of new ma-chinery.
10. "Scotland's industrial revolution was indeed revolutionary," con-cludes Whatley in his recent study.
11. The sevenfold increase in the number of patents granted in England is striking: 178 in 1725–1749, 1,273 in 1775–1799 (for textile patents, the numbers are 34 and 236, respectively).

12. The study of patents shows considerable inventive activity not only in branches that are recognized as technological leaders, but also in industries not normally associated with advancing technology.

13. Actually, for a long period, the redeployment of labor was in relative terms: in Britain, the absolute number of people employed in agriculture increased up to c. 1860, and there was no outflow of capital from agriculture to industry.

14. Alan Macfarlane traces it back to the unique character of English feudalism: England was a different kind of society, always "modern" in its attitudes, and the industrial revolution was only a consequence of that basic fact. In this regard, Temin (1997b) has stressed, on Weberian lines, the Protestant Anglo-Saxon culture, based upon individualism, which had a decided advantage in the age of machinery and factories. From these points of view, the industrial revolution had its roots in a *longue durée* process, across English history, of which it was both the continuation and the zenith.

15. Historians have also wondered, among other things, why the industrial revolution did not start earlier, in one of the countries that had been, in its time, more advanced than the rest of Europe (fifteenth-century Italy, sixteenth-century southern Netherlands, seventeenth-century Holland), rather than in England, a small country on the periphery that had been an importer of foreign technologies up to the seventeenth century (see chap. 2). Bairoch (1997) suggests that an industrial revolution had been more likely in medieval China than in late-seventeenth-century Europe but accepts that Britain was the only country where it could happen. Besides, some writers consider that growth is a normal condition, often inhibited by noneconomic factors. This view is not accepted here; we are looking for forces that changed the traditional pattern in England and produced the industrial revolution.

16. It has been calculated that the capital necessary to create one job in English industry c. 1800 was equivalent to the average wages for four or five months of one male worker. There was moreover an inflow of capital from Holland.

17. Some writers, however, consider that a very large city was rather a handicap; but London was quite different from Naples, Istanbul, or Edo.

18. Britain's coal output rose from 3 million tons c. 1700 to over 10 million in 1800—four times more than the whole Continent.

19. The importance of the "Glorious Revolution" of 1688, which gave to England a then unique form of government, should not be over-

estimated: stable property rights existed beforehand, while the industrial revolution started almost a century afterward. Moreover, eighteenth-century Parliaments were more obsequious toward the king's government than dominating.

20. Admittedly, property was safe from confiscation (as was also the case in many continental states), but Englishmen were heavily taxed, and taxation is expropriation. Besides, England adopted in 1624 a patent law that allowed inventors to reap the benefits of the use of their inventions (but only for fourteen years—not to delay progress). This raised the return on innovation and thus stimulated invention. However, it has been maintained recently that the eighteenth-century patent system did little to encourage invention.

21. According to a traditional view, several countries—such as France and Switzerland—did not have an industrial revolution, as technological and structural change there was slow and unspectacular. But we have seen that similar characteristics have been discovered in the British industrial revolution! Still, relative to Britain, nineteenth-century continental industrialization was belated and incomplete.

22. Because of this, continental governments—especially France before 1789 and Prussia after 1815—and businessmen had to send "spies" to Britain, to smuggle out machinery and to entice workers to go abroad (Harris 1998). After 1842, British engineering firms were very active in marketing their machinery abroad, as Bruland has shown in the case of Norway. They supplied "packages" involving information, machinery, skilled labor, and management expertise. This markedly eased problems for continental entrepreneurs and became a major channel of technological transfer.

23. The École Polytechnique was created in Paris in 1795; imitations followed in Prague (1807) and Vienna (1815).

24. The making of locomotives started in France in 1838, and no more imports took place after 1846. Equivalent dates for Germany are 1842 (founding of the firm Borsig in Berlin) and 1854. As early as 1842, 89 percent of steam engines at work in France had been made there.

25. Wallonia supplied coal, semifinished iron, and know-how to northern France and the Rhineland. The spinning mule was introduced in Catalonia from France in 1806. Quite early, many German experts worked in the industries of Poland (then annexed to Russia). French, German, and Swiss entrepreneurs played a significant role in the beginnings of the modern textile industry in Italy (1815–1861).

26. From 1871 to 1918, Germany had annexed northern Lorraine.

27. According to Ringrose, use of the term "Spain" does not make sense. See also the discussion above about industrial regions in Britain. The "clustering" of firms might cause competition for labor and rises in wages, but this was countered by immigration and vertical linkages between firms. Spatial concentration thus created an environment that encouraged further spatial concentration.

28. See chap. 2. Ireland is a special case, but in the nineteenth century, it was a region of the United Kingdom. Its uniqueness comes from the great famine of 1845–1849, which killed one million people and caused 700,000 or 800,000 to emigrate. Moreover, this massive emigration continued after the famine, so that population, which had been 8.2 million in 1841, fell to 6.3 million in 1851 (–24 percent) and 4.3 million in 1911. Ireland was the only part of Europe to suffer such a drastic demographic decline.

29. Lancashire concentrated almost the whole of the enormous cotton industry of Britain, while France had several cotton regions.

30. Even so, the number of mechanized cotton mills in France rose from 8 in 1790 to 37 in 1799 and to 234 in 1806.

31. Serfdom was also abolished in Spain, where the old regime was gradually liquidated and new property rights defined; but the main element of agrarian reform—the expropriation and sale of church, state, and town lands—was rather bungled. Emancipation was incomplete in Russia: collective constraints in village communes (*mirs*) were maintained. Its main economic consequence was not to make labor available for industry, but to stimulate serfs to participate in the market, in order to pay redemption charges.

32. It is surprising that Britain did not try to thwart what turned out to be the first stage of development of its chief economic rival. Rather, it watched with benevolence, wholly convinced of the correctness of the free-trade doctrine and of the superiority of the British economy.

33. However, Bairoch (in Mathias and Pollard) has maintained that during the early decades of the nineteenth century tariff barriers—plus the then prevailing high transport costs—helped the industrial revolution's diffusion, especially by allowing follower countries to start and develop capital goods and engineering industries as well as coal mining.

34. Though pre-1860 French protectionism has often been overestimated and anyway had been mitigated during the 1850s, the Franco-British treaty was an important turning point and was connected with changes in the nature of world trade, including rising price elasticity for French exports. The initiative came from Napoléon III, a

much maligned but far-seeing statesman (in 1867, he was to propose a single world monetary system; see n. 99). France was the treaty's main winner, but a kind of Anglo-French "commercial alliance" was established and lasted up to the 1880s.

35. The transalpine roads over the Cenis and Simplon passes, which Napoléon built, were the first major international links. Up to the emergence of electric tramways and the internal combustion engine for cars and trucks, all local, short-distance transport remained horse-driven. During the nineteenth century the number of horses greatly increased—as did pollution in towns.

36. Traffic on the Danube and on Russian rivers was relatively light. On the other hand, railroad competition put an end to traffic on many minor rivers and canals. It also hurt the coastal trade, which greatly declined (except where land travel was difficult, as in Greece and Norway). The numerous small seaports of traditional economies also declined (but for fishing), inasmuch as they could not receive the new large ships, and trade concentrated in a small number of large ports. Among them, Antwerp and Rotterdam handled much of western Germany's seaborne trade (and the former a good deal of northern France's as well).

37. A frequent way governments helped was to guarantee interest on companies' bonds. Conversely, governments exercised some supervision of railroads' operations, particularly of their fares. There were some early cases of repurchase and nationalization—in Germany starting in 1876, in Italy, 1905.

38. In late-nineteenth-century France, there certainly was too much investment in branch railroads. Many of them were pure pork ("electoral lines," in French). In other cases, it was hoped that they would stimulate industry and traffic, but results were disappointing.

39. The first transalpine railroads had been built farther east, in Austria (Semmering line, between Vienna and Trieste, 1854).

40. See "Stages of Industrialization," below. From 1870 to 1910, the share of freight costs in the price of wheat landed in Liverpool fell from 65 percent to 10 percent. The opening of the Suez Canal (1869) also played a part in the fall of freight prices.

41. The capital and credit shortage, for example, slowed down the mechanization of the Swiss cotton industry. In France and some other countries, notaries acted, on a rather large scale, as intermediaries between savers and borrowers. Despite convertibility of paper into specie, which prevailed in most countries up to 1914 (with some brief suspensions, because of war or crises), banknote circulation

spread slowly on the Continent, as did the use of new instruments of payment (e.g., checks, bank transfers).

42. Protestant banking (see chap. 2) remained important in the early nineteenth century but was later eclipsed by "native" and Jewish houses.

43. Actually, England and Scotland each had its own system, at least until 1845.

44. Eventually, they were the only private banks to survive, in their niche market, with their zenith before 1914.

45. Berend (in Teich and Porter) sees the German-modeled banks of Hungary as the prime and decisive mover in the acceleration of growth in that country after 1890.

    According to Cameron (1967), the banking systems that were the most favorable to economic progress were those of Belgium, Germany, and Scotland.

46. In Britain, the "big five" came about in 1918.

47. This periodization does not mean that we accept the hypothesis of fifty-to-sixty-year-long waves, or Kondratieffs. Crafts, Leybourne, and Mills are "skeptical of many of the proposed chronologies of growth" and state that "the volatility of trend growth" has been exaggerated —at least for industrial output. Among seven countries they considered, at least four display constant trend growth.

48. The cotton industry lost its dynamism after the "cotton famine" caused by the American Civil War (which had more economic impact than the short European wars of the period). On the other hand, the modernization of the wool and linen industries was stimulated.

49. The Netherlands had an economic renaissance; thanks to the spread of the steam engine, production and productivity grew fast in almost all branches of industry; textile work migrated from cottages to factories.

50. The situation in France was aggravated by phylloxera, a plant lice that devastated vineyards. The production of some industrial raw materials—wool, silk, dyestuffs—declined or even stopped in the face of competition from overseas producers and/or synthetic products. Sericulture was wiped out in France but was to peak in Italy in 1907.

51. Steel, which is stronger and more flexible than iron, had previously been an expensive product, but new processes enabled it to be produced cheaply and in large quantities. It is significant that, unlike in earlier periods, there was no time lag in the Bessemer and

Thomas-Gilchrist processes' diffusion between Britain and the Continent: it is proof of continental industry's maturity.

52. In the Netherlands, there was a rapid growth of heavy industry (e.g., engineering, shipbuilding). Despite the "great depression," Maddison's (1995) growth rates are higher for 1870–1913 than for the preceding half-century:

Growth of GDP at constant prices in twelve European core countries (percent per year).

	Aggregate	Per capita
1820–1870	1.7	1.0
1870–1913	2.1	1.3

The increase in growth rates is somewhat higher for his four countries of southern Europe and for eastern Europe.

Williamson (1997) gives the growth rates that follow for fourteen Old World countries (weighted averages, in percents):

	GDP per capita	Population
1870–1890	1.16	0.73
1890–1913	1.47	0.80
1870–1913	1.33	0.77

53. According to Bairoch (1997), c. 1870, Britain had 23 percent of the world manufacturing potential (traditional and modern).

54. There was also a slowing down of Britain's growth, which, according to some calculations, can be detected as early as the 1860s. On the other hand, the idea that there was a "climacteric" for British industrial output in the 1890s has been given up. According to Crafts, Leybourne, and Mills, its rates of growth slowly declined from the 1830s to 1900 and then stabilized, while a slowdown in the United Kingdom's GDP growth before 1914 would be almost imperceptible. Some experts are skeptical about this kind of calculation.

Britain's leading position compared to Germany's large companies comes about if services, especially distribution, and not only manufacturing, are considered.

55. For comparison's sake, consider that in 1880 the British and German shares of steel output had been 31 percent and 15 percent, respectively.

56. For example, Sheffield, with its many small firms, specialized in high-quality steels. Still, cotton manufacturers have been blamed for failing to establish professional management hierarchies.

57. Germany was the world leader in chemicals: by 1900, it was responsible for 80–90 percent of world production of artificial dyestuffs, but in electrical equipment it shared the lead with the United States. Still, it was the largest exporter of technologically advanced goods.

58. After the Anglo-French commercial alliance had lapsed (see n. 34), Germany reconstructed the European trade treaties network to its advantage. Even in France, Germany's archenemy, German firms were creating branch factories and buying iron-ore deposits; Thyssen built large steelworks in Normandy, near Caen. Siemens had two factories and in 1912 planned a joint venture with Schneider (a French firm) for the electrification of French railroads. However, after the international crisis of 1911, there was a nationalist reaction in France, which wanted to prevent this kind of penetration (and also to prevent the flow of French capital into Germany) and cooperation between French and German banks. On the other hand, German trade was going "global": 80 percent of it was with Europe in 1880, but it dropped to just 65 percent in 1913.

59. German population figures are based on the territory of the 1871 empire. There was a lag of almost a century between the falls in mortality and natality.

60. Population growth seems to have been an exogenous variable; if it was endogenous, it would be proof of the French economy's weakness. However, some writers consider that focusing on per capita growth underestimates the economic dynamism of prolific countries (like Germany) and overestimates the French performance.

61. At about 1840, with 0.2 percent of the world's population, Switzerland supplied 6–7 percent of the world's exports of manufactures. After midcentury, its exports were equivalent to a third of GNP (a higher ratio than Britain's).

62. By 1850, the Jura district (along the border with France) alone made a million watches per year, i.e., two-thirds of the world output. From 1860 to 1913, exports of watches grew at a rate of 4.7 percent per year.

63. Bairoch (1997) has made a distinction between, on the one hand, countries that exported primary products mainly to Britain, to which they became complementary and dependent, and that did not industrialize much (Denmark, the Netherlands); and, on the other hand, those that competed with the United Kingdom by exporting manufactures. But by 1913, they all had high incomes per capita, and Denmark was ahead of Belgium and Sweden.

64. These countries comprise Bulgaria, Greece, Romania, and Serbia (with Albania and Montenegro). Portugal might also be considered, as it was by 1913 one of the less industrialized and poorest countries and was among the lowest in agricultural productivity. This situation is often explained by its dependency upon Britain—going back to the Methuen Treaty of 1703. By 1870, Britain took 60 percent of Portuguese exports, of which 40 percent was wine.

65. Some railroad building started in the 1860s, and there was a minor boom in the 1880s. By 1913, the Balkans had 4 percent of total European railroad mileage (about 5,500 miles).

66. The first modern factories in the Ottoman Empire were established c. 1850 in southern Bulgaria, close to Istanbul, to make cloth for Turkish army uniforms. In Greece, the first steam-powered factory, a silk mill, was set up in Athens in 1854.

67. By 1910, the trade of the four Balkan countries was 2 percent of Europe's total trade. Greece had a relatively large merchant fleet.

68. The lateness of both the abolition of serfdom and other liberal reforms were factors behind this backwardness. Berend (in Teich and Porter) sees pre-1848 Hungary as frozen into its traditional feudal state.

69. GDP growth was possibly at 5–6 percent per year starting in the 1890s. However, new estimates—for Austria—by Schulze are much more pessimistic than those by Good: they put it near the bottom in terms of European growth, so that it continued to fall behind other countries. From 1860 to 1913, however, the value of Hungary's industrial output (at constant prices) increased by a factor of 14.

70. Russia built more than 15,000 miles of railroads from 1891 to 1902 and had a total of 42,000 miles in 1913, as opposed to 6,400 in 1870. Railroads were a prerequisite for industrialization in Russia due to the spatial dispersion of resources, e.g., for the creation of the steel industry of Ukraine (as mentioned earlier).

71. However, by value, textiles and food were ahead of steel and engineering.

72. The giant firms (and the flourishing of cartels from 1899) were the base of Lenin's view that Russia had reached the stage of "monopolistic capitalism"—the last stage of capitalism—and so was ready for socialist revolution.

73. Still, the finance minister Sergey Witte was certainly an industrializer, but some of his policies had negative effects.

74. From recent calculations by Good and Ma (based on Maddison's data), the performance of "central-eastern Europe" from 1870 to 1910 is somewhat better: its GDP per capita grew at 1.4 percent per year, versus an average of 1.2 percent for Europe and north-western Europe, and 0.9 percent for Mediterranean Europe, which was the laggard. Still, the catching up with the rich countries was limited.

75. O'Rourke and Williamson (1997, 1999) observe convergence between core and periphery, but they do not consider eastern and southeastern Europe. According to Crafts (1997), GDP per capita is not wholly adequate as a measure of the level or growth of living standards. In this respect, he prefers a "human development index" that takes into account changes in life expectancy and education. In such an index, the position in 1913 of the Scandinavian countries, the Netherlands, and Italy improves. But convergence is also confirmed.

76. The more general concept of "social capability" is also useful (though it has been seen as a confession of ignorance): a society is able to introduce into practice not what it knows, but what it can do.

77. O'Brien (1996) has shown that path dependency explains why the British model of industrialization is irrelevant to explain the supposed retardation of France. Path dependency also appears in economic policies, of which each country developed a specific one that was isomorphic to its political culture.

78. Still, in Britain, lack of adequate, publicly funded education did not retard industrial growth at the beginning of the industrial revolution (but the literacy rate was fairly high). On the contrary, it has been argued that, in the second half of the nineteenth century, investment in England for extending literacy did not contribute to economic growth, as most of the people who were made literate had unskilled jobs for which schooling was not a requirement.

79. Simpson has challenged the view that protection was the major factor in the poor performance of Spanish agriculture in the late nineteenth and early twentieth centuries; it was a consequence more than a cause of backwardness.

80. Actually, the latifundia of southern Italy and southern Spain were notorious for backward methods, extensive cultivation, and low yields. Conversely, microfundia, or microholdings, in some areas (Spanish Galicia and Polish Galicia) were intensely cultivated but overpopulated with poor peasants.

81. In 1910, in Britain, animal products were 75 percent of agriculture's final output (in value), but the ratio was smaller in other countries. There was, of course, a significant change in nutrition, at least in advanced countries: starchy staples declined (relatively) to the benefit of meat, fats, sugar, and, later, fruits and vegetables.

82. Europe produced 21–22 million tons of coal in 1820, 681 million tons in 1913; under one million tons of pig iron in 1800, and 45 million tons in 1913. Its total industrial output (Russia included) increased eightfold from 1800 to 1900.

83. Conversely, exports of capital from Europe to the United States and other "new countries" contributed to divergence between the two areas.

84. "There was a real business cycle among the European economic powers in the late nineteenth century," wrote Craig and Fisher, who, conversely, have found little causality between real outputs of European countries and the United States. Much earlier, Thomas had observed an inverse relationship between U.K. and U.S. cycles of residential building, and more generally an inverse rhythm of growth in the United Kingdom and the United States, which was connected with migration and capital exports. Still, some cyclical crises in America had serious effects in Europe. The problem of longer fluctuations has been mentioned earlier.

85. Moreover, there was a sharp contrast between the industrialized and rich northwest of Europe and the rest; and Europe was part of a global world economy.

86. Still, there was some investment by advanced countries in other ones, e.g., by Switzerland into France.

87. The distribution among other destinations was: 26 percent in the United States and other new countries, 19 percent in Latin America, 25 percent in Africa and Asia. The range of investment was rather narrow: government and railroad bonds, utility and mining stocks.

88. Actually, it had been active earlier than 1815, as we have seen, especially in the eighteenth century, but there was an interruption during the Napoleonic wars. After they ended, the London Rothschilds introduced an important innovation: interest on the foreign loans

they floated was paid in London, at fixed dates, at a fixed rate of exchange with sterling. Later, capital flows were stimulated by the payment of the huge war indemnity that France had to pay to Germany after its defeat in the war of 1870–1871.

89. In 1887, Chancellor Otto von Bismarck, who had fallen out with Russia, forbade the Reichsbank to accept Russian state bonds as collateral for loans, so Russia turned to France for loans. There was also some supervision of short-term capital movements.

90. A good example is Norsk Hydro (established in 1905 to make nitrogen in Norway), in which one French bank (Paribas), one Swedish bank, and a German chemical company cooperated. Despite their government's displeasure, French banks made short-term investments on the Berlin money market and collaborated with German banks in various projects, such as the Berlin-Baghdad railroad.

91. France also invested outside Europe, e.g., in Egypt and Argentina. And Russia also received Belgian, British, and German capital.

92. The Dutch invested more capital in U.S. railroads than in their own.

93. In Hungary—a country that was not very advanced—by 1910, a third of the population lived and worked in places other than their locality of birth. But many people eventually returned to their place of origin.

94. By 1914, 500,000 Poles lived in the Ruhr district, and they supplied 38 percent of the labor force in mining. However, up to 1880 Germany had also been a country of emigration, especially to the United States.

95. Still, some Jews played an important role in the textile and sugar industries of the "pale."

96. In 1881, 33,000 tourists (of whom 13 percent were Americans) stayed in Nice during the winter; c. 1910, 1.5 million passengers passed through French, Belgian, and Dutch ports that were connected with England. In 1912, Switzerland received 3.2 million guests from abroad. Tourism contributed to the integration of national railroad networks (harmonization of trains' timetables, exchange of rolling stock, etc.).

97. In late nineteenth-century Switzerland and on the Riviera, there was a good deal of investment in luxury hotels and other amenities.

98. As Britain's trade was very large relative to world trade, London was the natural intermediary, and bills on London were the natural instrument for the multilateral settlement of bilateral imbalances.

99. Napoléon III had hoped to establish a larger single-currency area, and an international conference in 1867 in Paris accepted his plans

in principle, but the British and Germans and the Bank of France were hostile, so France gave up the plan. As for the Latin union, it came to a de facto end in 1885 (de jure in 1926). (The word "Latin" had in fact been given by the British.) Monetary cooperation among the Scandinavian countries was established in 1873.

100. Still, there were relapses: the Italian lira was unconvertible during the *corso forzoso* of paper money, from 1866 to 1883. Spain never really adopted the gold standard.

101. Another result was the setting up of information agencies: Havas in Paris (1835), Reuter's in London (1851). The adoption by most European countries (except Britain and Russia) of the French metric system was also helpful to traders.

102. The international cartel of European rail-makers was the first to be established, in 1884 (but it was short-lived). It had been preceded by some agreements among a few firms in other industries (e.g., zinc-smelting, glass).

103. By 1905, Germany had 385 cartels and about 25 percent of its industrial output was cartelized. Austria-Hungary, with more than 200 cartels in 1912, may have been even more cartelized.

104. Of course, as was mentioned earlier, it had been common since the Middle Ages for firms to have bases of operations in more than one country, but they had been engaged in trade and banking. In industry, the French glassmaker Saint-Gobain was an early case: it rented works in Germany in 1857 and bought them in 1864; in 1888, it built works near Pisa, Italy; and in the 1890s, it became truly multinational, with works in half a dozen countries.

105. However, thanks to the huge hydroelectric potential of Switzerland, Sweden, and Norway, small Swiss and Swedish firms that made the relevant equipment (ASEA, Brown Boveri) were able to compete and expand. Many multinationals from small countries did more business abroad than in their place of origin. By 1913, 13 to 18 percent of multinational companies may have been Swiss.

106. A different case is "multinational" vertical integration; e.g., British and German steel firms acquired interests in foreign iron-ore mines in Spain, Sweden, and French Lorraine.

107. In the eastern Mediterranean, the Balkans, and even southern Russia, a diaspora of Greek merchants played a dominant role.

108. This is not to say that the mercantile community in Britain was not cosmopolitan: it had many German Jewish, Greek, and American houses.

109. Maddison (1995) gives the following rates for the growth per year

of exports (in volume) by twelve core countries: 1820–1870, 4.4 percent; 1870–1913, 3.2 percent.

110. The market share of northwestern Europe in world trade (volume) fell from 1871 to 1898 but recovered afterward, to two-thirds by 1913.

111. Europe was importing all its cotton, jute, and rubber, much of its wool, and an increasing share of the silk it used, plus nonferrous metals and ores. Despite large surpluses in Russia and Romania, it also imported, by 1913, a fifth of the wheat it consumed. Its dependence upon overseas supplies decreased for sugar, thanks to the rise in beet-sugar cultivation mainly on the fertile belt from the Parisian basin to the Ukraine.

112. Not until the 1860s did the United States surpass the United Kingdom in population and aggregate GDP.

113. A portent of things to come was that in 1900, during the Boer War, a share of a British loan was floated in New York.

114. On the other hand, there was a convergence of wage levels between the United States and some fast-growing European countries, like Sweden.

115. Maddison (during the conference "Economic Primacy among Nations," Harvard University, May 1994) added a third question: Why did the United States not do better? His answers were: diseconomies of scale (i.e., the cost of creating the infrastructure of a continent), the cost of the Civil War, and the drag by a backward South.

Four   Disasters, Renaissance, Decline

1. Because of this development, it is difficult, from 1914 onward, to isolate the economic history of Europe from that of other continents —and especially from that of North America. Even so, most trade of European countries was still with other states of Europe.

2. According to some British writers, it would have been better for Europe if Germany had won in a few weeks in 1914—as it nearly did. It would have dominated Europe (but not too harshly), they say, but millions of lives would have been saved (plus the British Empire), and the many catastrophes of the twentieth century would not have taken place.

3. Russia suffered heavily from the war, the 1917 revolution, and the civil war that followed, plus disease and famine: excess deaths from 1914 to 1922 are estimated at 16 million (of whom 3 million or more were soldiers). In the west, millions also died from the pandemic in-

fluenza of 1918–1919, and 7 million men who had been wounded remained disabled.

4. It was a typical yet absolutely new development in the 1920s that a currency could fall or rise by 50 percent within a few months. The new parity was made legal in 1928. The Belgian franc was also stabilized in 1926 (much below its prewar parity—likewise the Italian lira). In several central and east European countries, currencies were stabilized thanks to foreign loans, in return for some kind of international control upon their finances; this was also a new development.

5. According to Maddison's (1995) data, western Europe's GDP was, by 1919, 11 percent lower than in 1913—a level that was not exceeded before 1924. GDP per capita remained lower than in 1913 for one decade. Britain and Italy were the only countries to reach by 1920 their 1913 levels of industrial production. For some others, this only happened several years later (and for the Soviet Union by 1927–1928; see below).

6. For the fall in real GNP per capita, the extremes were 2 percent in Norway and Sweden and 35 percent in Poland. For Europe as a whole, it was 11 percent.

7. It has been maintained, however, that policy mistakes (for noneconomic reasons) rather than the gold exchange standard as a regime were responsible.

8. As a consequence, the use of petroleum and its by-products—mostly by motor vehicles and ships—greatly increased; Europe (Russia excluded), which is poor in oil, became a net importer of energy after 1930.

9. In retail trade, productivity grew thanks to the expansion of chain stores and the emergence of dime stores (in France, the first Prisunic opened in 1931).

10. When a human development index is used, the period 1913–1950 does not lag as badly behind the pre-1914 and post-1950 eras compared to when only per capita product is considered.

11. In Spain, the rate of growth of income per capita accelerated between 1910 and 1929, but by 1929 the country remained poor; then it suffered badly from civil war and isolation; by 1950, GDP per capita was no higher than in 1921.

12. France remained an outlet for emigrants—mainly Italians and Poles —in the 1920s, but many returned to their homelands in the 1930s for lack of employment.

13. The government pressured Paribas to invest in eastern Europe, but

after some disappointments it withdrew, in the 1930s, to France and its empire.

14. To Keynesians, a good deal of unemployment was policy induced, as it resulted from mistaken macroeconomic policies; to conservatives, it resulted from excessive real wages, which raised the natural rate of unemployment.

15. In France, the railroad companies, which were virtually bankrupt, were nationalized in 1937.

16. The rise of protection was the consequence and not the cause of the slump. Still, from 1915 onward, Britain had slightly twisted free trade—with duties on luxuries, antidumping duties—and business was calling for protection.

17. Some of those countries (and Germany, which also adopted restrictive policies in 1930–1932) had badly suffered from inflation in the early 1920s.

18. Actually, exchange control had been introduced in Germany in 1931, but the Nazis made it much more strict. Fascist Italy also adopted it.

19. Czechoslovakia was a country that suffered from restrictive policies because of its membership in the gold bloc: by 1937, output was below its 1929 level (likewise in Poland).

20. J. A. Garraty (*The Great Depression,* San Diego and New York, 1986, chap. 18, pp. 182–211) has found similarities between the policies of the New Deal and of the Nazis; but the latter were more successful in getting rid of unemployment.

21. This system fitted well the political regimes and economic structures of east European countries.

22. Socialism, defined by V. I. Lenin as "a state monopoly over the means of production," was considered a first stage in the process leading to communism. It meant a complete control of the economy by the state.

23. Some economists, however, wanted to develop agriculture as a priority, e.g., N. Kondratieff (of long cycles fame), who paid with his life for such views. Experts still discuss whether the NEP was compatible with fast industrialization.

24. According to the official Soviet index, GNP increased by a factor of 30 from 1928 to 1965; in the table below, for the same time period, it was a factor of 4.6. The five-year-plan targets were often not reached.

25. In the last years before World War II, a special effort was made in the area of armaments production, which increased by a factor of

2.5 from 1937 to 1940. In 1938 military spending was 20 percent of GDP. Research and development were concentrated in the military sector. Ten thousand aircraft were made in 1940—as compared to three hundred in 1930.

26. There were also four thousand state farms (sovkhozy), which employed hired labor. In kolkhozy, each member received a share of the final product—not much in general, as most of the crops had to be delivered to the state at low prices.

27. However, government spending on health and education increased.

28. In 1944, on a base of 1938 as 100, GDP was at 50 in France, 53 in the Netherlands, 87 in Norway, 84 in Belgium, 99 in Switzerland, 102 in Denmark, 121 in Sweden, 122 in the United Kingdom, and 124 in Germany (and 214 in the United States). The source for these figures, and for most quantitative data in the rest of this chapter, is Maddison (1995)—p. 72, table 3–8, in the present case. This writer is also indebted to Maddison for additional information.

29. The USSR may have suffered as many as 26 million (or more) excess deaths, plus a birth deficit of 11 million. This last—and worst —of the three demographic disasters it suffered brought its total losses of the period 1914–1945 to at least 74 million. On the other hand, losses of life in Britain, France, and Italy were lower than during World War I.

30. The smaller Jewish communities of Western Europe experienced lower losses, and their numbers were increased after the war by refugees from eastern Europe (who, e.g., again made Antwerp a major center of the diamond trade) and later from the formerly French North Africa. Seventy-five percent of French Jews survived World War II; the Jewish community of France is 530,000 strong (1999), the third largest in the world (after Israel and the United States).

31. The GDP of twelve Western European countries in 1945 was 14 percent lower than in 1938. In Germany, industrial production in 1946 was at 33 percent of its 1938 level.

32. Total aid granted from May 1945 to June 1947 was $6.4 billion. And loans of $5 billion were made by the United States and Canada to Britain in December 1945.

33. Because of British objections, the OEEC was not a supranational body and lacked authority.

34. According to Milward (1984), Western Europe was in no real danger of economic collapse. Moreover, though many people see the Marshall Plan as a proof of the decline of Europe, which only survived thanks to American charity, Milward suggests that the United

States rather became the hostage of Europe. There was no "Marshallization" of Europe, as Communists complained, despite some provisions to protect American interests and to give the United States some control over the economic and financial policies of receiving countries. And one can wonder why the United States helped a competitor to recover—but at the time, serious competition from Europe seemed a fancy.

35. In 1944, the governments of Belgium, Luxembourg, and the Netherlands decided to establish a customs union among their countries —the Benelux, which became operational in 1948. On the other hand, plans to create a customs union among the Nordic countries came to naught.

36. In 1967, there was a fusion of the ECSC High Authority, of the Euratom commission (which had been created at the same time as the EEC, for cooperation in nuclear research and development, but was not very successful), and of the EEC commission, to form the "European Commission."

37. From 1950 to 1989 the growth of Italy's GDP was second only to that of Japan.

38. Nonetheless, differences—sometimes significant—persisted among West European countries, in matters such as corporate governance, training and recruitment of managers, research-and-development policies, government intervention, business culture, etc. The different models of capitalism are discussed below.

39. The lag behind the United States was reduced at an average rate of 2 percent per year for the twelve core countries (while it had grown from 1870 to 1950 at 0.5 percent), and of 3 percent for the four periphery countries, where GDP per hour worked rose from 23 percent of the U.S. level in 1950 to 44 percent in 1973.

40. Broadberry (1998) has questioned the key role ascribed to technology transfers in manufacturing as a factor of convergence in productivity and has stressed the part played by services. To Denison, economies of scale—thanks to the widening of the market for consumer durables, which were suited to mass-production methods— had more effect in increasing productivity than the modernizing of equipment.

41. The productivity missions, which were a spin-off of the Marshall Plan, played a part in the transfer of U.S. technology and management methods, and also in mentality changes. This was a massive and unprecedented effort, as hundreds of missions went from European countries to America. Results were variable and selective but not

unimportant. Still, many other channels of transfer were used, particularly direct contacts and arrangements between American and European firms. There was also a rise of management education on American lines. Still, it has been maintained that the Americanization of European business did not go far enough, partly because of resistance by labor.

42. In the 1960s, gross domestic investment (housing excluded) was, in Western Europe, twice higher as percent of GDP than from 1920 to 1938, and higher in several countries than in the United States. Wage moderation was a contributor to high savings rates. Moreover, a good deal of American capital flew into Europe, while the latter did not export capital on a large scale during this period.

43. From 1949 to 1956, West German industrial production grew at a rate of 13 percent per year. On the other hand, the Italian miracle was achieved despite an uncongenial political environment, which included corruption, profligacy by the state, public-sector inefficiency, a sharp contrast between north and south, etc.

44. Emigration from Europe overseas (mainly to North America, Israel, and Australia) resumed after World War II but was never large. Still, Western Europe had a net migratory deficit at first, but since 1970 the net balance has been increasingly positive. Intracontinental migration was much bigger than emigration, as northwestern Europe attracted immigrants from Portugal, Spain, Greece, and Yugoslavia; owing to its increasing prosperity, Italy ceased to send emigrants, a trend followed after 1975 by Spain and Portugal. The major change—in comparison with the nineteenth century and the early twentieth—has been immigration into Europe from other continents: North Africa (and, to a lesser extent, Africa south of the Sahara), Asia (Turkey, India, Pakistan, etc.), and the Caribbean (to Britain). In the six founding members of the EEC, the number of foreign workers rose from 1.5 million in 1960 to over 4.5 million in 1973 (plus many illegal immigrants). Since 1973 governments have tried to reduce this inflow, but with little success, except in Britain. In the 1990s the EU received about one million immigrants (net) per year, who add to a settled foreign population of 18 million. Needless to say, there has also been much internal migration within European countries (see below).

45. From 1963 to 1973, Britain's share in world exports of manufactures fell from 11 percent to 7 percent.

46. This fits with the above-mentioned view that, during the golden age, differences in initial income levels had the largest single effect on

growth performance relative to the European average. Nonetheless, Switzerland stayed on top, and Greece at the bottom; and the countries close to the European average in 1975 were in the same position in 1994.

47. In 1950, labor productivity was lower in Germany than in Britain, but soon the former forged ahead. One cause was that low-productivity industries and sectors (i.e., services) had a bigger weight in the British economy than in Germany. Still, some British industrial branches performed well (I. Lescent-Giles, "La compétitivité de l'économie britannique au vingtième siècle: Mythes et réalités." In *Tendances récentes de l'historiographie britannique.* Paris, in press).

48. Moreover, political and social stability and the fact that Britain had won the war created feelings of superiority and complacency, which were uncongenial to change and competition.

49. To some writers the "German miracle" *stricto sensu* was limited to the 1950s: GDP grew at 9 percent per year from 1949 to 1960 and then slowed down gradually, to 4 percent in 1965–1973.

50. On 1 January 1953, a record figure of 5.5 million persons in the forced-labor system was reached; 1.7 million were in camps and 2.8 million in "special settlements"—they mainly belonged to national minorities, which had been deported for alleged collaboration with the Nazis.

51. Readers may wonder why the role of political leaders is stressed in the case of the USSR, but this is normal in a dictatorial command economy.

52. Actually, because of the region's climate, grain yields there were very erratic, and soils were eroded and exhausted within a short period. Moreover, as resources had been diverted from the rich "black soil" regions of southern Russia, their production fell.

53. These figures are, like all Soviet statistics, overestimates. Moreover, there was no transition to an intensive and balanced growth. Shortages and bottlenecks persisted; it was necessary to continue enormous investments in basic industries. Arbitration between consumption and investment was only possible in the short term (Asselain). Consumption per capita, as a percentage of its American level, rose up to 1965 (42 percent), then fell unceasingly (30 percent in 1986).

54. The military-industrial complex, however, was a closed circuit, with no fallouts for the civilian sector.

55. Romania broke away in the 1960s because its rulers wanted to develop all branches of industry. As a matter of fact, there was not much

division of labor (because there was little complementarity) and large cooperative projects were few (in one example, a gas pipeline was built from the Urals to Germany).

56. In the 1970s, the socialist countries tried to develop their trade with the West, but only raw materials could find markets there, as manufactured goods were of poor quality; and those countries became heavily indebted due to the trade imbalance.

57. By 1973, 58 percent of energy consumed in Europe was imported (this share was to fall to 38 percent by 1993). In the 1970s, important off-shore oil and gas fields began to be exploited in the North Sea.

58. By 1990, three-quarters of French electricity production came from nuclear power stations (76 percent in 1999). In western Europe, the ratio rose from 5 percent in 1973 to 32 percent by 1990. In 1998, 15 percent of the total energy supply of the EU was nuclear.

59. By 1982, oil was thirteen times more expensive in current dollars than in 1970, and six times in constant dollars; afterward, prices fell.

60. By 1992, in the twelve core countries, labor productivity (GDP per hour worked) was 87 percent of the U.S. level—against 72 percent in 1973 (in the four periphery countries, it rose from 44 to 62 percent). From 1973 to 1992, the productivity gap with the United States (where GDP per hour worked increased at 1.1 percent per year) was reduced at a rate of 1.16 percent per year in the core, and 1.76 percent in the periphery. Later on, however, the gap widened again (see below).

61. See table 4.7. Luxembourg—with the highest per capita product in the world ($39,300 in 1999)—stands out in front, ahead of the United States. It is interesting that the leaders are "small" countries, and the "large" ones come behind.

62. In France, GDP increased by 55 percent from 1973 to 1994, and GDP per capita by 39 percent.

63. Austria, Britain, Denmark, Ireland, Portugal, Sweden, and Switzerland are also in the first group, having markedly reduced unemployment during the 1990s. Belgium, Finland, France, Germany, Greece, Italy, and Spain are in the second. The fall of unemployment continued in the first months of 2000.

64. Employment rose by 14 percent in the United States from 1990 to 1999, but Ireland and the Netherlands created more jobs proportionately.

65. One can add that, in the 1970s, the supply of labor increased, as more women wanted to work and the baby boomers came of age;

on the other hand, as redundancies increased, many people retired earlier, willy-nilly, and young people stayed in school longer (many European students are actually in hidden unemployment). The average activity rate fell for men but increased for women between 1973 and 1992; it did not change for both sexes together. Women and young people suffered more from unemployment than adult males. The number of people living in poverty rose, of course, with unemployment, but varied greatly across the EU countries.

66. In the fifteen EU countries in 1998, agriculture employed 5 percent of the civilian labor force, industry 29 percent, services 66 percent. In 1988, corresponding figures had been: 7 percent, 33 percent, 60 percent. In Britain the fall in absolute numbers of industry's labor force started in 1965.

67. However, at constant prices, this share would have been stable for the last thirty years; as productivity grew faster in manufacturing than in services, there was a rise in the relative prices of services.

68. Admittedly, this phenomenon is especially obvious in France and mountainous parts of Italy. Were it not for the much-maligned Common Agricultural Policy of the EU, it would have been much worse.

69. An interesting case of a decline being stopped (thanks to innovation) is the clock and watch industry: in 1953, Switzerland supplied 83 percent of its world exports (by value); this share fell to 55 percent in 1970 and 28 percent in 1980 because of competition by Japan and Hong Kong and the invention of quartz watches. However, thanks to the Swatch (1982), the market share of the Swiss has stabilized (29 percent in 1993).

70. Albert, *Capitalisme contre capitalisme.* Actually, these views were too schematic and there is much diversity among national capitalisms: in Europe, only Britain, on one hand, and Germany, on the other, conformed to the two ideal types, which other countries fit imperfectly. A somewhat different idea juxtaposes the Anglo-Saxon market-oriented capitalism and the continental network-oriented capitalism, which is itself divided into two subvarieties: the Germanic (or social market type) and the Latin, which has a complex, closed, interlocking system of family-owned holding companies. Belgium and France would be somewhere in between. (On the "French exception," see below.) It has been also observed that western economies have more in common than these models suggest, and that models' differences are themselves often exaggerated.

71. The Deutsche Bank has moved stakes worth billions of dollars into several fund-management subsidiaries.

72. As for its welfare effects, in 1997, the three physically healthiest populations in Europe were those of Sweden, Norway, and Finland, which have extensive and strong public-health services.

73. In some countries, of course, these ratios are exceeded. In 1997, total tax receipts were 49.5 percent of GDP in Denmark and 51.9 percent in Sweden; France was at 45.1 percent; the lowest figure was Ireland, 33 percent; Britain was at 35 percent. A few countries recently reduced their tax burden.

74. Structural policies and the Common Agricultural Policy (CAP) have been attacked by free marketeers, who have also complained that liberalization has been too slow because of continued economic nationalism and protectionism by EU members (*Economist,* 9 Nov. 1999). In 1994, the European Economic Space achieved a partial union between the EU and the few surviving members of EFTA, but Switzerland refused to join.

75. Only 1.5 percent of EU citizens live in a member state other than the one in which they were born. Still, there is a good deal of cross-border migration of workers on a daily basis.

76. Actually, the criterion of 3 percent of GDP for budget deficit was proposed by France.

77. A French economist calculated that, from 1992 to 1998, preparations for the euro reduced the French rate of growth by 1.3 percent and created one million more unemployed. On the other hand, budget deficits have been cut down, inflation reduced to low figures, and interest rates lowered.

78. Indeed, from 1980 to 1997, GDP per worker increased faster in many European countries than in the United States, and in a few countries, productivity per hour worked was above the U.S. level, but participation rates and the number of hours worked per year were lower—and therefore so was product per capita. Moreover, from 1973 to 1997, the number of hours worked per person in employment per year increased in America, but fell in Europe. It was over 20 percent higher in the United States than in Germany.

79. According to Maddison (1995), from 1950 to 1996, the GDP of "capitalist Europe" grew at an average rate of 3.5 percent (thus it almost quintupled) and GDP per capita at a rate of 2.9 percent, increasing 3.7 times, roughly as much as from 1820 to 1950.

80. Admittedly, this ranking was made by the World Economic Forum, a strongly promarket body. A ranking for 2000 by another institution puts eight European countries (including Germany, Sweden, and Switzerland) among the top ten countries; Britain is fifteenth,

France nineteenth, Italy thirtieth. On the other hand, using a human development index, France and Germany are in top positions. According to other rankings, France, Germany, Italy, and Sweden get very bad marks for economic freedom.

81. This development is "devoutly" wished by some pundits. According to their views, the European economic and social model is in retreat and giving way to none other than the American one; national markets for corporate control are merging, not merely into one EU pool, but into a global (i.e., American-dominated) common market. A stiff dose of American competition and enterprise will have positive effects, like lower unemployment and higher living standards. So "what is the point of 'Europe' if Europe is turning out to be just another U.S.?" So "forget geography, forget culture" (*Economist,* 12 Feb. 2000).

82. A drastic solution might be a federal state, within a much enlarged EU, possibly uniting the original six of Charlemagne's Europe.

83. In 1997, Germany was the most important export destination for eleven EU countries (plus Switzerland) and six eastern countries. It was the most important source of imports for ten EU countries (plus Switzerland and Iceland) and an equal number of eastern countries —Russia included. For example, Germany is the first trade partner of France, who received 11 percent of German exports in 1997 and supplied 10 percent of German imports.

84. These difficulties concerned not only Germany, but France and other countries, as for long the Buba had fixed interest rates for most of the EU.

85. *Economist,* 6 Feb., 5 June, and 23 Oct. 1999.

86. Altogether, four countries of the periphery—Finland, Ireland (which grew at 7.3 percent per year, 1990–1998, and 9 percent, 1995–1999), Spain, and Portugal—have in recent years outperformed the rest of the EU, thanks to a big labor-cost advantage, and to massive FDI in the first two.

87. By 1965, Czechoslovakia was making as much steel per inhabitant as the United States and West Germany.

88. Labor productivity in agriculture (which, in 1990, still employed 20 percent of the working population) fell between 1978 and 1990 from 15 percent to 7 percent of the U.S. level. In manufacturing it had risen from 29 percent of the U.S. level in 1952 to 36 in 1978, but it fell to 18 percent in 1990, and 19 percent in 1997.

89. By 1987, Soviet GDP was 39 percent of the American, GDP per capita 33 percent (the ratio had been higher in 1976), GDP per man-hour 30 percent.

90. The two other major republics in Europe, Ukraine and Belarus, have fared worse than Russia. The first is a case of "arrested transition."

91. The demographic situation is also worrying, though not as bad as it is often said. Admittedly, the death rate rose sharply from 1990 to 1994, but it had been rising—though more slowly—under the Soviet regime since the mid-1960s, and it fell after 1994. On the other hand, the fertility rate has fallen to a very low level: 1.2. If it continues at this rate, total population might be only 140 million by 2010. In ECE also, life expectancy declined at first in some countries, but then it rose.

92. Since the late 1960s, their negative trade balance with the rest of the world forced them to borrow increasingly from the West—and to service their debt through "forced exports." In 1989, the foreign debt of East Germany was $1,300 per capita.

93. Romania was the worst case, under the rule of Ceausescu, a megalomaniacal tyrant: forced, misdirected, and overcentralized industrialization, plus pharaonic projects, resulted in immiserizing growth and in terrible performances of an oversized and obsolete industrial sector.

94. Roughly speaking, the private sector is now responsible for over 60 percent of production (the informal economy included); the ratio is higher in the Czech Republic, Hungary, and some other countries.

95. The share of trade with the CEEC in the EU's total trade is small. But an "unofficial," cross-border traffic has developed between ECE and Germany and Austria; it is carried out by short-term migrants —"tourist workers," pseudotourists, border-region peddlers (called "ants")—who shuttle back and forth. There are also illicit, but open, international markets and bazaars.

96. For the very long run—and independent of political regimes— Maddison (1995) has estimated that, from 1820 to 1992, GNP per capita increased by a factor of 13 in western Europe, 10 in southern Europe, 6 in eastern Europe (and 8 for the world at large). Good and Ma reckon that, over the period 1870–1989, the growth of ECE was close to the European average, which means that the lag with the West has not changed in the long run, hence a weak performance.

97. In 1980, the fertility rate in the USSR and its satellites was 2.3 (so their population increased fast up to 1990), but by 1997, it had fallen to 1.3; in that year the birthrate was 9 per thousand, the death rate 14 per thousand. If Russia is excluded, Europe has birth and

death rates of 11 per thousand. See also n. 91, above. The fall in population of the EU will be accelerated by the entry of ECE countries, as the latter's population will decline more rapidly than that of the core fifteen.

98. A. Perrenoud, "Le défi démographique." In Université de Genève, Faculté SES, *Bulletin du Département d'Histoire économique* 25 (Aug. 1994–July 1995): 30.

99. Ad M. van der Woude, "The Future of West European Agriculture: An Exercise in Applied History," *Review, Fernand Braudel Center* 15.2 (spring 1992): 248–49.

100. This ratio was reached by the EU fifteen in 1996. As for the over-sixty cohort, it rose from 12 percent of Europe's population in 1950 to 20 percent in 2000; by 2050, it will be 35–40 percent.

101. Quoted in the *Times Literary Supplement,* 24 May 1996, p. 10.

Selected Bibliography

This bibliography makes no claims to being comprehensive. It mainly includes books and articles by writers who are mentioned in the text and notes—and only their works that are direct sources. However, a number of important works that have been used but not quoted are also included. Most non-English works have been excluded.

For fuller bibliographies, I recommend consulting Cameron (1989) and Landes (1998).

The following abbreviations for journals' titles appear within the bibliography:
ECHR   *Economic History Review*
EREH   *European Review of Economic History*
JEEH   *Journal of European Economic History*
JEH   *Journal of Economic History*

Aldcroft, Derek H., and Anthony Sutcliffe, eds. 1999. *Europe in the International Economy 1500 to 2000*. Aldershot.
Aldcroft, Derek H., and Simon P. Ville, eds. 1994. *The European Economy, 1750–1914: A Thematic Approach*. Manchester.
Asselain, Jean-Charles. 1998. "Comment le capitalisme a remporté le conflit du siècle: Le basculement des années 1956–1968." Bordeaux. Mimeographed.
Bailey, Mark. 1998. "Peasant Welfare in England, 1290–1348." *ECHR* 41, no. 2: 223–51.
Bairoch, Paul. 1963. *Révolution industrielle et sous-développement*. Paris.
———. 1965. "Niveaux de développement économique de 1810 à 1910." *Annales. E.S.C.* 20, no. 6: 1091–117.

————. 1976. "Europe's Gross National Product: 1800–1975." *JEEH* 5, no. 2: 273–340.

————. 1979. "Ecarts internationaux des niveaux de vie avant la révolution industrielle." *Annales. E.S.C.* 34, no. 1: 145–71.

————. 1982. "International Industrialization Levels from 1750 to 1980." *JEEH* 11, no. 2: 269–333.

————. 1989. "L'économie française dans le contexte européen à la fin du dix-huitième siècle." *Revue Economique* 40, no. 6: 939–64.

————. 1997. *Victoires et déboires: Histoire économique et sociale du monde du seizième siècle à nos jours.* 3 vols. Paris.

Bardet, Jean-Pierre, and Jacques Dupâquier, eds. 1997–1999. *Histoire des populations de l'Europe.* 3 vols. Paris.

Berend, Ivan. 1999a. *Central and Eastern Europe: Detour from the Periphery to the Periphery, 1944–1993.* Cambridge.

————. 1999b. "The Further Enlargement of the European Union in a Historical Perspective." *European Review* 7, no. 3: 175–81.

Berg, Maxine, and Pat Hudson. 1992. "Rehabilitating the Industrial Revolution." *ECHR* 45, no. 1: 24–50.

Bergier, Jean-François. 1984. *Histoire économique de la Suisse.* Lausanne.

Blanchard, Ian. 1996. *The Middle Ages: A Concept Too Many?* Edinburgh.

Bordo, Michael D., and Lars Jonung. 1999. *The Future of EMU: What Does the History of Monetary Unions Tell Us?* NBER Working Paper Series, no. 7365. Cambridge, Mass.

Braudel, Fernand. 1982–1984. *Civilization and Capitalism: Fifteenth–Eighteenth Centuries.* 3 vols. New York.

Broadberry, Steve N. 1997a. "Anglo-German Productivity Differences 1870–1990: A Sectoral Analysis." *EREH* 1, part 2: 247–67.

————. 1997b. *The Productivity Race: British Manufacturing in International Perspective, 1850–1990.* Cambridge.

————. 1998. "How Did the U.S. and Germany Overtake Britain? A Sectorial Analysis of Comparative Productivity Levels, 1870–1990." In *Historical Benchmark Comparisons of Output and Productivity,* ed. Clara Eugenia Nuñez, 17–29. Seville.

Bruland, Kristine. 1989. *British Technology and European Industrialization: The Norwegian Textile Industry in the Mid-Nineteenth Century.* Cambridge.

Cameron, Rondo E., ed. 1967. *Banking in the Early Stages of Industrialization: A Study in Comparative History.* New York.

————. 1982. "The Industrial Revolution, a Misnomer." *History Teacher* 15: 377–84.

————. 1989. *A Concise Economic History of the World: From Paleolithic Times to the Present.* New York and Oxford.

Caron, François. 1976. *An Economic History of Modern France.* New York. (The revised French edition, *Histoire économique de la France, dix-neuvième–vingtième siècle,* Paris, 1995, is much preferable to this poor translation.)

———. 1997. *Histoire des chemins de fer en France.* Vol. 1, *1740–1883.* Paris.

Carpentier, Elisabeth, and Michel Le Mené. 1996. *La France du onzième au quinzième siècle: Population, société, économie.* Paris.

Chandler, Alfred D., Jr. 1990. *Scale and Scope: The Dynamics of Industrial Capitalism.* Cambridge, Mass.

Cipolla, Carlo, ed. 1969–1973. *The Fontana Economic History of Europe.* 6 vols. London.

———. 1976. *Before the Industrial Revolution: European Society and Economy, 1000–1700.* London.

Crafts, N. F. R. 1984a. "Economic Growth in France and Britain, 1830–1910: A Review of the Evidence." *JEH* 44, no. 1: 49–67.

———. 1984b. "Patterns of Development in Nineteenth-Century Europe." *Oxford Economic Papers* 36: 438–58.

———. 1985. *British Economic Growth during the Industrial Revolution.* Oxford.

———. 1987. "British Economic Growth, 1700–1850: Some Difficulties of Interpretation." *Explorations in Economic History* 24, no. 3: 245–68.

———. 1989. "British Industrialization in an International Context." *Journal of Interdisciplinary History* 12, no. 3: 415–28.

———. 1995. "The Golden Age of Economic Growth in Western Europe, 1950–75." *ECHR* 48, no. 3: 429–47.

———. 1997. "The Human Development Index and Changes in Standards of Living: Some Historical Comparisons." *EREH* 1, part 3: 299–322.

Crafts, N. F. R., S. J. Leybourne, and T. C. Mills. 1989. "Trends and Cycles in British Industrial Production, 1700–1913." *Journal of the Royal Statistical Society* 152: 43–60.

Crafts, Nicholas, and Gianni Toniolo. 1996. *Economic Growth in Europe since 1945.* Cambridge.

Craig, L. A., and D. Fisher. 1997. *The Integration of the European Economy, 1850–1913.* London.

Crouzet-Pavan, Elisabeth. 1995. *La mort lente de Torcello: Histoire d'une cité disparue.* Paris.

Davies, R. W. 1998. *Soviet Economic Development from Lenin to Khrushchev.* Cambridge.

Denison, E. F. 1967. *Why Growth Rates Differ: Postwar Experience in Nine Western Countries.* Washington, D.C.

Dormois, Jean-Pierre, and Michael Dintenfass, eds. 1999. *The British Industrial Decline.* London. (The most recent—but not the last—book on a controversial problem.)

Duby, Georges. 1974. *The Early Growth of the European Economy: Warriors and Peasants from the Seventh to the Twelfth Century.* London.

Eichengreen, Barry. 1992. *Golden Fetters: The Gold Standard and the Great Depression, 1919–1939.* New York and Oxford.

———, ed. 1995. *Europe's Postwar Recovery.* Cambridge.

Elvin, Mark. 1973. *The Pattern of the Chinese Past: A Social and Economic Interpretation.* Stanford.

Feinstein, Charles, ed. 1993–1997. *The Economic Development of Modern Europe since 1870.* 16 vols. Aldershot.

Feis, Herbert. 1930. *Europe, the World's Banker, 1870–1914.* New Haven.

Flandreau, Marc. 1995. *L'or du monde: La France et la stabilité du système monétaire international 1848–1873.* Paris.

———. 1997. "Central Bank Cooperation in Historical Perspective: A Sceptical View." *ECHR* 50, no. 4: 735–63.

Floud, Roderick, and D. N. McCloskey. 1994. *The Economic History of Britain since 1700.* 2d ed., rev. 3 vols. Cambridge.

Foreman-Peck, James. 1995. *A History of the World Economy: International Economic Relations since 1850.* 2d ed. Hemel Hempstead.

Gerschenkron, Alexander. 1962. *Economic Backwardness in Historical Perspective: A Book of Essays.* Cambridge, Mass.

Goldsmith, James L. 1995. "The Crisis of the Late Middle Ages: The Case of France." *French History* 9, no. 4: 417–50.

Gómez Mendoza, A. 1989. *Ferrocarril, industria y mercado en la modernización de España.* Madrid.

Good, David F. 1984. *The Economic Rise of the Habsburg Empire 1750–1941.* Berkeley.

Good, David F., and Tongshu Ma. 1999. "The Economic Growth of Central and Eastern Europe in Comparative Perspective, 1870–1989." *EREH* 3, part 2: 103–37.

Grantham, George. 1997. "The French Cliometric Revolution: A Survey of Cliometric Contributions to French Economic History." *EREH* 1, part 3: 359–405.

Gregory, P. R. 1982. *Russian National Income, 1885–1913.* Cambridge.

Habakkuk, H. J., and M. Postan, eds. 1965. *The Industrial Revolutions and After: Incomes, Population and Technological Change.* 2 vols. The Cambridge Economic History of Europe, vol. 6. Cambridge.

Harley, C. K. 1982. "British Industrialization before 1841: Evidence of Slower Growth during the Industrial Revolution." *JEH* 42: 267–89.

————. 1998. "Cotton Textile Prices and the Industrial Revolution." *ECHR* 41, no. 1: 49–83.

Harris, John. 1992. *Essays in Industry and Technology in the Eighteenth Century: England and France.* Aldershot.

————. 1998. *Industrial Espionage and Technology Transfer: Britain and France in the Eighteenth Century.* Aldershot.

Hawke, G. R. 1970. *Railways and Economic Growth in England and Wales, 1840–1870.* Oxford.

Heywood, Colin. 1995. *The Development of the French Economy 1750–1914.* Cambridge.

Hicks, John. 1969. *A Theory of Economic History.* Oxford.

Hoffmann, Philip T. 1996. *Growth in a Traditional Society: The French Countryside, 1450–1815.* Princeton.

Israel, Jonathan I. 1989. *Dutch Primacy in World Trade, 1585–1740.* Oxford.

Keynes, John Maynard. 1919. *The Economic Consequences of the Peace.* London.

Kindleberger, Charles P. 1978. *Economic Response: Comparative Studies in Trade, Finance and Growth.* Cambridge, Mass.

————. 1992. "Why Did the Golden Age Last So Long?" In *The Legacy of the Golden Age,* ed. F. Cairncross and A. Cairncross, 15–30. London and New York.

————. 1993. *A Financial History of Western Europe.* 2d ed. New York.

————. 1996. *World Economic Primacy, 1500–1990.* New York.

Komlos, John. 1983. *The Habsburg Monarchy as a Customs Union: Economic Development in Austria-Hungary in the Nineteenth Century.* Princeton.

————. 1989. "Thinking about the Industrial Revolution." *JEEH* 18, no. 1: 191–206.

Körner, Martin. 1980. *Solidarités financières suisses au seizième siècle.* Lausanne.

Labrousse, E. 1943. *La crise de l'économie française à la fin de l'Ancien Régime et au début de la Révolution.* Paris.

Landes, David S. 1969. *The Unbound Prometheus: Technological Change and Industrial Development in Western Europe from 1750 to the Present.* Cambridge.

————. 1983. *Revolution in Time: Clocks and the Making of the Modern World.* Cambridge, Mass., and London.

————. 1998. *The Wealth and Poverty of Nations: Why Some Are So Rich and Some So Poor.* New York and London.

Lévy-Leboyer, Maurice. 1964. *Les banques européennes et l'industrialisation internationale dans la première moitié du dix-neuvième siècle.* Paris.

Lévy-Leboyer, Maurice, and François Bourguignon. 1990. *The French Economy in the Nineteenth Century: An Essay in Econometric Analysis.* Cambridge.

Lüthy, Herbert. 1959–1961. *La banque protestante en France, de la Révocation de l'Edit de Nantes à la Révolution.* 2 vols. Paris.

Macfarlane, Alan. 1978. *The Origins of English Individualism.* Oxford.

Maddison, Angus. 1991. *Dynamic Forces in Capitalist Development: A Long-Run Comparative View.* Oxford and New York.

———. 1995. *Monitoring the World Economy, 1820–1992.* Paris. Quoted from the French edition: *L'économie mondiale, 1820–1992: Analyse et statistiques.*

———. 1998. *Chinese Economic Performance in the Long Run.* Paris.

Maddison, Angus, and Herman Van der Wee, eds. 1994. *Economic Growth and Structural Change: Comparative Approaches Over the Long Run.* Milan (papers by J. Blomme and H. Van der Wee, G. D. Snooks, B. Yun, P. Malanima).

Mathias, Peter. 1979. *The Transformation of England: Essays in the Economic and Social History of England in the Eighteenth Century.* London.

———. 1983. *The First Industrial Nation: An Economic History of Britain, 1700–1914.* 2d ed. London. Original edition, 1969.

Mathias, Peter, and John A. Davis. 1989. *The First Industrial Revolutions.* Oxford.

Mathias, Peter, and Sidney Pollard, eds. 1989. *The Industrial Economies: The Development of Economic and Social Policies.* The Cambridge Economic History of Europe, vol. 8. Cambridge.

Mathias, Peter, and M. M. Postan, eds. 1978. *The Industrial Economies: Capital, Labor and Enterprise.* 2 vols. The Cambridge Economic History of Europe, vol. 7. Cambridge.

Mendels, Franklin. 1972. "Proto-industrialization: The First Phase of the Industrialization Process." *JEH* 32, no. 1: 241–61.

Miller, E., Cynthia Postan, and M. M. Postan, eds. 1987. *Trade and Industry in the Middle Ages.* 2d ed. The Cambridge Economic History of Europe, vol. 2. Cambridge.

Milward, Alan S. 1984. *The Reconstruction of Western Europe, 1945–51.* London.

———. 1999. *The European Rescue of the Nation State.* Cambridge.

Milward, Alan S., and S. B. Saul. 1973. *The Economic Development of Continental Europe, 1780–1870.* London.

———. 1977. *The Development of the Economies of Continental Europe, 1850–1914.* London.

Mitchell, B. R. 1975. *European Historical Statistics, 1750–1970.* London.

Mokyr, Joel, ed. 1985. *The Economics of the Industrial Revolution.* Totowa.

———. 1990. *The Lever of Riches: Technological Creativity and Economic Progress.* New York.

————, ed. 1993. *The British Industrial Revolution: An Economic Perspective.* Boulder.

Morineau, Michel. 1998. "Malthus: There and Back from the Period Preceding the Black Death to the 'Industrial Revolution.'" *JEEH* 27, no. 1: 137–202.

Morrisson, Christian, Jean-Noël Barrandon, and Cécile Morrisson. 1999. *Brazilian Gold, Money and Economic Growth in France in the Eighteenth Century.* Paris.

Morrisson, Christian, and Wayne Snyder. 2000. "Les inégalités de revenus en France du début du dix-huitième siècle à 1985." *Revue Economique* 51, no. 1: 119–54.

Neal, Larry. 1990. *The Rise of Financial Capitalism: International Capital in the Age of Reason.* Cambridge.

North, Douglass C. 1981. *Structure and Change in Economic History.* New York.

North, Douglass C., and Robert Paul Thomas. 1973. *The Rise of the Western World: A New Economic History.* Cambridge.

O'Brien, Patrick. 1977. *The New Economic History of the Railways.* London.

————. 1991. *Power with Profit: The State and the Economy, 1688–1815.* London.

————. 1995. "The Great War and the Dislocation of the International Economy 1914–1929." In *Wirtschaft, Gesellschaft, Unternehmen: Festschrift für Hans Pohl*, ed. W. Feldenkirchen et al., vol 1, 245–65. Stuttgart.

————. 1996. "Path Dependency, or Why Britain Became an Industrialized and Urbanized Economy Long before France." *ECHR* 49, no. 2: 213–49.

————. 1998. "Imperial, Cultural and Biographical Components in the Technological Transformation of Textile Production in England, 1733–1822." In *Die Entstehung des modernen Europa 1600–1900*, ed. O. Mörke and M. North, 61–71. Vienna.

O'Brien, Patrick K., Trevor Griffiths, and Philip Hund. 1991. "Political Components of the Industrial Revolution: Parliament and the English Cotton Textile Industry, 1660–1774." *ECHR* 44, no. 3: 395–423.

O'Brien, Patrick, and Caglar Keyder. 1978. *Economic Growth in Britain and France, 1780–1914: Two Paths to the Twentieth Century.* London.

O'Brien, Patrick K., and Leandro Prados de la Escosura. 1992. "Agricultural Productivity and European Industrialization, 1890–1980." *ECHR* 45, no. 3: 514–36.

————, eds. 1998. *The Costs and Benefits of European Imperialism from the Conquest of Ceuta, 1415, to the Treaty of Lusaka, 1974.* Special issue of *Revista de Historia Económica.* Madrid.

O'Brien, Patrick, and Roland Quinault. 1993. *The Industrial Revolution and British Society.* Cambridge.

Olson, Mancur. 1982. *The Rise and Decline of Nations.* New Haven.

O'Rourke, Kevin H., and Jeffrey G. Williamson. 1997. "Around the European Periphery 1870–1913: Globalization, Schooling and Growth." *EREH* 1, part 2: 153–190.

———. 1999. *Globalization and History: The Evolution of a Nineteenth-Century Atlantic Economy.* Cambridge, Mass.

Palairet, Michael R. 1997. *The Balkan Economies c. 1800–1914: Evolution without Development.* Cambridge.

Parker, William N. 1984. *Europe, America and the Wider World.* Vol. 1, *Europe and the World Economy.* Cambridge.

Pirenne, Henri. 1939. *Mohammed and Charlemagne.* Trans. Bernard Miall. New York.

Pollard, Sidney. 1973. "Industrialization and the European Economy." *ECHR* 26, no. 4: 636–48.

———. 1974. *European Economic Integration, 1815–1970.* London.

———. 1981. *Peaceful Conquest: The Industrialization of Europe, 1760–1970.* Oxford.

———. 1997. *The International Economy since 1945.* London.

Postan, M. M., ed. 1966. *Agrarian Life of the Middle Ages.* The Cambridge Economic History of Europe, vol. 1. Cambridge.

———. 1983. "Feudalism and Its Decline: A Semantic Exercise." In *Social Relations and Ideas: Essays in Honour of R. H. Hilton,* ed. T. H. Aston et al., 73–87. Oxford.

Pounds, N. J. G. 1990. *An Historical Geography of Europe.* Cambridge.

Prados, Leandro, and Isabel Sanz. 1998. "Historical Comparison of Income: A Short-cut Approach." In *Historical Benchmark Comparisons of Output and Productivity,* ed. Clara Eugenia Nuñez, 31–47. Seville.

Rich, E. E., and C. H. Wilson, eds. 1967. *The Economy of Expanding Europe in the Sixteenth and Seventeenth Centuries.* The Cambridge Economic History of Europe, vol. 4. Cambridge.

Ringrose, David R. 1996. *Spain, Europe and the "Spanish Miracle."* Cambridge.

Rosenthal, Jean-Laurent. 1992. *The Fruits of Revolution: Property Rights, Litigation and French Agriculture, 1700–1860.* Cambridge.

Samuelson, Paul A. 1997. "Wherein Do the European and American Models Differ?" Banca d'Italia. *Temi di discussione del Servizio Studi* 320.

Schulze, Max-Stephan. 1998. "The Growth of Austrian National Income in European Comparison, 1870–1913." In *Historical Benchmark Comparisons of Output and Productivity,* ed. Clara Eugenia Nuñez, 123–34. Seville.

Simpson, James. 1995. *Spanish Agriculture: The Long Siesta, 1765–1965.* Cambridge.

Slicher van Bath, B. H. 1963. *The Agrarian History of Western Europe, A.D. 500–1850.* London.

Sombart, Werner. 1913. *The Jews and Modern Capitalism.* Trans. M. Epstein. New Brunswick, 1982.

———. 1915. *The Quintessence of Capitalism.* Trans. and ed. M. Epstein. New York, 1967.

Svennilson, Ingvar. 1954. *Growth and Stagnation in the European Economy.* Geneva.

Sylla, Richard, and Gianni Toniolo, eds. 1991. *Patterns of European Industrialization: The Nineteenth Century.* London.

Teich, Mikuláš, and Roy Porter, eds. 1996. *The Industrial Revolution in National Context: Europe and the USA.* Cambridge.

Teichova, Alice, ed. 1997. *Central Europe in the Twentieth Century: An Economic History.* Aldershot.

Teichova, Alice, Maurice Lévy-Leboyer, and Elga Nussbaum, eds. 1986. *Multinational Enterprise in Historical Perspective.* Cambridge and Paris.

Temin, Peter. 1997a. "The Golden Age of European Growth: A Review Essay." *EREH* 1, part 1: 127–49.

———. 1997b. "Is It Kosher to Talk about Culture?" *JEH* 57, no. 2: 267–87.

Thirsk, Joan. 1997. *Alternative Agriculture: A History from the Black Death to the Present Day.* Oxford.

Thomas, Brinley. 1973. *Migration and Economic Growth: A Study of Great Britain and the Atlantic Economy.* 2d ed. Original edition, London, 1954.

Toniolo, Gianni. 1998. "Europe's Golden Age, 1950–1973: Speculations from a Long-Run Perspective." *ECHR* 41, no. 2: 252–67.

Tortella, Gabriel. 1977. *Banking, Railroads and Industry in Spain 1829–1874.* New York.

———. 1994. "Patterns of Economic Retardation and Recovery in South-Western Europe in the Nineteenth and Twentieth Centuries." *ECHR* 47, no. 1: 1–21.

Trebilcock, Clive. 1981. *The Industrialization of the Continental Powers, 1780–1914.* London.

Van der Wee, Herman. 1963. *The Growth of the Antwerp Market and the European Economy (Fourteenth–Sixteenth Century).* 3 vols. The Hague.

———. 1986. *Prosperity and Upheaval: The World Economy 1945–1980.* Harmondsworth.

———. 1990. *The History of European Banking.* Antwerp.

———. 1999. "Was the Dutch Economy during its Golden Age Really Modern?" *European Review* 7, no. 4: 461–69.

Vries, Jan de, and Ad van der Woude. 1997. *The First Modern Economy: Success, Failure and Perseverance of the Dutch Economy, 1500–1815*. Cambridge.

Wallerstein, Immanuel. 1974–1989. *The Modern World-System*. 3 vols. New York.

Whatley, Christopher. 1997. *The Industrial Revolution in Scotland*. Cambridge.

Williams, Eric. 1944. *Capitalism and Slavery*. Chapel Hill.

Williamson, Jeffrey G. 1985. *Did British Capitalism Breed Inequality?* London.

———. 1997. *Growth, Distribution and Demography: Some Lessons from History*. NBER Working Paper Series, no. 6244. Cambridge, Mass.

Wrigley, E. A. 1987. *People, Cities and Wealth: The Transformation of Traditional Society*. Oxford and New York.

———. 1988. *Continuity, Chance and Change: The Character of the Industrial Revolution in England*. Cambridge.

Wrigley, E. A., and R. S. Schofield. 1981. *The Population History of England 1541–1871: A Reconstruction*. London.

Index

absolutist states, 85
Acapulco, 52, 59
Acco (Acre), 28
accounting, 34, 42
Adenauer, Konrad, 204
Adriatic sea, 8, 9, 266 n. 19
aerospace industry, 226
Africa, xiv, xv, 5, 27, 29, 33, 49, 50, 52,
    53, 54, 83, 120, 225, 226, 257,
    281 n. 87, 287 nn. 30, 44
aggression, 63, 69, 71, 73
agricultural revolution, 93, 107–8, 119,
    152, 153, 214
agriculture, 65, 72, 78–82, 99, 107–8,
    112, 119, 126, 127, 132, 135, 136,
    137, 141, 142, 143, 144, 145, 146,
    147, 151, 152, 153, 154, 168, 177,
    178, 180, 184, 185–86, 188, 194,
    210–11, 215–16, 218, 220, 224, 249,
    251, 254–55, 256, 271 n. 1, 272 n. 13,
    280 n. 79, 281 n. 81, 286 n. 23,
    292 n. 66; and industrialization,
    151–54
Airbus, 226, 241
aircraft industry, 138, 226
Airtouch, 229
Albania, 141, 143, 217, 279 n. 64
Albert, Michel, 228
Alexandria, 28
Algiers, 55
Alps, xvi, 10, 21, 31, 32, 43, 44, 60, 93,
    96, 124, 264 n. 5, 271 n. 3

Alsace, 118, 222
alternative agriculture, 269 n. 52
Amalfi, 27
America, xvi, 50, 51, 52, 53, 59, 64, 66,
    67, 68, 72, 82, 90, 91, 120, 124, 125,
    135, 136, 155, 156, 168, 180, 182,
    191, 195, 202, 205, 214, 223, 232,
    236, 237, 239, 240, 241, 243,
    266 n. 17, 281 nn. 84, 87, 284 n. 1,
    289 n. 44, 293 n. 78. See also United
    States of America
American aid, 202–3
American Civil War, 276 n. 48,
    284 n. 115
Amoco, 229
Amsterdam, 46, 47, 49, 55, 59, 67, 68,
    69, 70, 72, 79, 91, 265 n. 12,
    266 n. 26, 268 n. 41; treaty of, 244
Angell, Norman, 166
antiquity, xiv, 1, 3, 21, 22, 26
Antwerp, 44, 46, 54, 56, 67, 68, 69, 72,
    91, 141, 159, 164, 267 n. 36,
    268 n. 41, 287 n. 30
apparatchiks, 250
Arabs, xiv, 3, 16, 263 n. 19. *See also*
    Islam; Moslems; Sarracens
Aral Sea, 248
Argentina, 282 n. 91
Arianespace, 241
aristocracy, 2, 13, 20, 24, 86, 143
Arkhangel'sk, 266 n. 21
Arkwright, Richard, 102

Indian Ocean, 28, 29, 50, 54, 69,
 263 n. 23. *See also* East India
 companies; East Indies and East
 India trade
Indies, 69
individualism, 272 n. 14
Indonesia, 243
industrialization, 99–100, 130, 131, 132,
 133, 135, 136, 137, 142, 143, 144,
 146, 147, 148, 149, 150, 155, 158,
 159, 164, 165, 172, 183, 184, 192,
 193, 194, 195, 214, 216, 217,
 271 n. 1, 273 n. 21, 286 n. 23,
 295 n. 93
industrial revolution, 70, 73, 78, 93, 99,
 100, 103–7, passim in chapter 3, 132,
 133, 182, 224, 225, 271 n. 10,
 272 nn. 14, 15, 273 nn. 19, 21
industrialists. *See* entrepreneurs
industrious revolution, 92
industry. *See* coal and coalfields; cotton;
 iron; manufactures and
 manufacturing industry, rural
 industry; steel industry; wool and
 wool industry
inequality, 109–10, 222
inflation, 51–52, 66, 90, 166, 175–76,
 200, 206, 211, 221–22, 223, 231, 234,
 235, 240, 245, 250, 251, 253, 254,
 286 n. 17, 299 n. 77. *See also*
 hyperinflation
information agencies, 283 n. 101
information technology, 227, 240, 241,
 256
inland transport and trade, 41, 57–58,
 83. *See also* railroads
innovation, 100, 102, 103, 104, 105, 117,
 150, 248
institutional investors, 229, 239
institutions, 114, 122, 150–51
integration, of European economy,
 32–33, 58–59, 157, 166, 172, 203,
 219, 229, 240, 244, 246
interest rates, 111, 157, 231, 236,
 294 n. 84
internal combustion engine, 133, 182,
 275 n. 35
international banking, 43–44

international cooperation, 181, 202
International Monetary Fund (IMF),
 251
international monetary system, 134,
 160–62, 175, 180, 189, 223,
 275 n. 34. *See also* gold standard
Internet, 241
intervention by government, 187–88,
 201, 232–33. *See also* economic
 policy; government, role in the
 economy
interwar period, 162, 178 ff., 201, 208,
 222, 224, 225
invasions, xiii, 6–7, 9–10, 74, 75
inventions and inventors, 25–26, 34,
 38–40, 100, 101, 103, 106, 107, 110,
 113, 114, 115, 116–17, 141, 227,
 267 n. 38, 273 n. 20
investment and investment rate, 102,
 212, 248, 250, 289 n. 42, 290 n. 53
Iran, 8, 21, 57
Iraq, 3, 263 n. 23
Ireland, 7, 60, 109, 148, 156, 205, 208,
 214, 242, 245, 274 n. 28, 291 n. 64,
 294 n. 86
iron (industry, ore, works), 2, 26, 39, 61,
 75, 100, 101, 102, 115, 118, 119, 120,
 126, 130–31, 132, 134, 141, 143, 149,
 165, 271 n. 6, 273 n. 25, 281 n. 82.
 See also steel industry
Iron Curtain, 200, 217
Islam, 24, 28, 38, 76. *See also* Arabs;
 Moslems
Israel, 287 n. 30, 289 n. 44
Israël, Jonathan, 68
Istanbul, 75, 76, 124, 272 n. 17,
 279 n. 66. *See also* Byzantium;
 Constantinople
Italian companies, 33, 42
Italy, xiv, xv, xviii, 1, 2, 3, 5, 7, 14, 15, 17,
 20, 22, 24, 25, 27, 28, 29, 31, 32, 33,
 34, 37, 40, 43, 44, 46, 57, 60, 63, 64,
 65, 66, 70, 74, 76, 79, 81, 82, 90, 91,
 94, 119, 122, 123, 124, 125, 126, 128,
 129, 132, 133, 144–45, 148, 149, 151,
 152, 153, 156, 157, 158, 159, 160,
 183, 185, 187, 188, 195, 197, 200,
 204, 206, 207, 208, 211, 212, 213,

Thomas, Brinley, 281 n. 84
Thomas-Gilchrist process, 126
Thyssen, 278 n. 58
Tokyo, 239
Torcello, 5, 8
Tortella, Gabriel, 126
Total (company), 229
total factor productivity, 195, 206, 207
tourism, 141, 160, 227, 282 n. 96
towns, 2, 3, 6, 17, 20, 22–26, 79–80, 159,
    186, 194, 199, 262 n. 3, 267 n. 30;
    industrial, 109, 159
trade, 3, 5–6, 8, 23, 27–29, 30–33, 50,
    51, 52–57, 58, 123–24, 126–27, 136,
    140, 141, 142, 157, 164–66, 180,
    186–87, 188, 189, 191, 195, 203,
    204–5, 208–9, 213, 219, 221, 238,
    240, 255, 266 nn. 19, 21, 268 nn. 42,
    43, 278 nn. 61, 62, 279 n. 67,
    282 n. 98, 283 n. 109, 284 nn. 110,
    115, 291 n. 56, 295 n. 95; and
    economic development, 53–54,
    58–59, 112
trade treaties, 123–24, 274–75 n. 34,
    278 n. 58
trade wars. *See* tariff wars
tramways, 275 n. 35
transhumance, 20–21
transport, 83, 101, 112, 124, 127, 157,
    164, 269 n. 51; costs, 125, 126–27,
    132, 274 n. 33. *See also* freights
Transylvania, 16, 28
Trieste, 217, 275 n. 39
Troyes, 263 n. 29
tulip mania, 69
turbines, 102
Turkey, 76, 199, 289 n. 44
Turkish rule in the Balkans,
    consequences of, 76, 141–42
Turks. *See* Ottoman Turks
Tuscany, 25, 31, 34, 43, 55, 65, 265 n. 9
Tyrol, 90

Ukraine, 75, 77, 121, 126, 146, 147, 253,
    258, 279 n. 70, 284 n. 111, 295 n. 90
unemployment, 175, 178, 184, 185, 186,
    189, 190, 192, 195, 205, 221, 222,
    223–24, 227, 228, 231, 236, 244, 245,
    246, 252, 253, 254, 286 nn. 14, 20,
    291 n. 63, 292 n. 65
Unilever, 183
unions, 110, 200, 201, 228, 229, 230,
    231, 233, 244
United Kingdom, 100, 136, 155, 156,
    171, 207, 242, 274 n. 28, 279 n. 63,
    281 n. 84, 284 n. 112, 287 n. 28. *See
    also* Britain; England
United Provinces, xviii, 58, 67, 70, 71,
    112. *See also* Holland
United States of America, 96, 99, 109,
    122, 124, 130, 134, 135, 156, 158,
    159, 163, 164, 167, 168, 171, 173,
    174, 176, 177, 178, 179, 180, 181,
    182, 183, 184, 186, 187, 195, 200,
    202, 203, 205, 206, 207, 208, 210,
    211, 215, 216, 217, 219, 221, 223,
    224, 225, 226, 227, 228, 229, 232,
    235, 236, 237, 238, 239, 240, 241,
    242, 249, 252, 256, 271 n. 2,
    278 n. 57, 281 nn. 83, 84, 87,
    282 n. 92, 284 nn. 112, 114, 115,
    287 nn. 28, 30, 32, 34, 288 n. 39,
    289 n. 42, 291 nn. 60, 61, 293 n. 78,
    294 nn. 81, 87. *See also* America
"United States of Europe," 243
universities, 135, 150, 241, 292 n. 65
Ural(s), xiii, 1, 75, 194, 216, 244,
    291 n. 55
urbanization, 25, 79, 109, 159
Uro-Altaic people, 2
USSR, xiii, 174, 177, 188, 191–95, 196,
    197, 199, 200, 205, 210, 214–17, 218,
    219, 220, 248–50, 251, 252, 253, 255,
    285 n. 5, 287 n. 29, 290 n. 51,
    295 n. 97; "excess deaths" in, 192,
    194, 284 n. 3, 287 n. 29

Valais, 120
Valencia, 264 n. 6
values, 86–87
Van der Wee, Herman, 70, 96, 117, 201,
    203, 270 n. 67
Van der Woude, Ad, 70
Venice, xviii, 8, 24, 27, 28, 29, 32, 35, 43,
    48, 54, 57, 62, 63, 64, 65, 67, 68, 69,
    73, 74, 269 n. 57